Biography-Driven Culturally Responsive Teaching

Honoring Race, Ethnicity, and Personal History

3rd edition

SOCORRO G. HERRERA

Foreword by **Geneva Gay**

TEACHERS COLLEGE PRESS

TEACHERS COLLEGE | COLUMBIA UNIVERSITY
NEW YORK AND LONDON

A chapter-by-chapter discussion guide and instructional aids (templates, rubrics, and a checklist) for selected strategies are available for free download from the Teachers College Press website: tcpress.com. See page 192 for a list of the items available.

Permissions credit lines for reproduced figures appear below the individual figures.

Published by Teachers College Press, 1234 Amsterdam Avenue, New York, NY 10027

Text Design: Lynne Frost

Library of Congress Control Number: 2022931847

ISBN 978-0-8077-6648-4 (paperback)
ISBN 978-0-8077-6649-1 (hardcover)
ISBN 978-0-8077-8079-4 (ebook)

Printed on acid-free paper
Manufactured in the United States of America

For your limitless love and commitment to my craziness,
I will forever be grateful . . .

My children Dawn, Kevin, Jesse, and Isamari

For the hopes and dreams I have
for my grandchildren, Selah and Cyrus

Love you always!

Contents

Foreword

BOTH CONSENSUS AND CONTENTION exist among educators about teaching ethnically, racially, and culturally diverse students. The consensus is more ideological and the contention is largely methodological. The consensus tends to be on issues of "why," while "what" and "how" are more contentious topics. For example, most educators accept that ethnic, racial, cultural, and linguistic differences do exist among students, and that they have profound effects on educational opportunities and outcomes. Contentions are more likely to occur around how to understand these differences and what to do about them. Some educators promote bypassing these "existential realities" and dealing with diverse students from assumed higher philosophical planes, codified in phrases like "all students should be treated the same," "I am color blind; I see no difference when I look at students," and "in the final analysis individuality is what really counts." The counter-argument is that all students are culturally socialized, and they come to school with different social, ethnic, and experiential identities and heritages. In fact, diversity is inherent to the human condition and, invariably, it is embodied culturally. Since human culture and difference are indisputable, educational experiences for diverse students should likewise be culturally diverse. These claims are particularly compelling for racial and linguistic minority students.

Both perspectives sound even internally contradictory at times. For example, many educators who argue for treating all children the same simultaneously endorse honoring their individuality, and proponents of embracing cultural diversity concede that all individuals within cultural groups are not culturally identical. But, under closer scrutiny, what initially appears to be contradictory is not so. Instead, these claims symbolize human complexity and are indicative of the challenges (and opportunities) educators must address in creating authentic culturally responsive programs and practices for ethnically, racially, and linguistically diverse students. Yet the question of "how" is often so daunting for some that doing nothing is the response. Underlying the sense of helplessness is another point of contention. This one is between theorists or conceptualizers and practitioners. The practitioners accuse the theorists of proposing

lofty and abstract ideals without showing how to put them into practice—that is, how to get from idealized notions about cultural diversity into the exigencies of actual and authentic classroom actions. Conversely, some cultural diversity scholars view the efforts of practitioners as inadequate because of a lack of knowledge and genuine commitment to educational equity and excellence for ethnic and racial minority students. Both sets of perspectives have some valid points. Undoubtedly, theorizing on cultural diversity and multicultural education needs to include more functional strategies for practical implementation, and classroom practices need to be better aligned with theory. In the meantime, as these debates and divides between different segments of the professional community continue, many children of color are still being educationally neglected and left behind by teachers and other educators who are charged with doing the reverse—that is, opening up gateways of opportunity and making high-quality education accessible to them.

Interventions are needed to mediate these gaps between multicultural education theory and practice. A reasonable place to look for them is in the emerging body of new scholarship in the field. Many of these scholars have experienced the theory–practice divide personally because they were active classroom teachers not so long ago, and they received their academic degrees relatively recently. Socorro Herrera is one of these "new generation scholars," and she does a masterful job of mediating multicultural education theory and practice, specifically for culturally and linguistically diverse students, in *Biography-Driven Culturally Responsive Teaching*. She builds compelling and cogently constructed ideological and methodological bridges for teachers to cross over between theory and practice, as well as among different perspectives and paradigms within theory and practice. In so doing, she exemplifies many of the values, beliefs, and actions proponents consider essential to multicultural education and culturally responsive teaching. Among these are blending multicultural sensitivity and academic rigor; integrating cultural diversity into subject matter content and all other aspects of teaching and learning; and promoting academic success without compromising the cultural identities and affiliations of ethnically, racially, and linguistically diverse students.

Herrera uses several techniques in building these bridges within and between culturally responsive theory and practice that are worthy of emulation by other educators. First, she develops a comprehensive and eclectic ideological foundation for using the personal life experiences of culturally and linguistically diverse (CLD) students as content and method in teaching them more effectively. This student-centered framework incorporates ideas from different bodies of scholarship about human growth and development, theories of learning, second language learning, sociocultural funds of knowledge, cultural studies, and culturally responsive teaching. The result is a complex and richly textured paradigm for accessing, characterizing, and employing the biographies of CLD students in teaching and learning. Second, Herrera offers detailed, pragmatic suggestions for doing culturally responsive teaching with CLD students in a wide variety of grades, subjects, instructional settings, and school contexts. After a careful reading of this book, teachers will be hard pressed to not find some strategies that they can incorporate into their own instructional repertoires with little or no modification, or feel empowered to create their own strategies given the models provided throughout the book. Yet, this is not a handbook of cookie-cutter, prescriptive strategies that teachers are expected to memorize and mimic in their own classrooms. Instead, the teaching techniques presented are intended to illustrate what conceptualized and theorized ideas about cultural responsiveness look like in actual (not contrived) classroom teaching. These action strategies are accompanied by explanations of how they exemplify various elements, beliefs, and ideas about culturally responsive teaching. Thus, teachers listening to and reading Herrera have a better chance of understanding theoretical ideas about the interactions among culture, teaching, and learning, and becoming more effective culturally responsive teachers. This is so because they can see theory and practice juxtaposed with one another and simultaneously they receive interpretative assistance from the author in making these connections transparent. Thus, in reading this book teachers learn on multiple levels and in different ways some of the fundamentals of teaching CLD students, as they are expected to help their students do likewise.

In addition to content that is scholarly yet very readable by different members of the professional community, this book is positive, affirming, and celebratory of CLD students. So much of educational scholarship about, and reform proposals for, teaching students of color is pathologically oriented and paints dismal portrayals, as if there is nothing redeeming about the prospects. Kudos to Herrera for resisting these inclinations! Instead, she speaks of her constituency with respect, honor, care, grace, and affirmation, as much by the nuances, tone, and "feel" of her text as by explicit declaration. These are children worthy and deserving of dignity, first and foremost because they are children beginning their life journeys and they deserve the unequivocal support and assistance from those who teach them. Even her choice of title conveys this sense of care and grace for the children for whom she is advocating. Rather than presenting CLD students as statistics, she humanizes them through references to *their biographies* throughout this book. Her messages are persistent and unequivocal: that effective teachers must first know and respect culturally and linguistically diverse students before attempting to teach them; that children cannot be genuinely known by attempting to deculturize them; that educational excellence for diverse students is contingent on using multiple and diverse cultural texts and instructional methods; and that, since learning is strongly influenced by cultural socialization, strategies used in teaching students must be informed by this socialization. To do otherwise is untenable, unethical, hegemonic, and pedagogically questionable. These are also some of the most important ideological and methodological anchors of culturally responsible teaching in general as well. *Biography-Driven Culturally Responsive Teaching* is a valuable resource for improving the education of ethnically, racially, and linguistically diverse students by *teaching them through who they are,* and regardless of where, what, and who is involved in the instruction and learning.

—*Geneva Gay, University of Washington, Seattle*

Preface
My Life, My Work

THE TRAJECTORY of my life as an immigrant, migrant, and second language learner has opened up a space in my professional world to live in the realm of possibilities. The last few years have brought forth all the emotional trauma that I try so hard to keep deep inside my soul, as I traverse the minefields of far too many educational spaces. My experiences afford me fuel to live in a world of possibilities, while the truth is that I often work in spaces that are riddled with pain and deficit thinking. A *deficit perspective* basically assumes that the differences students bring to school (e.g., home culture, native language, religious beliefs) are irregularities to be fixed before the learner can be expected to excel in a grade-level classroom. This type of deficit thinking and the limiting educational practices that result are realities that arise less from the amazing educators who live and work in those spaces than from systems and structures that prioritize efficiency over caring.

As I complete the third edition of this book, I have, of late, been forced to examine who I am and where I want to focus my future efforts for culturally and linguistically diverse (CLD) families and students during this phase of my career. The battles and conversations surrounding Black Lives Matter, the COVID-19 pandemic, critical race theory, and, of course, the ever-widening opportunity gap are so polarized that they seem to offer little hope. I am now in my fiftieth year of this journey that we call public education. At times I ponder what else can be said—what will heal the pain that many teachers feel as they try to balance the official space of the school with emergent efforts to honor and respect the history—the life potentials—of the learners they teach. Through this book, I extend to the reader a path toward a brighter future. I tell the following story in the hope that you as an educator may identify with much of it and feel the *power* that you can and often do bring into the classroom, the school, and the community in which you teach.

When Was the First Time . . . ?

In the last three years, I have attended and presented numerous diversity trainings in response to all that is happening in our current society. The question most often asked of me at these gatherings is "Do you remember the first time you realized you were *fill-in-the-blank*?" For me, it is *Mexican American.* Is this question asked often in your school and system?

The space you inhabit growing up teaches you so many lessons as you make your way through an unknown culture, in and out of school. In some spaces, you might be perceived as insignificant—as if, were you to disappear, no one would notice. In others, you would give anything if only you could disappear. You typically don't tell stories like these. Instead, you bury them deep inside of you, for fear others will know how you really don't fit in. My response, my story follows.

On a cool, dark night, in a world where you didn't ask any questions and you just followed the lead of the two humans who risked everything to open up new pathways for your future, the night did not go as other nights. The stillness of the one-room house in which we lived seemed to have a dark cloud hovering over it. This was very unusual for a household that was always buzzing with the stories of the day.

After dinner, the *storm* revealed itself—we would be leaving the farm where we had been working for almost a year. There was no explanation, although as the language broker, I knew we had not been getting paid. For the last two months, the food we had been eating had come from the eggs we gathered from the chickens, the food our extended family gave us on the weekend, and, of course, *los quelites* (weeds) we picked from the fields. Even today, I'm reminded of *healthy weeds* when I eat spinach. We were always told that's where our brain power and energy would come from as we struggled in the fields and in school. I assumed, as we tiptoed around gathering our things, that our leaving was connected to need. I just didn't understand why we were going through the motions of eating dinner, cleaning up, turning off the lights, and going to bed, if we were going to leave. That was soon to be revealed in a way that, to this day, I wish I could forget.

Late in the night, I felt a tug on my pajamas. It was time to leave. Quietly, as if we were escaping some place where we no longer fit, we each climbed into my dad's lime green Chevrolet pickup. *Mi mami* sat in the front, with me and brothers in the metal bed of the truck. Gently, my father threw in a minimal number of belongings, those things like the Virgen de Guadalupe that we never seemed to leave behind, even though it was big and bulky. He quietly tossed an old canvas tarp over us. Then, with the truck lights off, he put the truck in neutral and he started to push us onto the road. For what seemed an eternity, he pushed and pushed. Finally, he climbed into the truck, started the engine, and down the road we went. Somehow, the fear of the dark and the unknown added to the discomfort of that smelly, ugly, dirty tarp.

It was only a few minutes before the angry shouting of an all-too-familiar voice pierced the darkness of the night. I felt the truck pull over and another one pull alongside. I felt my body tighten. I wanted to scream, to run, to go back home to my cousins in Mexico. I wanted to be anywhere but there. It wasn't two more minutes before a flashlight and a rifle were pointed directly at me.

I don't remember all that I had to language broker on that night. I do, however, remember the piercing words that I still carry in my soul. "I want you to translate for your dirty, filthy, Mexican father," our recent boss shouted. "I could kill you Mexicans. You are on my land. You are stealing from me. I could kill all of you and no one would care. . . . That's how worthless you are. You're all damn lucky that I am letting you go." To this day, I don't know if I have ever been so frightened or shocked at our plight as I was that night.

Sometimes I relive the emotions of that night. His words and our fears still permeate every cell in my body. This happens especially when I find myself in unaccepting racialized spaces, such as some of the classrooms or schools where I have worked, both nationally and internationally. It prompts in me that unmistakable sense of fight or flight. In these spaces, too often learners' abilities are still defined by the color of their skin, their culture, and their home language. At times my inner voice sends messages that things will never change within these marginalizing spaces. It is then that I remind myself why teachers matter and why those who are culturally responsive and sustaining in their pedagogy truly do change lives.

You Are Unique and Powerful in This World

Trauma, language, culture—for us as teachers, each of these can hang on our shoulders like heavy bricks in schools inhabited by a deficit mindset and focused on looking for resources that will "fix" CLD students. Our schooling systems often respond with a plethora of programs intended to accelerate language development, mitigate trauma, manage behavior, and bolster academic achievement. Most of these quick-fix, technocratic solutions are implemented without regard for how their apparent "efficiencies" leave teachers fragmented in their approach, treating CLD and community differences as broken components that must be put back in order. Too often, this expected order of things seeks conformity to dominant cultural norms and use of only English from the learner, parents, and family. The multitude of ways in which CLD students have navigated and negotiated racialized landscapes, sometimes relying heavily upon their cultural and community wealth to persist and persevere, are disregarded.

And so, I ask: How can we, as educators, create ecologies of trust and respect if the technocratic gurus and the initiatives of our systems perceive these learners, families, and communities as broken or deficient, as irregular components to be fixed? Indeed, what is forgotten in the frenzy to *fix* diversity are the powerful professionals who practice their craft on a daily basis in classrooms, zoom sessions, and online environments. Who better to understand, respond to, and affirm human potential? Who better than teachers to differentiate learning for the inescapable reality that CLD student populations are increasingly the norm in our educational settings? Despite the appeal of their supposed efficiencies, "one size fits all" curricula and initiatives are increasingly money machines that, at their foundation, are out of touch, unresponsive, dysfunctional, and inappropriate for the new majority of our classrooms, pre-K–16.

In my own youth, I was taught only by White, monocultural educators. Some treated me as invisible or transitory. Others pitied my existence but had no answers. However, a select few looked me in the eye and radiated excitement for what we could accomplish together. Thanks to them, I found in me the fire, the drive, the skills to achieve and, ultimately, to succeed where so many of my friends did not. These classroom teachers saw in me not deficits but the potential that could be realized through humanistic and socioconstructivist pedagogies. They realized that I knew more than I could share, I cared more than I could show, and I was capable of more than I knew. Although I didn't know much English, they took the time to surface the wealth of what I did know about crops, such as cotton, sugar beets, sweet potatoes, and peanuts, and how to grow them. I also had the skill-set to recognize and communicate to farmers that hired my family when our pay was short, and whether the discrepancy was five dollars or a hundred and five dollars. Those teachers who *saw* me, who looked me in the eye, who built upon what I *did* know, created classroom spaces that empowered me as a learner and survivor. Each of the caring ones demonstrated empathy and believed that all the Mexican American learners in their classroom had something to say, could learn, and were capable of so much, given their life experiences. They laughed, learned about us, and reminded us of how worthy each of was to be in their space. They valued our contributions and learned from us as well, as they listened to us talk about our journeys.

As I teach my classes, conduct research, and write, I often reflect upon how my most influential teachers enacted what we refer to today as a *culturally responsive/sustaining pedagogy,* long before it was "cool" to do so. I remember how they called out their colleagues who bought into a deficit narrative. I think about the conditions each created to intentionally include the culture and language of the students they taught, while at the same time opening up doors and windows to other spaces for us to see that there was a whole unexplored world waiting for us.

In my first visit to the public library as a sixth-grader, Mr. Rowland looked down at me and said, "Here, there are hundreds of more books to read, books written about the histories of Mexican Americans, Native Americans, and African Americans. These books are powerful. You should continue reading because there is power in the words that are written by different people at different times." He knew that I lost *and found* myself in books, and there were indeed so many books there. After that day, he made sure to check on me to see if I needed more books. He put in my hands books that would teach me about the possibilities that were out there for the taking.

My best teachers also reminded me that the decisions my parents made were no different from those of other parents. Many students had some hidden sort of pain (i.e., some type and degree of trauma). Some had alcoholic fathers. Many experienced family financial difficulties. Still others suffered abuse. Many struggles were the same ills that students endure today. Back then, they told me that although my challenges were real, I was also charting a new and very different path for myself. Although there was little they could do, they often reminded me that the pain in my life would make me stronger, and that they would always be there for me.

Yes, these were rural, White teachers who, despite risks, cared about and scaffolded lessons for Mexican American learners in a system that focused on their deficits and expected conformity and assimilation. Like many systems today, it was a system in which test scores limited my entry and participation in a variety of mainstream activities. Yet, my favorite teachers taught me that reading, writing, and arithmetic could be learned. The pace might be different for some, and the depth might be different for others. However, we all are capable of learning. They assured me that learning to write, especially, was a lifelong process. In this system, I also taught myself that "playing the game" was the way to get ahead—the way to manage when I had to *be* a certain way to fit in.

As we advanced through the education system, my peers and I realized that middle school and high school were very different ecologies, and the game to be played was more demanding. Learning who might be accepting, supportive, and nurturing took more energy, more risk-taking. In these spaces, it was not difficult to figure out what some teachers thought about their students and families from *the other side of the tracks.* Their meaning perspectives about Mexican American and poor children were evident in their practices and in the *pobrecito* label that they placed on learners, especially regarding the possibilities of attending college.

To game the system here was more difficult, but with probing, experimentation, and a few setbacks, I found exceptional teacher allies and learned to manage two selves. My *conformist self* was essential in most of my social and academic interactions with school educators. This self projected the behaviors that most of my teachers and administrators expected to see, no matter how it felt inside. My friends often asked questions like "What happened to you? Why are you wanting to be White?" I wanted to scream because I just wanted to survive, yet reach my goals.

To accomplish this, my *driven self* recognized that many of the skills I had developed in elementary school led to opportunities not otherwise available to Latinx students. Developing those skills had required a willingness to negotiate with allies and being up to the challenge. This self was determined to be literate in English and a high school graduate. This driven self searched for teachers who held the same dispositions as those who had helped me in grade school. It listened for language that conveyed a caring attitude. It asked risky questions about perceptions and beliefs.

In response to this management of my two selves, I left middle and high school scarred on the inside and fragmented in my identity, but ahead on my goals. It wasn't so much the poverty and trauma that affected my identity. It was a system and the structures within that system that regularly reminded me: you are poor, you don't belong, you are behind, you don't write well, and more. I sought to actively and persistently challenge those disabling messages with the counternarratives from my family and from my ally teachers. Over time, these teachers taught me cognitive, metacognitive, and social-affective strategies for self-motivation and to scaffold my own learning. For example, through self-talk I reminded myself that I was still growing and sharpening my skills for survival and success in the future. I was locating and relying upon allies who knew what it took to play the new game as I transitioned to college.

My father, who in his own way was trying to protect me, always told me that I was only a guest in these White spaces. I was to lower my head, play *their* game, and keep moving toward the end goal of getting an education. Among my ally educators, the ends, the goals that were possible, could be leveraged so as to endure the means. For my father, the attainment of the goal to acquire a good education was the aspiration that would yield liberatory outcomes. Education was something that no one could *ever* take away. However, what my allies and some members of my own family didn't see was how much of my culture and language/identity I was having to mask in order to succeed academically.

I often battled with my conformist self, my soul urging me to look around and see the consequences and causalities of those who gave up their culture and, through assimilation, aligned their inner self and their external ways with a culture they really didn't understand or fit into. I will always be haunted with the question "Would I have been accepted by teachers if I had just been me?" I erased or buried so much of my identity in order to succeed. It became a source of guilt and shame that haunted me for years.

Like many others, I have not just a few stories of the teachers who nurtured me through my crazy life. They reminded me that the life I led as an immigrant, migrant, and emergent bilingual was going to be a powerful part of the history, the *biografía*, that drove my success as a learner and as a graduate. It would become what made me unique. They encouraged me to believe that my challenges would not limit my possibilities for the future. And, in fact, I did later heal in my own time, with the care, empathy, and love from those around me. Many were very open about the racialized spaces in which I would find myself—where others would not see what they saw. But together, these nurturers gave me the social language and the inner voice to not let others define me.

Your Identity *Es Tu Fortaleza* (Is Your Strength)

Throughout my public-school experience, I did not have one teacher of color. Not a single one. Yet, I graduated with a cognitive belief system instilled by many, but not all, of my teachers who gave me the strategies to succeed academically. They frequently reminded me that I could do anything that I set my mind to accomplish, if I just worked hard enough. Or at least this was the story I told myself. In my inner being, I denied the pain of facing the "-isms" of the universe we navigate every day. I used my driven self and my allies to overcome the many microassaults on my potential, capacities, and knowledge that I suffered in high school and in college. The following are but a few examples of these disempowering messages I received in those years: "I can tell you are a second language learner. You don't write, do you? Should you be attending classes when you have a child? Most Mexican women get married really young—I hope you make it! You work and go to school—that must be really hard."

It wasn't until I found my support group—a Latina faculty member and Latinx peers who were on the same journey as I—that I became whole again. I finally had a peer, a mentor,

a teacher, and an advocate who looked like me. She proved to be a powerhouse Latina who was *bien Chingona*. I was and still am in awe of this woman. When I first met her, my academic and cultural/language identities were like a neglected plant that refused to die. Yet my mentor knew how each of our histories, those of my cohort peers and my own, defined our place within the social and academic contexts of education. She could see how our own identity formation as Latinx college students would inform the way we interacted with communities, families, and learners. She recognized that many of us wore a mask of survival, and behind that mask lay years of identity denial that needed to be healed and unpacked if we were to be prepared to teach for social justice in culturally responsive and sustaining ways.

We were not all ready to critically reflect. Doing so meant having to admit that there was part of me that existed only in another world. It was a world I loved, but negative messages swam through my mind, circulating recurrent themes that I was not worthy of participation in any collegial conversation. No one wants to admit that deep within the soul, much is hidden in order to survive White spaces and achieve success.

I will forever be grateful for the six years I spent at Eastern New Mexico University preparing to be a bilingual teacher and counselor. My mentor sheltered but also challenged as she guided a Mexican girl who carried her identity in her heart but could navigate different cultural and linguistic spaces in order to be heard. When I began teaching in my first classroom after graduating from the teacher education program, my expectations for what I was going to accomplish with my students and families were high. I was prepared to teach students like me, but the system was not yet ready to change. My mentor supported my navigation of this challenging space, reminding me to draw on the same assets that had always given me strength.

Reflecting for years on this trajectory, on my life experiences in two distinct worlds, I have come to understand the power I have as a Latinx woman. I'm in a long process of letting go of the guilt and fear, positioning myself in a world where I belong. There, I must recurrently remind myself that I have a social and academic voice, bound by all that I am. Further, I am now mostly free to bring my voice and identity into a range of challenging spaces. Although my identity may not always fit in the box expected by the systems in which I work, I am confident that I empathize, I listen, and I can help schools reach and teach CLD and other students in humanistic, sociocultural ways that align with their "nontraditional" socializations. As we enter the third decade of the new millennium, it is time to know who we are, and to reconcile with ourselves as we find our own agency in schools and classrooms. We must challenge ourselves and others to do what is right for the rapidly growing population of CLD and other marginalized students in our schools and families in our communities.

Positionality: *Y Ahora Que?* (And Now What?)

As I conclude, I think of a script that some amazing BESITOS students (BESITOS/Herrera Terry, 2004) wrote and performed. In the first act of the *teatro*, they strived to remind all educators of their positionality. They wrote: "I am here today. Take a look at me. You will see. I have a different point of view." Each and every one of us—educators, community members, families, and students—socially construct our world based on the multiple identities that we have chosen or those that have been imposed on us by societal/external forces.

I often remind myself of the importance of understanding the educators I collaborate with across the country and the world. We have constructed our own identities based on the roads we have traveled throughout our primary, secondary, and tertiary socialization. Therefore, if I critique, it is my responsibility as an educator to walk alongside/collaborate with educational peers in order to find out where our positionalities intersect and to determine how we can work together to harness the resources we each have to accomplish what we want for *all* students. A strong sense of self-worth, deep-rooted identity, self-confidence, and knowledge are powerful and have the potential to generate the agency we need to question the many top-down initiatives in our school systems and their fit with the realities of our communities, families, classrooms, and students.

We don't all arrive at readiness at the same time or in the same way. What is important is to recognize is that all human beings need spaces that acknowledge who they are and how they learn. It is tragic when our labels become so taken for granted that we forget the dynamic nature of being human. Consider, for example, the dynamic manner in which the brain rewrites our story in a new way through every interaction, every single day of our lives.

We live and work in racialized spaces. For CLD learners, the color of their skin, their language, their socioeconomic level, their gender, and their academic potential frequently are viewed through a deficit lens clouded by a set of presocialized, unquestioned assumptions, many of which alter teachers' perceptions and expectations of CLD student potential at the subconscious level. Pullout programs and practices (e.g., ESL pullout classes) that tend to arise from these assumptions deny CLD students adequate access to the grade-level curriculum necessary for academic success. When we teach students whose home language, culture, or ethnicity differs from ours, it is pivotal to our efficacy as educators to regularly surface these taken-for-granted assumptions. We can then question and explore their validity. If they are in error, we can consider when/where in our prior socialization we developed them. We educators are actors within the system; we will either chose to continue using scripts that are based on point-in-time evaluations of (and assumptions about) CLD populations that overemphasize what students do *not* have, do *not* know, and *cannot* accomplish, or we will create culturally responsive/sustaining conditions for learning and build upon students' strengths.

As I cross new thresholds in my fifty-year journey from CLD student, to preservice teacher, to teacher, to professor, researcher, and writer, I am thankful for those insightful, open-minded White teachers who nurtured my early academic capacity building. There is much work to be done if future White teachers are going to be prepared to understand the cultural, linguistic, and cognitive dimensions of the learner as assets to be nurtured and built upon. I continue my collaborations with colleagues to increase the number of teachers of color (TOCs) in all of our schools, K–16. It may be that their most meaningful contributions cannot be technocratically evaluated, as they, just by their presence, serve as role models and professionals capable of inspiring a new generation of CLD graduates.

Some days the prescriptive initiatives, policies, and practices dictated by systems with high numbers of CLD students seem to confound any semblance of rational decision making and make me feel as though I should run and not look back. Yet, then I enter a different highly diverse school or classroom and witness teachers in action, a sparkle in students' eyes, a learner's excitement to show what she knows, and walls filled with student work products that reflect a wealth of culturally and linguistically influenced knowledge co-created by the classroom community. It's in those moments that I know my responsibility to collaborate with and build up teachers. Through our shared expertise, we can move conversations forward and push back on practices and structures that are deficit driven.

It is my hope that in this text you will find caring teachers who, although they could so easily be buried by initiatives, instead choose to differentiate their practices in socioconstructivist and asset-driven ways. May they inspire agency and advocacy for CLD students so that learners are no longer forced to decide which self they will show, but instead can apply their full potential toward personal and academic excellence. I invite you to become a biography-driven ally teacher, as we strive to change the status quo.

Acknowledgments

MY WORK on this book has reminded me of the many educators, students, and families who bless my world with their talents, passion, and limitless giving. Dr. Shabina Kalid Kavimandan, you have for over 15 years encouraged me to question, believe, and advocate as we have collaborated with teachers, administrators, coaches, students, and families. Your balance of art and science in praxis has helped me ground and authenticate my work in these voices from schools and their communities. Melissa Holmes, you have brought to this book the scholarship and reflection that embodies *pushing the boundaries* and making the connections that make this book possible. Every page in this book has been sprinkled with your magic! Throughout the process, both of you have provided constructive criticism with compassion and guidance in order to stretch the limits of thinking, creativity, and authenticity. Without your support, my goal of putting more of my life's work into written format might never have been possible.

I also acknowledge the Center for Intercultural and Multilingual Advocacy (CIMA), where much of the work with the teachers highlighted in this book has taken place. I appreciate and value the colleagues, graduate and undergraduate students, and friends who have collaborated with me there to fill in the gaps, when the rest of us had little energy left to spare. I am indebted to Drs. Éder Intriago Palacios, Maria Antonieta Morales, and Paolo Fabre Merchan, and to Latania Marr y Ortega. Thank you for participating in our brainstorming sessions, maximizing technology in the development process, and sharing your experiences from the field. My love and thanks go to each and every one you at CIMA who have contributed.

I extend my heartfelt appreciation to the many *teachers across the country* who have contributed their creative voices and talents to this project. I don't believe that a week has passed without at least one of you sharing your encouragement, a picture, a quote, or a sample of student work that exemplifies what biography-driven instruction (BDI) is all about in classroom practice. Without your words, images, and outcomes of what is possible with culturally and linguistically diverse (CLD) student populations, this book would be only a dream. You have taken theory to the highest levels of accommodative classroom practice and have stepped outside the box to provide *all* students with the education that they deserve, regardless of current or past political agendas. *You are the individuals who make a difference!* I treasure your friendships and your willingness to share of yourselves. To educators in the state of Kansas and across the country, I will be forever grateful.

Energy and excitement are what I find in the schools of the many *schooling leaders* with whom I have had the privilege to collaborate during the process of writing this book. I humbly thank you for creating spaces and places where teachers are cherished and celebrated. I have personally witnessed your encouragement of teachers' professionalism by supporting them to push the envelope in order to do what is best for all learners. It is through administrator support that the teachers described in this book have been able to soar beyond sociopolitical and other boundaries that often threaten teacher voice and action. Many of their combined efforts in the support of biography-driven practices are documented and illustrated in this edition of the BDI text. Their innumerable contributions toward more equitable educational practices for CLD and other students offer each of us hope for a better society. In particular, this edition of *Biography-Driven Culturally Responsive Teaching* has been expanded, focused, enhanced, and refined in response to the committed leadership and example of those who challenge, encourage, and support all educators to be increasingly responsive to learners' assets and needs. Such individuals include Dr. Scott Springston, Chris Wendt, Michele Ingenthron, Kristina Bowyer, Martha Mendoza, Diana Mendoza, and many others who believe that fidelity to the curriculum does not come before the learners and families they serve. Thank you for acknowledging the assets that CLD students and families bring to teaching and learning. Your efforts to change the system and structures that serve the fastest growing student populations in this country are admired and greatly appreciated by the those of us who believe in cultural and linguistic responsivity and sustainability in public education.

My heartfelt thanks go also to Jean Ward. Regardless of the day or time, Jean has been only a phone call away. It is difficult to find the words to express how I feel about her and the support that she has afforded me throughout the entire process of bringing this new edition of the BDI text to completion. It has been almost two decades since I met her and, in that time, she has never stopped believing that this book, and each edition of it, would be written. It brings warmth to my heart to think of the many times, across the country and at multiple education conferences, we have had dinner together. Across our collaborations, she has always embraced the *Latina way,* smiling when, for example, a dinner turned into a CIMA family gathering. She has never hesitated to generously welcome anyone who came to join us.

Jean, you have been a guiding light to me in navigating the ideas as well as the challenges of generating this and our other books. Your own efforts to expand access to the ideas in this book show me new angles of advocacy. Your voice, persistence, and determination will forever strengthen my resolve to meet the challenges of writing and bringing to light the beauty and wealth of knowledge and experience that CLD students, families, and communities contribute to our collective learning. Thank you for your immeasurable contribution to fostering teacher agency and advocacy for emergent bilinguals and diverse thinkers of tomorrow.

Finally, I wish to express my love and gratitude to Drs. Kevin Murry and Nancy Kole. It's hard to believe that for three decades both of you have believed in this work and have provided the emotional support that makes our work in really difficult spaces possible. Kevin, you are forever the voice in my head that tells me I must continue this work and believe in myself. Your words have helped me navigate the intersection of research and practice. Nancy, your gentle spirit and love for my kids have made it possible for me to maintain the schedules, appointments, and late hours necessary to negotiate access, reach teachers' hearts and minds, and persuade change in schools and educational systems. It is people like you who make the third space a possibility.

Introduction

THE DIVERSITY OF STUDENTS in today's classrooms challenges us as educators to invest our hearts and minds in our teaching efforts with each and every student. Yet with competing agendas tugging at our time, energy, and professional understanding of how best to address the needs of culturally and linguistically diverse (CLD) learners, we often struggle to make sense of it all and to have our voices heard above the rhetoric that surrounds teaching. With extensive research and ongoing conversations, the third edition of this book has been created as a continued response to the voices of thousands of teachers I have had the privilege to work with across the United States—teachers who daily step out of the box and teach with students and families in mind. Although the journey remains difficult at times, the passion and commitment of these educators serves as their catalyst for clearing the path for the academic achievement of CLD student populations.

The following discussion provides a brief overview of the evolving path set forth in this book. It is a path that I hope will lead you to discovery of the great rewards that can be reaped through the use of biography-driven instruction—an instructional framework for enriching every CLD student's academic experience. Teachers dedicated to seeing CLD students succeed in the classroom place the biographies of learners at the center of their practice. In this way, they are able to use students' knowledge, skills, and words as entry points to learning and as the foundation for culturally responsive and sustaining teaching.

Chapter 1 provides updated demographic data that accurately reflect our classrooms today. This chapter situates biography-driven instruction within the context of prominent efforts toward liberatory practices, including culturally relevant pedagogy, culturally responsive teaching, and culturally sustaining pedagogy. The chapter also looks particularly at the work of Vygotsky, with his emphasis on the importance of working from each student's "zone of proximal development." Connections are made between the work of Vygotksy and that of Krashen. Together, their research supports ideas presented in this book regarding the critical nature of using the biographies of all of our stu-

dents to make our instruction more comprehensible and their learning more successful. The chapter describes the teacher's role in creating the "third space," in which the members of the learning community collaborate to maximize the wealth of their knowledge, strengths, and experiences. This chapter provides new insights from current brain research. Finally, the chapter previews the three phases of lesson delivery, which are used to create effective academic conditions for CLD students.

Chapter 2 foreshadows the four dimensions of learning that are discussed in this and subsequent chapters. It also provides a revised, in-depth exploration of the biopsychosocial history. The term "biopsychosocial" encompasses the entirety of the human experience, with considerations for the biological, psychological, and social aspects of a person's history. Understanding this concept is essential to the academic success of CLD students because learners carry more than their backpacks to school. They carry with them intrinsic traits and lived experiences that shape their knowledge, skills, and ways of being. By delving into CLD students' culture, background, and emotions—and sometimes stepping outside of our own comfort zones—we teachers can begin to understand those elements that influence students' engagement, cognitive belief system, and motivation to learn. When we incorporate the sociocultural dimension of the CLD student's biography into the classroom, we can better advance the learning and development of each member of our classroom community.

Chapter 3 addresses the processes by which emergent bilinguals acquire a second language and how that affects their academic progress. Just as a student's sociocultural history creates rules for living, laughing, and loving, in much the same way a learner's linguistic background establishes a guide for how he or she understands verbal communication. To help educators maximize a student's linguistic repertoire, I discuss fundamentals of second language acquisition, such as the relationship between basic interpersonal communication skills (BICS) and cognitive academic language proficiency (CALP). We teachers must understand CLD students' cultures and English language learning processes to effectively plan instruction. Using the knowledge we gain through observation, we can determine how to most effectively plan instruction that allows students to view concepts and texts through the lens of their life experiences, while drawing upon their existing and developing language skills. Our efforts to this end will result in more meaningful lessons that will support students' retention of content in permanent memory and use of new language and skills in authentic communication.

In Chapter 4, I address the question *Why do we think the way we think?* Vygotsky suggests that language and sociocultural experiences determine thought and development. When we understand the role of cognition and culture in shaping how our brains are accustomed to working, we can tailor our culturally responsive instruction, learning strategies, and assessments to ensure the best fit for CLD students. Instructional moves, materials, and tasks that make sense to us educators, because of our own frames of reference, may be confusing, awkward, or even alienating to students. In this chapter, I provide multiple types of learning strategies to scaffold students' engagement with cognitively complex content. I also explore how we promote students' comprehension of academic concepts, skills, and vocabulary when we value and build upon their ways of knowing, thinking, and applying.

Chapter 5 discusses the critical need for educators to provide CLD students with access, engagement, and hope. At times, even our best intentions can fall short of ensuring that all students have equal access to a rich, challenging curriculum. In an effort to assist teachers to design and implement instruction that promotes the engagement of *every* student in the meaning-making process, I focus on engagement, which is important in moving CLD students one step closer to ever greater gains in academic and literacy development. Key to this process is our demonstration of respect and care for each student, both as an individual and as a learner in our classroom. The CLD Student Biography Card is included as a helpful tool for getting to know students and planning instruction that is culturally responsive and biography-driven. This chapter also includes a discussion and related appendix resources to guide teachers through the process of critical reflection, in which they reflect on how their teaching practices are influenced by long-standing perceptions and belief systems.

Chapter 6 explores concrete strategies for creating a biography-driven classroom. By looking at the contextual and situational processes of teaching, which encompass the classroom ecology and in-the-moment learning dynamics, we can learn how to best create a learning community that supports CLD student achievement. Students' affective filters lower and they become more open to instruction and interaction when we create a climate that takes into account their voices, motivations, and socioemotional mindsets. New for this edition is an updated explanation of the biography-driven instructional framework. In this third edition, I also offer a lesson planning guide to support teachers' implementation of consistent, effective practice with CLD students. In biography-driven instruction, we teachers begin each lesson as a participant-observer, uncovering what students already know and have experienced. Then we incorporate the various kinds of knowledge students bring to the classroom into our teaching, using their funds of knowledge (home assets), prior knowledge (community assets), and academic knowledge (school assets) to guide our actions and decisions. Putting student knowledge to use in the classroom sparks new learning and supports academic achievement for all learners.

Chapter 7 looks at the teacher's job as one of continuous discovery—recognizing students' assets and potential and using what they bring culturally and linguistically to facilitate learning. It addresses the difference between this kind of facilitation and the more traditional practice of simply transmitting knowledge. Optimal instruction for CLD students begins when we consider their biopsychosocial histories, biographies, and background knowledge in planning lessons. We then make efforts to be transparent in our teaching by explicitly telling students what we expect them to take away from the lesson. When we share content and language objectives with students, we create a sense of hope and expectation in the classroom community. In this chapter, I provide a new BDI lesson planning template. In addition, this chapter incorporates updated research on how the brain processes information and provides considerations for vocabulary lessons that can support students in storing newly acquired information in their permanent memory.

Chapter 8 provides teachers with tools to scaffold instruction for CLD students, giving students the support they need to stand on their own while learning and to show others what they know. This kind of support begins with active listening and creating comprehensible input that aligns with students' individual biographies. Biography-driven instructional *strategies,* as differentiated from one-time activities, can help us provide such comprehensible input and scaffolding. To illustrate, readers are provided with an in-depth exploration of the DOTS strategy as a means of making academic content and language accessible and engaging. Cognitive, metacognitive, and social/affective strategies can aid students in present learning situations as well as in future endeavors. Such strategies help students gain a sense of ownership, take greater responsibility in their learning, and develop interpersonal skills as they collaborate to make sense of new concepts. By having students work together in pairs or small teams, we provide CLD students with low-risk opportunities to practice their language skills and share their unique cultures and perspectives. These opportunities for interaction and discussion support us as we monitor and navigate students' socio-states of mind (e.g., anxiety, fear, boredom) during instruction.

Chapter 9 offers a review of critical concepts related to biography-driven instruction, which leads us to focus on new ways to view assessment, emphasizing the need to celebrate what students *do* know and *can* do. Standard forms of assessment tend to show what students do *not* know and are *in*capable of doing. Consider for a moment CLD students' socioemotional states when they take a test or see their resulting grade. Students learn through trial and error and through discovering meaning in ways that are relevant to them. Memorizing information for standardized tests rarely results in learning that lasts. By using formative assessments before and during the lesson, we can discover what and how students are learning and determine how we can best modify instruction to guide students from the known to the unknown. Reviewing and providing closure at the end of the lesson gives students one more chance to confirm their learning, helps alleviate any anxiety they might feel, and gives us teachers a chance to evaluate how the class as a whole has met the learning objectives. When it comes time for summative assessment, we can take into account learners' individual biographies as we tailor assessments to yield the most informative data about the content and language development students have achieved.

Chapter 10 offers a more in-depth look at the standards that inspired biography-driven instruction as it is presented today, including research demonstrating the effective use of this instructional framework. Additionally, this chapter provides insights from educators in the field, who relay how biography-driven instruction has had an impact on CLD students in their schools and classrooms. These educators discuss their unique student populations and the benefits of culturally responsive pedagogy for the entire learning community. These administrators and teachers share their thoughts about the importance of dialogue, collaboration, and critical reflection as they continually work to transform their programs, models, curricula, and instruction to enhance learning opportunities for CLD students. By listening to their stories, we can better visualize what biography-driven instruction might mean in our own professional settings.

I HAVE ALWAYS viewed this book as a practitioner's guide—a way to help educators recognize the assets that their CLD students bring to the classroom. This third edition has been re-organized for greater readability and comprehensibility. This new edition makes more explicit how biography-driven instruction provides a basis for transformation of our educational spaces. It uses bold type to highlight additional key concepts and terms introduced in each chapter and includes a corresponding glossary at the end of the text. Even with a firm grasp on theory, at times we educators may not know how to put these new ways of thinking into practice. To better support theory-into-practice applications, this edition new figures and samples of student work that are used to illustrate critical ideas and concepts. A classroom observation tool to support coaching, mentoring, and self-assessment is also provided. Available online is an updated Discussion Guide, organized around activities entitled Collaborate, Elaborate, and Conclude (CEC), to encourage individual and group study of the key concepts in each chapter. Whether you are reading through the book on your own or are conducting a structured book study with colleagues, the CEC activities will help guide you in formulating new goals and action plans for working with your CLD students.

1 The Foundations of Biography-Driven Instruction

GUIDING QUESTIONS

Do the educational program and the curriculum come before the learner? To what extent do we consider our knowledge of learners as integral to teaching and learning? What goals can be achieved, questions be posed, and policies be challenged, if we let go of old ways of teaching?

See the online Discussion Guide for opportunities to further explore answers to these questions and connections to chapter content with a colleague or team. Available for download from the Teachers College Press website: tcpress.com

THE FOUNDATIONS of biography-driven instruction (BDI) stem from four decades of wide-ranging educational practice, research, and theory, as well as my own experience growing up as a culturally and linguistically diverse migrant student. The depth of my understanding has come from working with teachers in diverse classrooms nationally and internationally and from the conversations I have had with families and students along the way. In this book, I strive to present what I have learned in the most straightforward and practical manner possible, elaborating on important theoretical constructs that provide the power we need to do the right thing in classroom practice. However, this pedagogy is approached without ever losing sight of the sociopolitical threats we face and the realities of the contradictory contexts in which we as educators work every day.

At times, it may seem impossible even to think about how to integrate BDI into a teaching practice that already is subject to so many competing demands, including district and state standards, multiple administrative agendas, and constant curricular changes—to name just a few. To mitigate this frustration, readers might keep in mind the metaphor of a journey, which is employed in this chapter and throughout the book. When we travel to a new place, the best way to get to know the landscape and the culture and language of the people is to be *present* within the space we are occupying and keep our senses attuned to the details of what we are seeing, hearing, and feeling. What is important is how we experience each encounter at the "gut" level, and critically reflecting on our expectations and our responses

when what is happening is not aligned with our existing frame of reference. If we take our time and remain focused on deliberately reaching our goal, the destination, a life-changing process of discovery may unfold before us.

As we continue on this journey of teaching and learning, we can think about the changing landscape of our classrooms. The learner's race, ethnicity, identity, culture, and language have become, and will continue to be, essential considerations for educators regardless of grade level or content area. We must acknowledge and own the reality that our demographics have changed.

Consider the following: According to an analysis of data from the most recent U.S. Census by the Brookings Institution, the predominant component of the nation's growth, between 2010 and 2020, is attributable to a "diversity explosion" (Frey, 2021, p. 1). Among groups of Americans associated with this change are those who identify as (1) Latino/Hispanic (the fastest growing group), followed in growth rank by those who self-identify as (2) from two or more races, (3) Asian American, (4) Black American, (5) from other races, (6) Hawaiian/Pacific Islander, and (7) Native/Alaskan Native. Together, these diverse groups now comprise more than 40 percent of the U.S. population (Frey, 2021), and they are projected to comprise 56 percent by the year 2060 (Krogstad, 2019). The group that self-identifies as White has dropped by more than 5 million people (or about –2.6 percent), the most notable decline since 1790 (Frey, 2021).

Looking more closely at youth under age 18 in the United States, Frey's (2021) analysis highlights that the youth population overall has declined. One of the most dramatic changes is the drop of close to 1 million White youth, who now comprise approximately 47 percent of this age-group. The youth population growth would be even more stagnant if not for increasing numbers of youth from diverse groups, especially those who self-identify as Latino/Hispanic, roughly 26 percent of the population. The group that contributed most to this age-group's gains, however, was those who identified as two or more races. This trend reflects the ongoing diversification of our country. Frey (2021) reminds educators that the majority of American youth in 21 states are persons of color, and this diverse group comprises over 40 percent in an additional eight states.

In many ways for us as educators, this new landscape—where we can no longer relegate culturally and linguistically diverse learners to subgroups within our classrooms—serves as a call to action for defining how we will navigate sociopolitical agendas and corporate-driven curricula, and deal with the implications each has for our work in diverse contexts. How will we build the currency, defensibility, and futurity (Herrera & Murry, 2016) necessary to be efficacious in culturally and linguistically diverse classrooms? How will we be prepared to look at the "science of teaching and learning" through an alternative lens, one that moves us beyond the deficit perspective that underlies prescriptive curricula and single-lens interventions that fail to attend to the history, experience, and assets of diverse learners, their families, and the community?

For decades, beginning with the No Child Left Behind agenda and continuing to the present day, our response to diversity in the classroom has been to "fix" the learner, using curricula devoid of authentic representations of the student, often driven by teach-to-the-test agendas that measure discrete skills without attention to the individual's processing and learning. This line of thinking is considered a **deficit perspective**, in which teachers and administrators see students as liabilities who become identified as needing to be (and possibly unable to be) "fixed" by our current educational system (Darling-Hammond et al., 2020; Gorski, 2010; Hammond, 2015; Kressler & Cavendish, 2020).

Instead of viewing our students from a deficit perspective, we need to shift our mindset to an **asset perspective**. Each learner who arrives in a classroom brings with him or her a richness in language and culture, a history or biography that is much more meaningful than points scored on a test. Students carry with them experiences, native languages, academic backgrounds, and other resources that can inform decisions made about placement and programming. As educators, our becoming current on the alternative science that can more effectively inform our work with culturally and linguistically diverse learners and families is critical.

For this book and the work that I do in the field, I find the term **culturally and linguistically diverse (CLD)** to be the most representative and inclusive of this population. For teachers, it serves as a reminder that when the student's culture differs from that of the school, there is a high probability that their language may also conflict with that of the school curriculum. It also reminds us that in our efforts to address academic language development for all, and language acquisition for those learning a second language, we must be attentive and understand how culture influences language and learning. Such readiness sets the stage for us to draw upon a diverse range of knowledge, skills, and talents that students already possess.

The term CLD includes not only emergent bilinguals, who are learning English as an additional language, but also native English speakers who use various dialects and registers that do not adhere to the expectations of Dominant American English (DAE) (Paris & Alim, 2014) (often referred to as Standard American English [SAE]). Like English learners, these native English speakers also inhabit cultural identities different from those of the majority teacher population. Being mindful of the wider implications of the term CLD impels teachers to develop classroom practices that encourage, promote, and celebrate students' diverse backgrounds.

Today, it is more important than ever to find ways of providing equitable educational opportunities for all learners. Although we can choose from among multiple paths, answers to many challenges already exist within our own classrooms. At times, influences beyond our control can affect our efforts to provide students with a high-quality education that promotes both their academic and their linguistic development. In these moments, we must acknowledge that each of us has a role in exploring and advocating for alternative pathways and bridging them into our classrooms to address the multidimensional and exciting points of departure that learners bring to the educational space.

The Influence of Politics on CLD Student Education

Federal laws, jurisprudence, and constitutional mandates have had a significant impact on the educational system of America. *Plyler v. Doe* (1982)—a landmark case that sought to exclude immigrant students from American schools, with the resolution guaranteeing the rights of undocumented immigrants to a free public education—is a prime example of how the U.S. Supreme Court has been instrumental in shaping our educational policies. Court rulings have also served to illuminate aspects of what it means to provide learners with an equitable education. In *Lau v. Nichols* (1974), for example, the Court ruled that an equitable education is *not* ensured "merely by providing students with the same facilities, textbooks, teachers, and curriculum; for students who do not understand English are effectively foreclosed from any meaningful education." Similarly,

Title VI of the Civil Rights Act of 1964 has heavily influenced decisions made at the state and the local level to safeguard students from discrimination.

At the same time, the trajectory of our nation's schools has been shaped by the political landscape. Differences in agenda directions or ways mandates are implemented are commonly attributed to a political party with a given ideology and a Secretary of Education belonging to a specific administration. Yet, often missing from the larger conversation is discussion of the problematic scenario in which political ideologies and their frequently uncompromising adherents get to determine the "flavor of the year" initiative depending on the majority party's outlook toward education. Shouldn't our educational policies be determined based on the context in which our school systems operate? Shouldn't educators, families, and the communities that the school districts represent be front and center in decision-making processes?

In recent years, diversity, equity, and inclusion (DEI) initiatives in many school districts have come under increased scrutiny. On one hand, school districts want to maximize the potential of their diverse student body, and on the other, states are placing limits on whether and how teachers can discuss race and race-related issues in schools (Romero, 2021). Recent state legislatures, and specifically governors, have worked to restrict the language teachers can use in classroom conversations that involve race. Such actions reflect the power of policy mandates to influence the education that youth in our country receive. In the wake of such sweeping mandates, it becomes even more critical to consider ways educators can build upon and foster the academic and linguistic potential of CLD learners.

Regardless of mandates that come and go, teachers hold the power—through their pedagogy and instructional practices—to cultivate students' knowledge and skills, foster perspective taking, and develop critical thinkers prepared to use what they learn to transform their communities and the world around them. In this book, I provide educators with tools and techniques to support them as they engage CLD learners by first considering their unique biopsychosocial histories (discussed in Chapter 2). Such daily efforts on the part of teachers serve to bolster the learning of students and counter detrimental effects of decontextualized educational practices.

Access Denied: Limiting Programs for CLD Learners

In surveying the historical response to the diversification of our schools and classrooms, one pattern is especially clear. Education has become addicted to programs and models that claim to meet the needs of all learners yet feed a "one size fits all" mode of efficient practice that is technocratic in nature. Driven by politics, corporate America, and "experts"

who often have limited knowledge of the needs and assets of CLD learners, schools and systems rely on resources that promise "rigor and relevance for all" but fail to attend to the individual learner. In our urgency to address test-driven, deficit-oriented agendas such as No Child Left Behind, we as school systems have bought into programs that purport to "accelerate learning" and attend to the culture and language of the learner. Across areas including special education, social-emotional learning, college and career readiness, advanced placement, and of course reading, programs abound to ensure that all students across the country meet standards of success for the future. Yet, if we take time to follow up on how these programs have fared, we find that they commonly fail to support learners who are culturally and linguistically diverse.

Consider the Reading First program, which resulted from the No Child Left Behind Act of 2002. To address identified needs, the goal of this response was to test more and be data driven, intervention focused, and resource rich. Educators were to isolate the problem, drill and practice, retest, and repeat, if necessary, without regard for the literacy-rich backgrounds of CLD learners. Such responses were limiting for students as well as teachers. According to Berlak (2003):

> The most obvious consequence of using highly prescriptive reading packages is the loss of flexibility—the ability of classroom teachers and schools to use their own judgment in selecting teaching materials and methods that respond to children's learning differences as well as to differences in culture and language. (p. 15)

Responsiveness to the individual backgrounds and continually changing needs of learners is a defining hallmark of effective education, yet as systems we have failed to apply this criterion to our programming and instructional decisions.

Programming designed for English learners has fared no better. Despite the wide range of diversity in the language and cultural backgrounds of youth, schools often continue to be guided by outdated programs, and learners frequently are taught by teachers not afforded the preparation they need, experience curricula that are reductionistic in nature, and are provided few, if any, opportunities to leverage the richness of the experiences, knowledge, and skills that they bring into the educational space. Again, based on a need to be efficient and systematic, program and placement decisions are often made by educators relying on predetermined criteria, without knowledge of the learner and his or her family.

Academic programs for students who are learning English, although clearly described in the literature, come to life based on the interpretation of the people who implement them. The needs of the population being served—or the politics of the school, district, or state in which teachers operate—influence the selection of a given program and the implementation of curricula. The instructional models utilized can also vary within each type of program. An overview of current program types is provided in Figure 1.1.

One common distinction among program types is made between **additive programs**, where the goal is for students to "add on" English as an additional language, and **subtractive programs**, where the primary purpose is to transition students from their native language to English, thereby "subtracting" their first language from their knowledge base (Howard et al., 2018). Additive bilingual programs are associated not only with increased student achievement in the content areas, in both English and the native language, but also with increased self-esteem and more positive cross-cultural attitudes (Howard et al., 2018). On the other hand,

subtractive language programs have been shown to have detrimental effects on CLD students' school performance and on their learning of a second language (Collier & Thomas, 2009; Ovando et al., 2011; Thomas & Collier, 2012). Subtractive programs lead to native language loss, which correlates with lower levels of second language proficiency, diminished academic achievement, and even the development of psychosocial disorders (Howard et al., 2018; Lindholm-Leary, 2014).

Some readers may recognize that while research supports additive program types, they may be teaching in a subtractive program. While program type can be a constraint, it need not dictate all aspects of instruction. By focusing on the holistic development of CLD students and by using their biographies to guide instruction, we can respond to their sociocultural, linguistic, cognitive, and

---

FIGURE 1.1
Language Instruction Program Types

Subtractive Programs—
Development of Students' Native Language Is Not Fostered

English as a Second Language (ESL)	• Provides students with instructional support (e.g., scaffolding, cooperative learning) to transition students to an English-only instructional program without native language support (Faltis & Hudelson, 1998; Linquanti, 1999).
	• More effective programs are based on grade-level curriculum and incorporate both language and content objectives; less effective programs employ language objectives and treat language learning as a process isolated from content learning (Berman et al., 1992; Faltis & Hudelson, 1998; Herrera & Murry, 2016).
	• Multiple variations
	  ◦ Push-in programs: Students remain with grade-level peers for the full day with support provided in the classroom; depending on program design, an ESL teacher might team-teach or assist in making lessons comprehensible, or an instructional aide might provide differentiated support.
	  ◦ Pull-out programs: Support provided outside the grade-level classroom for a portion of the day; most costly, stigmatizing, and least effective program type (Collier & Thomas, 2009; Thomas & Collier, 2012).

Sheltered Instruction (SI)	• Provides students with instruction that integrates grade-level content development and language learning (Herrera & Murry, 2016). • Content-area teachers modify instruction to make content comprehensible for CLD students (Echevarría et al., 2016). • Native language support provided through more proficient bilingual peers and supplemental materials (Herrera & Murry, 2016). • Classes usually taught by grade-level teachers, not ESL teachers.
Transitional Bilingual Education (TBE)	• Goal is gradually transitioning students from content-based instruction in the native language to an English-only environment; also known as "early exit programs" (Ramirez, 1992). • Has a subtractive effect: As students' English language proficiency increases, their native language fluency decreases (Díaz-Rico, 2008). • Short-term (2–3 years) nature hinders students' development of grade-level academic language (Berman et al., 1992; Díaz-Rico, 2008; Ovando et al., 2011).

(Continued on the next page)

FIGURE 1.1	
Continued	
Additive Programs— **Development of Students' Native Language (and English) Is Fostered**	
Developmental Bilingual Education	• Also known as "maintenance bilingual education" or "one-way dual language programs"; implemented in a wide variety of ways (Thomas & Collier, 2012). • Teaches content-area subject matter in the CLD students' native language and in English, with the goal of increased student proficiency in *both* languages (Herrera & Murry, 2016). • Rooted in the belief that CLD students bring cultural and linguistic assets to be incorporated into the classroom environment (Cummins, 1998). • Encourages involvement of parents who may not speak English fluently (Herrera & Murry, 2016). • Typically begins in early years of schooling (K–1st grade) and continues as long as is feasible in the school district.
Two-Way Immersion Programs	• A form of bilingual education; also known as "two-way dual language programs" (Thomas & Collier, 2012). • Designed with the linguistic and academic needs of both CLD students and native English speakers in mind. • Typically takes place during elementary school years. • Main goals: (1) Students obtain high levels of proficiency in native language and English; (2) Both groups attain academic proficiency at grade level; (3) Students develop respect and positive cross-cultural attitudes (Howard & Christian, 2002). • Criteria include: At least ⅓ of students are native/heritage speakers of the partner language or are native English speakers; these two groups are integrated and interact in content-area lessons (Thomas & Collier, 2012). • Some heritage language/indigenous language programs can be categorized as two-way immersion programs.

academic needs in a more comprehensive manner, despite the program type in which we work. I explore these four dimensions of the student biography in detail in Chapters 2–5.

What's Love Got to Do With It? Everything

As we continue to experience changes in the makeup of our classrooms, the "How to?" question becomes ever more relevant to our practice. We often look for answers in professional development and come away discouraged, wondering how the take-away activities, strategies, and techniques could possibly effect change in the academic success of CLD students. Or we question how their use would be realistic, given mandates, lack of time, and required fidelity to the curriculum. Knowing where we as teachers fit—and understanding our need for flexibility and autonomy to deliver instruction that attends to community, family, and learner assets—is lost in the sociopolitical sphere in which we practice. The espoused (what we say) often gets lost in translation when it comes to what happens in practice. All the relationship building, socioemotional support, and cultur-

ally responsive acts of empathy and love get lost in teaching the "one size fits all" curriculum within the designated time frames and according to test-driven expectations that influence our daily lives.

For decades, the mantra surrounding the richness of diverse knowledge and skills that can be "harvested" from the community, family, and learner has been heavily advertised and yet absent or only superficially present in schools and classrooms. The ideal of *what should be* and the practical side of *what is* continue to push back against each other. When I ask preservice or in-service teachers why they chose this profession, the responses are often "Because I believe in what's possible when you reach and teach students" and "I love my students." Holding that this is true for most of us, as educators we must ask what "love" means within the technocratic, "one size fits all," corporatized world in which we teach. Will love overcome all the oppressive forces? Will we find the agency and will to "balance both worlds" and bring the community, family, and learner to the epicenter of our teaching and learning space? What action will be evident in our daily practice?

If we espouse that we are committed to using families' and students' funds of knowledge, being culturally relevant, culturally responsive, and culturally sustaining, and using strength-based/asset pedagogies, how will we let go of the deficit perspective that is narrated loud and clear during our data-driven decisionmaking meetings? How will we ensure that our planning is grounded in this work? Most importantly, how will we navigate and negotiate the delivery of instruction to document and build classroom community using the language, skills, knowledge, and history of the population we serve? Daily, hourly, and situationally every minute we are serving our families and students. How will we make love a reality in our educational spaces?

This book seeks to help teachers turn the espoused into reality through approaches to planning, delivering, and assessing instruction in ways that keep the CLD student—and each of our students—at the center of our practice. This transformation of our classrooms and systems involves investigating what CLD students know and applying such knowledge and skills to our process of fostering academic and linguistic growth. It also requires each of us to reflect on our own professional practice and to assess the opportunities we provide students to meaningfully integrate their prior knowledge and experiences (Hagevik et al., 2012; Souto-Manning, 2012). What kinds of teaching and learning dynamics offer us the greatest level of information about students? How can we use this information in our teaching to achieve our curricular goals? In this book, I propose the **biography-driven instruction (BDI) framework**, which provides educators with the guidance they need to tailor their pedagogy in ways that promote the success of all students—especially CLD students—in their classrooms.

The Foundations of Biography-Driven Instruction

The BDI framework and its related methodology give us a practical way of applying what others have shared about culturally responsive/relevant teaching and culturally sustaining pedagogy, which are explained in more depth later in this chapter and throughout the text. Some of the foundational research and scholarship includes:

- Gay (e.g., 2000, 2002, 2010, 2018)
- Ladson-Billings (e.g., 1994, 1995a, 1995b, 2017)
- Nieto (e.g., Nieto, 1992, 2000; Nieto & Bode, 2018)
- Ogbu and Simons (1998)
- Paris (e.g., Alim & Paris, 2017; Paris, 2012; Paris & Alim, 2014, 2017)

BDI has evolved from the work of many educators and researchers whose findings continually remind us of the power of students' assets in the classroom, including:

- García (e.g., García, 2017; García & Wei, 2014; García et al., 2017)
- Moll (e.g., Esteban-Guitart & Moll, 2014; Moll, 2019; Moll et al., 1992)

- Thomas and Collier (e.g., Collier & Thomas, 2009; Thomas & Collier, 1997, 2012)
- Vygotsky (e.g., 1978)
- Krashen (e.g., Krashen, 1984/2005, 2009; Krashen & Mason, 2020)

Through its emphasis on integrating student knowledge with the school curriculum, BDI creates opportunities for teaching and learning in the "third space," as explained later in this chapter. Influential work on this important space includes:

- Bhabha (1994)
- Benson (2010)
- Gutiérrez (e.g., DiGiacomo & Gutiérrez, 2017; Gutiérrez, 2008; Gutiérrez & Johnson, 2017; Gutiérrez et al., 2003)
- Moje and colleagues (2004)

BDI also incorporates what we know from research on how the brain learns, including:

- Hammond (2015)
- Jensen (e.g., 2006, 2008)
- Semrud-Clikeman (2015)
- Sousa (e.g., 1995, 2011, 2017)
- Willis (e.g., Willis, 2006, 2010; Willis & Willis, 2020)
- Zadina (2014)

The theme that unites these theory- and research-based strands is the necessity of fully including CLD students at the center of our educational efforts by first getting to know them as individuals and then using the resulting knowledge and insights to inform our instruction.

Charting the Course Toward Liberatory Practices

In *Pedagogy of the Oppressed*, Freire (1970) writes clearly about the power of language in learning spaces. He paints a picture of what could be achieved if only we provided a context, spaces where the teacher would understand and facilitate the learner to work from the known (their own experiences and history), and where teacher and learner would engage in sharing the power that historically has been possessed solely by the teacher. Imagine what would be possible if we teachers fully recognized that the space we inhabit is governed by the truths of the world experienced by learners and by the community that supports the validity of those truths.

Freire further posits that it is through learners' experience with naming their world and relating it to their new learning that they find their social and academic place in the educational space. This will require a move away from the type of direct instruction that mirrors the notion of banking education (Kavanagh & Fisher-Ari, 2020), in which CLD students are seen as devoid of any knowledge that matters in schools. Recently, I was told by a school administrator that teaching students using their own knowledge and words would lead to disastrous outcomes for all: chaos in classroom management, more work for the teacher, and most importantly, learners failing to develop the necessary skills they lacked or build the background needed to succeed in school. The comment was loaded with the language and assumptions of No Child Left Behind, the kind of deficit thinking that views the learner as possessing no knowledge that could be of any value in the classroom.

For all the rhetoric on equity, relationship building, and social-emotional learning, our systems, programs, and practices continue to reflect an outdated, reductionist approach for all learners "at risk" of perceived failure. The belief is that more direct and explicit instruction, testing, and data-driven decisionmaking will lift students from the empty academic world in which they live. Often, any attempt to talk about alternative approaches—such as inquiry-based, asset-driven, and liberatory practices—is seen as a threat to ensuring the success of the most marginalized students. This type of response signals a lack of understanding that the "science of learning" must be balanced with liberatory practices deeply rooted in the assets, skills, and knowledge that the learner brings to the educational context. In these kinds of limiting educational contexts, I find that "science" only refers to the curricular aspects of education. The science of the learner, on the other hand, is considered "fluff"—something to be aware of, but not something that will "move our testing scores forward." This mindset keeps us anchored in the current conditions that continue to fail CLD learners and their families as well as their teachers.

As educators deeply committed to social justice, antiracist education, and equity, centering our instruction on learners to create liberatory spaces is about doing the right thing. We must become knowledgeable about these areas of study and remind others that liberatory practices are deeply rooted in theories and constructs dating back to Giroux, Freire, Dewey, Socrates, and others—the science that highlights the importance of humanizing the teaching and learning process, drawing on the interwoven sociocultural, linguistic, cognitive, and academic dimensions of the learner. Until learners are allowed to use the strength and power of their experiences, languages, and knowledge, no educational equity will exist.

Culturally Relevant Teaching

Often educators in schools ask, What is the difference between culturally relevant teaching and culturally responsive teaching? Are they one in the same? Yes, and no. Gloria Ladson-Billings (1994) introduced the notion of teaching as an act of providing opportunities for CLD learners to use their knowledge, skills, and histories as springboards for academic achievement and for their healing and wellbeing, and as movement toward political action. Culturally relevant teaching is not something we *do*. Rather, it is what *results* through the empowerment of learners, which is only possible when we understand our own positionalities in teaching (and in the larger world) and our beliefs about what is possible with communities, families, and learners. Questions that bear to be asked are, How far we are willing to go to critically question our curriculum and the spaces in which we teach, in relation to the population we serve? At the end of the day, what is most important to us as educators?

Mezirow (e.g., 1991, 2018) reminds us that our meaning perspectives drive our actions. Often without realizing it, we carry out instruction based on the "templates" we have been socialized to believe. As a result, either we believe that the communities, families, and learners we serve have the capabilities, knowledge, and skills to succeed in life and education, or we accept the narrative focused on tests scores and deficit thinking. When educators question their socialization, they can re-evaluate their thinking about what is possible with CLD learners.

Thinking critically about our assumptions has the potential to move our teaching forward. Creating spaces that speak to the population we serve will not be achieved by our merely planning activities that highlight the culture and language of the learner. Rather, the history, language, knowledge, skills, and perspectives of learners must become the linchpin of our daily practice. In other words, our planning, resources, instruction, and assessment must be informed by the communities, families, and learners we serve.

Culturally relevant teaching pushes us toward creating democratic schools where equity, respect, and belonging abound—spaces where the identity of the family and learner are central to decisionmaking processes. Classrooms can too easily become places where drill and practice, rote memorization, and project completion become the norm, without "harvesting" the gifts of the learner. It is important to resist a focus on preparing learners to fit the same pattern, to leave behind their histories, joys, and language and become just another face in a single file. As educators, we must prepare to transform the space in which we teach. As Geneva Gay (2018) reminds us, through culturally responsive teaching we have the power to transform education as it exists today.

Culturally Responsive Teaching

No one would intentionally deny any student the opportunity to bring his or her "historical self" into the classroom. Nor would we ever want to deny students their language or culture while we teach. However, creating a learning ecology that is culturally relevant and responsive to CLD students requires more than good intentions. To do so effectively involves thoughtful planning, continuous learning, and conscious reflection on our most deeply held beliefs and assumptions.

Over the last three decades, much as been written about what it means to teach in culturally responsive ways (e.g., Gay, 2000, 2018; Nieto, 1992; Nieto & Bode, 2018; Ogbu & Simons, 1998). Each of these educators and researchers agrees on the need for:

- Holding high expectations
- Valuing families' and students' ways of being
- Creating contexts where all voices are provided an opportunity to be heard
- Creating classroom ecologies that care for and respect the student, regardless of background
- Using what is learned about students' biographies to plan lessons that are meaningful to the learner

Working in schools, I am guided by the ideas and words of Geneva Gay, who describes what it means to be culturally responsive in classroom practice. She states:

> *Culturally responsive teaching* is defined as using the cultural characteristics, experiences, and perspectives of ethnically diverse students as conduits for teaching them more effectively. It is based on the assumption that when academic knowledge and skills are situated within the lived experiences and frames of reference of students, they are more personally meaningful, have higher interest appeal, and are learned more easily and thoroughly (Gay, 2000). As a result, the academic achievement of ethnically diverse students will improve when they are taught through their own cultural and experiential filters. (2002, p. 106)

I am continually reminded that we cannot hope to achieve our goal of having CLD students reach their individual potentials unless we know who they are and what they dream of becoming in the future. When classrooms become places where failure is seen as just another opportunity to learn, students risk without fear. According to Gay (2018), "Culturally responsive teaching is a means for unleashing the higher learning potentials of ethnically diverse students by simultaneously cultivating their academic and psychosocial abilities" (p. 21). This can only happen in contexts that care for, respect, and validate the uniqueness of every student.

In culturally responsive classrooms, teachers not only make decisions about their teaching based on students' biographies, but they also often take on the challenge of doing so in sociopolitically charged environments. Such environments draw out the courage of educators, enabling them to become advocates for doing what is right for CLD students. Thanks to the courage of such teachers, all students can be challenged and supported to become critical thinkers and learners who look forward to taking the next steps in reaching their dreams.

Culturally Sustaining Pedagogy

The greatest level of respect a family and learner can be shown is our honoring and utilizing their heritage and community practices and the funds of knowledge of the home that have sustained and anchored the wealth of assets present. Schools have the potential of becoming spaces that acknowledge and utilize students' historical, cultural, and linguistically bound ways of being and ways of knowing to transform education. The work of Django Paris (e.g., Paris, 2012; Paris & Alim, 2014, 2017) serves to illuminate the present condition. Educators who are committed to creating and exploring culturally relevant and responsive classrooms are asked to hold a mirror up to their own practices in an act of self-critique. What have efforts to date accomplished? Where have we fallen short?

When pedagogies that include "culture" in the name become buzzwords in our hallways, we must ask ourselves, What observable evidence confirms that our instructional practices are different from those found in any other classroom? The goal of culturally sustaining pedagogy is "to perpetuate and foster—to sustain—linguistic, literate, and cultural pluralism as part of the democratic project of schooling" (Paris, 2012, p. 93). How do we work, within the context of our daily lessons, to sustain the languages, literacies, and cultures of the learners in our classroom communities?

To effectively sustain something, it is important to perceive and understand threats to its survival. It can be tempting to think of the four walls of our classroom as a protective firewall, buffering us from outside sociopolitical influences. Yet, it is those very forces that create the conditions that place CLD students and their families at the periphery. The classroom is the place for exploration, analysis, and critique—for ourselves and for learners. It is only through interactions with others who bring histories, experiences, and perspectives different from our own that we have opportunities to expand our understanding of self and society. After all, what do we mean by "real-world applications" if our view of the world is limited to our own slice of reality?

By actively engaging the community, learning from the family, and understanding the biography of the learner, teachers actively empower themselves to have defensibility of practice (Herrera & Murry, 2016; Herrera et al., 2020). With the ability to articulate the *what* and *why* behind our pedagogical practices, we are better prepared to perceive and question the dominant ideologies that undergird practices in classrooms and schools that become oppressive for CLD students and families. We also are positioned to take an active role in envisioning and helping to create more equitable conditions that speak to the historical and sociopolitical realities of our specific context and the community we serve.

BDI, therefore, serves as framework for our collective movement from culturally relevant, responsive, and sustaining *theory* to pedagogical *enactment*. It provides a lens for assessing what we know, believe, and do against the benchmark of CLD student engagement, wellbeing, and success. BDI brings the CLD learner to the center of our efforts, building on what we know about the social nature of human learning and development. It is to these foundations of learning that I now turn.

I Need You, and You Need Me: Learning as a Social Practice

In the name of efficiency and standardization, policies, programs, and practices are developed to advance the learning of CLD students, assuming that educators hold the answers. This severely underestimates the power and potential of *learners* within our classroom communities. The resulting conditions frequently involve students being placed in relatively homogeneous groups to focus on increasingly isolated types of skill development. In doing so, *all* learners lose out on the diversity of thought, skill, and experience that is essential for expansive learning opportunities. Vygotsky and Krashen stand out among theorists who have provided foundational insights into the conditions needed to bolster learning and language development for CLD students.

Vygotsky and the Zone of Proximal Development

Within sociocultural theories of learning, the **zone of proximal development (ZPD)** (Vygotsky, 1978) is one of the core constructs that helps us understand students' developmental patterns and the type of input that must be provided to foster their growth. The ZPD was conceptualized by Lev Vygotsky in response to observations he made of learners engaged in individual versus mediated performance assessment. The ZPD is used to explain the relationship between learning and development and reflects ideal learning conditions.

Vygotsky (1978) defines the ZPD as "the distance between the actual developmental level as determined by independent problem solving and the level of potential development as determined through problem solving under adult guidance or in collaboration with more capable peers" (p. 86). Vygotsky posits that all individuals have the potential to learn, and that learning is highly dependent upon the particular context, situation, and social interaction. Vygotsky's characterization of the ZPD is built on the assumption that to understand child development, one must take into account how the child interacts with his or her environment. Such social interactions also are reflected in the learner's biopsychosocial history.

Aljaafreh and Lantolf (1994) describe the ZPD as "the framework, par excellence, which brings all of the pieces of the learning setting together—the teacher, the learner, their social and cultural history, their goals and motives, as well as

the resources available to them, including those that are dialogically constructed together" (p. 468). The classroom spaces that we seek to create involve teachers intentionally supporting learning and development by engaging with students and providing opportunities for peer interaction. These purposeful interactions push learners to think about new concepts, use new vocabulary and language, consider issues from multiple perspectives, and negotiate meaning together.

Krashen and the Input Hypothesis

The work of Stephen Krashen also has contributed to our understanding of how to take students from their current point of development to the next level. However, unlike the work of Vygotsky, Krashen's research focuses on second language acquisition and learning. At the core of this research is Krashen's (1984/2005) **input hypothesis**, which suggests that language is acquired "by understanding input containing $i+1$; that is, by understanding language that contains input containing structures that are a bit beyond the acquirer's current level" (p. 40). In other words, teachers might think of Krashen's small "i" (in "$i+1$") as a snapshot of the individual student at the present moment of his or her language development.

In light of this widely accepted theoretical construct, one would expect classroom plans and processes to be organized around the student's biography. Additionally, one might predict that pedagogy would be orchestrated to place English learners in contexts and situations designed to carry them linguistically to $i+1$, meaning that the students would be continually stretched just beyond the current limit of their language abilities. At present, however, there appears to be a gap between what Krashen's input hypothesis suggests and what actually happens in classrooms that serve CLD students.

Typically, teachers endeavor to provide comprehensible input by using traditional components of sheltered instruction, such as visuals, guarded vocabulary, cooperative learning, and hands-on activities (Herrera & Murry, 2016). Although these efforts can be helpful for comprehension at the surface level, they do not take us far enough to promote meaningful learning through connections between the known (students' background knowledge) and the unknown (new curriculum and language). As Krashen (2009) argues, rather than planning for *comprehensible* input, our emphasis should be on ensuring that input is *comprehended*. This type of transformative comprehensible input (Herrera et al., 2017) can only happen if our classroom processes support learners in sharing with us how they are making sense of the new information. Throughout this book, readers will find steps and examples for providing a "tool in the hand" for students to first make connections to their lives and what they already know and then document new learning within the same artifact. Using these tools, along with implementing strategic grouping configurations, revoicing student contributions, and allowing time for students to confirm/disconfirm connections, are ways teachers can scaffold comprehension throughout the lesson.

When considering how they will effectively apply the input hypothesis to classroom practice, teachers utilize information about the following aspects of the emergent bilingual learner:

- Native language
- Proficiency in listening, speaking, reading, and writing the native language
- Stage of English language development
- Schematic connections to the topic at hand
- Cultural discourse patterns
- Preferred types of interaction

The student's ability to notice, comprehend, and respond to potential input during the teaching and learning process depends on the existence of suitable learning contexts and conditions within the classroom. Teachers striving to create opportunities that support students to progress one step beyond their current level of performance not only understand the theoretical underpinnings of second language acquisition but also reflect upon how a student's biopsychosocial history and individual biography influence language learning. Chapter 3 of this book elaborates on how Krashen's findings can assist this process.

Commonalities in the Contributions of Vygotsky and Krashen

It is easy to understand how comparisons of these two great thinkers, Vygotsky and Krashen, have come to be part of discussions regarding the education of CLD students. Long-standing conversations have drawn a parallel between Vygotsky's ZPD and Krashen's $i+1$ construct (R. Ellis, 1997; Nyikos & Hashimoto, 1997). For example, Guerra (1996) notes that Krashen's i "is what Vygotsky called the actual development of the child" and "the $i+1$ stage is the equivalent to Vygotsky's zone of proximal development. It refers to the kind of input that is at a level of difficulty which immediately follows the i stage" (p. 7). Using these two theories in conjunction to inform practice has the potential to move CLD students one step beyond, both academically and linguistically. However, we must guard against oversimplifying what it means to determine the i, or the actual development of the student. We must value multiple perspectives on what counts as "knowledge" rather than allowing our view of a student's current level of development to be limited by the results of standardized tests.

Even before we think about strategies and tactics for taking theory into practice, we must examine the attitudes and beliefs guiding our current efforts with CLD students. Take a moment to reflect upon the following questions:

- What factors influence the way my daily instruction looks?
- How do I document the actual developmental linguistic and academic levels of my students?
- What kinds of strategies do I use to move students from their existing knowledge and skills to more advanced understandings of new curricular materials?
- What types of observations do I make throughout the lesson to gain insight into how CLD students understand (or do not understand) vocabulary, concepts, and tasks?
- How do I use grouping configurations to promote social interaction and learning?
- How do I incorporate observations regarding CLD students' information processing to enhance and/or modify my lesson in the moment?

In classrooms where cultural and linguistic diversity is increasingly the norm, it is essential that instruction be designed to take *all* learners beyond their current level of development.

According to Vygotsky (1956), "Instruction is good only when it proceeds ahead of development. It then awakens and rouses to life those functions which are in a stage of maturing, which lie in the zone of proximal development. It is in this way that instruction plays an extremely important role in development" (p. 278). The strategies and activities used during the lesson "rouse" each learner's developing understandings and skills, which are anchored in past experiences and existing knowledge. As learning continues to progress, the students and teacher continually connect the past to the present, and the present to the future, through social interactions such as instructional conversations. For this reason, teaching and learning that are organized around Vygotsky's and Krashen's constructs must involve planning, teaching, and assessing with the biographies of the learners in mind.

Students are asked to brainstorm about the events and experiences they consider most important in their life. The teacher then connects the things that the learning community has in common. *(Image courtesy of Jamie Williams, Bilingual 3rd Grade, Iowa)*

Teaching and Learning in the Third Space

Across the country, CLD students and their teachers are brought together in classroom spaces to make sense of multiple institutional agendas and expectations of schooling. The conditions created in these spaces can be transformative or oppressive, depending on how teachers make decisions and organize learning environments. When educators work to move beyond the status quo, CLD students' biopsychosocial histories, biographies, knowledge, and Discourse are valued and utilized beyond superficial attempts to "celebrate" students' culture and language. Gee (1990) defines Discourse (with a capital D) as commonly shared "ways of using language, of thinking, believing, valuing, and of acting" (p. 143). Discourse shapes our way of knowing as we interact with popular culture and our traditions while simultaneously building relationships with our families and communities, including our classroom communities (Moje et al., 2004).

Gee's conceptualization of Discourse is closely linked to the idea of **funds of knowledge** (Moll et al., 1992), which highlights the wealth of knowledge and resources that students accumulate from their homes, families, and communities. Discourse and funds of knowledge, although tied to a student's culture, are situated within a student's unique, individual biography. Esteban-Guitart and Moll (2014) more recently utilized **funds of identity** to describe the historically accumulated, socially distributed, and culturally developed resources that are key to a person's self-understanding, self-definition, and self-expression. The individuality of the learner as well as his or her socially situated relationships and activities are among influences that determine which resources are most relevant and useful. Teachers who capitalize on students' ways of knowing and interacting with the world understand that CLD students' assets have the potential to accelerate learning and create true teaching and learning communities (Benson, 2010; Esteban-Guitart & Moll, 2014; Moje et al., 2004).

Often, however, CLD students' assets are left untapped because the classroom does not provide a place for them to become part of the curriculum. Teachers often have not been prepared to recognize this kind of information or use it to differentiate instruction. Kris Gutiérrez and colleagues (e.g., DiGiacomo & Gutiérrez, 2017; Gutiérrez, 2008; Gutiérrez & Johnson, 2017; Gutiérrez et al., 1995) conceptualize a classroom "space" where the negotiation of disparate assets, demands, expectations, and needs becomes possible. Uncovering, discovering, and utilizing students' funds of knowledge and Discourse during instruction enables us to bring together what Gutiérrez and colleagues (2003) refer to as the "official space," characterized by the teacher's Discourse and the school curriculum, and the "unofficial space," characterized by the students' background knowledge and thoughts related to the curriculum. Teachers

co-create this new "**third space**" with learners in the moment; it cannot simply be willed into being or built into a lesson plan (Gutiérrez & Johnson, 2017). Through responsiveness to contributions of individual learners and the voice of the collective classroom community, teachers dive deeper into the sensemaking process *with* students. Together, they jointly negotiate Discourse and knowledge, utilizing all linguistic and cultural repertoires of practice (DiGiacomo & Gutiérrez, 2017; Gutiérrez & Rogoff, 2003). This type of interaction makes the curriculum truly relevant to students in relation to their communities and the larger world. This third space is an indicator of culturally relevant, responsive, and sustaining classrooms.

According to Gutiérrez and colleagues (2003), in third spaces "alternative and competing discourses and positionings transform conflict and difference into rich zones of collaboration and learning" (p. 171). Taking students to their zones of proximal development requires more than superficial ways of thinking about and using prior knowledge. When teachers create conditions and situations in which they activate, connect, and affirm the multiple dimensions of CLD students' biographies, third spaces become the norm. The joint construction of meaning through interactions that disrupt typical teacher–student power dynamics makes it possible to turn classrooms into sites of learning within a *collective* zone of proximal development (Gutiérrez, 2008; Gutiérrez & Johnson, 2017). Teachers and students learn from one another as they harness the power of their distributed knowledge and experience toward increased understanding.

These oftentimes uncomfortable spaces center questioning, ambiguity, acknowledgment of tensions and contradictions, and critical social thought (DiGiacomo & Gutiérrez, 2017). Third spaces encourage youth to use their cultural past "as a resource in the present and a tool for future action" (Gutiérrez & Johnson, 2017, p. 253). They value imagination and collective social dreaming for a more just world, as well as movement toward the ideal in the here and now (Gutiérrez, 2008; Gutiérrez & Johnson, 2017). By creating such contexts that counter default teaching scripts and make new forms of participation and support possible, teachers foster relational equity that promotes students' ability to contribute authentically to classroom activity, shape knowledge production, and assume increased responsibility (DiGiacomo & Gutiérrez, 2017).

Research Into How the Brain Learns

If the ZPD and *i*+1 prepare us for asking questions about what contexts and situations are best for taking students—regardless of background—to the next level academically and linguistically, current brain research sets the stage for us to understand the kinds of learning conditions that support the brain in perceiving input, making sense of it, and effectively storing it for future use. Cognitive science reminds us of the relationship between the body, the brain, and the social and cultural context. Bondebjerg (2017) emphasizes that our networks and connections are grounded in social and cultural similarities and proximity, with emotions often playing a central role. Let's take a moment to reflect on the congruence of students' cultural and linguistic backgrounds with our own instruction. In what ways do we build on the home literacy practices of CLD students and their families? How do we create classroom conditions that encourage students to use their native language skills as resources for learning? In what ways do we structure activities and interactions to allow for multiple entry points to the content, as well as diverse ways of exploring issues and solving problems?

The impact of culture on learning and cognition is far reaching and frequently overlooked. Veissière and colleagues (2019) contend, "Although it is clear that specific developmental experiences—governed by explicit social norms and contexts—shape these perceptual, cognitive, and attitudinal processes, most of cultural learning appears to be *implicit,* in the sense that it occurs without explicit instruction" (section 1.1). This means that teachers and students come to shared learning spaces with only implicit understandings of how their culture has shaped their ways of perceiving, interpreting, and interacting in the world. All members of the learning community have been socialized to view their ways of knowing, understanding, and interacting as logical, sensible, and comprehensible to others. Given our highly diverse classrooms, pivotal questions become, In what ways are we as educators accounting for culturally influenced understandings and experiences of the curriculum? How are we creating instructional ecologies that attend to the perceptual, cognitive, and attitudinal processes with which students come equipped?

Learners are shaped by their backgrounds and experiences, both in the classroom and beyond (Kieran & Anderson, 2019; Sousa, 2017; Willis & Willis, 2020). Although people from shared heritage backgrounds might have many cultural aspects in common, their lived experiences make their individual ways of knowing unique. According to Sousa (2017):

> The total of all that is in our long-term storage areas forms the basis for our view of the world around us and how it works. This information helps us to make sense out of events, to understand the laws of nature, to recognize cause and effect, and to form decisions about abstract ideas such as goodness, truth, and beauty. (p. 58)

Students bring this view of the world, which Sousa calls our **cognitive belief system**, when they enter our classrooms.

Often, we educators speak about the importance of students' schema, or background knowledge. Neuroscience also reinforces that a learner's existing neural network and connections to it throughout the learning process are critical (Zadina, 2014). However, our actions in the classroom do not always demonstrate adequate consideration for the diversity of knowledge students possess, and often reflect assumptions about the relevance of their previous schooling experiences. Kieran and Anderson (2018) argue that educators must consider the extent to which students' prior learning experiences were actually meaningful and linked to their lives. This awareness is especially important when considering the past schooling experiences of CLD students, who have been historically marginalized or oppressed. Our ability to construct knowledge and effectively store information in long-term memory requires that *sense* and *meaning* characterize the new information to be learned (Sousa, 2017). Relationships and semantic associations must be made between the new information and the information already stored in our memories (Bjork et al., 2013; Zadina, 2014). In learning spaces that fail to provide these conditions, students are left at a disadvantage.

Many teachers find themselves needing support to help students activate and bridge from the worldview constructed in their past to the present, and from the present to the future. We must prepare lessons that take learners from what they know to an understanding of the unknown, new information. Engaging the brain requires that learners be motivated and supported to actively learn (e.g., through connecting, elaborating, interpreting, and interrelating) (Bjork et al., 2013). This, according to Sousa (2017), requires teachers to use strategies that promote students' personal connections to the curriculum and that hold every student accountable for his or her learning. To this end, strategies in the chapters that follow support teachers in facilitating those essential connections between the students' worldviews and the curriculum.

This book cannot fully do justice to cognitive science by providing an in-depth guide to what brain researchers tell us about the self in relation to learning, but it offers introductory ways to think about how CLD students' background knowledge relates to our **classroom ecology**—that is, to the students, the teacher, the community, and all the other dimensions and dynamics of classroom practice. Manipulating the ecology in effective ways then becomes a matter of asking questions that are not so much, What do I need to make my CLD students academically successful? but rather, Who is here? and What does this mean for my teaching practice? Jensen (2006) poses the following suggestion: "Think less in terms of what *one thing you can do* and start thinking in terms of *creating conditions for contrast*" (p. 207). In saying this, he refers to the need for us to create places where students are always anticipating the challenge and excitement of the new learning that lies ahead. Figure 1.2 suggests ways to create these conditions in practice, which will be discussed in detail throughout this book.

What the teacher does before, during, and after the lesson creates the "contrasting environments" to which Jensen refers—environments that provide opportunities for students' exploration, learning, and growth. These kinds of

---

FIGURE 1.2
Monitoring Our Inclusive Practice

- Get to know the biographies of your students. Who are they?
- Listen to what students have to say, and use their voice as your point of departure to make lessons meaningful.
- Create an environment that values interaction for both social and academic tasks.
- Select strategies that maximize students' self-knowledge, create low-risk learning environments, and support students in integrating new information with their existing understandings.
- Make time to affirm and celebrate language, culture, and learning.

---

environments are possible only when the classroom provides conditions and situations that are "substantially richer" than what the student already is exposed to or knows. Much like the constructs of Vygotsky and Krashen, brain research reminds us that in order to "invite" the brain to learn, the teacher must value what each student brings to the learning situation and create engaging circumstances to challenge each brain. I call this process "getting oxygen to the brain," and it requires that teachers:

- Keep students "on their toes" as they engage in the lesson
- Allow students to negotiate the curriculum in a variety of ways and through interaction with multiple people
- Work with students to co-create new models for information by integrating the curriculum with the knowledge that each member of the learning community, regardless of background, brings to the learning endeavor

Strategies and activities can be used to support students as they construct meaning by activating what they know and working with others to build understanding. Ultimately, our guidance should result in students using their new-found or elaborated knowledge and skills to analyze, synthesize, evaluate, and create ideas relevant to their learning. This is what taking students "one step beyond" is all about. Information that is linked to the past, experienced in the present, and taken into permanent memory is more likely to be available to the learner in the future.

Many classrooms where CLD students find themselves today do little to invite students, with their unique histories, experiences, knowledge, and personalities, to engage in learning. Jensen (2006) says it best when he reminds us:

Many students struggle through school, never finding out . . . their passions, their strongest talents, or their preferred modes of communication. This puts them

at a tremendous disadvantage because it is their strengths that will help them cope and even thrive in this world. (p. 209)

Even though they may be operating within a context of standardized testing, educators can rise to the challenge to strategically and systematically select strategies that respond to the needs of all learners, rather than succumb to the more "drill-and-kill" approach, where students are asked to "repeat after me" in lessons that are so scripted that even the teacher's brain struggles to remain engaged. Such lessons leave little hope that students will be motivated to learn. In classrooms where the culture and language of CLD students are not valued, the brain often shuts down, and little or no thinking takes place.

For optimal thinking and learning to occur, all aspects of the classroom must be designed with the learner in mind. When we think about the classroom only in terms of a physical environment—for example, as related to arranging desks in a certain way because it meets the demands of "the way I teach"—we limit our opportunities to create brain- and student-compatible places where activities and strategies can bring school and learning to life for CLD and other students. Furthermore, when envisioning ways to create contexts and situations conducive to learning, it is helpful to think about the lesson in three distinct phases: *activation* (before), *connection* (during), and *affirmation* (after). I offer a brief introduction to these phases here; each will be further elaborated in subsequent chapters of this book.

- **Activation.** If we believe, as brain research tells us, that new information is learned only if the new information can be attached to something that is known or has meaning for the learner, it becomes critical that teachers look for ways to activate CLD students' **background knowledge**. Strategies implemented before the lesson can provide opportunities for students to share, or make public, what they know about the curricular concepts, language, and skills being covered. But what good is it to ignite, or activate, background knowledge, and then leave it in the dust as we proceed into the lesson to introduce new concepts? Successful activation requires that we remain present to observe when and how the student activates the brain, listening and watching for insights about his or her knowledge that can be taken into the lesson. To support students in making meaningful links to new learning, we must first learn what they know!
- **Connection.** Cognitive research tells us that the human brain has roughly a 30-second holding pattern for new information that enters (Sousa, 2017). This means that if a student determines that the information is of little or no importance, it's gone. If, in the activation phase, we have made note of the knowledge and associations that students already possess related to the lesson, we

can more easily find ways during the lesson to make the curriculum relevant to the students. In this way, students are more likely to retain new information in their memory for a substantially longer period of time, long enough to actively make sense of it. During the lesson, the teacher takes on the role of facilitating learning and creating conditions that encourage learners to practice and apply new vocabulary and concepts in meaningful and interactive ways. It takes multiple meaningful exposures, with different people and for a variety of purposes, for students to come to a thorough understanding and take ownership of the new information.

- **Affirmation.** Regardless of an individual student's academic or linguistic starting point, all learners need to have their learning affirmed. The importance of this principle cannot be overstated. Affirmation must be given in a way that lets students know their effort during the lesson was worth it: "Look at what you have learned!" By providing time in the "after" phase of the lesson for one final review and rehearsal of the new information, we prepare students to individually demonstrate their learning. Then, at the end of the lesson, we can ask learners to complete assessment tasks, knowing that we have provided students with the tools and understandings they need to succeed. Students do not want to be asked to produce something that is out of reach—they want a chance to show others what they have learned. Acceptance and affirmation lead learners to not fear taking risks in their learning, because they already know the teacher and their peers value them as learners. When we expect everyone to learn and hold everyone accountable for learning—*believing and communicating to students that everyone has potential*—we will begin to see the results we work so hard to achieve!

Brain research provides insights that can help us as we strive to create the conditions that allow students to reach their ZPD and receive *i*+1 input. Such research enables us to better understand how learners perceive, work with, and store new information. The key to all these processes is our knowledge of each student's biography (Semrud-Clikeman, 2015). Rather than relying solely on the results of standardized tests to tell us what students know and can do, the most effective educators of CLD and other students employ strategies that delve into students' long-term memories to expose the wealth of their knowledge and experiences, which combine to form the fundamental core beliefs and understandings that affect their interpretation of new material. Using these student understandings to guide our subsequent decisions about instruction and assessment results in biography-driven decisionmaking.

The use of relevant strategies before, during, and after the lesson will support students' comprehension and storage of new content and language input. As Willis and Willis (2020) state, educators must learn how to "hone strategies to guide students' brains to more effective focusing, sustained attentiveness, and active construction of understanding and memory so that they can store, connect, and retrieve, and extend learning to new applications, problems, and innovations" (p. 2). In this way, we can enable students to move from memorizing isolated facts to internalizing understandings that are personally relevant in the present and available for the future (Willis, 2010). No one can be forced to learn. We can only encourage, support, and thus motivate students to join the community of learners on their educational journey.

Making It Happen!
How This Book Can Guide
Next Steps

Now more than ever it is important to understand teaching and learning from a more sociocultural and humanistic perspective, using a "lens" that focuses our attention on the student and not on current political agendas. As educators, each of us wants to do what is best for all students; yet we can often become overwhelmed with all that comes our way from the sociopolitical climate we work in, the school culture we find ourselves in, and the magnitude of the curricular and assessment demands that are imposed upon us.

For too long we have danced around what it means to be "student centered" when it comes to instructional practices for this growing population. In this book, I make more explicit what it means to teach CLD students. I discuss the four dimensions of the student biography, which is at the heart of how students learn and retain new information. Furthermore, this book adds to the discussion of sheltered instruction, differentiated instruction, and other methods and philosophies that work to enhance educational opportunities for all students.

In biography-driven instruction for CLD students, *the journey truly is the destination.* Just as it is for our students as they navigate new content in our classrooms, *every successful step along the way constitutes its own arrival.* As you undertake this journey, I encourage you to think about what you already do in your teaching that is connected to the perspectives and strategies recommended here, while remaining open to other approaches you may never have considered before. It is not possible, nor is it necessary, to perfectly incorporate every new idea as soon as you are introduced to it. Rather, begin the journey with a simple willingness to shift perspective. This openness to re-envisioning what is possible has the potential to keep our feet on the path to enhanced classroom practice, and our hearts on the academic success of all students.

2

Biography-Driven Instruction

GUIDING QUESTION

What role does using the biopsychosocial history of the learner play in building relationships and creating instructional spaces of hope and learning?

See the online Discussion Guide for opportunities to further explore answers to this question and connections to chapter content with a colleague or team. Available for download from the Teachers College Press website: tcpress.com

EVERY JOURNEY we make begins with planning for learning, acknowledging that there is much to see, hear, listen to, feel, and learn. The journey might be for business, pleasure, a family visit, or in response to an unexpected event. In our educational space, the journey of becoming increasingly skilled in working with culturally and linguistically diverse (CLD) students in the classroom is no different.

For most of us, part of the decision to become a teacher hinged on our interest in children, adolescents, and young adults as individuals—in the unique character of the students we could imagine ourselves teaching. Our vision of these learners was framed by our own experiences in classrooms and the community in which we were socialized. However, the reality we may have faced when we arrived in our first classroom, and the reality we more frequently face in our classrooms today, is usually far removed from the initial idea of teaching we once held. Part of what has changed in our classrooms is the sense that on a daily basis we must juggle political pressures, "one size fits all" curricula, and testing—while at the same time pursuing the myth (within spaces that do not allow for alternative/innovative ways of using different tools) that we can do all of it and also attend to the socioemotional, linguistic, and cognitive dimensions of students. Yet, it is not an either/or situation. The journey toward becoming a more culturally responsive teacher begins with the intent to raise our own awareness of how the uniqueness and individuality of each learner factors into student learning.

This chapter introduces and describes the elements that comprise the *biopsychosocial* history of the CLD student.

This complex term encompasses the many facets that define the individuality of each student in a classroom. This chapter also describes the four interrelated dimensions of the CLD student biography that were introduced at the end of Chapter 1—the sociocultural, linguistic, cognitive, and academic dimensions—and explores the sociocultural dimension from two different perspectives. The goal in this chapter is to move beyond school-initiated definitions and notions of the sociocultural dimension and toward culturally responsive teaching pedagogy. As described by Gay (2018), culturally responsive teaching places students at the center of teaching and learning. When we take the risk of stepping outside the boundaries often set in schools, we provide opportunities for students to express knowledge and understanding that is more deeply rooted in their culture, language, and life experiences. In this way, we, as part of an educational system, begin the journey of accelerating CLD students' academic development.

This chapter guides you to explore the following questions:

- How is the sociocultural/emotional dimension tied to my teaching, students' learning, and our cognitive belief systems?
- What role does the sociopolitical climate and related dynamics play in classroom teaching?
- How does the climate of the school/classroom make a difference in academic learning?

For every concept presented in this chapter, there is an *exception to the rule*. Every thought and action will take its own unique path based on the biographies of the students and families in your specific setting. As you read this chapter, remind yourself that it is *you* who will use the information to create your own pathway—often a road less traveled—toward optimal learning. By exploring the biographies of your students, their families, and the context in which they live and learn, you will come to realize the many unique opportunities you have for reaching every CLD student in your classroom.

Biopsychosocial History

For educators, the last two decades have proven to be a steep and ever-changing journey of unanticipated learning curves, requiring us to attend to competing curricular and testing agendas, while at the same time being responsive to the learner. I often ask educators, What is most important within your educational space: families and students, curriculum, or instruction? The response is always a resounding "families and students," followed by the "however" statement to sum up how contradictory the messages are that they receive about planning and delivering instruction for students who do not fit the mold. With frustration and exhaustion, teachers describe the reality of curricular mandates that change every year, along with the latest rhetoric on building relationships, socioemotional learning (SEL), and culturally conscious discipline, each supposedly grounded in becoming culturally responsive. These agendas become mantras to post on our walls and espouse at community and family meetings. Yet, culturally relevant, responsive, and sustaining theories are left in books and meetings or in shallow professional development sessions that often do not go deep enough to effect real change.

A deeper exploration of how to enact each of these theories in practice is made more complex by the reality that while students may have the same country of origin, race, ethnicity, culture, and native language, they each bring their own biopsychosocial background and experiences, or history. The concept of biopsychosocial history might best be understood by thinking about the many facets of our own lives. By understanding our own unique complexity, we educators can begin to understand the CLD student. **Biopsychosocial history** is a term used to describe the most basic elements of human experience, which include the *biological, psychological,* and *sociological* aspects of an individual (Engel, 1977; Gates & Hutchinson, 2005; Herrera et al., 2020; Saleebey, 2001).

The Biopsychosocial Model

George Engel developed the biopsychosocial model in the 1960s and 1970s. This model represented a revolutionary way of understanding and responding to disease and illness in the medical field (Borrell-Carrió et al., 2004; Engel, 1961, 1977, 1980; Smith, 2002). The prevailing model up to that point was the biomedical model, which guided health professionals to approach medicine from a very analytic perspective that relied heavily on biological cause–effect relationships. Patient care tended to be performed in an objective and frequently dehumanizing manner. Little attention was given to the patient's subjective experiences (Borrell-Carrió et al., 2004).

The biopsychosocial model reflects increased awareness of the complexity surrounding health issues and the multitude of factors—including those at the molecular, individual, and social levels—that affect someone's well-being. The psychosocial dimensions of an individual ("personal, emotional, family, community") are considered in addition to the biological aspects (Smith, 2002, p. 309). Biopsychosocially oriented patient care attends to the patient's fears, concerns, and expectations. Health professionals develop caring relationships with their patients and offer empathy, generosity, and compassion throughout diagnosis and treatment (Borrell-Carrió et al., 2004).

The biopsychosocial model has since been applied in other fields as well, such as psychology, education, and social work (e.g., Melchert, 2013; Rotatori et al., 2014; Saleebey, 2001). We do not have to know how to spell *biopsychosocial* or commit the order of the component parts to memory. We *do* have to know and understand how these aspects impact the motivation, engagement, and learning of each and every one of us. Within our students' biopsychosocial histories, we can begin to find the keys to unlock their potential for academic success.

My research and exploration of the biopsychosocial history of the CLD student began two decades ago as an attempt to better account, in BDI, for the complex, nuanced, and, at times, conflicting backgrounds, knowledge, skills, and experiences—reflective of the collective history of the learner, family, and larger community—that each student brought to the classroom. The biopsychosocial history served as one way to acknowledge and synthesize the educational literature pertinent to student-centered factors that most influence the efficacy of promising practices for CLD students (Herrera et al., 2020). Effective practice, we know, requires answers to questions such as, What has prompted this student and his or her caregivers to relocate? Has the transition been stressful, dangerous, or depleting? What has been the individual's history of education? What is the home language? Has the student fled a war-torn country? Has the student experienced or witnessed violence? Does the student live in a supportive community, a dangerous community, or both? Is there a level of fear, stress, or anxiety? What cultural connections or community agencies may be able to ameliorate the transition challenges for this student and her or his caregivers? Although the biopsychosocial history of the individual has been utilized in the literature of medicine and psychology, within those domains it has been criticized as too *fluffy* and lacking diagnostic and scientific grounding (Henriques, 2015).

Envisioning Biopsychosocial History in Educational Contexts

In our work as teachers, we would be the first to admit that we are not doctors and that we are fully aware that a wide range of factors outside the classroom and the school may impact CLD students' success in school. Therefore, what may be considered *fluff* in some areas of study has profound relevance in education, such as knowing the following:

- What are the biological realities of the learner (e.g., skin color, developmental age, physical health)?
- Is the learner psychologically present, or is he or she distracted by stress and anxiety related to the community, school, or home?
- What societal supports will the learner have in the home, school, or community to support and sustain the native language and culture? To adapt to a new community, school, and second language?

A focus on the biopsychosocial history of the learner in the classroom broadens our perspective from considering primarily cognitive and academic factors to addressing other sometimes more urgent and crucial factors impacting the CLD student's readiness for learning, engagement with the curriculum, lesson comprehension, and school success.

The working model of the adapted biopsychosocial history complements and provides the foundation for what BDI refers to as the *biography of the CLD student* (Herrera & Murry, 2016). The CLD student biography, discussed later in this chapter, prompts teachers to explore the sociocultural, cognitive, linguistic, and academic dimensions of students' challenges and processes in learning and schooling. As we prepare to take a deeper look at each part of the biopsychosocial history, we must keep in mind that no conceptualization of the student will ever be able to encompass the full story of what the learner and family experience. All educational spaces are surrounded and influenced by forces of the sociopolitical context. All too often, resulting school contexts reflect a history of conditions that have failed to live up to the promise of liberatory praxis—failed to provide "oxygen for the soul" that CLD students and families need to thrive. In such spaces, it can be difficult for administrators to lead and for educators to teach. Where do we begin as we seek to change course and chart a new future?

As educators, we must consider both the official and the unofficial space as we carry out our craft. We do this, in part, by acknowledging threats from external forces (e.g., national, state, or local anti-immigrant sentiment), which must be navigated and negotiated in order for us to be culturally responsive in the classroom. Culturally responsive and sustaining educators become artists, utilizing all resources to find a balance where threats are acknowledged, teaching is informed by critical reflection on practice, and families become true collaborators in our shared goal of preparing learners who believe in their own potential and have the capabilities and agency to take the next steps toward a future they co-create.

Confronting Our Reality: Invisible External and Internal Forces

As we take a closer look at each part of the biopsychosocial history, we must remember how closely they are intertwined. Together, the biological, psychological, and sociological distinctions serve to expand our awareness and perception of pivotal factors that influence students and their learning. Our ability as educators to be responsive to the individual learners in our classrooms depends on our understanding their histories.

Biological Aspects

I have long posed questions about the meaning perspectives that we as educators hold in relation to the students of color, youth living in poverty, and linguistically diverse learners that we serve. According to Alcoff (2006), as humans we become actors within public spaces who take on the characteristics and expectations of those around us. Figure 2.1 illustrates the biopsychosocial realities/planes in which we teach and learn. As we consider the biological aspects of the learner, we may think first of those biological aspects that are determined well before the time the student arrives in school. We can be concerned about the development and physical well-being of the learner, asking questions such as these:

- Has the student had an eye examination?
- Has the student had a hearing test?
- Does the student have any special needs?

CLD students may not have had access to regular checkups to ascertain their physical needs, and such circumstances can have implications for their learning.

Migrant children, for example, have a high incidence of hearing loss due to lack of medical care at a young age. Often ear infections go untreated, and this can lead to difficulty in learning to read using current programs based on knowledge of English sounds, such as phonics. Although we cannot control biological factors, we can observe and seek attention for the medical needs of our students. Frequently, schools provide students with hearing, speech, and vision exams. If such services are not available at the school, referrals to appropriate clinics or organizations can be given. Similarly, school services are in place to provide equitable access to learning for students with special needs.

One of the most visible of biological traits is skin color. The visible identities of students of color are met with a full range of responses from those of us who teach. As educators, our socialized self has the potential to influence how

FIGURE 2.1
Biopsychosocial History

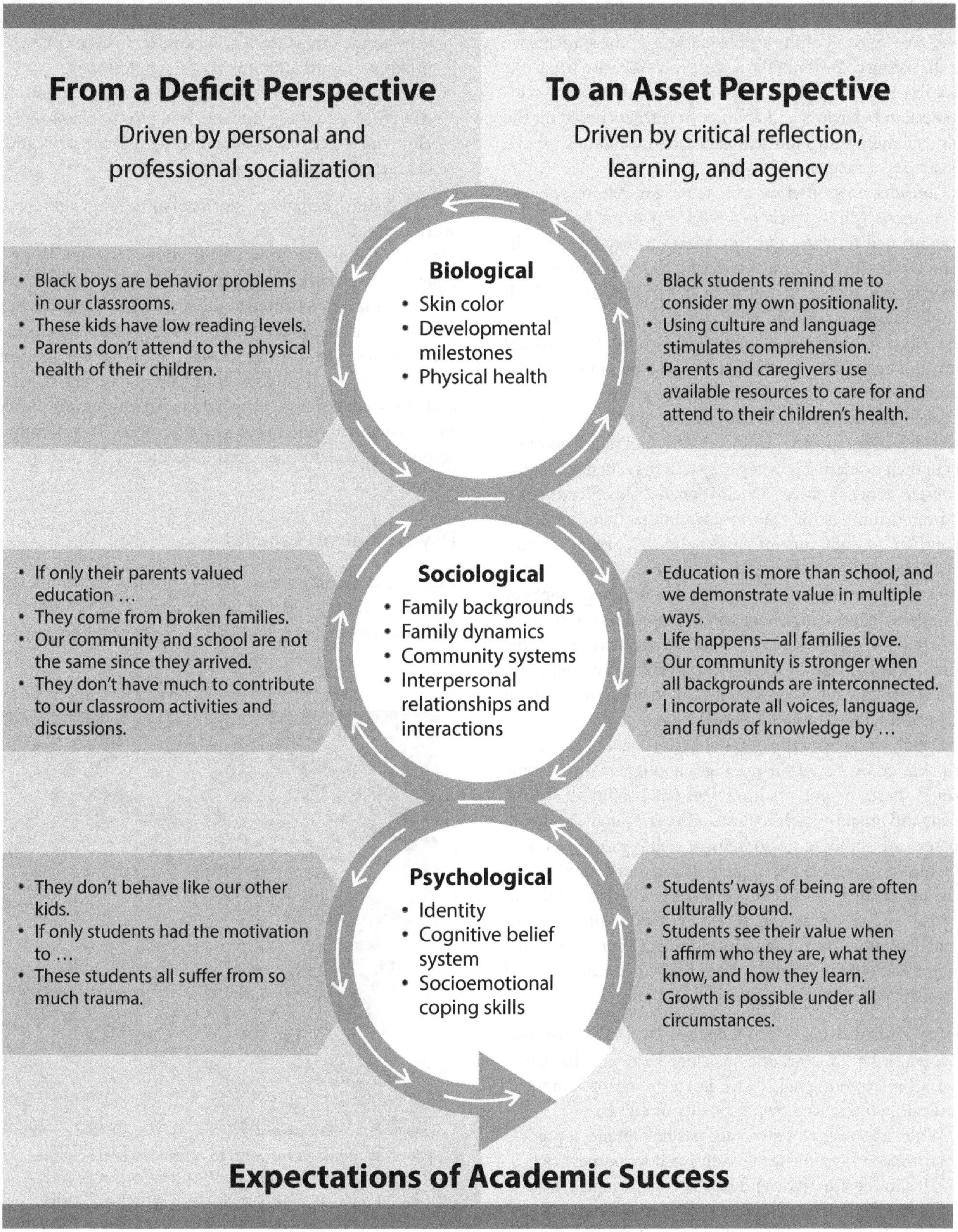

From a Deficit Perspective

Driven by personal and
professional socialization

To an Asset Perspective

Driven by critical reflection,
learning, and agency

Biological
- Skin color
- Developmental milestones
- Physical health

- Black boys are behavior problems in our classrooms.
- These kids have low reading levels.
- Parents don't attend to the physical health of their children.

- Black students remind me to consider my own positionality.
- Using culture and language stimulates comprehension.
- Parents and caregivers use available resources to care for and attend to their children's health.

Sociological
- Family backgrounds
- Family dynamics
- Community systems
- Interpersonal relationships and interactions

- If only their parents valued education …
- They come from broken families.
- Our community and school are not the same since they arrived.
- They don't have much to contribute to our classroom activities and discussions.

- Education is more than school, and we demonstrate value in multiple ways.
- Life happens—all families love.
- Our community is stronger when all backgrounds are interconnected.
- I incorporate all voices, language, and funds of knowledge by …

Psychological
- Identity
- Cognitive belief system
- Socioemotional coping skills

- They don't behave like our other kids.
- If only students had the motivation to …
- These students all suffer from so much trauma.

- Students' ways of being are often culturally bound.
- Students see their value when I affirm who they are, what they know, and how they learn.
- Growth is possible under all circumstances.

Expectations of Academic Success

we enact our craft based on the assumptions and messages we have received about the CLD students we serve, as well as the deeply rooted ways of doing that already texture our pedagogy. Although many teachers work under the mantra "I don't see color" or "I see all learners as part of the human race," we *do see* all of the visible markers of the students we teach. Seeing color is not the issue. Problems arise when our socialized ways of responding to color result in our ascribing certain behaviors and abilities to learners based on the color of their skin (and associated connections to social constructs of race and ethnicity).

Consider how often we hear messages that, in one way or another, say it is typical of a Black boy to not be engaged or motivated to learn. Our socialization may have conditioned us to think this way, especially if we work in technocratic spaces that adhere to a model of efficiency, which simplifies our understanding and responses by providing a prescribed roadmap to facilitate the work we do—a model devoid of attending to the history and biography of the learner. Figure 2.2 summarizes many of the differences between systems that utilize a technocratic rather than an asset-driven perspective. Unfortunately, CLD students often begin their academic journey in spaces that often stay at the lowest level of cognitive participation, devoid of instruction and opportunities for collaborative interaction that could take them to their zone of proximal development (Vygotsky, 1978) and provide *i*+1 (Krashen, 1984/2005). In such spaces, the conditions perpetuate a self-fulfilling prophecy of underachievement, where societal messages are so common that learners begin to buy into the narrative and incorporate a self-image of themselves as failures or deficient, and where low test scores lead only to more prescribed/scripted interventions and more drill and practice.

Deficit thoughts, not always conscious, about the learner's skin color, based on messages about racial or ethnic groups, have the potential to cloud one's ability to see the needs and innate gifts that students bring. Human beings all possess the ability to do something well regardless of gender, race, national origin, language background, or physical/learning challenges. Teachers do well to check their thinking habits by daily asking how they may be limiting students' potential by subconsciously setting conditions that do not scaffold the learner toward his or her academic and linguistic potential. Consider the following:

- For students labeled "too talkative," "too social," or "too loud," we need to ask the question, Through what lens am I interpreting talk? Is the learner's way of communicating influenced by personality or culture?
- When a learner of a given age has not yet met a predetermined milestone for learning or development (e.g., "He's in the 4th grade and he still can't read it."), how do we respond? Developmental stages account for approximations with regard to age and performance. Yet, expectations about which skills to begin learning

or to emphasize for students of particular ages or in different levels of schooling can differ across cultures and contexts. When culturally loaded expectations are not met, do we consider the milestone a lost cause and switch to a "damage control" mentality? Or do we find ways to maximize the learner's assets to accelerate progress toward attainment of the milestone?

- For students who have physical or learning limitations, what assets do these students bring to the classroom? How can we encourage and highlight those skills and characteristics for their peers to see?

If students' behaviors, performance, language use, or worldviews do not align with the expectations of typical U.S. schools or our own socialization, we often begin to assign characteristics to groups of learners (e.g., Asian students as the model minority, Latinx learners as having a *mañana* attitude, Black youth as loud). A deeper understanding of students gained through conversation, listening, and observing will guide us to the unique potential, assets, and gifts found within each student. All learners are entitled to have opportunities to become their best selves. Culturally responsive educators set conditions that make such growth possible.

Psychological Aspects

Most CLD students who arrive in our classrooms from another country did not ask to leave their community, their native language, and their culture to come to a new

Asking students to respond to questions and activities that provide insights into their lived experiences and states of mind as they participate in school and daily activities helps us connect to their emotional and psychological needs.

FIGURE 2.2
Asset-Driven Versus Technocratic Perspectives

Criterion	Asset-Driven	Technocratic
Purpose of Education	Maximization of the human potential/ family and learner	Efficiency in the educational system (e.g., schools, classrooms)
School Leadership	Values the autonomy of knowledgeable, racially/culturally responsive, ethical, and caring educators	Values top-down, business-like, administration of efficiency maximization, cost minimization, and quantitatively measured accountability in schools/classrooms
Teachers	Are mostly autonomous facilitators of asset-based, student capacity building through a humanistic perspective/authentic *cariño*, that values learner diversity	Follow top-down decision making; conform to standardized protocols with fidelity; are accountable for standardized assessment scores among students
Learners	Bring a diverse range of characteristics, home environments, experiences, ways of knowing, languages, and more to the classroom	Prepared using a curricular scope and sequence that adheres to rigid cognitive/ developmental benchmarks for each grade level, with socioculturally bound expectations (e.g., are familiar with practices, values, and institutions of the dominant culture)
CLD Students	Bring a diverse range of characteristics, experiences, ways of knowing, and languages that are approached in the classroom as strengths for constructivist teaching and learning	Bring challenges (deficits) that reduce the efficiency/efficacy of classroom teaching and learning and, therefore, must be remediated
Diversity	Enhances the range of knowledge, experiences, perspectives, problem-solving, learning, and more, to which students are exposed	Challenges and limits the standardization and efficiency of classrooms, schools, and the larger educational system
Dominant Teaching & Learning Philosophy	Constructivism	Behaviorism
Typical Emphases of Teaching and Learning	Whole to part; active, student-centered learning; democratic environment; teacher as facilitator; autonomous/student-accountable learning	Part to whole; teacher centric learning through stimulus-response, repetition, and memorization; externally motivated learning using positive reinforcement/ punishment

Sources: Mehta (2013); Murry and colleagues (2020).

and exciting place. They often must transition quickly from an environment that includes friends and close family ties to an environment a great distance from "home." Learners in this scenario must deal with uncertainty on a daily basis.

Whether born in the United States or abroad, *all* students—including those who are living in poverty, struggling with trauma, grappling with a learning disability, learning a second language, or facing racial discrimination—come to our classrooms to engage and become equal participants in the classroom community. Almost immediately, learners who are the most vulnerable and marginalized are tested, sifted into "ability groups," and routinely removed from the content or grade-level classroom based on the assumption that they could not possibly perform in that context. Before we explore what is possible through inclusionary practices that maximize each learner's knowledge, experiences, and language, decisions are made and the scaffolding and interactions key to students accessing and engaging in rigorous academic content are removed.

These types of processes, which are so common in our educational systems, present unpredictable experiences for students. They also send powerful messages about what is expected and valued that can affect learners' psychological well-being. Often their cognitive beliefs about harnessing their academic potential or learning the English language become dimmed by self-doubt. Policies that place the primary emphasis on testing serve as a path that leads many CLD students to believe they are not capable of achieving the same success as many of their peers.

Educators have all witnessed the power of our own thinking and how it influences what we believe is possible. As adult learners, we are capable of positive self-talk, critical analysis, critical reflection, and letting go of thoughts that are self-destructive. However, children, adolescents, and young adults have yet to achieve the socioemotional and cognitive processes to fully navigate and push back on voices that send messages about the color of their skin, their language, or their academic abilities. The messages received have the potential to affect their cognitive belief system (Sousa, 2017). How learners perceive they fit into a learning space has a significant impact on their motivation and engagement to produce. Ask yourself how the culture and climate of the school and the practices of your classroom set learners up for success. What aspects of each might lead to (or hinder) positive psychological states of mind for the learners in your classroom? How does the learning community become a social space, before it becomes an academic space?

We as educators must navigate and positively influence the psychological states of our learners if they are to reach their full potential (Ainley & Ainley, 2011; Cholewa et al., 2014; Linnenbrink-Garcia & Pekrun, 2011). This begins by moving beyond the superficial behaviors and responses of learners and observing the student throughout the learning process. Consider the following questions to more deeply explore the classroom messages students receive that may impact their psychological well-being:

- How do I create opportunities for the student's identity to be shared and affirmed within the community throughout the lesson?
- What conditions do I set for attending to the socio-emotional dimension of the learner?
- How do I ensure that all learners experience the same content, learning goals, lesson objectives, and opportunities to interact with the classroom community?
- What words do students use to describe themselves, their friends, and their family members?
- How often do I monitor students' states of mind?
- What intentional grouping configurations do I design and use during lessons, considering students' language proficiencies, countries of origin, and affective needs, as well as the empathy levels of peers?

At times, we may feel as though we are probing into the lives of students and asking for information they consider private. Although this can be a concern, learning more about a student's life can inform us about the psychological factors that may be supporting or inhibiting his or her learning. Therefore, do not be afraid to gently learn from the student and the family about their fears, frustrations, and successes. Sharing our stories and reaching out is what connects us as human beings—and as teachers and learners.

Sociological Aspects

We rarely think about the influence that society has on what we teach, how we teach it, and why we teach it. Such influences can come from individuals with anti-immigrant sentiments and can be observed in media coverage that marginalizes CLD students and their families who have moved to this country. Often, racist and discriminatory messaging targets those who have lived their entire lives in the United States. These societal influences, which are often political, have implications for us as teachers and for CLD students as learners.

How often do we feel disappointed by decisions made about the program and curriculum that must be followed, or about the assessments that will be used to determine the level of students' academic growth? The decisions about programming, curriculum, and assessment that influence what happens to learners are often dictated by the politics of the day or district mandates driven by individuals who may not understand the needs of CLD students and families or the realities of different schools and classrooms.

In the midst of these outside pressures, we must continually reflect on why we teach. For most of us, our commitment to teaching might involve the desire to reach students and develop the citizens of our country and world. By asking ourselves the following questions, we become better able to navigate the politics of our school, community, state, and nation, and we ready ourselves to move forward in doing what we were prepared to do—teach.

- Is the surrounding community welcoming toward immigrants and those who bring diverse languages, cultures, and religious beliefs?
- What language is used to describe the population we serve in my educational context?
- Do I critically reflect on and discuss media portrayal of CLD families and students with my class?
- Do I know where I stand and what I believe about teaching CLD learners?
- What is the impact of the current national, state, local, and school messages sent to CLD families and students in my setting?
- In what ways do I set create conditions for open discussion about local issues and those presented in the media?

- In what ways are discussions to prepare students to be part of the community and for global citizenship based on what they have to contribute?

Those of us that serve CLD families and students often find that our own psyche plays tricks on us. As we receive societal messages that give way to defining what it means to come from a linguistically diverse home, a single-parent home, or a low socio-economic background, we begin to assimilate those messages, which paint a picture of the many challenges we face in being effective with learners that fit into such categories. We forget that families have rich experiences, language, and histories that may be different from what we or the system values, yet are assets that could serve to reimagine the way we plan and deliver curriculum in schools.

Unfortunately for our families and students, the wealth they bring in experiential assets often does not fit into our typical systems or structures, which frequently only serve to limit and exclude their funds of knowledge. At the same time, these institutional ways of engaging in the educational enterprise often do not allow or open spaces for us to apply our professional selves—to use our own creativity and innovation in classroom practice, so that we might learn and use the experiences and assets that students bring to the classroom.

What if all educators learned, planned, practiced, and critically reflected on teaching decisions through a biopsychosocial lens? What might change if we always questioned how these three aspects of the learner were influenced by outside forces, or how long-standing deficit perspectives might be driven by our own socialized meaning perspectives? Biological and sociological factors have an incalculable impact on the psychological well-being of the families and students we serve. As we actively work toward becoming culturally responsive, culturally sustaining educators, our enhanced understanding of students' biopsychosocial histories can set us on the path toward an asset-based pedagogy. Figure 2.3 depicts how we can glean information about each of the aspects of students' biopsychosocial histories through the classroom work they produce.

FIGURE 2.3
Biopsychosocial History in Classroom Practice

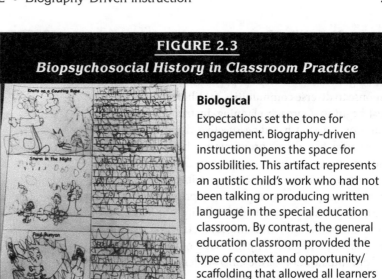

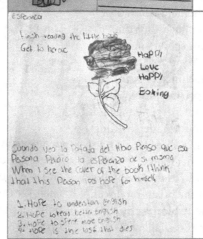

Biological
Expectations set the tone for engagement. Biography-driven instruction opens the space for possibilities. This artifact represents an autistic child's work who had not been talking or producing written language in the special education classroom. By contrast, the general education classroom provided the type of context and opportunity/ scaffolding that allowed all learners to maximize their potential.

Psychological
Teachers can gain insights into the psychology of the learner by providing opportunities for students to share about their dreams, aspirations, and emotional responses to the curriculum.

Sociological
Allowing learners to connect their lived experiences to the content using their full repertoire of language resources provides the greatest information about family and community assets.

So . . . Now What?

Educators who are putting together the puzzle of understanding their diverse student population realize that in our response to diverse communities, families, and students, we must begin to approach planning, instruction, and assessment from an asset-based perspective, deciding how to best move past deficit-driven programs, methods, and models of instruction. An essential step is constant "habit checking" of assumptions about what is possible. Understanding threats, staying current on promising practices, and having research that supports our defensibility of practice is the point of departure in advocating for instruction that is biography driven and guided by the assets of the learner.

Conceptualization of the CLD student biography builds on the work of Thomas and Collier (1995, 1997, 1999, 2002). Their multisite, multidimensional longitudinal research guided my efforts as a researcher and educator for decades. Thomas and Collier (1995) outlined four dimensions that greatly influence CLD student success in school. The four dimensions—*sociocultural, linguistic, cognitive,* and *academic*—form the basis for all teaching and learning. Together, they are encompassed in the **prism model**, which is depicted in Figure 2.4. These four interdependent and complex dimensions are the foundation for understanding linguistic and academic growth of CLD students. While crucial for CLD students, this model benefits all.

Building on this foundational work, I collaborated with others to expand on the dimensions of the prism model to develop the concept of the **CLD student biography**. The CLD student biography accounts for the challenges and processes associated with each of the four dimensions. Successful educators explore and understand these dimensions through multiple lenses—like a photographer trying to fully represent the many dimensions of a subject. Grounding our work in the *biography* of a student's learning experiences, funds of knowledge, and ways of knowing can support teachers in providing culturally responsive, sustaining education that liberates. The four dimensions at a glance are as follow:

Sociocultural Dimension. This dimension represents what a student brings to school from the resources he or she has learned from birth. Although these understandings and skills may differ from prevailing definitions of what counts before a child enters school, for CLD students they represent the treasures of their life. Exploration of this dimension must move beyond simple interest surveys and toward an understanding and utilization of students' funds of knowledge, as they relate to the content of our daily lessons.

Linguistic Dimension. Language is not a static number on a test. Rather, language is the dynamic tool we use to express our thoughts and to communicate about, and comprehend, the daily interactions that surround us. To educate CLD stu-

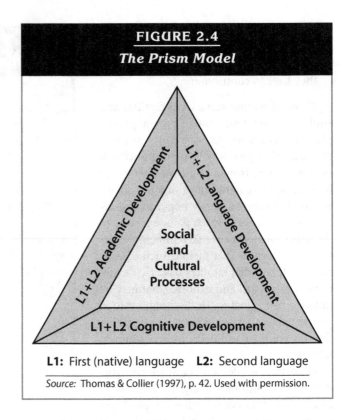

FIGURE 2.4
The Prism Model

L1+L2 Academic Development

L1+L2 Language Development

Social and Cultural Processes

L1+L2 Cognitive Development

L1: First (native) language   **L2:** Second language

Source: Thomas & Collier (1997), p. 42. Used with permission.

dents involves the skill of listening beyond the spoken word, where our efforts to understand become a gift that allows us entry into the student's heart and mind. Many say that our language cannot be separated from our culture. Our instruction can profit more from active listening and making connections to a student's culture than from knowing a student's score on a particular test.

Cognitive Dimension. Have you ever been fascinated in watching a student and wondered how it was that he or she creatively solved the problem at hand without you? When we teach, questions related to students' approach to problem solving can seem perplexing at times. Yet, we know that all individuals take different paths when making decisions, solving a problem, or sharing a story. A student's culture has great influence on his or her way of thinking, knowing, and applying information. If throughout lessons we provide a "gallery" for students to "exhibit" their thoughts and learning, we provide an opportunity for their culture and language to make themselves visible that otherwise would not likely exist in the school.

Academic Dimension. Academic success can usually be equated with the level of access that has been afforded to the individual, particularly if a high-quality education has been denied due to a student's level of linguistic ability or socioeconomic background. How is it then that we can profess to provide an equitable opportunity for every CLD student who enters school? Every CLD student has the potential to learn and become proficient in the English language. If we rely less on the test and focus more on the learner, then we may move forward toward creating places where every child's potential is realized.

IN THE NEXT SECTION of this chapter, we will begin our "deep dive" into the how we as educators can come to more fully understand the human potential that is reflected in the individual learners of our classroom communities.

The CLD Student Biography

By becoming aware of the many changing family and individual dynamics of our students, we can set positive conditions for learning, harvest what is known throughout the lesson, and assess what students bring to our classrooms. It is also important to foster a safe environment for students to tell their stories so that we, as educators, can understand the multiple layers that inhibit or accelerate language and academic learning.

We must use what we learn before, during, and after our lessons to assess students' language and academic growth and to strive to understand them from both a school and a cultural perspective. To begin, take a few minutes to assess your current understanding of what the sociocultural, linguistic, cognitive, and academic dimensions represent in classroom practice. Figure 2.5 provides a brief activity that

can help guide your self-assessment. As you learn more about the first dimension of the CLD student biography, begin to ask yourself how you might plan, teach, and observe student behavior through the prism of your new insights and learning.

The Sociocultural Dimension

Transitions: Viendo hacia un futuro

Un futuro
  Un futuro de historia
   Todos tenemos historias
    Por eso estoy aquí
   We all have stories
    I am here
     Get to know me and you will see
      I have a different point of view.
—*BESITOS/Herrera Terry (2004)*

The complex variables that influence our way of life, our definition of love, and what makes us laugh also influence a student's motivation and engagement to learn. This **sociocultural dimension** of the CLD student biography is at the heart of language acquisition and learning. The sociocultural dimension includes the adjustment and development processes that students go through as they learn to

---

FIGURE 2.5
Hearts Activity

1. Take a piece of paper and draw hearts on the page to mirror those illustrated here.

2. For each layer of the heart, do the following:

   • *Outside Layer of the Heart.* Record the words that come to mind when you hear the words *sociocultural, linguistic, cognitive,* and *academic*. What are some challenges that students face in these areas?

   • *Middle Layer of the Heart.* Record tools and strategies you use in practice when considering the dimensions of your students.

   • *Center of the Heart (or outside the heart for additional space).* Write about an experience from your classroom practice that comes to mind when you think of the sociocultural, linguistic, cognitive, and academic dimensions of the CLD student biography and the challenges you face.

3. Read the rest of the chapter and consider connections to your own practice, as reflected in your completed heart. More specifically, what are some of the assets you could draw upon from your students' backgrounds to enhance your teaching practice?

A template for classroom use is available for free download and printing from the Teachers College Press website: tcpress.com

respond to unique, idiosyn-cratic ways of being and be-having both in and out of school. Sociocultural devel-opment is driven by:

- *Social institutions*, including the home, school, and societal interactions
- *Affective influences*, including self-esteem, anxiety, and motivation
- *Social interactive phe-nomena*, including bias, prejudice, and discrimination

These images reflect how two different educators approached the teaching of nouns. The picture at the right provides a biography-driven perspective to literacy development, in which the language and knowledge of the learner are used to bridge into grade-level concepts.

Independently and together, each of these factors creates a variety of complex language and learning issues, including student/teacher/family interactions, a student's learning process, and other dynamics of teaching and learning.

Traditional School-Initiated Responses

In response to these dynamics, school environments have long focused on learning about the sociocultural dimen-sions of a child's life by using tools that provide information related to the culture and language of the student, family, and community. Some of the most typical efforts include:

- Learning about the traditions of different ethnic groups and celebrating important aspects of those cultures
- Making sure the environment and curriculum in some way mirror the lives of the students in the classroom
- Using the student's native language when necessary to increase communication
- Using interest inventories to learn about the students and their families
- Celebrating holidays

Many educators have broadened their horizons by going further, through:

- Learning the language(s) of their students, or at least enough vocabulary to demonstrate interest and respect
- Visiting the communities where their students live
- Conducting interviews with community members to learn about the students and families in the community

One of the most important ways teachers learn more about their students is through home visits. A home visit can illustrate and strengthen a teacher's understanding of the multidimensional facets of students' lives. Home visits enable teachers to become more aware of:

- Family structures and roles

- Students' learning styles, acculturation levels, and lan-guage development at home
- Communication patterns within the family

When teachers enter households not with the purpose of discussing a student's reason for absences or failure to thrive at school but as genuine ethnographic researchers wanting to gather information, they are able to dip into the palette of opportunities to create an all-encompassing portrait of their students. By learning about and drawing upon fami-lies' household resources, networks, and survival strategies, teachers can play the role of cultural mediators between the school culture and the home culture.

Home visits allow us to see nontraditional forms of lit-eracy development and evidence of student skills that we may not see demonstrated on traditional classroom assign-ments. At times, home visits may also force us to live in the moment and delve deeply into the challenges of over-crowded living, multiple jobs, and beginning levels of pro-ficiency in English. If we consider the influences these con-ditions might have on a student in relation to academic success, access to English language models, and accultura-tion, we may begin to understand the student behaviors and responses we witness in our classrooms. In addition, home visits help us see our students as creative explorers who are dynamic and adept members of their families and communities. Through newfound understanding of the variables that bring our students love, life, and laughter, we are better able to create a sense of belonging among the learners in our classrooms.

The following excerpt exemplifies the kind of insights educators can gain from a home visit:

> As I visited the parents, something else I found very intriguing was that Dad usually gave Amla and Amaan choices about their culture versus American

culture. Many festivities that we have are not celebrated in Jordan—Halloween, music activities, etc. Dad said he gave Amla a choice in those situations. He said if she wants to participate in music at school, it would not be a big problem. Amla always asks her dad what he would want her to do and he replies he would prefer her not to, but it is her choice. So she does not participate in music here at school or celebrate Halloween. She remains very true to her country and culture and is very proud of where she is from and her family background.

This actually made me realize that the students truly are living two worlds at the same time and are so adept at making choices. If that is the case, then why don't I present Amla with situations where she can make different choices about content in the classroom.

—*Brooke Jones, Elementary Teacher*

Think about how home visits can take a teacher one step beyond in her own teaching. Although making home visits can be challenging because it often requires going into spaces that are outside our comfort zone, doing so can prove pivotal to our discovering student assets and eliminating barriers in our classroom practice. Figures 2.6 and 2.7 provide tips and an example guide for conducting home visits.

Home visits, as well as the other aforementioned ways of learning about the sociocultural aspects of a student's life, have long been documented in the research and practical literature of the field (Herrera et al., 2013; McCarthey, 2000; Reid, 1996). Educators who use what they have learned about CLD students and families in their teaching move beyond the "institutional curriculum" to one that is more inclusive, participatory, and ultimately transformative. By capitalizing on students' cultures, educators increase the likelihood of students' active engagement in learning. Figure 2.8 depicts the school-initiated responses common to the sociocultural dimension, as well as those related to the linguistic, cognitive, and academic dimensions, which are discussed in Chapters 3, 4, and 5.

Socioculturally Speaking: *i*+1

The aspects of the sociocultural dimension discussed thus far affect our decisions for planning instruction, buying curricular materials, interacting with students, and teaching lessons. Yet, traditional ways of learning about the sociocultural dimension of students tend to yield somewhat limited information for teaching lessons, because they frequently provide a point-in-time understanding of a student's way of life outside school. Without additional sources of information to provide context for a particular event or particular data, our understanding of a student may be limited to the interpretations we make of what was learned in that moment. Systematically contextualizing our lessons to include the assets, skills, and knowledge students bring enriches the lesson delivery process. If we fully understand what living arrangements, language brokering, traditions, and language use are found in the home, we are better prepared to teach.

As educators, it is always important to be able to shift our ways of thinking. Homes that are non-normative are actually more interesting than we might expect and hold more potential than we could ever imagine. This change in thinking, however, will require language use that does not focus on the aspects of how a family lives and interacts that might seem odd to us. Rather than casting aside experiences that do not align with our own frame of reference, it is better to celebrate the ways that others actually live (e.g., different

---

FIGURE 2.6
Tips for Teachers Conducting Home Visits

1. Go into the homes of students as an ethnographer. That is, do not go into the home with an agenda; rather, go in with an open mind and with the goal of learning as much about the students and their families as possible.

2. Pose open-ended questions such as:
   - What would you like me to know about your child?
   - What goals do you have for your child?
   - How do you think I can best support your child to meet these goals?
   - What questions do you have about me and/or my classroom?

3. Encourage parents to share information about their children informally (e.g., likes, dislikes, personality traits, strengths, areas where they might need support).

4. Advocate for home visits as a powerful tool for learning about your students while taking into consideration district guidelines.

5. If possible, identify and bring a paraprofessional or other volunteer who can translate if necessary.

6. Be sure to follow up with parents via verbal and written communication regarding the date and time of the home visit. Remember to work around *their* schedule.

7. After you have completed the home visit, take time to document your observations and insights as they relate to the sociocultural, linguistic, academic, and cognitive dimensions of the CLD student biography and think about ways you can bring these into the classroom.

FIGURE 2.7
Guide for Home Visits

Home visits (duration about 45 minutes to an hour) can provide an amazing source of information regarding the sociocultural, linguistic, cognitive, and academic dimensions of CLD students. When talking with caregiver(s), it is important to consider that most caregivers hold teachers in very high regard.

Observations During Home Visits	Sample Questions

• In some cultures, parents are not the ones who are directly responsible for their children; oftentimes, the grandparents are important caregivers (e.g., in families from India). Who is/are the student's primary caregiver(s)?
 	
• What types of learning opportunities are available to the student at home?
 	
• Do the parents/grandparents/siblings/extended family members read to the student?
 	
• What role do stories play in the student's language development?
 	
• What insights are revealed about the student's cultural learning style?
 	
• What are the family's goals for the educational, vocational, and personal development of the student?
 	
• What general expectations do the caregivers/parents have for the student? This often varies across cultures.
 	
• What roles does the student play at home? Sometimes students perform the role of caregiver for younger siblings while parents work in the evenings.
 	
• What is the level of acculturation of the child and his or her family?
 	
• What are the cultural norms of the family (e.g., not looking another in the eye while speaking)?
	• *Ask open-ended questions:*
	  ◆ What would you like me to know about [student's name]?
	  ◆ What do you think he/she does especially well?
	  ◆ What did you want to do when you were young?
	  ◆ What do you wish for your child?
	
	• *Ask about the student's language opportunities at home:*
	  ◆ Does the student get to go to the grocery store? Make a grocery list?
	  ◆ Does the family discuss television shows (e.g., novelas)?
	  ◆ What role does music play in the home?
	  ◆ Are there any books that the family reads together?
	  ◆ Do the parents/siblings/extended family members tell stories? For what purposes (e.g., to entertain, to teach lessons) are the stories told?

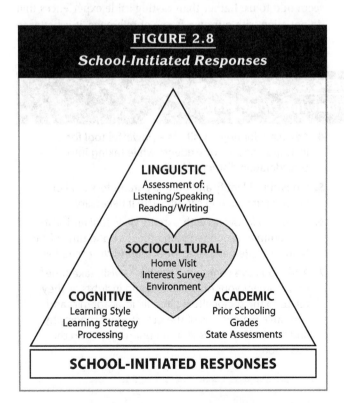

FIGURE 2.8
School-Initiated Responses

family structures, different living arrangements, different traditions) and use these new experiences to provide an encouraging and rich classroom community.

Given the pace of life in schools, we do not give much thought to allocating some of our time before the lesson to learning about how the student's life experience might manifest itself in the lesson we are going to teach. Little attention is given to how a student's emotions might relate to the vocabulary or topic to be taught. The following sections move us one step further in considering new lenses we can use to observe the students in our classrooms so that we will be better able to feel and think *with them* as we teach. Chapters 7, 8, and 9 provide practical strategies to help reveal the sociocultural picture of students' lives—a picture that reflects the heart of their experiences.

Life: The Wide Angle

In my current work in schools, I have been exploring the effect that a student's life has on his or her engagement in the classroom and motivation to risk sharing about the ways he or she personally relates to a lesson. *Life* can be defined as the entirety of what an individual has experienced and what he or she is experiencing in the present. These experiences determine our psychological, sociological, linguistic, and academic thoughts and actions. At the end of each day, many students leave school to participate in home and community situations that often do not fit within our own frame of reference; yet these experiences can enrich our teaching.

As you read the following vignette, consider ways this student's experiences could contribute to your classroom learning community:

> After school Cecilia walks home from her 6th-grade classroom with her four brothers. A long afternoon awaits her because she has to make sure dinner is cooked for all the family. She also must make sure that the house is ready, because six members of her mother's family will be joining them this evening. The relatives just lost their jobs in Colorado and will be living with Cecilia's family until they can decide what will happen next. Cecilia lives in an efficiency apartment with her brothers and parents (and soon the six members of her extended family). She looks forward to everyone getting together because that means staying up until early morning, laughing, and listening to the adults tell stories about their struggles in the United States. Often Cecilia wonders how losing a job can be amusing. For now, she needs to focus on getting ready. She needs to rearrange the furniture and figure out where everyone is going to sleep before *mama y papa* come home from work. She also needs to figure out how to make the potatoes, meat, and flour feed 12 people instead of six. She looks forward to all the craziness of everyone being together again, if only for a short time.

Life happens, and we all must play the game with the cards we are dealt. As children, we rarely ask questions about what is happening. It is what we know and live, and it can bring love and laughter to our life.

Given the right tools, we educators can create environments where we can become part of the fabric of our students' lived experiences. We can draw on our CLD students' experiences, knowledge, and problem-solving skills and frame them within the contexts of our academic world. For example, given the scenario just described, we could certainly find ways to integrate aspects of Cecilia's life into mathematical explorations of dividing portions, discussions of efficient use of electricity and other resources, and so forth. We can provide what I call a "canvas of opportunities" for students to think about and talk about, and we can celebrate their contributions. Tapping into the resiliency factors that contribute to students' abilities to manage life outside school has the potential to accelerate language and literacy development. These opportunities help create the

Sharing our past experience with others and then taking our combined perspectives to text increases the likelihood that what we are learning will be more meaningful. *(Image courtesy of James Callahan, High School, Kansas)*

classroom conditions needed for students to become valued members within the academic learning community.

Love: The Group Shot

Our life is filled with emotional and social aspects that often influence our attitudes, thoughts, and behaviors. The ways we demonstrate *love,* and what we love, are heavily influenced by the life we have experienced in and out of school. Often we teachers wonder how it is that parents can make certain decisions related to our students. At times we may think, "Can they truly love them? If they do, why don't they make decisions that make sense? Why do they not support them in learning English? Why do they not read to them at night? Why do they send their children thousands of miles away to a new and unknown country to live with friends and extended family? Why do they take them out of school for so long? How can this be love?" Consider the following vignette about Angelica. How would you interpret and react to the family's decision about Angelica's education?

> Since arriving in the United States at the age of 13, Angelica had been the perfect daughter. As the oldest of four children, she was the first to learn English and thus became the language broker of the family. When things went wrong because of her father's drinking, she was there every Monday to translate with the judge. When it came time to ask *el patron* for the family's paycheck at the end of a long week in the fields, it was Angelica who was there to deal with the sarcastic remarks about the "kids" not earning their pay. There was no dating, no talking on the phone, no, no, no, to anything that was "American." "You know those girls are not like you," her mother would say, "They have no morals, no rules."

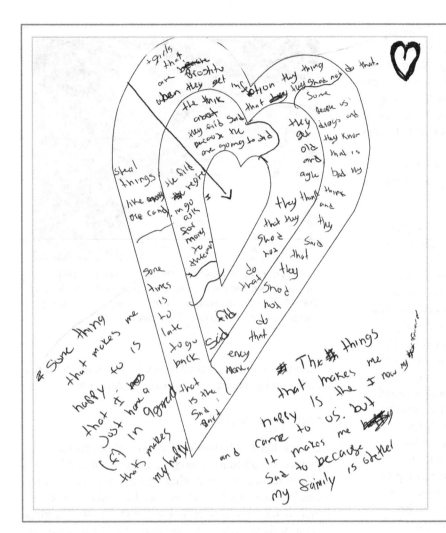

**Hearts Activity:
One Teacher's Perspective**

I used this activity to introduce *Bleachers,* by John Grisham. One of the major themes is regret. I introduced the word and then we started on the outside with examples. The middle heart was used to document feelings associated with regret. Students used the center heart (or outside of the heart) to write about personal regrets or fond memories.

Working individually, in pairs, or in small groups, the students were able to understand what it means for a text to have a "theme." By providing them an opportunity to link the story to their own experiences and share with each other, the activity promoted sociocultural con-nections and language development as they discussed with each other what they wrote. For preproduction and early pro-duction (students not ready to write in English), I had them write in their native language and then get assistance from a peer who could translate. This lowered the students' anxiety and they were more engaged. I observed the students thinking in ways that connected themselves to the standard I was trying to teach, one that is difficult to get across in traditional ways.

—*James Callahan, High School, Kansas*

(Remember, every immediate family has its own unique value system.)

In school Angelica excelled, always keeping up with everything, no matter where her year started or where it ended. Her senior year came and it was time to graduate with honors and make a decision about which college she would attend. Her counselor was excited about the many possibilities and the scholar-ships coming her way. This was Angelica's dream. So, when Angelica came and told her that she would not be attending college and that instead she would con-tinue to work, the counselor was devastated. How could Angelica's family do this to her? How could they take away this opportunity? Did they not love her?

The answer for Angelica's family was quite simple: Her parents loved her so much that they wanted to protect her from all harm that might exist outside their familiar environment and circumstances. Send-ing Angelica to a place that was beyond their scope of understanding represented a risk too great to take for their only daughter.

Gaining insight into what it meant for Angelica's parents to live in a new country with new rules, and at the same time try to protect their children from harm, can give us a new perspective about why families and students make decisions that are not always within our own cultural boundaries of understanding. It becomes our role to step out of our com-fort zone, care about how our students define what they love, and explore the histories of our students and their families. Such efforts can help us understand the love-cen-tered motives behind others' actions and illuminate ways we can work *together* with families to support our students. Gay (2018) finds that teachers who really care about stu-dents' humanity move beyond the parameters defined in school and toward a more caring way of teaching.

Laughter: The Close-Up

What does not make you laugh can sometimes make you cry. Which would you prefer to do? We often look at stu-dents' lives and wonder how they can be so resilient given the many life challenges they face. Through my own lived experiences and the stories my students have shared over the years, I have come to realize that laughter and humor

By creating classroom contexts and opportunities before the lesson that are risk-free and that allow students to disclose what they bring to the lesson, we gain valuable insights that we can use during instruction. The Vocabulary Quilt (see Appendix E) is one strategy that provides the opportunity for such disclosure by allowing each student to make connections with the content, see other's connections, and reveal connections to teachers that can help the teacher bridge from what students know and clear up misunderstandings. *(Image courtesy of Kendra Herrera, 3rd Grade, Texas)*

are deeply embedded in the resiliency and persistence of my successful students. It is their stories filled with faith and laughter that can make teaching meaningful in ways that are often absent in our teacher preparation programs and professional development training. Consider the following teacher reflection on how Jaime's experience with *el coyote* provided a link to content concepts.

I remember Jaime's story to his friends about the time he crossed from Guatemala. The many adventures that he had experienced culminated with him and his family being left in Mexico, thinking they had reached the United States. I only understood bits and pieces of the story the first time I heard it, given my initial "disinterest" in what was being talked about and my concern that the conversation was too loud for my own comfort level.

Later that semester, the border crossing story resurfaced. The laughter of the group surrounded Jaime's tale of his family's entry into the United States years earlier, when the person helping them cross into the United States (*el coyote*) had left them at a Walmart just across from the U.S. border, still on the Mexican side. He had told them that this was a U.S. store and that a phone and food were available for them before they continued their journey to their destination. By the time he reached my class, Jaime's

family was documented, and he found the story something to laugh about.

I decided to "hook" into what I had learned from Jaime's story and make connections to globalization. As a class we discussed the fact that Walmart is no longer a chain of stores found only in the United States. Other students added to the discussion by chiming in with the names of additional companies whose influences have crossed national boundaries. Those were the connections that students in class never forgot.

Young and Hadaway (2006) point out that any type of "conceptual hook" with the experiences a student has had in the past increases the chance that the information will make it into the student's permanent memory. Memories closely related to personal life experiences make for great opportunities to create a community of learners that values each member's prior knowledge. Drawing on one student's experience signals to all students that their experiences are respected and valued, too.

What makes us laugh is very much culturally bound, and the joy we experience in our community is heavily connected to our own ethnicity, socioeconomic level, and educational background. Gay (2018) asserts that planning instruction that takes into account the complex, interactive, and dynamic yet stabilizing force in human life—that is, a student's culture—paves the path to culturally relevant pedagogy. I believe that understanding the sociocultural dimension of each student beyond our standard school-initiated definitions and moving toward a pedagogy that encompasses and is defined by the content of life, love, and laughter can lead to a new way of using students' experiences to ensure their academic success. Figure 2.9 illustrates the dimensions of the CLD student from a biography-driven perspective. Take time to create an ecology of laughter and joy in your own practice.

Reflections on the Sociocultural Dimension

I began this chapter by discussing the importance of the biological, psychological, and sociological aspects of our humanity. In the context of classroom learning, these aspects play out in the four dimensions of the CLD student biography—the sociocultural, linguistic, cognitive, and academic dimensions. This chapter focuses on the sociocultural dimension. As educators, we must be attentive to the sociocultural dimension as it relates to both the assets that we can draw from and the challenges that may be keeping our students from moving forward. We can remember that prior to arriving in our classrooms, our students have already learned to love and learn within their own families and communities. Their lives are filled with experiences we

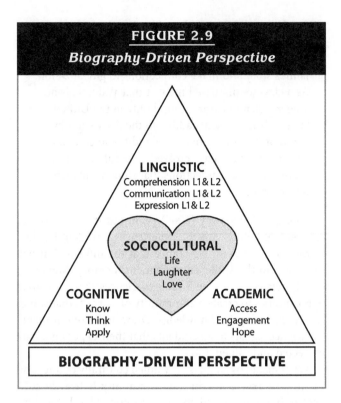

FIGURE 2.9
Biography-Driven Perspective

LINGUISTIC
Comprehension L1 & L2
Communication L1 & L2
Expression L1 & L2

SOCIOCULTURAL
Life
Laughter
Love

COGNITIVE
Know
Think
Apply

ACADEMIC
Access
Engagement
Hope

BIOGRAPHY-DRIVEN PERSPECTIVE

dents are immediately starting from a disadvantage. Everything they have learned about life and the world up to this point is being dismissed as irrelevant to school learning; there are few points of connection to curriculum materials or instruction and so students are expected to learn in an experiential vacuum. Students' silence and nonparticipation under these conditions have frequently been interpreted as lack of academic ability or effort, and teachers' interactions with students have reflected a pattern of low expectations, which become self-fulfilling. (pp. 2–3)

We educators must first recognize the gifts that our students possess, no matter how far removed they may be from our own reality and the reality of our school. The gifts are more varied than we can begin to imagine. By building on the background knowledge students bring to the classroom, we can provide conditions that will promote CLD students' motivation and engagement in the learning process. The scenarios presented in this chapter include examples of the challenges students face each day. We must move beyond thinking such ways of life inhibit students intellectually; on the contrary, for many students, the kaleidoscope of languages, cultures, and communities provides a source of energy to continue to move forward despite all the challenges life presents both in and out of school. Our charge then is to draw upon our students' gifts and assets and use those to bridge to the content we teach. Chapters 7, 8, and 9 provide practical ideas for making this a reality in our classrooms.

can learn from and draw on in the classroom to transform their educational experience. Cummins (1996) best summarizes the influence of the sociocultural dimension on students' learning by noting:

When students' language, culture and experience are ignored or excluded in classroom interactions, stu-

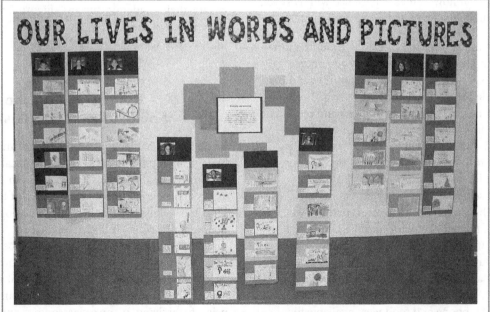

Share these student events with the rest of the classroom and school. Create communities where every language, culture, and experience are celebrated and become a source of learning inside and outside of the school. *(Image courtesy of Dennis Stanton & Marie Kane, Elementary, Kansas)*

3

Language of the Heart

GUIDING QUESTION

In what ways can students' cultural assets contribute to teaching and learning to support language development and use?

See the online Discussion Guide for opportunities to further explore answers to this question and connections to chapter content with a colleague or team. Available for download from the Teachers College Press website: tcpress.com

THERE IS no greater magic than having someone listen to and validate what we have to say in our native language, the language of the home. In Spanish, there is a saying, "*cada cabeza es un mundo*"—every head is its own world. When we communicate effectively, we succeed in crossing the distance from our world to the world of another. However, we do not always succeed in crossing that distance. Much gets lost in schools, where teachers have not been given the tools or liberty to use the native language of many learners. Currently, educational institutions tend to focus on learning about the linguistic proficiencies of students through the narrow lens of formal language assessment. This chapter first reviews school-situated aspects of language and then takes the educator into the heart of communication by exploring how language is inextricably tied to culture.

The Linguistic Dimension

My life made a complete turn.
  Un cambio radical.
    Questions rushed through my head.
    Tengo que hacer un extra esfuerzo.
    Para speak and read in English.
      I felt like a part of myself was missing.
      I am here today.
                    —*BESITOS/Herrera Terry (2004)*

As demographics have shifted and the number of CLD students has grown, great attention has been paid to what teachers should understand to be successful with these students. College courses and professional development trainings abound that aim to provide preservice and in-service

teachers with the fundamentals of second language acquisition and demonstrate how this process is relevant to classroom practice. Yet before we explore the varied dynamics of second language acquisition, let us first look briefly at the way we acquire our first language.

We do not begin life as fluent speakers of our first language. With much encouragement and support, we spend our early years acquiring the basic sound patterns, vocabulary, sentence structures, and communicative skills that we later take for granted. We then continue to improve our linguistic capabilities through formal schooling and our interactions with others. Although by age 6 we have completed 50% of the process of acquiring our first language, we continue to spend the rest of our lives acquiring additional vocabulary and refining our language skills (Akmajian et al., 2017; Herrera & Murry, 2016).

The process of second language acquisition is markedly more difficult than that of first language acquisition. Second language learners rarely have the opportunity to spend years merely becoming acquainted with the sounds and structures of the new language. The communicative competence that is often expected from students as they transition through grade levels requires grammatical knowledge as well as social knowledge—knowing how to use the utterances appropriately (Larsen-Freeman, 2018). As we situate this within the context of daily language instruction, it becomes imperative to reflect on the reality that emergent bilinguals are expected to:

- Quickly acquire enormous amounts of vocabulary
- Recognize and use complex sentence structures that may be very different from those typical of their native language

- Grasp subtle nuances of the new language that are key to in-depth comprehension and effective communication

Continuing the discussion of the four interrelated and complex dimensions of the prism model, I will now review the most commonly known aspects of teaching linguistically diverse students.

Traditional School-Initiated Responses

At the beginning of each school year, both novice and seasoned teachers who work within school systems with high populations of English learners are likely to take part in professional preparation related to fundamental concepts and theories that set the stage for understanding second language development and teaching. Similarly, within teacher preparation settings, preservice educators might take a class or two that give them a peek into the theories of second language acquisition, although such coursework is not guaranteed. In the following sections of this chapter, I will provide highlights related to:

- Distinction between basic interpersonal communication skills (BICS) and cognitive academic language proficiency (CALP)
- Krashen's theory of second language acquisition (SLA)
  - ◆ Acquisition–learning hypothesis
  - ◆ Monitor hypothesis
  - ◆ Natural order hypothesis
  - ◆ Input hypothesis
  - ◆ Affective filter hypothesis
- Stages of second language acquisition
- Distinction between common underlying proficiency (CUP) and separate underlying proficiency (SUP)
- Formal assessment of oral language proficiency
- Communicative and sociolinguistic considerations

For each concept and theory, I will include a brief discussion as well as suggestions for their application in classroom practice.

BICS and CALP

When considering students' levels of proficiency in both their first and second languages, we must take into account their listening, speaking, reading, and writing abilities in those languages. We must also differentiate between their level of **basic interpersonal communication skills (BICS)**, commonly described as conversational playground language, and their level of **cognitive academic language proficiency (CALP)**, which refers to the more decontextual-

FIGURE 3.1
BICS and CALP

Language as an Associative Function	Language as a Cognitive Function
BICS: **B**asic **I**nterpersonal **C**ommunication **S**kills	**CALP:** **C**ognitive **A**cademic **L**anguage **P**roficiency
Social communication/ playground language	Academic communication/ classroom language
Language processing and production are less cognitively demanding.	Language processing and production are more cognitively demanding.
The brain is focusing on ideas.	The brain is focusing on ideas and language production.
Similar to discussing familiar topics in one's first language.	Speaking in a second language requires a greater degree of mental effort.
The language learner's schema fits the experiential and conceptual knowledge as well as the linguistic and/or cultural context of the situation.	The language learner's schema does not fit the experiential and conceptual knowledge and/or the linguistic or cultural context of the situation.

ized, abstract language that is often used in academic settings (Cummins, 1981). Figure 3.1 provides basic information about BICS and CALP that may be helpful in understanding CLD students.

According to Cummins (2008), the distinction between BICS and CALP was introduced to draw educators' attention to the timelines and challenges that second language learners encounter as they attempt to catch up to their peers in academic aspects of the school language. This distinction explains why CLD students might be able to converse quite effectively with their peers in English, yet not grasp the English vocabulary needed to comprehend an academic lesson. The BICS/CALP distinction further reveals the important role that our instructional actions can play as we facilitate students' language development by supporting them to build on their own linguistic repertoires and their emerging English language capabilities as they work toward increased understanding of more nuanced skills.

Did you know that social language can be used as a springboard to academic language? I have heard many teachers consistently claim that their second language learners speak English well, but these same educators express frustration when attempting to move students to academic conversations. Teachers, you already have the tools, and your language learners have the ability to speak academically. We must remember that social language is the starting point for academic conversations. Using tiered vocabulary, language learners can move from BICS to CALP. In Chapter 7, I provide a more detailed description of how to use Tier 1, 2, and 3 words to promote academic language.

The BICS/CALP distinction has implications for planning instruction, interpreting assessment data, and understanding the reluctance of some students to fully participate in classroom activities. Consider the following two tasks: (a) Tell me about your last family outing or vacation, and (b) Write a paragraph describing the solution formed in a chemistry experiment using the words *solute, solvent,* and *concentration.* While both tasks require students to describe, synthesize, and summarize information through their own schematic connections, the second one requires use of context-specific academic vocabulary, complex cognitive processing, and background content knowledge. The second task represents the type of work we often require of CLD learners in the classroom without providing adequate **scaffolding** that would support their CALP development and thus increase the likelihood of their academic success. Therefore, it becomes of utmost importance that we provide adequate scaffolding, linguistic supports, and comprehension checks that would support their CALP. As teachers, we can support students' CALP development by:

- Providing visuals to support the required task
- Ensuring that students have opportunities to interpret visuals in their own words and from their own perspectives
- Teaching and posting the academic vocabulary
- Allowing learners to create visuals that show their understanding of vocabulary words and content concepts
- Using grouping configurations that help enhance students' understanding of words through discussion and elaboration
- Allowing peer-to-peer collaboration to paraphrase what was learned
- Maximizing use of the native language to pre-teach, clarify, or elaborate on critical academic vocabulary and concepts
- Encouraging learners' strategic use of the native language to activate conceptual and linguistic background knowledge, build on existing literacy skills, and confirm understanding of new information,

Krashen's Theory of Second Language Acquisition

By shattering old myths, introducing new subtleties, and challenging the conventional wisdom, Stephen Krashen changed the way we think about language in the classroom.

In his seminal works, Krashen (1981, 1982) describes his theory of second language acquisition by outlining five key hypotheses.

Acquisition–Learning Hypothesis. "A person cannot learn by grammar alone." Krashen distinguishes between the processes of *acquiring* and *learning* a second language. Acquiring a language is a largely subconscious process in which the learner picks up the language in a natural environment by using the language for a variety of real communication purposes. In contrast, learning a language requires conscious effort and involves being able to understand and apply grammar and other formal language rules.

Monitor Hypothesis. "Usage is the only path to fluency." Krashen demonstrates how it is only by *acquiring* a language that the learner gains fluency. For this reason, it is crucial to create a school environment that allows CLD students to hear and use the English language in meaningful contexts. Language *learning* merely assists individuals in self-monitoring and correcting their language production; it does not help learners use the language with natural ease.

Natural Order Hypothesis. "Errors are normal and often disappear on their own." Krashen describes how English language learners acquire the rules of the English language in a predictable order. He finds that regardless of age, students make certain grammatical errors as they progress through the stages of acquiring English. These errors are developmental and highly predictable. They are usually temporary and begin to disappear with modeling of the language. Therefore, it is important for educators to avoid "error correction" of CLD students' language production. An emphasis on mistakes can lead to student apprehension and prevent learners from moving forward in acquiring the English language. If a grammatical error persists for a long time (becoming what has been referred to as "fossilized"), then it may become necessary for the teacher to use explicit techniques to address the error.

Input Hypothesis. Beginning where they currently stand, learners advance step by step. First and second language learners need to receive **comprehensible input** as they acquire literacy skills. Comprehensible input is new language material that learners are able to understand, in spite of its unfamiliarity, because measures have been taken to ensure that connections are made between the new information and what the learners already know. Krashen's "*i*+1," discussed in Chapter 1, describes this kind of comprehensible, new material. The "*i*" represents the learner's existing linguistic capabilities and the "+1" signifies that the new material is one step beyond where the learner currently stands (Krashen, 1985). Tying language and content to meaningful experiences is crucial because students cannot

FIGURE 3.2
Comparison of First and Second Language Acquisition Processes

L1 Acquisition	L1 and L2 Acquisition	L2 Acquisition
• Parents or caretakers are the primary language models for first language learners. • First language learners have innumerable opportunities to interact with language models. • Most first language learners acquire a high level of first language proficiency. • First language acquisition is arguably internally motivated by an innate cognitive process, although environmental factors shape development. • Most people develop a first language.	• Through a process called overgeneralization, a language learner may indiscriminately apply a language rule to many different situations (e.g., *He goed to the store yesterday*). • Learners acquire language by interacting with others. • Learners go through a silent period. • Learners need comprehensible input. • A highly contextualized, language-rich environment will facilitate language acquisition. • During the initial stages of language acquisition, learners may need more time to process information. • Language acquisition is cognitively demanding. • Language acquisition involves conceptualizing information in new ways and developing new ways of processing information. • Language acquisition occurs in predictable stages. • Language acquisition is a dynamic process during which learners actively construct meaning using prior knowledge, experience, and context. • Second language learners can lose a first or second language if they do not use that language.	• Second language learners already have a language for communication and thought. • Second language learners can transfer knowledge about language (metalinguistic awareness) and thought processes from the first to the second language. • Peers and teachers are the primary language models for second language learners. • Second language learners have a greater repertoire of language learning strategies. • The second language learner may make language mistakes in the second language because he or she is applying rules from the first language to the second language. • Second language learners can code switch, which involves using both languages to create greater meaning than could be achieved by relying on only one language. • Second language learners can use cognates to comprehend new words in the second language. • Second language learners often have greater prior knowledge and experience to rely on as they acquire the second language. • Second language acquisition is arguably externally motivated by sociocultural factors, although innate cognitive processes facilitate the acquisition process. Not all people develop a second language at the same rate. • Second language learners who reach high levels of bilingual proficiency tend to have greater cognitive abilities than monolingual language learners.

Source: Adapted from Herrera, Socorro G.; Murry, Kevin G. *Mastering ESL/EFL Methods: Differentiated Instruction for Culturally and Linguistically Diverse (CLD) Students,* 3rd Ed., p. 65, © 2016. Reprinted by permission of Pearson Education, Inc., New York, New York.

learn something that they do not understand. Consequently, successful educators focus their efforts, regardless of students' literacy levels, on the attainment of meaning. Teachers do this by actively engaging students in the learning environment and by using strategies that contextualize content (e.g., role playing, experiments, field trips, visuals). As students learn from and about language embedded in rich and varied contexts, they develop their language proficiency.

Affective Filter Hypothesis. "It's hard to learn when you're scared." Learning a second language can be more difficult than acquiring a first language because second language learners often are inhibited by what Krashen refers to as an **affective filter**. CLD students are aware that they are not as proficient in their second language as their native-speaking peers. Therefore, they may struggle with anxiety about saying the wrong thing, making grammatical errors, or incorrectly pronouncing what they say. The affective filter controls the extent to which students are able to actually take in what they are supposed to be learning. If students feel comfortable in their learning environment and know their language efforts will be met with support, they are more likely to comprehend the material and take risks with their language production (Sousa, 2011). However, in stressful situations, the affective filter of students is raised (much like a defense mechanism), and the result often involves a decrease in student motivation, engagement, and language production.

Stages of Second Language Acquisition

Often we educators learn about the stages of second language acquisition in professional development sessions or graduate level classes; however, many of us leave this knowledge behind when we exit the training environment. Applying an understanding of these stages is crucial to conducting instruction that will allow our students—regardless of stage—to feel that they are contributing and comprehending key conceptual ideas. Fully grasping these stages allows teachers to situationally deliver instruction that will take students one step beyond as they progress through the stages.

The process of second language acquisition mirrors the process of acquiring a first language in many ways. In both processes, learners go through a silent period—a period during which they are trying to internalize the common sounds, words, and patterns of the language. Although students in the silent period are actively acquiring language skills, they might use only nonverbal forms of communication (e.g., nodding, shrugging, or pointing) until they feel adequately prepared to take on the challenge of verbal communication. This preproduction stage of language acquisition may last for several months (Ovando et al., 2011). Students then pass through the early production, speech emergence, intermediate fluency, and advanced fluency stages as they gain proficiency in the second language (Krashen & Terrell, 1983). (These stages are discussed further—in the context of assessing a student's progress in language acquisition—later in this chapter.)

One major difference between the processes of first and second language acquisition is the context in which each takes place. Learners acquire their first language in the context of the home. They are surrounded by those who support them socioemotionally and who use the language to engage them in daily life practices that are essential to the functioning of the family unit. Students acquire their second language within the context of a school. The degree of encouragement and support they receive is highly dependent on the teacher and the classroom conditions created. To what extent are learners provided tasks that encourage use of the second language for expression of original thought? What types of opportunities do learners have to practice and use the new language to develop peer relationships that foster a sense of belonging and offer socioemotional support? How are learners supported to let go of the fear of "saying it wrong" to instead make English a living part of their continually expanding linguistic repertoire?

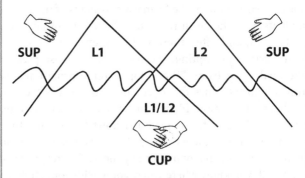

FIGURE 3.3
The Iceberg Metaphor

Academic language starts with basic literacy skills, and the demands increase as a student continues through school. Fluency and literacy in the native language (L1) allow the optimal **_transfer of skills_** to the second language (L2). Therefore, the more literate and schooled a student is in his or her L1, the easier it is for the student to transfer skills and concepts from the L1 to the L2 with appropriate instruction and support. This is where the interdependence and relationship between the L1 and L2 can clearly be seen.

SUP: **S**eparate **U**nderlying **P**roficiency
(L1 and L2 do not interact)

CUP: **C**ommon **U**nderlying **P**roficiency
(L1 and L2 do interact to promote L2 acquisition)

SUP   L1   L2   SUP

L1/L2

CUP

Source: Adapted from Cummins (1981), p. 24. Used with permission.

Figure 3.2 compares and contrasts first and second language acquisition processes.

CUP and SUP

The optimal learning environment for CLD students is one that leads to literacy skills both in the student's native language and in English. Why is it necessary to use students' native language when building their academic knowledge? In short, skills and knowledge gained in the native language transfer to the second language. The student's core of knowledge that is accessible through either language can be illustrated through the concept of **common underlying proficiency (CUP)** (Cummins, 1981). For example, regardless of the language educators initially use to teach the process of addition to students, the students will be able to perform the mathematical operation. The iceberg metaphor depicted in Figure 3.3 illustrates that while CLD students may not possess the English surface features to effectively explain how addition works, they might completely understand the concept of addition. They do not need to learn the concept twice, only the language to express their understanding in a new language. Unfortunately, some educators misunderstand students' background knowledge as being a **separate underlying proficiency (SUP)**. The SUP viewpoint regards access to knowledge as limited to the specific language in which students originally learned the concepts or skills (Cummins, 1981). As a result of this misunderstanding, such teachers believe that curricular material must be retaught in English, and they often fail to notice the wealth of content knowledge that CLD students already possess.

Formal Assessment of Oral Language Proficiency

According to the International Literacy Association (2017), oral language proficiency is critical for advancing English learners' academic success. Students' word knowledge is considered an important facet of their language production and academic success. Yet, ask a group of educators who are not ESL teachers what the formal assessments of their CLD students have shown in relation to their level of language proficiency, and often there will be silence in the room. With further prompting, the responses of those present likely will range from, "That is top secret information only available in the office for official use," to "That is the ESL teacher's information. I have too many students to keep up with that. I have the scores but I don't know what they mean," or "The students in my class have been exited so their scores don't really matter any more." My response is, "How will you know where you're going with your students if you don't know where they have been?"

Every district that has CLD students is required by law to administer a language test prior to assigning or placing a student in a program. These tests vary in the types of information they gather, yet whatever information is gleaned from the process can serve as a window into students' linguistic abilities. Figure 3.4 provides a list of the tests most used by states across the country to assess the linguistic and literacy abilities of CLD students, along with brief information that can guide you in understanding what the scores on each test mean. Often states choose to use tests that have been developed to meet the needs of students within their districts. We as educators can benefit from learning how CLD students are assessed and from using the results of those assessments to inform our understanding of each student's biography.

Standardized tests, along with informal observation of students' second language acquisition (SLA), help us to more effectively plan instruction. Thus, we need to be familiar with tools used to observe language development and get into the habit of using them daily in our classroom. Figure 3.5 provides an overview of the stages of SLA and student actions that may be observed by the teacher during each stage. As students progress through each stage, it is important that we recognize the steps of that progression so that we can appropriately scaffold and support their learn-

ing through our teaching strategies. Figure 3.6 illustrates what student production for a Thanksgiving activity can look like for each stage of SLA.

We enhance our ability to successfully support students' development of oral language proficiency in the classroom when we:

- Know the biographies of our students
- Tap into learners' experiential and linguistic capital
- Utilize the stages of SLA as fluid considerations for grouping configurations, scaffolding of instruction, and differentiating postinstructional assessment products
- Conduct formative assessment throughout the lesson
- Provide postinstructional opportunities for students to articulate their learning

Understanding the linguistic biographies of CLD students increases our chances of successfully differentiating instruction to aid the progress of each student. In later chapters, I explore how knowledge of SLA stages is used to plan, teach, and assess student learning during every lesson.

Communicative and Sociolinguistic Considerations

Just as the sociocultural dimension encompasses students' implicit, often unverbalized, rules for loving, laughing, and living, the **linguistic dimension** relates to their internal guide for comprehending the world of verbal communication, with all its hidden cultural messages. Before a student enters the classroom, avenues of communication already have been paved for appropriate ways of asking a question, responding, and making sense of what is communicated in different contexts. Hymes (1972) referred to this as "communicative competence." Teaching is often contextualized within the "norms" of the English language. These subtle aspects may differ from the modes of communication used by CLD students. Our students have learned how to express what they know, resolve conflict, react to nonverbal cues, and navigate their emotional state based on the cultural context to which they have been socialized. Effective cross-cultural communication is essential to the teaching and learning process.

To date, the standard focus in schools has involved:

- Supporting students' understanding of the grammatical rules of the English language by comparing English to the native language
- Supporting students' sociolinguistic knowledge by teaching students to write for specific purposes, considering audience and setting
- Teaching students to use discourse in appropriate ways to ask questions and organize written thought
- Teaching students how to be strategic communicators in classroom settings

These and other support systems have been employed to help students navigate and become competent users of the

FIGURE 3.4
Formal Assessments of Language Proficiency

Language Assessment	Key Characteristics
The Dos Amigos Verbal Language Scale (Critchlow, 1996)	This assessment uses 85 pairs of opposites in Spanish and English to measure conceptual linguistic knowledge. Qualitative results provide information about relative proficiency in each language. The provision for qualitative interpretation also facilitates a more holistic picture of proficiency levels in the two languages as they are demonstrated separately and in unison.
Preschool Language Assessment Scale (Pre-LAS 2000) (Duncan & DeAvila, 1998)	This assessment is designed to measure the developing language and preliteracy skills of preschool-age children to inform the placement of these young language learners into the most appropriate classroom settings. It is available in English and Spanish.
Language Assessment Scale—Oral (LAS—O) (Duncan & DeAvila, 1990)	This assessment measures the listening and speaking skills of students in grades 1 through 6 and 7 through 12. Like the Pre-LAS, it is available in English or Spanish and is useful in assessing primary language development or to identify students for placement in, and exit from, bilingual/ESL programs. The LAS—O contains an optional observation form that can be completed by another examiner to further support or triangulate findings used to determine whether a student is ready for redesignation.
The Bilingual Verbal Ability Tests Normative Update (BVAT-NU) (Muñoz-Sandoval, Cummins, Alvarado, Ruef, & Schrank, 2005)	This assessment takes into consideration both the native and second language and comprises three subtests from the Woodcock-Johnson III Tests of Achievement (Woodcock, McGrew, & Mather, 2001) that have been translated into 18 languages (now including Hmong and Navajo). The BVAT scoring software generates a report that differentiates among the student's bilingual verbal ability, student's cognitive academic language proficiency (CALP) skills, and relative language proficiency in languages assessed.
Language Assessment Scale—Reading/Writing (LAS—R/W) (Duncan & DeAvila, 1990)	This assessment measures reading and writing skills in English or Spanish L1 ability levels. It may be used to identify students for placement in, and exit from, bilingual or ESL programs. The test combines selected response and writing sample evaluations to assess vocabulary, fluency, reading comprehension, mechanics, and usage.
IDEA Proficiency Test (IPT) (Ballard & Tighe, 2004)	This assessment offers oral, reading, and writing versions available in Spanish and English. It is also designed to assess both social and academic language. Like other assessments of this type, the IPT may be used to measure primary language skills but is most often employed for the identification, placement, and (re)classification of CLD students who are acquiring English in appropriate classroom contexts.
Woodcock-Muñoz Language Survey Revised (WMLS-R) (Woodcock, Muñoz-Sandoval, Ruef, & Alvarado, 2005)	This assessment is another popular measure of Spanish and English that comes with a computerized scoring program. This scoring program generates a narrative that describes the CALP in English or Spanish, or the relative proficiency between languages if both versions of the test are administered.
Receptive One-Word Picture Vocabulary Test (ROWPVT) (Brownell, 2000b) and its companion, the **Expressive One-Word Picture Vocabulary Test (EOWPVT)** (Brownell, 2000a)	These assessments, originally developed for English speakers, have been translated into Spanish and are normed on bilingual students in the United States. These assessments credit correct responses in either language (conceptual scoring) in addition to rating relative proficiency in Spanish and English.
Stanford English Language Proficiency 2 (SELP2) assessment (Harcourt Assessment, 2003)	This assessment measures the English listening, reading, writing, and speaking skills of K–12 students. Now with four forms, SELP2 can be used at the beginning of the school year to establish a baseline and then administered periodically to obtain multiple data points to evaluate progress. SELP2 assesses student language proficiency and mastery of skills included in the CCSS and WIDA standards and is a predictor of how well students will perform on high-stakes state assessments. If employed during the school year, results can be used to help prepare students in advance of the standardized testing required by states.

FIGURE 3.5
P-EP-S-I Ahh!

P-EP-S-I Ahh! is a teacher-friendly mnemonic device to help you recall the stages of second language acquisition. Knowing which stage your CLD student is in will help you plan and implement instruction that supports English language acquisition and student achievement.

Acronym		Student Behaviors	Teacher Tips
P	Preproduction	• Gain familiarity with sounds, rhythm, and patterns of English. • Rely more heavily on picture clues for understanding. • Respond nonverbally by pointing, gesturing, or drawing.	• Pair students with more advanced learners. • Use many visuals, physical movements, gestures, and verbal cues to support and expand students' language acquisition process. • Avoid forcing students to speak prematurely by allowing for a silent period. • Try to help students use their background knowledge by making connections to their native language and previous experiences.
E **P**	Early Production	• Use one-word type utterances; may verbally identify people, places, and objects. • Manipulate objects and ideas mentally. • Start using knowledge of letter–sound relationship. • Use routine expressions independently.	• Provide students with an increasing number of visual cues to help them integrate phonics and context cues. • Use authentic and rich literature in classroom instruction. • Teach key vocabulary and concepts to increase students' comprehension. • Have students label or manipulate pictures and/or real objects.
S	Speech Emergence	• Understand grade-level concepts. • Engage in much more independent reading as a result of increased oral language proficiency. • Apply and manipulate writing according to their needs.	• Guard vocabulary and introduce concepts through the use of multiple strategies. • Model responses to literature for students by explaining, describing, comparing, and retelling. • Focus on communication in meaningful contexts and expression in speech and print. • Respond genuinely to student writing and hold conferences that highlight students' strengths and progress.
I	Intermediate Fluency	• Explore and utilize extensive vocabulary and concepts in content area. • Write and read a wider range of narrative genres and content texts with increased comprehension.	• Structure and guide group discussions to facilitate more advanced literature studies. • Provide for a variety of realistic writing experiences. • Continue to shelter instruction and check for understanding.
Ahh!	Advanced Fluency	• Produce language with varied grammatical structures and vocabulary. • Construct multiple hypotheses and viewpoints.	• Continue to support ongoing language development through integrated language arts and content-area activities.

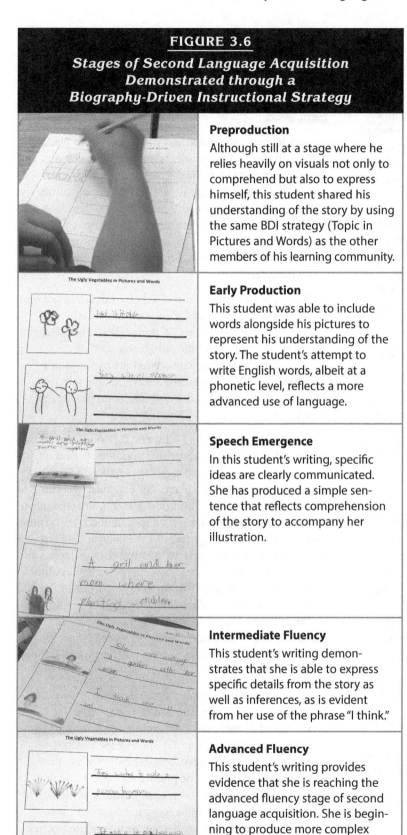

FIGURE 3.6

Stages of Second Language Acquisition Demonstrated through a Biography-Driven Instructional Strategy

Preproduction

Although still at a stage where he relies heavily on visuals not only to comprehend but also to express himself, this student shared his understanding of the story by using the same BDI strategy (Topic in Pictures and Words) as the other members of his learning community.

Early Production

This student was able to include words alongside his pictures to represent his understanding of the story. The student's attempt to write English words, albeit at a phonetic level, reflects a more advanced use of language.

Speech Emergence

In this student's writing, specific ideas are clearly communicated. She has produced a simple sentence that reflects comprehension of the story to accompany her illustration.

Intermediate Fluency

This student's writing demonstrates that she is able to express specific details from the story as well as inferences, as is evident from her use of the phrase "I think."

Advanced Fluency

This student's writing provides evidence that she is reaching the advanced fluency stage of second language acquisition. She is beginning to produce more complex sentences and to use vocabulary from the text (e.g., "wiggled") in contextually appropriate ways.

(Images courtesy of Lara Evans, 2nd Grade, Kansas)

English language. What often is absent (and will be addressed in the subsequent chapters of this text) is evidence of teachers' valuing and bringing into the learning process CLD students' culturally embedded notions of communication, expression, and comprehension. Such scaffolding can increase students' communicative competence in a new culture and language.

Linguistically Speaking: *i*+1

For CLD students, communicative competence is situated in the discourse of their family unit and community ("primary discourse"). Primary discourse reflects the native language and our socialized way of interacting with others, which is based largely on our primary socialization in the family during our formative years. Often the primary discourse is in conflict with that of dominant curricula and assessment tools in public education ("academic discourse"). According to Gee (2001), discourses can be defined as "ways of combining and coordinating words, deeds, thoughts, values, bodies, objects, tools, and technologies, and other people (at the appropriate times and places) so as to enact and recognize the specific socially situated identities and activities" (p. 721). My work with teachers and students relies heavily on observation of culturally situated discourse. I have found that culturally situated discourse has important implications for successful teaching and the advancement of student learning.

Communication

> What might a language full of nouns tell us about a culture? How about a language full of verbs? A language with no past tense? No future tense? A language with no word for "read" or "write"? A language with six words for love?
> —*Linda Christensen (2000, p. 106)*

From the moment young children begin to interact with their primary caregivers, they have models for every act of communication. They learn nonverbal cues, from a wink that means "I love you" to a motherly look that says "Just test me." According to Boggs (1985), the attitudes and behavioral patterns that are most important to children are those involved in communication. Given this information, how often do we teachers consider and use our students' culturally embedded communication patterns in our teaching? Is there a chance that we may interpret what we see based on our own cultural filters?

McDaniel and colleagues (2012) note that in order to understand communication, we must also understand culture. In our classrooms, we must begin to move beyond framing communication as teaching the content/structure of language and toward understanding the sociocultural aspects of language development and communication. According to Boggs (1985):

> Communication entails much more than the content and structure of written and spoken language, and it serves purposes greater than the mere transmission of information. Sociocultural context and nuances, discourse logic and dynamics, delivery styles, social functions, role expectations, norms of interaction, and nonverbal features are as important as (if not more so than) vocabulary, grammar, lexicon, pronunciation, and other linguistic or structural dimensions of communication. (p. 301)

Boggs contends that the "form of exchange between child and adult and the conditions in which it occurs will affect not only what is said, but how involved the child will become" (p. 301). Exploration of how communication impacts student motivation and engagement can inform the way we conduct business in our schools.

Ask yourself the following questions:

- How do I consider students' cultural and linguistic references when modeling student learning strategies that involve asking questions?
- In what ways do I consider cultural patterns of communication when designing different tasks and configuring my groups for each?
- How do CLD students communicate with others in their first language (L1) versus English (L2)? Do these interactions vary based on the people involved (e.g., parents, peers, teacher, and others)?
- In what ways do I provide space for students to borrow from their own linguistic register?
- How do I support learners to connect their new learning to their already established frames of reference?
- In what ways might culturally bound discourse patterns impact reading, writing, and class participation for my CLD students?
- What opportunities do I provide for students to take on the role of teacher?

Consideration of the role culture plays in students' classroom responses can influence our interpretation of their behavior. According to Bowers and Flinders (1990), behavior can be understood as the communication of thoughts in culturally prescribed ways. Understanding that students use their culturally bound systems to communicate during the lesson moves us to recognize that we must structure and manage our own communication styles to establish conditions that will encourage students to bring their identities into every act of communication.

Expression

As an educator and researcher, I have elected to place special emphasis on how students' expressive behaviors and actions contribute to or hinder their comprehension of academic concepts. Classrooms are full of opportunities for students to express thoughts and ideas as teaching and learning unfold. As educators, we are always asking students to read with expression, respond to the prompt, define words, or write paragraphs. Seldom do we ask ourselves the following questions:

- Given the student's cultural background, is this the best way for him or her to express personal ideas?
- Does the student feel free to express his or her thoughts without fear of giving the wrong answer?
- Have I, as the teacher, considered my own ways of expressing what is expected and selected a way that will be best understood, given the biographies of my students?

Observing and reflecting on ways CLD students use language and communication systems to express their thoughts and ideas moves us one step closer to creating effective pathways for learning to take place. For example, according to Heath (2000), textbook questions often require students to provide straightforward answers to demonstrate learning. This type of questioning may lead to inappropriate answers from students whose primary discourse uses metaphor and imagination or emphasizes the generation of hypotheses. Expression of needs and learning is especially critical to the success of students whose first language is not English.

Consider the following scenario, and ask yourself if your interpretation of the student behavior would reflect the cultural norms of the classroom where you find yourself today.

> A few years ago I was asked to visit a kindergarten classroom where a teacher wanted me to observe a child she thought was in need of special services. I was asked to participate during the whole-group rug/reading time so that I might observe the disruptive behavior the child, Jamal, was exhibiting while the teacher was reading. The problem seemed to be that Jamal did not wait to be asked questions by the teacher; rather, he would ask questions and make comments while the teacher was reading. The teacher had already used all her classroom management tools to try to get this student to be like the other students and wait to speak until she asked questions or asked for comments on the book.
>
> As I observed, she was absolutely right in her observations. Jamal was very engaged in what the

teacher had to say and wanted to immediately add to or pose questions related to what she was reading. After the lesson, I took Jamal aside and asked:

Herrera: Did you enjoy the story?

Jamal: I liked it a lot.

Herrera: It was a great story! Why did you not wait for the teacher to ask you questions about the book?

Jamal: I answered the questions.

Herrera: Sometimes you talked when the teacher had not asked a question. Why?

Jamal: M'am, because in my church when you feel it, you just have to tell it!

I will never forget this exchange or the many similar exchanges I have experienced since then. CLD students generate "expressive acts" that are consistent with their own frames of reference. Educators do the same and have expectations of their students consistent with these frames of reference. We may interpret student behavior as nonattentive, evasive, or disrespectful and proceed to respond according to what we perceive. Although a student's behavior may be outside the lines of *classroom management*—that is, outside our *expectations* for student participation and ideas about what is acceptable and what is not—we must remember that as different cultures become part of our classroom fabric, it becomes necessary to *bridge* ways of expressing thoughts and feelings in new ways.

By using strategies that provide opportunities for students to express thoughts, ideas, and learning in multiple ways, we can begin to observe for the often subtle messages

Providing opportunities for students to voice what they have learned before moving forward gives each student one last chance to *get it right*. In this picture, students in small teams are sharing their personal perspectives on the topic and associated key vocabulary terms. Students had recorded their ideas on the Magic Book tool and in their teams were provided with structured opportunities to stop and discuss what they had added. At the end of the lesson, the students incorporated relevant personal connections to the new information as they summarized their learnings. *(Image courtesy of Scott Calder, High School, Kansas)*

that our students send about their culturally embedded ways of expressing their understanding and knowledge. In the case of Jamal, the teacher might have gained greater understanding about his behavior and guided his participation by asking the following types of questions during strategy implementation:

- Jamal, I see that you get really loud and excited about the vocabulary quilt. Is there something you really like about this activity?
- Jamal, what could we do to have you wait to share all the exciting things you know until we finish with the quilt?
- Jamal, I am wondering what you thought about this word. Do you think you could raise your hand and tell me in a quiet voice what you are thinking?

Spending time with Jamal's small group during the activity would support his transition from culturally appropriate to classroom-appropriate ways of responding to learning. Understanding his behavior through the lens of his cultural response would set the stage for rerouting his actions by talking to him about his excitement during participation. It may take time to move from a student's cultural/home response to classroom-appropriate behavior, but the time invested will be well worth it. The process may even provide new ideas for class participation that all students might enjoy. Chapters 7, 8, and 9 further discuss explicit ways of supporting student expression.

Comprehension

In schools, the ultimate goal of teaching is for students to comprehend what was taught and to take that information on to the next level. That is, students must store new knowledge in their permanent memory so that it is accessible in the future. In the classroom, we teachers often go about the act of teaching by using all the prescribed methods and materials and sprinkling them with our own techniques to achieve the goal of having everyone learn. Yet frequently we are surprised at the interpretations our students have come to by the end of the lesson. We ask, "How did this happen?"

According to Säljö (1996) and Wertsch (1998), learning and meaning-making are seen as inseparable from the learner's situational and sociocultural circumstances. Our conceptualization of "literacy" has shifted from being text-driven to instead emphasize the active transformation of texts (Hiebert, 1991). According to Hughes and Talbott (2017), students' literacy experiences inside and outside of school influence their ability to understand text and engage with specific reading tasks. This can have huge implications for how CLD students view the text and create meaning. Further, Vaughn and colleagues (2017) suggest that English learners often are able to master the foundational skills of word reading with adequate fluency, but that as the syntax, vocabulary, and background knowledge of texts become more complex, students' reading difficulties manifest. Considering this, it becomes all the more important for us to create situations in our classrooms where we support students to reflect back on their schemas and known frames of reference.

Eisner (1998) reminds us that literacy "is not limited to text" (p. 15). Rather, it is related to the individual's ability to construe meaning from any of the forms used in the culture to create and convey meaning. Consider the following scenario and note your initial reaction to the students' discussion.

A few years ago I had the opportunity to observe and co-teach in a middle school where the teacher had been reading *The Scarlet Letter* by Nathaniel Hawthorne. Because they were deep into the book by the time I visited the class, we decided to use a strategy called "The Relevance Scale" to have the students review for me what they deemed important from the story. Each group was assigned a chapter and asked to find the three most important details and be ready to share. As each of the groups debated what they were going to share with me, I noted from my observations how their sociocultural background was influencing what they considered important.

At the end of the lesson, the students were asked how the details they had selected as most important might differ if they were from another culture or country. Following is a glimpse of the path that students' responses took:

Student 1: Well, you know, I think if you sleep with someone else it doesn't matter, so why would that be important?
Student 2: Well, in my family a woman who does that is trash and no one would accept her.
Student 3: Well, then I think her sleeping around is important and she should be punished.
Student 2: My family and I would vote for that.
Student 1: Well, do we think we need to know that she slept around?

Many of the groups followed the same pattern of discussion, identifying relevance according to their own culturally bound ideas of what was important and why. After much discussion and debate on the students' *culturally situated* thoughts on the novel and class consensus building related to the overarching themes of the novel (e.g., compassion, withholding judgment), the teacher took the discussion to the present day. He asked student groups to consider the identified themes in relation to current environments or situations where inhumane actions, lack of compassion, and so forth have repercussions on the present-day lives of people. An assessment of student comprehension in this scenario would need to consider the pathways of thinking and analysis that each group took to arrive at the universal themes of the novel and apply those themes to various situations in the world today.

As we plan and deliver instruction designed to promote CLD students' comprehension of curricular content, we must find ways to elicit students' interpretation of text through the lens of their life experiences. We can then use these insights to better scaffold instruction and guide students toward the knowledge and understandings we want them to possess and be able to apply to future learning. The following questions can guide us as we move beyond school-initiated responses to linguistic diversity and consider differences related to how students comprehend new information:

- What kinds of opportunities do students have to individually respond to visuals in order to share from their own point of view?
- When introducing unfamiliar concepts, in what ways are connections that are culturally familiar to CLD students used to explain the new material?
- How are CLD students encouraged to communicate with their peers about their life and experiences so that all students can make multiple connections to content?

Reflections on the Linguistic Dimension

Increasing the academic achievement of our CLD students means thinking about language from multiple angles. Currently in schools, we focus heavily on understanding language from "one side of the coin," that is, language learning that emphasizes grammar, vocabulary, pronunciation, and limited sociolinguistic aspects. Moving beyond this limited focus means creating situational and social contexts in which we can learn through observation about the ways students communicate, express, and comprehend classroom instruction based on their cultural and linguistic socialization.

Considering students' linguistic capacities to communicate and express themselves, Delpit (1988) states that it is important that we "coach those voices to produce notes that will be heard clearly in the larger society" (p. 296). Mays (2008) further challenges us, saying, "Educators who take the time to learn the primary Discourse of their students are helping to close the achievement gap and value the voice of ELLs often stifled by the academic Discourse predominately used in schools today. Can you hear them? Each one has something to say" (p. 418). When we fully consider the linguistic dimension of the CLD student biography, we recognize that language, literacy, and learning are greatly influenced by the culture and community in which a student has been socialized. We begin to understand the importance of providing opportunities for students to participate in the learning process and demonstrate their understanding in ways that differ from those traditionally found in schools. Our ability to act on newfound insights about the linguistic dimension of our CLD students is bolstered by reflection on our current habits of mind and action.

4   Culture-Driven Thought and Learning

GUIDING QUESTION

How does understanding the cognitive dimension influence planning and delivering instruction?

See the online Discussion Guide for opportunities to further explore answers to this question and connections to chapter content with a colleague or team. Available for download from the Teachers College Press website: tcpress.com

What we talk about; how we talk about it; what we see, attend to, or ignore; how we think; and what we think about are influenced by our culture.

—_Porter and Samovar (1991, p. 21)_

THE THIRD and most overlooked dimension of the CLD student biography is the cognitive dimension. Cognition can be thought of as a broader yet more precise term for "thinking." It encompasses how a student's brain processes and learns what is taught (Lightbown & Spada, 2013; Ortega, 2009). For each of us, our thought process is part of who we are as individuals, and how we respond is based on our biographies or biopsychosocial histories. Often as teachers we fail to see or cannot understand why CLD students take their own path in writing, responding, or engaging in activities that have been explicitly modeled in the classroom. Knowing that students' thought processes are influenced by their biographies can give us insights into their actions, especially if we are aware of, and listen and observe for, the impact of the cognitive dimension on the learning process.

When considering the cognitive dimension in a professional development setting, teachers' socializations commonly are limited to school-situated definitions and perceptions. Very little is presented on culturally defined patterns of processes and pathways nurtured within the boundaries of our immediate family and community culture. Teacher preparation also frequently fails to ready us to observe for the culturally bound ways that students process what they are learning, not only in the moment but also throughout the lesson. Often we perceive that the challenge lies in the prescriptive curriculum, the lack of time, or the number of

students we are charged to teach. This chapter will help uncover the nuances of the cognitive dimension, allowing us as educators to approach our students from a culturally responsive and sustaining perspective.

The Cognitive Dimension

The **cognitive dimension** is often neglected for a variety of reasons, including the following:

- Limited understanding of the influence culture has on ways of thinking
- Limited perspectives on how cognitive processes can be demonstrated in the classroom
- Limited knowledge of the role cognition plays in acquiring a second language
- Limited understanding of how to account for varying levels of language proficiency when designing cognitively challenging tasks
- Limited knowledge and skills to differentiate tasks in order to vary the level of cognitive demand required for learning to occur

Often teachers may view cognition through a limited lens, leading to flawed interpretations of what is possible during instruction. For example, L2 learning challenges (e.g., comprehension, pronunciation, or length of time needed for second language acquisition) frequently are viewed as a hindrance to academic success or as a sign that, given the English proficiency of the learner, he or she may not be able to participate fully in classroom activities that require certain cognitive processes. For example, many teachers cite the "silent period" as a reason for not asking questions of newly arrived students (McLaughlin, 2012; Mohr & Mohr, 2007). Consider Jorge's story:

> When I arrived in the United States I was eager to begin school and learn English. My father, a U.S. citizen, had great dreams of my receiving an education that would lead to something. At first I was happy when many of the teachers would skip me when asking questions or ask questions that required me to answer yes or no. After a few weeks I figured out that the teachers thought I was not capable of thinking, that my not speaking English was somehow connected to my intelligence level. I wanted to scream and say, just because I don't speak English does not mean I cannot think. I am so happy that some teachers made things happen for me. Here I am today at the University, having come to the United States just three years ago.

Many CLD students have had K–12 schooling experiences similar to those of Jorge. They often are not challenged cognitively during instruction and instead are taught lower-level skills (Chamberlain, 2005; Gaddy, 1999; McLaughlin, 2012; Nieto & Bode, 2018). According to Waxman and Tellez (2002), lower teacher expectations may lead second language learners to lower achievement throughout their educational experience.

Considering different perspectives on the role of cognition in second language acquisition can support educators to better understand the theoretical foundations of instructional practices used with CLD students. With a more thorough understanding of *why* we do what we do, we can more effectively reflect on our current practices as we continue to move forward and enhance our instruction with CLD students.

Evolving Thought on Cognition and Second Language Acquisition

This chapter's general overview of theories of cognition is intended to provide a foundation for understanding how cognitive theories of learning shape effective classroom practices for second language learners. Undoubtedly, research efforts will continue to expand our knowledge of factors and processes that influence how CLD students acquire linguistic and academic knowledge. My hope is that this section will give educators a context within which to reflect on their own perspectives on cognition and the role it plays in learning.

In the past, thought on second language acquisition reflected **behaviorist theories** and considered the acquisition of language a stimulus–response activity based on the establishment of habits. Current views on the acquisition of language have largely emphasized **information processing theories,** in which "the human mind is viewed as a sym-

Classrooms where students sit in straight rows and work only on individual assignments provide little opportunity for students to make public what they are thinking, why they think the way they do, and how they are making sense of the information presented during the lesson.

bolic processor that constantly engages in mental processes" (Ortega, 2009, p. 83). Although the thinking on second language acquisition and cognitive processing has changed, there are still district-mandated curricula that use a noncommunicative, linear, drill-and-practice approach to teaching. This way of thinking tends to place limits on the academic achievement of learners. Movement away from stimulus–response ways of teaching allows us to explore *performance* rather than behavior to assess student learning. In classrooms where diversity is part of the classroom fabric, an in-depth analysis of student performance enables us to attend to the needs of individual students throughout the learning process.

According to information processing theories, students' processing of knowledge used for learning can occur through both automatic and controlled operations. As the term implies, automatic processes "require small effort and take up few cognitive resources"; as a result, multiple automatic processes can take place at the same time (Ortega, 2009, p. 83). When students are learning in a language they understand (i.e., the native language), some of their learning occurs with little cognitive effort, particularly when they have background knowledge related to the topic. However, for CLD students who are learning in a language that is unfamiliar to them, cognitive processing is often much more controlled, or conscious, on the part of the learner.

Consciously controlled processes require greater cognitive resources, are voluntarily controlled by the learner, and are intricately linked to goal-directed motivation. Because these processes require the learner's attention, only one process can be carried out at any given moment. As Ortega (2009) notes, "performance that draws on controlled processing is . . . more vulnerable to stressors" (p. 84). The student's capacity for performance of automatic versus controlled processes in the classroom has significant implications for teachers of second language learners. Performance in the classroom is enhanced when the teacher aligns instruction and situates the learner's biography within the ecology of the classroom to meet the cognitive processing needs of diverse learners. Teachers can do this by:

- Creating risk-free or low-risk opportunities for students to share what they know
- Selecting strategies and techniques that vary the degree of cognitive demand required of the students to complete a task
- Considering how the students' state of mind or emotions impact learning
- Considering the culture of CLD students when introducing potentially foreign concepts
- Setting up situations in the classroom where student talk occurs often
- Allowing students to use their native language to make sense of new information and check their comprehension of new language and content
- Observing and documenting student conversations for insights into how students process information
- Using resulting insights and information about student learning to modify instruction or student groupings, as needed

The information processing theory known as *skill acquisition theory* has had a great deal of influence on instructional practices for second language acquisition. Ortega (2009) explains: "Skill acquisition theory defines learning as the gradual transformation of performance from controlled to automatic. This transformation [or *automatization*] happens through relevant practice over many trials" (p. 84). It is important to note that the process of automatization is skill specific. If practice emphasizes receptive comprehension in the second language, then comprehension skills will be the focus of automatization; if practice emphasizes L2 production, then production skills will be the focus (Ortega). Therefore, a balance of attention to both receptive (i.e., listening and reading) and productive (i.e., speaking and writing) skills is needed for CLD students.

Imagine, for a moment, that you are a second language learner in a grade-level classroom. During instruction, you are not provided with the support you need to acquire the academic vocabulary of the lesson or to use what you already know to comprehend the lesson. Instead, you are forced to move quickly through the lesson with little time to link ideas and make sense of what you are being asked to do. CLD students often experience this kind of scenario with reading programs in which they are asked to merely "mirror" what the teacher is demonstrating, without opportunities for meaningful and relevant practice. What often

results is little development of student knowledge with regard to either language or content. Communicative, constructivist settings, on the other hand, provide students with opportunities to actively discuss and create meaning during learning.

Segalowitz (2003) posits that a qualitative change takes place when automaticity has been achieved. Automaticity means more than the learner simply becoming faster at a skill, or accumulating skills mastered through practice (Ortega, 2009). Rather, Ortega explains, "prolonged and repeated practice *changes the knowledge representation itself* [italics added] by making the stored knowledge become more elaborated and well specified" (p. 85). Such is the case, for example, with vocabulary learning. When a word becomes automatic, a reader is able to readily decode it when reading. Because teachers are concerned with the degree to which students' knowledge of a given word reflects both strength (i.e., ability to automatically recognize the word and to use the word) and depth (i.e., elaborated, structured understanding of the word and the subtle nuances of its use across contexts), it is important to focus CLD students' attention on the cognitive processes they engage in to comprehend words.

The most recent developments in understanding the cognitive processes involved in second language acquisition relate to **emergentist theories**, which evolved from information processing theories. Emergentist theories emphasize the learner's desire to make sense of the linguistic environment in which he or she interacts (Ortega, 2009). The learner's brain strives to (a) identify recurring examples of language use; (b) make guesses based on the best possible evidence, context clues, most current relevant information, and so forth; and (c) adjust accordingly based on whether a given prediction is confirmed or disconfirmed (Chater & Manning, 2006; N. C. Ellis, 2002, 2006a, 2006b, 2007; Ortega, 2011). In classroom practice, this can occur only through multiple exposures to vocabulary, content and context-embedded activities, and the use of multiple grouping configurations where CLD students can encounter different perspectives and different ways of expressing the same information.

Emergentist theories emphasize usage-based learning, which Ortega (2009) defines as the idea that "language use and language knowledge are inseparable, because we come to know language from using it" (p. 104). N. C. Ellis (2007) describes the language learning process as "a dynamic process in which regularities and systems emerge from the interaction of people, their conscious selves, and their brains, using language in their societies, cultures, and world" (p. 85). I believe we teachers have much to gain from understanding how researchers' knowledge and theories have changed over time regarding how language is acquired and processed, and the implications of such changes for classroom practice.

Traditional School-Initiated Responses

Within the classroom context, teachers have defined and have attempted to address the cognitive dimension of CLD students in the following ways:

- Varying the complexity and difficulty of the task CLD students are asked to accomplish
- Using learning style inventories to discover students' learning style preferences
- Using cognitive learning strategies to support student learning

The sections that follow provide a brief introduction to these school-situated responses to the cognitive dimension, which teachers often employ to address CLD students' development of academic content and English language proficiency.

Cognitive Complexity and Difficulty of Task

The cognitive demands that CLD students experience in the classroom depend on the types of academic tasks and supports they are provided. Contextual clues such as visuals, manipulatives, and concept-related objects can help students as they try to make sense of curricular concepts. Figure 4.1 provides examples that demonstrate the range of contextual support and degree of cognitive involvement in communicative activities. Any student who is continually asked to participate in cognitively demanding tasks without time to periodically allow the brain to "relax" will likely lose the motivation to continue to be engaged in the lesson.

By varying the complexity of tasks, educators can increase CLD student engagement and understanding of the lesson. Students who are learning a new language also need opportunities to be challenged at varying levels while they are learning new content material. Selecting strategies that allow for variance in cognitive demand increases the likelihood that each student will be able to more fully participate in classroom activities that accelerate language and academic development. Figure 4.2 illustrates how a lesson on insects was designed to incorporate tasks that varied in cognitive complexity.

When teachers reflect on ways to vary the cognitive complexity of a task, they often look to Bloom's taxonomy, which was originally conceptualized to include the following six levels, organized in order of increasing complexity: knowledge, comprehension, application, analysis, synthesis, and evaluation (Bloom et al., 1956). L. W. Anderson et al. (2001) revised the taxonomy; the revised version is depicted in Figure 4.3. In describing the differences between the

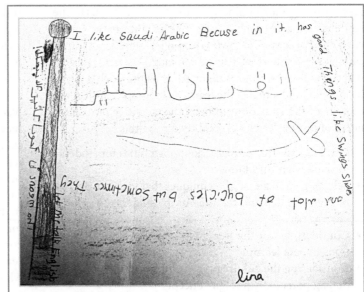

I read *Candy Corn* and *Just Around the Corner* by James Stevenson to the whole class. As a follow-up, I showed them how to write a shape poem—choose a topic and then write the poem in a representative shape. Then I asked them to write their own.

In an earlier lesson, we had read some Spanish poetry and listened for the rhythm and rhyme, noting that we could hear the play with words even in another language. As a class, I had the students chorally read some of the easier poems. As a result, some of the children wanted to write poetry in their own languages.

One student immediately decided that she would write a poem about Saudi Arabia. She wrote the poem in the shape of a flag, and she added lines in Arabic. Her poem shows pride in her culture and language and an awareness of English even in her home country. When she was done, she also wrote in Arabic about her relationship with her brother.

Although I know almost nothing about Arabic and was not able to read what this student wrote, I think it is still essential to provide students with opportunities to think and write in the language in which they are most fluent, which is their native language. Students can illustrate what they wrote, with the hope that some meaning will be apparent from the illustration. Then I can have follow-up conversations with them in English about what they wrote. *(Image courtesy of Leellyn Tuel, 2nd Grade, Kansas)*

two versions, Sousa (2017) notes that the revised taxonomy "changes the labels to verb form, renames three levels, and interchanges the top two levels. The dotted outline suggests a more open and fluid model, recognizing that an individual may move among the levels during extended processing" (p. 290). Because we want students to be able to use the information they are learning for future purposes that are personally relevant, it is fitting that *Create* now receives emphasis as the highest level of complexity. When we support learners to engage in the upper three levels (Analyze, Evaluate, and Create), we foster their ability to utilize *divergent* thought processes, in which they make new discoveries and arrive at insights not part of the original material (Sousa, 2017).

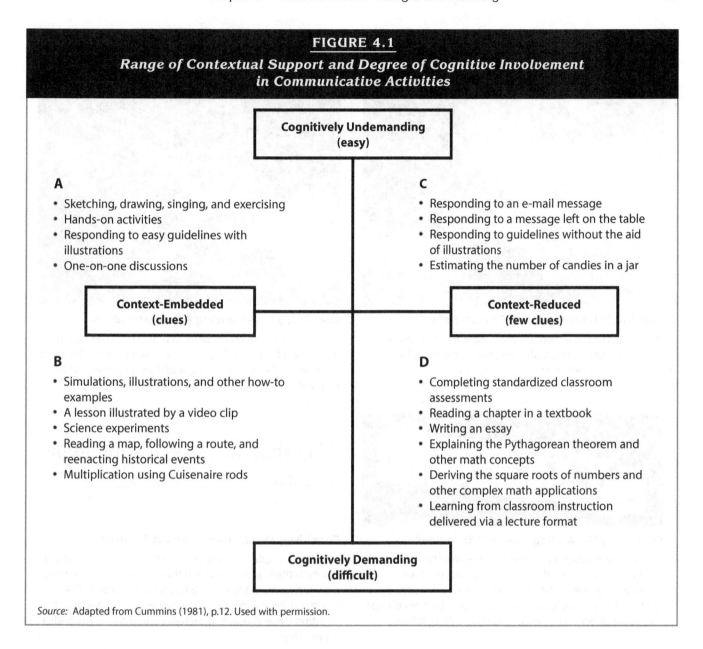

FIGURE 4.1

Range of Contextual Support and Degree of Cognitive Involvement in Communicative Activities

Cognitively Undemanding (easy)

A
- Sketching, drawing, singing, and exercising
- Hands-on activities
- Responding to easy guidelines with illustrations
- One-on-one discussions

C
- Responding to an e-mail message
- Responding to a message left on the table
- Responding to guidelines without the aid of illustrations
- Estimating the number of candies in a jar

Context-Embedded (clues)

Context-Reduced (few clues)

B
- Simulations, illustrations, and other how-to examples
- A lesson illustrated by a video clip
- Science experiments
- Reading a map, following a route, and reenacting historical events
- Multiplication using Cuisenaire rods

D
- Completing standardized classroom assessments
- Reading a chapter in a textbook
- Writing an essay
- Explaining the Pythagorean theorem and other math concepts
- Deriving the square roots of numbers and other complex math applications
- Learning from classroom instruction delivered via a lecture format

Cognitively Demanding (difficult)

Source: Adapted from Cummins (1981), p.12. Used with permission.

Sousa (2017) urges educators to remember the distinction between *complexity* and *difficulty* when putting Bloom's taxonomy to use with learners in classroom practice. As he explains, "Complexity establishes the level of thought while difficulty determines the amount of effort required within each level" (p. 297). Often teachers think the tasks they have designed will lead to more complex thought, when in reality the tasks only require greater effort at the same lower level of thought. For example, asking students to name the seven continents is equally complex as asking students to name all the countries on each of the seven continents. Both of these tasks require students to *remember*. The second task, however, is much more difficult.

Student ability is more closely related to difficulty than to complexity (Sousa, 2017). Even slower learners can think complexly; it simply takes them more time to learn the con-

cept and to sort the subcomponents or supporting understandings when deciding which aspects of the concept to let go of and which to retain for future use. Unfortunately, the time allotted to instruction of a given concept frequently does not afford slower learners the opportunity to fully learn the concept and perform the needed sorting. As Sousa notes, "This explains why fast learners are usually fast retrievers: They have not cluttered their memory networks with trivia" (p. 296). Fast learners have had ample time to both learn and sort.

Similarly, for emergent bilinguals who must contend with the cognitive load required for language acquisition in addition to that generally associated with learning grade-level content, sufficient time must be allotted for processing curricular concepts. In practice, this means that we teachers must identify the core concepts of our curriculum that are

---

FIGURE 4.2

Student Tasks That Vary in Cognitive Complexity

Cognitively Undemanding & Context-Embedded

In this part of the lesson, students were asked to draw the body parts of an insect. Students were able to look at examples of insects throughout this task.

Cognitively Undemanding & Context-Reduced

Students later worked in pairs to practice and discuss the vocabulary for the body parts of an insect. They listened to the teacher define the words, and they identified the corresponding terms on a vocabulary strip.

Cognitively Demanding & Context-Embedded

As the lesson progressed, the students were provided with the pictures they had drawn to share what they had learned in sequence. This task was context-embedded (pictures); however, it did require that the students discuss the information in sequence (cognitively demanding).

The abdomen has the important organs.

Cognitively Demanding & Context-Reduced

Students completed the lesson with a writing assignment in which the teacher provided them with a sentence strip on which a main idea of the lesson was written. The teacher then asked students to write a paragraph incorporating three supporting details related to the main idea on the strip.

(Images courtesy of Erica Bonderson & Nichole Zoeller, Elementary, Iowa)

---

absolutely essential for all students to learn. By emphasizing depth rather than breadth of content coverage, we increase the likelihood that all students will have time to fully understand the content and build from there to become adept at creative and critical thinking.

Learning Styles

The concept of "learning styles" emerged on the scene in the 1950s and gained popularity beginning in the 1970s (Papadatou-Pastou et al., 2021). This notion, which reflects the idea that we each have preferred modalities of instruction through which we are able to more effectively learn, makes

intuitive sense. Yet, despite widespread use among educators, the concept has been heavily criticized and is now considered a *neuromyth* (e.g., Hood et al., 2017; Krätzig & Arbuthnott, 2006; Papadatou-Pastou et al., 2018, 2021; Pashler et al., 2008; Rohrer & Pashler, 2012; Stahl, 2002; Will, 2019).

According to Papadatou-Pastou and colleagues (2021), criticism of learning styles reflects four primary themes:

1. *Lack of shared meaning surrounding the definition of the construct.* In fact, Coffield and colleagues (2004) identified more than 70 different constructs referred to as learning styles. Among these, 13 were considered dom-

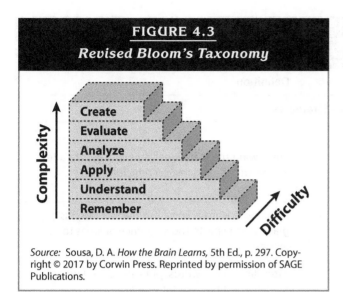

FIGURE 4.3

Revised Bloom's Taxonomy

Source: Sousa, D. A. *How the Brain Learns,* 5th Ed., p. 297. Copyright © 2017 by Corwin Press. Reprinted by permission of SAGE Publications.

inant. Included in this review were conceptualizations promoted by Dunn and Dunn (Dunn, 1990; Dunn & Dunn, 1993). Many researchers would also include theories such as Gardner's multiple intelligences (Gardner, 1992, 1993).

2. *Lack of scientific research affirming the rationale for learning styles.* Reviews of research on learning styles have yielded mixed results (Hayes & Allinson, 1993) or have demonstrated insufficient experimental support for the concept (Pashler et al., 2008).

3. *Lack of evidence to substantiate the use of learning styles in the classroom, and the potential for negative repercussions if they are used for guiding instruction.* Few systematic studies have been undertaken to examine the effectiveness of delivering information through different modalities for increased classroom performance. Those that have been conducted have failed to support the concept of learning styles (Krätzig & Arbuthnott, 2006; Rogowsky et al., 2015; Willingham et al., 2015).

4. *Lack of valid and reliable learning style assessment tools.* In a study involving the psychometric properties of 13 common learning style tests, researchers found insufficient internal consistency and test–retest reliability (Coffield et al., 2004). Furthermore, many classifications rely on student self-assessment or teacher assessment based on observation, and studies have shown little consensus between student- and teacher-determined learning styles (Marcus, 1977; Papadatou-Pastou et al., 2018).

In effect, a focus on learning styles diverts time, energy, and financial resources away from instruction grounded on we do know: Among its multiple parts, the brain makes use of multiple types of input to support our sense-making processes (Sousa, 2017; Zadina, 2014).

As educators, we can support learning that lasts by providing all students with rich classroom experiences that uti-

lize multiple types of information. Such instruction allows learners to use *multiple* modalities. When we also maximize the potential of peer interaction, we make it possible for learners to witness and engage in diverse ways of working with concepts and language.

Student Learning Strategies

Learning strategies "are conscious mental and behavioral procedures that people engage in with the aim to gain control over their learning process" (Ortega, 2009, p. 208). In the education of CLD students, the most widely recognized research on learning strategies was conducted by Chamot and O'Malley of George Washington University. Their research and writing (e.g., Chamot, 2009; Chamot & O'Malley, 1994; O'Malley & Chamot, 1990) documented types of learning strategies and their association with particular academic tasks. One of the central components of their work is the use of student learning strategies to support academic and language development of second language learners. An overview of the three primary types of strategies detailed by Chamot and O'Malley (1994) is provided in Figure 4.4.

Oxford (1990) also extensively researched learning strategies, developing a model that includes six groups of strategies and their associated subsets of strategies (p. 17). In total, Oxford discusses 62 strategies. Figure 4.5 depicts the relationships among the various strategies in Oxford's system.

Student learning strategies, when introduced and modeled by the instructor and gradually released for student learning, provide students with the necessary tools to take responsibility for and scaffold their own learning. This type of responsibility is often an expectation of the gifted student or is modeled by parents in homes where parents have a college education. However, because school may be students' first exposure to such strategies, it becomes essential in classrooms with diverse students that we, as teachers, take responsibility for including learning strategies as part of our daily practice so that all students have access to tools that lead to academic achievement.

Although much of the research done on learning strategies has been inconclusive, there is evidence to support use of learning strategies such as self-regulation and metacognitve skills to bolster learning (Dinsmore et al., 2008). According to Ortega (2009, 2011), strategy use by the individual is highly dictated and controlled by the teacher. This control manifests itself in the learning objectives and goals the teacher selects. Other factors that influence the learner's strategy use include the following:

• The student's motivation to learn the target language

• The particular learning task

• The cultural appropriateness of various strategies for the learner

FIGURE 4.4
Chamot and O'Malley's Three Types of Learning Strategies

Strategy	Description	Definition
Metacognitive Strategies		
Planning		
Advance organization	Preview Skim Gist	Previewing the main ideas and concepts of a text; identifying the organizing principle
Organizational planning	Plan what to do	Planning how to accomplish the learning task; planning the parts and sequence of ideas to express
Selective attention	Listen or read selectively Scan Find specific information	Attending to key words, phrases, ideas, linguistic markers, and types of information
Self-management	Plan when, where, and how to study	Seeking or arranging the conditions that help one learn
Monitoring		
Monitoring comprehension	Think while listening Think while reading	Checking one's comprehension during listening or reading
Monitoring production	Think while speaking Think while writing	Checking one's oral or written production while it is taking place
Evaluating		
Self-assessment	Check back Keep a learning log Reflect on what you learned	Judging how well one has accomplished a learning task

- The student's ability to make sense of the strategy and how it supports his or her learning

Without a conscious inventory of these factors, the teaching of learning strategies may leave students, particularly CLD students, without any new skill or tool for uncovering, monitoring, or evaluating their own learning.

Although there is much to be learned about learning strategies and their true impact on the student, we do recognize that explicit strategy instruction can enhance the likelihood of CLD students' achievement of linguistic and academic success. The role that a student's sociocultural and linguistic biography plays in his or her selection and use of learning strategies, including when and how they are applied in different content areas and within different contexts, demands further research. By proactively seeking to understand how a CLD student has gained knowledge about the world, the types of thought processes he or she frequently uses to make sense of new information, and the ways he or she is most adept at applying information, the

educator can gain insights into the learning strategies the student currently uses.

My work with colleagues seeks to operationalize the use of learning strategies by providing teachers with tools that support learners to better understand how they process information and that students can use to scaffold their own learning. Autonomous learning may not be achieved if students do not audit their own processing and make decisions about strategies that support them to take control of their own learning. Students must also understand how strategies become more powerful when they modify them to meet their own individual ways of learning and performing tasks. This customization ultimately supports learners' increased English development at the same time they are becoming more acculturated to the context and content of the learning environment.

It is important to plan for and teach learning strategies that are aligned with the teaching objectives, curriculum, and CLD student biography. We must remind ourselves that merely teaching learning strategies will not result in greater

FIGURE 4.4
Continued

Strategy	Description	Definition
Cognitive Strategies		
Resourcing	Use reference materials	Using reference materials such as dictionaries, encyclopedias, or textbooks
Grouping	Classify Construct graphic organizers	Classifying words, terminology, quantities, or concepts according to their attributes
Note-Taking	Take notes on idea maps, T-lists, etc.	Writing down key words and concepts in abbreviated verbal, graphic, or numerical form
Elaboration of Prior Knowledge	Use what you know Use background knowledge Make analogies	Relating new to known information and making personal associations
Summarizing	Say or write the main idea	Making a mental, oral, or written summary of information gained from listening or reading
Deduction/Induction	Use a rule/Make a rule	Applying or figuring out rules to understand a concept or complete a learning task
Imagery	Visualize Make a picture	Using mental or real pictures to learn new information or solve a problem
Auditory Representation	Use your mental tape recorder Hear it again	Replaying mentally a word, phrase, or piece of information
Making Inferences	Use context clues Guess from context Predict	Using information in the text to guess meanings of new items or predict upcoming information
Social/Affective Strategies		
Questioning for Clarification	Ask questions	Getting additional explanation or verification from a teacher or other expert
Cooperation	Cooperate Work with classmates Coach each other	Working with peers to complete a task, pool information, solve a problem, get feedback
Self-Talk	Think positive!	Reducing anxiety by improving one's sense of competence

Source: Chamot, Anna Uhl; O'Malley, J. Michael, *The CALLA Handbook,* 1st Ed., © 1994, Table 4.1, pp. 62–63. Reprinted by permission of Pearson Education, Inc., New York, New York.

learning. Rather, the strategies selected for instruction must lend themselves to supporting students' attainment of the objectives and understanding of the content.

These strategies must become part of the daily routine of lesson delivery and must be used throughout the lesson. Students will only come to know the value of a strategy if it is used consistently, if it is modeled by the teacher, and if the student receives feedback on how the strategy supports him or her in learning the language and content.

In addition, learning strategies must be culturally responsive and relevant, as certain learning strategies may be inappropriate for some students (e.g., students from non-Western cultures may not be accustomed to providing corrective feedback to peers) (Ortega, 2009, 2011). In such instances, specific efforts should be made to provide explicit instruction and guidance in using the strategy to enhance learning. By incorporating use of multiple types of strategies in the classroom and continually reminding students

FIGURE 4.5
Oxford's System of Learning Strategies

Memory Strategies

Creating mental linkages
- Grouping
- Associating/elaborating
- Placing new words into a context

Applying images and sounds
- Using imagery
- Semantic mapping
- Using keywords
- Representing sounds in memory

Reviewing well
- Structured reviewing

Employing action
- Using physical response or sensation
- Using mechanical techniques

Cognitive Strategies

Practicing
- Repeating
- Formally practicing with sounds and writing systems
- Recognizing and using formulas and patterns
- Recombining
- Practicing naturalistically

Receiving and sending messages
- Getting the idea quickly
- Using resources for receiving and sending messages

Analyzing and reasoning
- Reasoning deductively
- Analyzing expressions
- Analyzing contrastively (across languages)
- Translating
- Transferring

Creating structure for input and output
- Taking notes
- Summarizing
- Highlighting

Compensation Strategies

Guessing intelligently
- Using linguistic clues
- Using other clues

Overcoming limitations in speaking and writing
- Switching to the mother tongue
- Getting help
- Using mime or gesture
- Avoiding communication partially or totally
- Selecting the topic
- Adjusting or approximating the message
- Coining words
- Using a circumlocution or synonym

Metacognitive Strategies

Centering your learning
- Overviewing and linking with already known material
- Paying attention
- Delaying speech production to focus on listening

Arranging and planning your learning
- Finding out about language learning
- Organizing
- Setting goals and objectives
- Identifying the purpose of a language task (purposeful listening/reading/speaking/writing)
- Planning for a language task
- Seeking practice opportunities

Evaluating your learning
- Self-monitoring
- Self-evaluating

Affective Strategies

Lowering your anxiety
- Using progressive relaxation, deep breathing, or meditation
- Using music
- Using laughter

Encouraging yourself
- Making positive statements
- Taking risks wisely
- Rewarding yourself

Taking your emotional temperature
- Listening to your body
- Using a checklist
- Writing a language learning diary
- Discussing your feelings with someone else

Social Strategies

Asking questions
- Asking for clarification or verification
- Asking for correction

Cooperating with others
- Cooperating with peers
- Cooperating with proficient users of the new language

Empathizing with others
- Developing cultural understanding
- Becoming aware of others' thoughts and feelings

Adapted from Oxford, *Language Learning Strategies,* pp. 17–21, 1E. © 1990 Heinle/ELT, a part of Cengage Learning, Inc. Reproduced by permission. www.cengage.com/permissions.

that we all have "tricks" that support our learning, we can provide CLD students with assurance that strategy use should be flexible to their specific learning needs.

Pedagogy that values student biographies in the exploration and use of learning strategies requires a move away from pre-set, reductionistic taxonomies of how learning strategies are taught and used in classroom practice. Instead, by observing, listening, and documenting CLD students in action, we teachers can create more opportunities for students to integrate strategy use that is effective—based on how *they* as individuals know, think, and apply knowledge.

Cognitively Speaking: *i*+1

It is easy to get stuck in what has been researched or prescribed within our own teaching cultures and pay little attention to the cultural context of the student or the role of individual motivation in the learning process. Yet as Jensen (2008) reminds us, "In order to get learners to be creative and have greater subject interest, higher self-esteem, and the ability to be reflective, there must be intrinsic motivation" (p. 124). We are more likely to encourage that motivation, and to accomplish our teaching goals, when we focus on CLD students' ways of learning.

Multiple Ways of Knowing

The way we come to know things from an early age is a result of our interactions with others in our family, in the community, and in the world. We learn to ask questions, respond, tell a story, and interpret the voices and actions of both the communicator and the message itself. Students' knowledge and their revelation of it reflect the words, understandings, and perspectives of those whose voices, actions, and thoughts they have learned to imitate. Every student enters the classroom with knowledge and with expectations about the way things are going to work. It can be difficult to see beyond our initial ways of knowing. Consider the following scenario:

> I remember being asked to write, to tell my stories. My stories had to include everyone because in my family nothing ever happens to just one person. I remember when a snake bit my little brother in the fields. Lots of things were happening and they didn't happen in a line the way my teacher wanted me to tell them. My story happened in a zigzag, with many little things that I had to tell about before I could get to the point. These little things are what made my stories funny. In my family, you have to make your stories funny, even the serious ones. That's how we survived the really hard times, like not having a place to live, running out of gas, or praying for the chicken to lay an egg so we could eat. My families' stories are very funny. I *know* how to tell stories. Ever since I was little

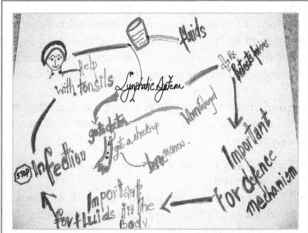

The use of mind maps (Buzan, 1983) as a strategy for allowing students to document what they know and to share what they have learned increases the likelihood that all students, even those who have not reached a high level of proficiency in English, will be active participants in learning. The mind map allows for both linguistic and nonlinguistic representations of student learning. *(Image courtesy of Jeremy Pride, Middle School, Kansas)*

> I could tell the best stories. My teacher didn't like the way I told my stories. She thought I needed to pay more attention to what the book said and tell my stories in a line. I still don't think she knows how to tell stories like I do.

In classrooms that I observe, I frequently find teachers trying to "fix" CLD students' ways of knowing. They ask students to imitate their actions, and often an interaction between the teacher and student can take multiple repetitions before the teacher gives up hope that the student will ever get it right. Seldom are questions asked about the student's way of knowing and how it has implications for the task at hand. The teacher does not typically explore whether, or how, the CLD student is making sense of the requested task, or what meaning the student brings to the task he or she has been asked to perform. Often we leave aside the student's cognitive processes and consider them the private thoughts of the learner rather than ask the student directly how he or she came to a conclusion. Much is lost in practice when the only processing we document and value is that which is prescribed by the grade-level curriculum. As an outsider looking in, I am encouraged when I see a teacher ask a student why he or she approached a task in a way other than what was prescribed by the curriculum.

The ways students come to "know," referred to by Byers and Byers (1985) as "the organization of the processes of human communication," is based on their particular culture and the "template for the organization of knowledge or information in that particular culture" (p. 28). The experiences CLD students have had in life will greatly influence their ways of knowing, and thus will have implications for what happens within the classroom. How students interpret information and respond when asked to answer a question or provide a written response will vary, as each student's knowledge and ways of sharing that knowledge will reflect their unique histories.

So what can a teacher do to ensure that CLD students' ways of knowing are central to their education? Here are a few suggestions:

- Listen closely to what is communicated both verbally and nonverbally.
- Look for patterns in responses. After multiple interventions, ask yourself if the type of intervention being used is culturally appropriate.
- Create the conditions for multiple ways of knowing to be allowed during the course of a lesson.
- Consider allowing cultural knowledge to be valued as highly as the prescribed answer.
- Explore ways for documenting the thought processes of the learner in relation to the content and language objectives throughout the entire lesson.

Ways of thinking and knowing have implications for learning, feedback, and the way educators manage their classroom. Gay (2018) perhaps says it best when she reminds educators that "far from being simply a means for reporting experience, language is a way of defining experience, thinking, and knowing" (p. 93). Sapir (1968) similarly noted that "language is a guide to 'social reality' . . . [and] a symbolic guide to culture" (p. 162). In becoming culturally responsive educators, we must strive to ensure that our views on knowledge, thought, and the application of knowledge do not place limitations on our CLD students.

Why We Think the Way We Think

We teachers always are looking for ways to tap into what students are thinking as they listen, interact, and work with the information that is shared during the lesson. Most documentation of their thought processes results from students articulating their content understanding during the lesson or through their submitted work. What we often fail to do is observe and listen for cultural aspects of what students are thinking. According to Nieto and Bode (2018), there is an undeniable connection between students' thinking processes and the influences that have been shaped by their cultural background. Vygotsky (1934/1962) discusses the interrelatedness of learners' thought, language, and culture. In his work, he states an "indisputable fact": "thought and development is determined by language . . . and the sociocultural experience of the child" (p. 51). Although culture cannot force us to think in a certain way, it does shape our way of thinking (Joy & Kolb, 2009; McDaniel et al., 2012).

Ji and colleagues (2004) explored such cultural influences on thought in a study on ways Chinese and European

Americans' reasoning styles differed. It appears that bilingual Chinese individuals are more "relational," whereas European Americans are more "categorical" when organizing objects. In the study, these differences remained, regardless of the language in which the participants were tested. Observation and research on differences in thinking when CLD students are asked to perform different tasks can lead to the identification of best practice strategies for CLD students of a given cultural background.

Students' ways of thinking are absolutely critical to literacy development. As I work with students from diverse backgrounds and we collaborate to make sense of text, I am continually reminded that we educators do not do enough to create places and spaces in our lessons where we can discover CLD students' ways of thinking. Consider the following quote and reflect on what it means for classroom practice:

> It is the culturally appropriate way of thinking, not the act of reading or writing that is most important in the development of literacy. Literacy thinking manifests itself in different ways in oral and written language in different societies, and educators need to understand these ways of thinking if they are to build bridges and facilitate transitions among ways of thinking. (Langer, 1991, p. 13)

If we teachers simply begin our lessons with the information that we want students to learn and focus on students' acquisition of the requisite skills, we forget one of the primary goals of literacy instruction: students should be able to read and write effectively for real purposes and for real audiences. This means that we must apprentice students to thinking about literacy acts in ways that are appropriate to the culture of formal education, and we must begin by valuing students' own ways of thinking about and enacting literacy.

Applying What We Know and Think

The ultimate goal of any lesson is for all students to reach a level of internalization of knowledge that allows them to apply that knowledge in the present and in future learning situations. This application of what has been learned is most often observed for during and after the lesson, when students are asked to respond to questions, complete a project, or write about the topic. Students' application of knowledge and thinking frequently is evaluated by teachers who, at these moments in the lesson, see their role as that of a judge who determines the extent to which expectations (often set arbitrarily without regard to students' biographies) have been met. When our perspectives on assessment and evaluation are void of any understanding of how a student's biography may influence how he or she represents new learning, we educators may miss opportunities to celebrate success. Chapter 9 explores how classroom assessment that is centered on students' biographies can inform our teaching as well as encourage students to continue their learning efforts.

According to Bruner (1996), what we think and what we learn will always be situated within our cultural resources. Therefore, it is through our understanding of the particular culture of the student that we will find additional meaning in what students share about their learning with the rest of the classroom community. It is important to ask questions related to the cultural conflicts that may be present when we ask students to apply information in ways that may be inconsistent with their cultural paths of knowing, thinking, and applying. If what we ask students to do is inconsistent with their patterns, the resulting "evidence" that we have to evaluate may result in a shallow interpretation of a student's ability to apply new learning.

Although we should continually seek to open new avenues for application to students, we must do so in ways that first value the students' familiar ways of demonstrating learning and then guide them to new ways of applying what they know. For instance, students from Korea might be unfamiliar with the expectations traditionally associated with summarizing a chapter. They might repeat what the teacher has already mentioned about the topic, or copy some parts of the chapter. Korean students often are accustomed to teachers pointing out what is important and needs to be memorized. Therefore, independent study or classroom tasks that require students to decide what is important about a topic or to identify the key information from a chapter might be seen as confusing. A teacher might help such learners as well as other students in the classroom to gain an understanding of the process of summarization by:

- First identifying key concepts from a passage or lesson and then asking students to locate textual explanations/support for each concept or to record points of the lesson related to each concept
- Providing explicit instruction on how to differentiate key information from supporting details
- Incorporating opportunities for students to work together to practice differentiating essential information from nonessential details (The Relevance Scale strategy, discussed in Chapters 3 and 9, can be particularly effective with CLD students.)
- Supporting students in individual summarization tasks by providing a hand-held scaffolding tool, such as a foldable or a graphic organizer, to help guide their thinking
- Providing students with examples of written summaries and modeling for students how information contained on a scaffolding tool can be used to develop a written summary of content knowledge

Consciously placing the biography of the student at the forefront of learning ensures attention to the impact that cul-

ture may have on CLD students' cognitive processing and their learning before, during, and after the lesson. According to Gay (2018), "the processes of learning—not the intellectual capability to do so—used by students from different ethnic groups are influenced by their cultural socialization" (p. 202). As Ramírez and Castañeda (1974) explain:

> The sociocultural system of the child's home and community is influential in producing culturally unique preferred modes of relating to others . . . culturally unique incentive preferences, . . . as well as a preferred mode of thinking, perceiving, remembering, and problem solving. All of these characteristics . . . must be incorporated as the principal bases upon which programs for instituting changes in the school must be developed. (p. 32)

Understanding cognition from a cultural perspective sets the stage for a different approach to planning, teaching, and assessing CLD students, and it has implications for the way we design learning tasks, interpret students' emotional and behavioral responses, and select and model learning strategies. Providing students with the scaffolding strategies/tools to support their own learning throughout the lesson, while simultaneously creating a systematic way to document what each student comprehends as the lesson unfolds, is critical to the success of all learners.

Reflections on the Cognitive Dimension

High expectations and cognitively challenging instruction must be hallmarks of our professional practice with every student. CLD students must be held accountable for their learning of grade-level content and their development of English language skills. At the same time, we must guide students in using strategies that will enhance the effectiveness of their learning processes.

The key for us as educators is to remember to use our students' biographies to center our instructional efforts. Moving beyond activities in the classroom that produce few results for students who seem to lack motivation, are seldom engaged in the lesson, or are at risk of failing will require us to make a conscious decision to use learning strategies every day. We can provide students with opportunities to share with us how they have come to know the world, in relation to what we are teaching. We can encourage students to openly share their ways of understanding curricular content and relationships among concepts and vocabulary words. As we gain insight into students' culturally influenced ways of knowing and thinking, we can better provide avenues that will allow each student to demonstrate fully his or her academic knowledge and linguistic skills, as well as progress made along the way.

5

Academics
More Than a Test Score or Grade

GUIDING QUESTION

How does adherence to academic measures or markers limit planning and assessment for student potential, guided by grade-level/content standards?

See the online Discussion Guide for opportunities to further explore answers to this question and connections to chapter content with a colleague or team. Available for download from the Teachers College Press website: tcpress.com

IMAGINE WHAT LIFE in schools would be like if academic achievement were viewed from the lens of student potential rather than a standardized score. If school meant a place where planning, lesson delivery, and assessment were about openly setting conditions to create a canvas of opportunity for the learner? If classroom instruction demanded high cognitive engagement, collaboration, and cooperation with other community members who could support everyone to reach their ZPD? Would the results improve for students who are failing? This chapter explores from a slightly different perspective what it means to look beyond standardized tests, test scores, and grades. It asks that we think about the kind of access that has been provided or denied to students, which is beyond their control. At the end of each day, one of the most important elements of teaching is giving students a reason to return the next day ready to engage and learn—that is, providing students with hope that tomorrow will be an even better day.

The Academic Dimension

The fourth and final dimension of the CLD student biography is the **academic dimension**. This dimension incorporates all content-area school instruction and learning from the first years of formalized education through adult education. With each progressive grade level, learners' knowledge base increases and their language expands. The optimal learning environment for CLD students is one that reflects understanding of how the brain processes information and knowledge of how to utilize technology to build literacy skills both in their native language and in English.

Educational scholarship has extensively documented the need to support students in "naming their world," that is,

working from the known to the unknown in order to bring meaning to what we teach in schools. Prescriptive curriculum that is not framed around the leaners' "known world" and their language repertoire immediately sets up the learning space for an uphill struggle in working with and taking new knowledge to long-term/permanent memory. Why is it necessary for students to use the knowledge they have accumulated as active participants in the world they inhabit? Why is it important that students use the words they have available to them in English and the native language when building their academic knowledge? Simply put, we store information in sets of words associated with concepts/ideas/stories that connect to our lived experiences (Marzano, 2004; Zadina, 2014). Additionally, research has long documented that skills and knowledge gained in the native language transfer to the second language (e.g., Goldenberg, 2008). This core of knowledge that is accessible through either language can be conceptualized as a student's common underlying proficiency (CUP) (refer to Chapter 3 for a discussion of CUP).

Traditional School-Initiated Responses

> Don't judge me
> by my skin.
> Don't judge me
> by my language.
> Don't judge me
> by my test scores.
> Take a minute to talk to me
> And learn who I "really am."
> —*BESITOS/Herrera Terry (2004)*

We teachers have been taught to make all kinds of decisions based on data that CLD students present at the time they arrive in our classrooms and from the many standardized assessments we conduct throughout the year to assess academic growth. This is especially true for reading and math, the two areas where CLD students are most likely to fail. Decisions are made related to the capacities CLD students have in reading, math, writing, and other academic areas based on these limiting types of information. Often, these scores begin to define what, when, and for what amount of time the learner will receive interventions to address identified "gaps." As students participate in these well-intentioned interventions, they often miss out on receiving the higher-level academic content that many of their grade-level peers receive. For decades, this model has persisted in education with minimal documented results for our lowest performing students.

In my work with youth, I have found—as reflected in the quote above—that there exists a need to use such data as a point-in-time measure of the gaps that *may* exist and to respond by developing culturally relevant, responsive, and sustaining lessons to address such potential needs. More importantly, however, we must *not* use the data, especially single measures, to make decisions that segregate the learner. Decisions have the potential to remove the student from effective academic and English development models, limit the building of interpersonal relationships with members of their classroom community, and have lifelong implications (e.g., through denial of access to higher-level courses, grade-level curricula, and high-quality instruction).

> I was placed in lower Math
> Lower Language Arts
> Because of this ONE test in the 6th grade.
> —*BESITOS/Herrera Terry (2004)*

Traditional school-initiated responses to the academic dimension frequently reflect perspectives on academics that are defined simply by:

- Entry point profiles
- Standardized test scores (formative and state end-of-year tests)
- Grades
- End-of-year records

These sources of information often present a limiting, ethnocentric perspective on CLD students' academic abilities and achievement. Such a perspective may set the stage for instruction to be reductionistic in scope, leaving students further and further behind their grade-level peers. Students are placed in lower-level, drill-and-kill curricula and in programs that view learning in a linear fashion and do not accelerate, but instead remediate. Literature on this topic is saturated with voices decrying the consequences that reductionistic programs have on CLD students (e.g.,

Delpit, 2006; Gay, 2010; Ladson-Billings, 2009; Nieto, 2005). These authors urge educators to view CLD students' existing knowledge and skills as assets that can be used to accelerate academic growth and make decisions related to effective programming and instruction.

Frequently, the attitudes, beliefs, and lifelong assumptions that we educators hold regarding what is possible with CLD students can negatively impact their academic progress and success (Herrera, 1996; Khong & Saito, 2014). Expectations have a way of turning into the reality we see and the actions we take in our professional life. If we believe, for example, that using heterogeneous groups when teaching will have negative implications for the advanced or "gifted" students, we translate this into the way we approach our practice. For every daily decision we make in classrooms, we must ask ourselves what "evidence" supports what we believe is true. We must also ask whose evidence it is. From what point of view is the research undertaken and written? The ultimate question then becomes, How do we collect or seek out evidence that is aligned with the populations we serve? This will take critical reflection and risk-taking that goes against the stream of common practice—practice that may be limiting the possibilities for CLD and all other students.

An audit of the way we feel, think about, and act on a situation involving our teaching with CLD students can reveal whether our initial thoughts were based on assumptions, misconceptions, past experiences with other students, or even just a "gut feeling" that stems from the school-situated information that is available to us. Consider the following teacher's reflection as she struggles with maximizing the resources available to support CLD students' participation in the grade-level curriculum.

> I attended a professional development where the leader shared strategies for getting students to be more engaged and work at higher levels of Bloom's taxonomy. Although I participated and enjoyed talking to my peers, in my mind I was rolling my eyes. I knew that this outside "guru" did not understand the reality of my Black and Brown students and their families. Our work in this school is to minimize the chaos, to make sure we have established routines. If students are not controlled, they will run wild, just like they are allowed to do at home. I love these students and would be excited if they could use the novels that I love to teach them, but their Lexile levels do not allow for that. They still don't have the reading skills or background knowledge to really do the cool stuff. So, this is another day wasted learning from someone that does not understand me or the kids I teach!

In this journal activity, the teacher felt annoyed, frustrated, and a little angry that she was being asked to sit and listen to an all-day presentation on strategies for culturally responsive teaching. However, after leaving the session, she kept going back to the presentation in her mind, with a nagging feeling about the portion in which the presenter had talked about critically reflecting on challenges educators face when teaching in diverse contexts. She wondered, What assumptions have I made, about both the professional development and the content? What assumptions have I made about the students and the curricula? As she dug deeper, she recognized the following assumptions in her own thinking:

- I assumed that the students in my classroom who were poor or did not speak English could not possibly access the content curriculum.
- I assumed that what I was teaching was what students needed to learn.
- I assumed that after so many years of teaching, culturally responsive teaching was not for me. After all, I loved all my students equally.
- I assumed that, given the Lexile level of the students, they could not participate in reading high-level novels.

She also came to the realization that, in her profession, she seldom questioned how her teacher preparation program or the district and school initiatives would impact the CLD students she was teaching. She came to the realization that it was much easier to accept the deficit views for educating the bottom tier of learners. Doing otherwise required going against long-standing ways of doing. She was always resistant to outsiders coming in and telling her how to teach "Black and Brown students" in her classroom. As she thought back to the session, she questioned and wanted to learn more about the strategies and research that had been presented.

    Figure 5.1 provides an overview of the Reflection Wheel Journal process this teacher undertook as she examined an "event" from her own professional life in her educational context with CLD students. It is important to remind ourselves that how we respond to the work we do is based on our own knowledge and experiences. We must look at the pressure/tension points—these represent possible areas for critical reflection, new ways of thinking, action, and transformation. These "events" serve to either move us forward or hold us back in doing the right thing. The full journal entry of the teacher, along with detailed guidelines for the process, are presented in Appendix A as an example of what this journaling procedure can look like in practice. When we make **critical reflection** a regular part of our professional practice, identifying and examining the assumptions we make in our efforts with students becomes second nature. The result is our increased capacity to make decisions that promote the success of CLD students in our classrooms and schools.

The "Hearts" activity that was introduced in Chapter 2 is an excellent strategy for supporting students in making connections from self to text.

Academically Speaking: *i*+1

Throughout the previous chapter, the discussion focused on the role that culture plays in CLD students' processing of new information. We learned that culture is the lens that individuals use to make meaning socially and academically. It also influences learners' interpretation of the input they receive. Just as this is true for CLD students, it is also true for us as teachers. Our culture influences the way we teach. As Gay (2018) notes, "Even without our being consciously aware of it, culture strongly influences how we think, believe, communicate, and behave, and these, in turn, affect how we teach and learn" (p. 8). Key to CLD students' success in school is the degree to which they are assured of access to equitable educational opportunities, provided with learning environments that actively seek their engagement, and supported by teachers and other educators who inspire hope for their future.

    By being mindful, intentional, and present throughout the lesson to the community we are serving, we set the conditions necessary to establish an "ebb and flow" between the language and cognition evident in what students say and produce, and the curriculum/content we are teaching. In the third space, we place our shared humanity at the center as we engage with learners in ways that disrupt typical power differences. We allow students to teach us about their experiences, realities, and views of the world. We encourage learners to use all their language resources to express their thoughts and share how the content connects with their lives. After all, it does not matter whether teachers understand the content (we already assume they do) or can use the language with ease. What *is* of concern is the degree to which students see the relevance of what we are teaching for

FIGURE 5.1

Reflection Wheel Journal: Process

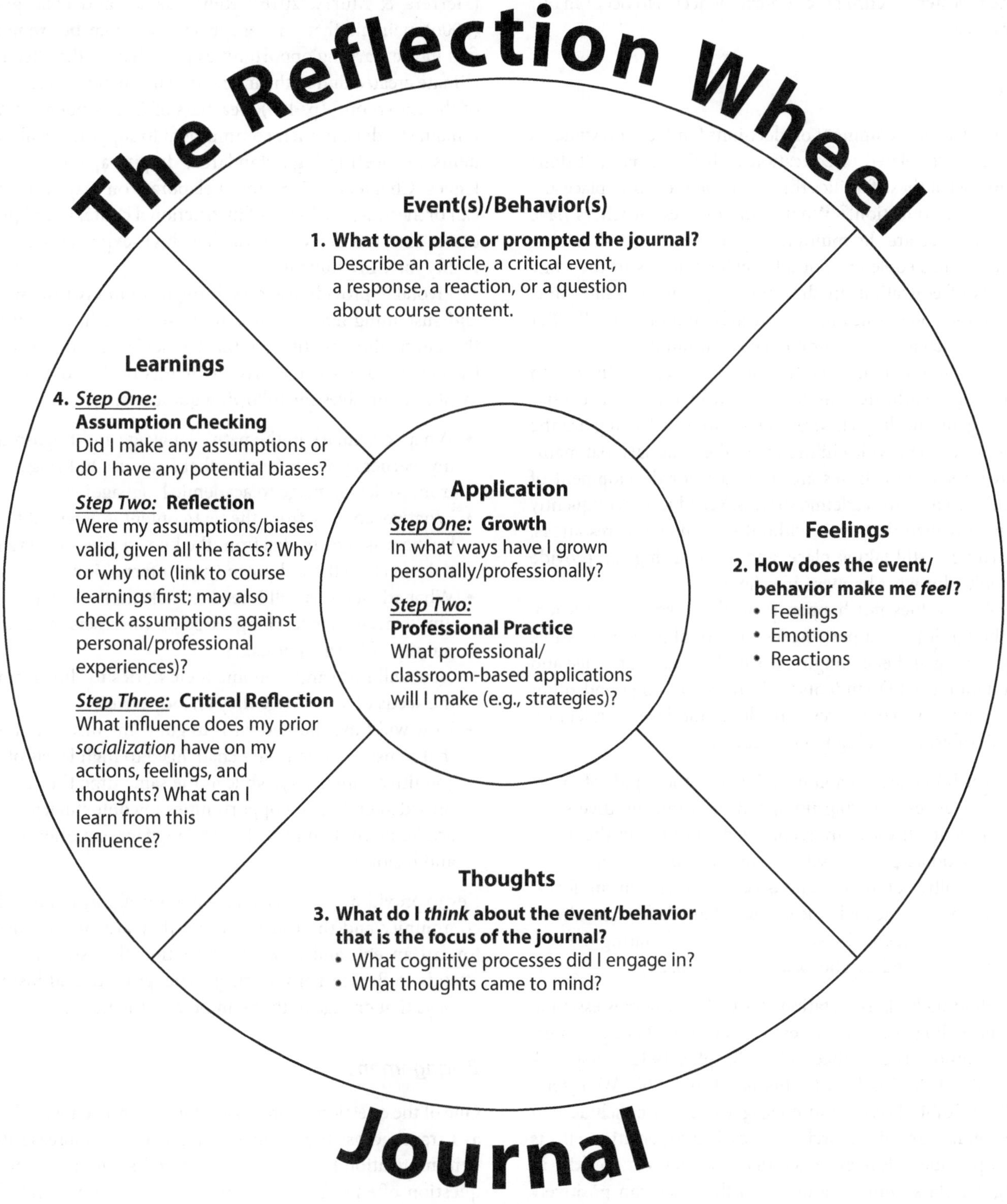
The Reflection Wheel
Event(s)/Behavior(s)
1. What took place or prompted the journal?
Describe an article, a critical event, a response, a reaction, or a question about course content.
Feelings
2. How does the event/behavior make me *feel*?
• Feelings
• Emotions
• Reactions
Thoughts
3. What do I *think* about the event/behavior that is the focus of the journal?
• What cognitive processes did I engage in?
• What thoughts came to mind?
Learnings
4. *Step One:* Assumption Checking
Did I make any assumptions or do I have any potential biases?
Step Two: Reflection
Were my assumptions/biases valid, given all the facts? Why or why not (link to course learnings first; may also check assumptions against personal/professional experiences)?
Step Three: Critical Reflection
What influence does my prior *socialization* have on my actions, feelings, and thoughts? What can I learn from this influence?
Application
Step One: Growth
In what ways have I grown personally/professionally?
Step Two: Professional Practice
What professional/classroom-based applications will I make (e.g., strategies)?
Journal

their daily lives, and whether they are able to use their language repertoire to meet their needs and life goals. Our role as educators is to be a facilitator, navigator, and negotiator of the biography of the learner and the standards we teach. The first step is setting the context for access to occur in our practice.

Access

Often teachers comment on decisions families and students have made related to education with the remark, "I don't know what these families think—no one seems to place any value on education!" What many of these teachers have failed to see are the multiple ways of defining and valuing education. People are not all provided access to the same kinds of education, in the same ways, at the same time. Therefore, how education is perceived and valued will differ within each and every immediate community.

Most homes that CLD students grow up in are filled with the hope, faith, determination, and love needed to raise strong and healthy children. Often what is lacking are the resources to provide children with the materials that mainstream society believes are necessary for development of skills essential to academic success. Yet educators frequently fail to realize that even without such material resources, learning is still taking place, and this learning can provide "hooks" for what happens in school.

Access does not happen from the curricula we teach, although it plays a part. Access in school is made possible by valuing and encouraging use of the native language and by tapping CLD students' cultural knowledge and other strengths to make success in the grade-level curriculum achievable. According to Gay (2018):

> Much intellectual ability and many other kinds of intelligences are lying untapped in ethnically diverse students. If these are recognized and used in the instructional process, school achievement will improve radically. Culturally responsive teaching is a means for unleashing the higher learning potentials of ethnically diverse students by simultaneously cultivating their academic and psychosocial abilities. (p. 21)

Holding high expectations for CLD learners is essential to providing equitable access to education. Citing numerous authors (i.e., Babad, 1993; Brophy, 1982; Cooper & Good, 1983; Good, 1987; Jussim et al., 1998; Weinstein, 2002), Rubie-Davies and colleagues (2006) conclude that "Several years of research into teacher expectation effects has provided clear evidence that expectations do exist in regular classroom situations and that they can positively and/or negatively influence student performance and achievement" (p. 429). Demanet and Van Houtte (2012) likewise reference research from four countries (Belgium, France, the United Kingdom, and the United States) and

arrive at the same conclusion. Although most teachers assert that they hold high expectations for all of their students, there often exists a gap between what is espoused and what is demonstrated in their daily instructional practices (Herrera & Murry, 2016). Rubie-Davies and colleagues (2006) maintain that teacher expectations "may be exemplified in the learning opportunities provided, in the affective climate created and in the interactional content and context of the classroom" (p. 430). Teachers of CLD students must remain steadfast in their commitment to supporting all students in meeting high standards, despite apparent challenges. Chapters 6, 7, 8, and 9 elaborate on ways teachers can orchestrate the kinds of instructional contexts and processes that are likely to turn their high expectations into reality for CLD students.

Pivotal to providing access through culturally responsive and sustaining instruction is understanding how to bring the curriculum to life for the particular community of learners we are teaching. As facilitators of the content, we must ask ourselves the following questions:

- What vocabulary in the native language and English do my learners possess (assets) that I can use to bridge from social language to academic language?
- What vocabulary from the text/content is essential for learners as they bridge from the known (their experiential assets) to the unknown (new information)?
- What adaptations will I need to make to the curriculum to accelerate learning based on the assets my community of learners possess?
- How will I use and combine their stories to "lift" from the seeds of knowledge they already have?
- How will I use the standards to guide my instruction so that I ensure students are challenged to high levels of cognitive complexity, while at the same time they are provided embedded opportunities to contextualize academic content in their own language, experiences, and history?

Key to providing access is our agency and ability to meet the community and the learner where they are, and to move toward an ebb and flow of instruction that situationally attends to the learner's language, background, and history in ways that engage both the mind and the heart.

Engagement

One of the questions I am most frequently asked by teachers as I travel across the country is, How do you increase student motivation to learn? From where I stand, this type of question often reflects a continued focus on a search for external factors that limit CLD students' motivation. The question of motivation should be one that educators consider from the perspective of pedagogy, asking themselves, Have I done enough to plan and deliver lessons that take into account the biographies of the students? Planning lessons that spark a desire to learn and that allow CLD students to be equal contributors, regardless of their linguistic or academic ability, is essential to student engagement in the classroom. Therefore, we as educators must understand motivation and engagement in terms of our own discovery of how best to involve CLD students throughout the learning process.

How then does motivation relate to engagement? According to Wlodkowski and Ginsberg (1995), "Engagement is the visible outcome of motivation, the natural capacity to direct energy in the pursuit of a goal" (p. 17). Without motivation, there is no engagement. Engagement cannot exist without the student being motivated to become part of the learning. Newmann and colleagues (1992) view engagement as "the student's psychological investment in and effort directed toward learning, understanding, or mastering the knowledge, skills, or crafts that academic work is intended to promote" (p. 12). Their description of engagement captures what it means to be engaged in the lesson beyond the realm of prescriptive curricula that follow "strict" processes, which often fail to create space for the learner to be able to make public and transparent what they know and what remains to be learned. For example, often our reading programs follow an outdated stimulus–response approach to phonics instruction that is worksheet-bound, where learners sit and wait to be called on to answer a question, repeat abstract rules, or read aloud from a book that has no connection to their schema.

The educator's task is to set up conditions during instruction that will promote students' investment in learning. This investment for the learner is first about having a cognitive belief system, an inner voice, affirming that they fit in the space and have something worthy to contribute to move the learning forward. As a researcher and collaborator in classrooms, the following questions come to mind when planning (setting the context) and delivering instruction (situationally monitoring engagement):

- How do I set the context to deliver my instruction in ways that allow the learners to engage with me and their community of learners, using their assets as a point of departure for social and academic conversation?
- How do I intentionally engage my learners by valuing their connections and stories as I deliver instruction?
- How do I define motivation and engagement? What do they look like in the classroom? What is my role in influencing these for students?

In describing the construct of engagement, Appleton and colleagues (2008) emphasize its multidimensional nature, encompassing cognitive engagement, behavioral engagement, and emotional engagement. The extent to which a student engages in academic work is influenced by myriad

Using strategies at the beginning of the lesson that activate the knowledge (words) students have related to the topic or target vocabulary increases the likelihood that students will use what they know to scaffold their own learning. *(Image courtesy of Jennifer Wilk, 3rd Grade, Kansas)*

factors. A primary concern is addressing the student's **state of mind**. Student feelings of anxiety, alienation, incompetence, frustration, or boredom must first be addressed in order that motivation and engagement toward meeting the objectives of the lesson can be promoted. A student's perceptions of competence and control (*I can*), values and goals (*I want to*), and social connectedness (*I belong*) all weigh heavily into levels of classroom engagement (National Research Council & Institute of Medicine, 2004). Regardless of the sociopolitical climate of the times, the culture of the school, or any other threats to teaching, the teacher has the potential and control to create classroom conditions that will increase student motivation and engagement. Chapters 6, 7, and 8 explore in detail these aspects of classroom practice with CLD students.

Hope

> My teacher made me smart. She made me smart because she cares about me. She always tells me that I am learning so much and someday I'm going to be her superstar. My teacher makes me feel like I am so smart. I love my teacher because she cares about me.
>
> —3rd-Grade Student

CLD students are aware of their grades, test scores, and prior schooling experiences. Hope is found in being held to high expectations, feeling like a worthy contributor to the learning space, and, most importantly, *being noticed*—not as a test score, not as the learner who has spotty attendance or the child who has behavior challenges—but as someone special who is gifted in ways too many to count. In their stories, second language learners often share feelings of isolation, a sense of disconnectedness, and thoughts of never being able to be part of the class because they often do not see where their experiences, skills, and knowledge fit. When they share about their home and community, what is shared disappears into an emptiness—in return are messages that communicate that their knowledge does not align with the curriculum or the conversation of the moment. This often leads to feelings of hopelessness, which then can lead to a "Why try?" attitude that manifests itself in low motivation, engagement, and desire to learn. We educators can address this disconnectedness from learning through actions that demonstrate a sense of caring—first about the person we are teaching and, as a result, about the learning we are helping them achieve. A place where each individual is cared about can give students hope that the dreams and goals they have for the future are attainable. Too often the fast-paced nature of our school systems and the testing-oriented mandates pressure us to forget what we know from decades of research about creating places of care and hope in our schools.

Hope is essential to students' ability to cope with often unfamiliar, difficult, and unpredictable cultural and academic situations. Snyder and colleagues (1991) describe hope as having two distinct, yet reciprocal and additive, elements—agency and pathways—that support individuals in moving toward the goals they wish to accomplish. Agency refers to "a sense of successful determination in meeting goals in the past, present, and future" (p. 570). Pathways, on the other hand, are related to "the perceived availability of successful *pathways* related to the goals" (p. 570). In other words, hope is the feeling that there exists a road on which to walk and that one is capable of the journey. These two components of hope work together in setting the stage for a student to have a sense of hope that he or she will be a successful member of the learning community. Following are questions to ask about creating spaces for hope to be alive in our educational settings:

- How is all knowledge valued and used during the lesson?
- How do you listen in order to be present to the message of the *learner* versus the message's connection to the content?
- What pathways are open to make public and transparent students' strengths in language, knowledge, and culture, so that you can bring together a community of learners that moves forward in learning based on what each contributes to the learning and academic content?

Students approach specific learning endeavors with different types of accumulated experiences with goal attainment (Snyder, 2002). Some learners are assaulted by negative emotions from scarring past experiences even as they take initial steps in pursuit of a goal. Others bring a history

of success in reaching similar academic goals in similar contexts and are ready to take on a new challenge accompanied by powerful positive emotions. Becoming aware of what we teachers do to orchestrate a learning environment that promotes (or hinders) a sense of hope is important to developing a pedagogy that is both culturally responsive and relevant to the CLD student. Supporting students to identify possible pathways to reach their goal and encouraging them and scaffolding their success along the way can help them develop the type of "*I can*" agency-related thinking that will support their attainment of not only the current goal, but future goals as well.

One of the most important ways we "give" or "take away" a sense of hope is in the way we provide feedback. In this era of testing mania, many students see their plight as having no hope for improvement, given the value placed on point-in-time standardized assessments. Consider, however, the way the teacher in the following scenario talks with the student and provides feedback that sends the message that there are multiple paths for attaining the goal of becoming a better writer.

> I always hoped to be a better writer and I knew that with practice I could accomplish anything I set my mind to do. When I was in the seventh grade my teacher, Ms. Porter, used to tell me: "Darling you write like you talk!" What she meant is that I could go on forever without putting in any kind of punctuation in my writing. I wrote to tell my stories or meet the assignments she was always giving. She made us write and write. Every time she handed something back it was another little mini-conference to talk about how I could make my grammar better, and every time I listened, I was always hoping that my next paper would be better.
>
> What I liked best about Ms. Porter's corrections was that they always came with a "but." She would say, "I want you to keep working, working, working on that grammar, but in the meantime, don't ever hand in a paper without having someone edit your work. You know, there are these people out there called editors, and that's all they do is edit for people like you—people who have all the ideas and experience, who are unique and special like you. With that "but" she gave me hope that someday I would learn to write just like she wanted me to do; but regardless of my writing skills, my ideas were always good and I could always look for editors. Today I'm grateful to Ms. Porter for filling my life with hope. I still use an editor, grammar check, and any other resource I can to support my becoming a better writer, because I have discovered that writing is a lifelong process.

This idea of seeing the future as a time when what we are working toward now will potentially be a reality is a perspective on learning that CLD students crave as they sit in classrooms today.

As learners, we all want to:

- Experience a sense of hope about what we can accomplish
- Have a place where relationships of support and encouragement are part of daily interactions
- Actively participate in learning situations that are low risk and accepting of current abilities and understandings, yet always challenging us to higher levels of understanding
- Have discussions in which our thoughts and perspectives are valued
- Experience a sense of accomplishment with regard to content and language development
- Have opportunities to be evaluated in ways that reflect the meaningful work we have produced in classroom endeavors

It is this validation from both peers and the teacher that gives students a sense that they are valuable members of the learning community. In this way, hope can become a source of student motivation that is greater than any learning strategy or instructional technique that we can bring to a lesson. According to Kuhrt (2007), hope "is the factor that allows even the poorest most destitute individual to succeed" (section 7.3.4). As teachers, our goal is to use our interactions and orchestration of learning to set conditions that give our students—regardless of sociocultural, linguistic, cognitive, or academic background—the hope they need to become motivated and engaged learners in our classroom.

In these times of adverse political agendas, we must be very clear about where we stand in our beliefs about teaching and learning. Do standardized tests, grades, and cumulative folders close the door to the hidden potential of our CLD students? Or do we intentionally design our classroom and instruction to encourage students' sharing and use of their talents and background knowledge to accomplish the academic goals we have set? Our attitude and approach to instruction with diverse learners will set the stage for interactions among all learners and the potential for hope in our classroom.

CLD Student Biography Cards

Our ability to respond to students' needs and to validate students' assets requires that we first *know* our students. As the National Research Council and the Institute of Medicine (2004) note:

> Instruction that is appropriately challenging for all students requires considerable knowledge of each student's understanding and skills. Instructional decisions about tasks and next steps also need to be

informed by data on student learning. Standardized testing done annually does not provide useful information for these purposes. (p. 214)

We teachers must find ways to explore each dimension of our students' biographies. Creating a **CLD Student Biography Card** for each diverse learner in our classroom can be an especially helpful first step for getting to know our students and beginning to plan instruction with the student biography in mind. Although biography cards can be tailored to each teacher's specific classroom needs, consideration should be given to each of the four dimensions—sociocultural, linguistic, cognitive, and academic. Figures 5.2 and 5.3 provide an annotated sample of a CLD Student Biography Card that can be used with students of all ages. A card such as this enables teachers to document both school-situated and biography-situated information. Figure 5.4 shows an example of a completed card. A template for the CLD Student Biography Card for classroom use can be found in Appendix B and is available for download from the Teachers College Press website: tcpress.com

Although CLD students will be able to share with us many of the most basic aspects of each dimension through informal conversations, surveys, and so forth (at times along with the help of a parent, sibling, peer, or translator), we as teachers also need to incorporate opportunities for students to share connections and ways of thinking in each of our lessons. It is by capitalizing on these student insights, connections, and associations that are directly linked to the content that we are able to provide students with pedagogy that is culturally responsive and biography-driven. Chapters 6, 7, 8, and 9 explore how to provide such opportunities and ways teachers can capitalize on student assets and background knowledge to advance the learning of the classroom community.

Reflections on the Academic Dimension

Perhaps the most important finding of recent research (e.g., Murry et al., 2020) and Thomas and Collier's work (e.g., 1995, 2012) is the understanding that the biopsychosocial history is the bridge to deeper understanding of the four components of the prism model, or the four dimensions of the CLD student biography. Recognition of the interdependence of the history and the strengths and assets of the learner reminds us of the importance of providing a historically grounded, culturally responsive, and sustaining school environment that nourishes natural language growth, cognitive development, and academic progress founded on the biography of the learner. Teachers who place an inordinate focus on CLD students' needs and deficits and postpone their exposure to core content knowledge actually increase the time that it takes for students to

FIGURE 5.2

CLD Student Biography Card: Front

CLD Student Biography Cards can support teachers in documenting student progress, making decisions about grouping configurations, and continually scaffolding to meet students' sociocultural, linguistic, cognitive, and academic needs.

Insert a photograph of the student (this is a helpful visual reminder for you as a teacher).

Name:

Age:

Grade:

Country of Origin:

Time in USA:

L1: _____
R: _____
W: _____

L2 Proficiency
(LAS/IPT/Other):
O: _____
R: _____
W: _____
SLA: _____

Student Processing:

Learning Preferences:

Prior Academic Experiences:

Preferred Grouping:

School-Situated

Sociocultural

Complete the student's **demographic information** by interviewing the student, his or her family, or a past teacher.

Linguistic

Step One: Determine (informally or formally):

L1: Student's First Language
R: First Language Reading Proficiency
W: First Language Writing Proficiency

Step Two: Determine the CLD student's English language proficiency (scores can be obtained from the district/school ESL teacher as needed).

O: English Oral Proficiency (speaking/listening)
R: English Reading Proficiency
W: English Writing Proficiency
SLA: Stage of Second Language Acquisition

Cognitive

How does the student **process information** (e.g., solve a math problem, complete a science experiment, summarize a story)?

What **learning preferences** should be taken into account for this student?

Academic

What **prior academic experiences**/exposure does the student have to promote content learning and transfer of knowledge?

In what **grouping** configuration is the student most comfortable (i.e., total group, partner, small group, or independent)?

FIGURE 5.3

CLD Student Biography Card: Back

Sociocultural Dimension
Home + Community + School =
Background
Knowledge

_____
_____
_____
_____
_____
_____
_____

Linguistic Dimension
Valuing L1 & L2

_____
_____
_____
_____
_____
_____
_____

Cognitive Dimension
Implications for Practice

_____
_____
_____
_____
_____
_____
_____

Academic Dimension
+   State of Mind   –

_____
_____
_____
_____
_____
_____
_____

Biography-Situated

Sociocultural

Consider insights gleaned from conversations and inter-actions with students, parents, and colleagues (in both academic and non-academic settings) about what brings the student **life**, **laughter**, and **love**.

- What assets does the student bring as a result of living within his or her culture and family?
- What role does the student play in the family? What is he or she learning in that role that would be of benefit at school?

Linguistic

Consider aspects of **comprehension**, **communication**, and **expression** in both the student's first language and second language.

- In what ways do the patterns of communication within the student's family and culture have the potential to be assets in the classroom?
- In what ways could these assets be used to increase the student's engagement and learning?

Cognitive

Consider ways the student's culture might influence how he or she **knows**, **thinks**, and **applies** new learning.

- In what ways does teaching align with patterns and expectations for knowing, thinking, and applying within the student's family and culture?
- In what ways can the student use his or her patterns of cognition as a resource to access information and demonstrate learning in the classroom?

Academic

Consider factors that are helping or hindering the student's **access** to equitable educational opportunities, **engagement** in instruction, and **hope** for success in the learning community and in the future.

- What resources are available to the student to set the stage for success in the classroom?
- What opportunities can be provided for the learner based on assets he or she has available at home?

FIGURE 5.4
Example of a Completed CLD Student Biography Card

Name: _____

Age: 11

Grade: 5th

Country of Origin: SAUDI ARABIA

Time in USA: _____

L1:
R: Reads Quran (Arabic) proficiently
W: writes some vocab in Arabic

L2 Proficiency (LAS/IPT/Other):
O: 4
R: 3
W: 2
SLA: overall 3

Student Processing: _____

Learning Preferences:
Is a very visual learner.
Primarily likes highlighted text.

Prior Academic Experiences:
Has studied in Saudi Arabia
Did half-day in Arabic &
half-day in English Is good at Math

Preferred Grouping:
Small groups / partners.
Prefers to work with girls.

School-Situated

Sociocultural Dimension
Home + Community + School =
♡ Background Knowledge

family is actively involved in the Arabic community. She attends Arabic classes at the mosque. Often shares associations of the stories heard within her own community to the content being discussed in class

Linguistic Dimension
Valuing L1 & L2

family's literacy practices revolve around parents telling stories to their kids. She often uses a similar story telling format while summarizing her own learning in the class.

Cognitive Dimension
Implications for Practice

Due to the visual nature of her native language, she always tries to find her own visual associations to the content being presented.

Academic Dimension
+ State of Mind —
←—————————→

Through family's active community involvement within the arabic community, she has learned to reach out to peers when she needs help. As a teacher, I just need to be mindful of her academic needs during Ramadan.

Biography-Situated

70

close the academic achievement gap in English (Collier & Thomas, 2009; Thomas & Collier, 2012). Second language learners need simultaneous linguistic, cognitive, and academic development.

We can promote such development for CLD students when we proactively find ways to ensure their access to the grade-level curriculum. Students need opportunities to build their content and language proficiencies in ways that first value what they already know. By considering students' backgrounds and states of mind in our planning and implementation of instruction, we can more effectively ignite student motivation and increase their engagement in our classrooms.

Perhaps the greatest harm we as educators can do to our culturally and linguistically diverse students is to maintain a belief system that informs us only of what is *not* possible for this population. Basing our practice and decisions on very limiting information can have long-lasting and detrimental consequences for students and their families. Once we recognize that not all learning happens in the classroom, we can begin to explore a wider range of assets and discover more fully the potential within all learners. Through critical reflection on our teaching, we move to open doors and expand possibilities for CLD students who are frequently marginalized and viewed through a narrow lens. As we continue to encourage, support, and build on students' current progress and success, we demonstrate the care and respect that provide learners with hope for their own achievement.

6

Biography-Driven Planning, Teaching, and Assessing

GUIDING QUESTION

What aspects of traditional ways to plan and deliver lessons are reconceptualized in the biography-driven instruction method?

See the online Discussion Guide for opportunities to further explore answers to this question and connections to chapter content with a colleague or team. Available for download from the Teachers College Press website: tcpress.com

THE FOUR PRECEDING CHAPTERS focused heavily on the complex and multidimensional aspects of the CLD student biography. The prism model provided a point of departure for exploration of the sociocultural, linguistic, cognitive, and academic dimensions of the student from two perspectives—the school-situated perspective and the culturally responsive perspective. Both perspectives have an important role to play in teachers' planning, delivery, and evaluation of instructional practice.

This chapter takes us further on our journey beyond "business as usual" in schools, moving toward an understanding of what culturally responsive pedagogy looks like in practice by providing an *overlay* to use in the classroom. I have chosen the term "overlay," rather than "guide" or "steps," because I have found in my work in schools that most teachers are already using school-prescribed lesson plans or curricula that outline both the scope and the sequence of the material to be taught. In architecture, overlay refers to a set of beneficial adaptations that can be made to an existing blueprint or building as it is being constructed or remodeled. This chapter provides a culturally responsive, classroom-based overlay for planning and delivering instruction and moving beyond the obvious—standards, objectives, and prescribed ways of teaching. Such fundamentals are essential and are discussed in detail in Chapter 7. First, however, it is important to understand the larger picture as we approach lesson planning, delivery, and assessment from a biography-driven perspective. In addition to providing an overlay that teachers can apply to their existing programs and curricula, the chapter discusses processes and factors that can either inhibit or increase student learning. It also explores the role

of the teacher as participant observer within the learning community.

Contextual and Situational Processes

The classroom is a place of constant change that demands continual reflection as we negotiate the processes of teaching and learning on a daily basis. As educators, we create the conditions necessary to ensure that we are culturally responsive to students as we differentiate, scaffold, and orchestrate instruction by navigating the curriculum of the school as it relates to our students' lives. We are the "masters of our domain." We are clearly in charge of setting the tone and conditions for learning within our classrooms. It is true that the learners in our classrooms help create the atmosphere, but we have the power to arrange and rearrange the "ecology" and the "actors" within that ecology to remove limitations on the learner. We can all relate to learning situations in the past that either created an opportunity or denied us the access we felt necessary to our success. As adults, we can usually circumvent a problematic situation (or take advantage of an opportunity) and access what we need to make "it" happen. CLD students, however, often depend on the *teacher* to establish and manipulate contextual and situational classroom conditions to maximize their learning.

Contextual Processes: Classroom Ecology

Contextual processes in teaching are the things we do with the physical setting in which we teach, the curriculum, and the community of learners in our classroom.

72

Together, these factors constitute the *context* in which learning takes place. Talk among educators often focuses on creating a friendly, culturally inclusive environment—a place where students feel welcome and see their culture and language represented within the classroom. In most cases, we teachers work hard to have books that represent the cultures and languages of our students and to build classroom word walls that use the native language to facilitate transfer of information. These and numerous other efforts help to create places that are representative of our students. However, we may be limiting our focus to the physical *environment* and not considering the overall *ecology* of our classroom.

In considering the distinction between ecology and environment, we can begin to reflect on the complex dynamics that take place in classrooms, that is, the role of classroom relationships and their interdependence with teaching and learning. Borrowing from Memari and Golamshahi (2020), ecology relates to the habitat, "the physical niche or context with characteristic purposes, dimensions, features, and processes that have consequences for the behavior of occupants in that setting" (p. 2). Keeping this thought in mind, it becomes all the more important for educators to consider the effects of various aspects of their instructional planning and facilitation on the ecology of the classroom. **Classroom ecology** encompasses the structures, arrangements, events, and processes that influence student and teacher action (and reaction) in the classroom. Just as in nature, the **classroom environment** is "physical" in character and includes elements such as the arrangement of chairs and desks, bulletin boards, wall decorations, and so forth. Classroom ecology, on the other hand, specifically involves the inherent interconnectedness of the multiple agents and aspects at play. Outdoors, ecology describes the complex interactions of various forms of plant and animal life within a particular physical environment, be it a marsh, a tallgrass prairie, or a mountain range. In the classroom, ecology emphasizes the human element in the context of the particular environment determined by the curriculum and physical space. Both the environment and the larger ecology of our classrooms—including the way we design our classrooms, select materials, plan instruction, and build the classroom community—should reflect our valuing of students and their needs.

A teacher's belief system influences his or her decisions related to the classroom environment, but it has an even greater impact on the classroom ecology. The teacher's intentional decisions, as well as unexamined actions, are rooted in the **meaning perspectives** that he or she holds about education and CLD students and families. A meaning perspective can be defined as the "structure of assumptions within which one's past experience assimilates and transforms new experience" (Mezirow, 1991, p. 42). Our meaning perspectives provide us with a set of expectations that

This is an example of a cultural quilt (Herrera et al., 2013), in which students record important biographical events and turning points that reflect cultural and family values. By using the cultural quilt with her students, the teacher was able to gain valuable insights about each of her students that she was then able to use for developing a classroom community that values and builds upon students' diverse backgrounds.

"serve as an orienting frame of reference or worldview (Wessels et al., 2011, p. 3). They develop over the course of our lives and are influenced by our socialization and ongoing experiences in a particular family, community, and larger world context. Meaning perspectives are difficult to identify and to change because they reflect our tacit beliefs that have developed over time (Wessels et al., 2011). Yet they have far-reaching effects on our decisions about contextual processes that either expand or limit the opportunities we provide to CLD students.

Contextual processes in classroom practice are shaped by the ethnic and cultural identities of both the teacher and the learner. The culturally responsive teacher is aware of, and asks questions related to, everyday classroom dynamics. Reflect on the following questions:

- How do I currently set the stage for a climate of trust and respect of diverse cultures and languages?
- How much do I know about my students' lived experiences and their lives outside of the classroom?
- In what ways do I tap into the home and community experiences and knowledge of the students I teach?

- In what ways do I invite parents and family members of CLD students to share lesson-specific knowledge and experiences that can be used as resources in my teaching?
- How do I use observations of students' experiences to hook onto and bridge to what students bring to each lesson?
- In what ways do I check my habits of teaching and actions based on the culture of the school, curriculum, or previously held expectations for CLD students?

To create basic contextual conditions that will optimize learning, we as educators must understand our power to conceptualize and create an ecology in which every student feels safe to share his or her cultural identity without fear of ridicule. Teachers who are conscious of contextual factors and bear them in mind when planning, making decisions about curriculum, and setting up their classrooms increase the chances that students will be engaged and motivated to learn. For each lesson—and overall—contextual factors that must be considered include the following:

- Biographies of the students
- Content and language objectives
- Grouping structures/configurations
- Applicability of lessons to the real world
- Standard(s) to be addressed during lessons
- Physical aspects of the classroom that support learning
- Curriculum and applicability to students' frames of reference

Explicit attention to the context in which each lesson will take place prepares us to move forward with more confidence, knowing that classroom conditions for learning have been designed with the sociocultural, linguistic, cognitive, and academic *assets* and needs of the students in mind.

Situational Processes: Teaching in the Moment

Situational processes are the means through which teachers orchestrate teaching and learning dynamics "in the moment." This concept applies to each and every student and teacher action and reaction in classroom practice. Think about the dynamics at play during any given lesson; there are many "contingencies" during instruction that could not have been anticipated. Every task we ask students to perform is subject to contextual factors and is interpreted and cognitively processed in ways unique to each individual student. Each action and reaction must be "mediated" by the teacher, who continuously navigates and negotiates the sociocultural, linguistic, cognitive, and academic biography of the student, as well as the objectives of the lesson.

Situational processes enable us to guide students to achieve the goals we have for their social and academic development, and to support students to meet the learning

In this 8th-grade classroom, Ms. White has students from four different countries. She creates an effective learning ecology by attending to both contextual and situational factors. At this point in the math lesson on graphing, Ms. White has students work in pairs seated throughout the room so students are able to share their diverse perspectives about the terms and concepts and she is able to listen to their conversations and observe their learning. This allows Ms. White to support students in making meaningful connections and to re-teach and re-route as necessary. *(Image courtesy of Julie White, Middle School, Kansas)*

objectives we have set for the lesson. We must be attuned to students throughout the lesson, monitoring and documenting the learning experiences CLD students are having as they participate. Situational factors that we as teachers should consider include the following:

- Students' states of mind
- Language demands on students
- Levels of student interest during the lesson
- Opportunities for, and students' comfort with, native language use
- Development of student responsibility and autonomy
- Adequacy of "think time" provided to students
- Students' cognitive processes related to sense and meaning making
- Feedback and validation of student connections

If our goal is to have a climate where trust, respect, engagement, and academic achievement are part of the ongoing dynamic of the lesson, we must commit to an ongoing consideration of situational factors such as these.

Attending to situational factors requires us to manipulate the context of the lesson as it develops, to create conditions in which students can be socially and academically successful. Such decisions require planning as well as on-the-fly reflection and problem solving. For example, we may need to reflect on contextual factors that might be hindering student learning, in which case we will have to identify possible solutions in the form of contextual changes and modifications. Therefore, the situational conditions for learning might change throughout the course of the lesson, and such changes are in direct response to what is happening with the dynamics of student learning. Reflecting on current classroom practice, we can all think of some examples of how we have modified a planned lesson in progress to better suit the situation as it occurred in real time. By challenging ourselves to attend explicitly to the situational factors relevant to CLD students, we can greatly improve their chances for social and academic success.

Contextual and Situational Teaching

As stated by Gay (2018), "Teaching is a contextual, situational, and personal process" (p. 28). Optimally, contextual and situational teaching takes into account each student's biography and aligns teaching and learning to respect the prior experiences, community settings, cultural backgrounds, and identities of every individual in the classroom (Gay, 2018). Educators who take into account their own **positionality** and who continually monitor and document contextual and situational processes set up a community of trust and respect where students carve out their own place in the community. Students fully understand and believe they are contributing members of the classroom in both social and academic ways.

Knowing how best to design our ecology and make adjustments during instruction requires that we understand how the strategy we select will support us to encourage, observe, document, interpret, and utilize students' social, cultural, linguistic, and cognitive responses during the lesson. The contextual and situational opportunities we create will be only as good as the teaching and learning strategy we use. As discussed in previous chapters, understanding the biography of each student provides the teacher with a guide for consideration of the factors that might accelerate or pose threats to student learning. Honest, critical reflection on our own beliefs and assumptions is key to this process.

According to Gay (2018), students often are "taught from the middle-class Eurocentric frameworks that shape school practices" (p. 28). Regularly assessing our perspectives helps ensure that our teaching practices actually reflect the ideals we have for CLD students' learning. Teachers can proactively reflect by doing the following:

- Considering the culture and sociopolitical climate of the school
- Exploring the visible environment and asking questions about what is invisible
- Viewing curriculum from a "student biography" perspective versus a "prescriptive response to learning" perspective
- Becoming informed about the myths and misconceptions that may have negatively influenced their expectations of CLD students

- Examining pedagogical perspectives for any indications of a deficit perspective (i.e., one that does not maximize learning by building on students' assets and documented potential)
- Noting whether (or to what degree) social interactions among students in the classroom are based on a mutual respect of student biographies, which results when each student understands that knowledge and learning are uniquely shaped by the multiple languages and cultures represented in the classroom

Such reflection is the catalyst for aligning ecology, curriculum, student biography, teacher biography, and learning with a "what is possible" mindset, rather than dwelling on challenges to be overcome. This kind of reflection also shifts our teaching in ways that accelerate student learning and move us beyond reductionistic practices or efforts to simply create a positive environment. A classroom ecology that exemplifies what we would like to see in society is one in which there is clear evidence that learners and teachers trust each other and respect what each brings to the classroom community. When educators actively create classroom ecologies of trust and respect, the chance for motivation, engagement, and hope in the learner is exponentially increased.

Community Climate

Classrooms are small universes. In those universes, we learn to accept and appreciate one another's variances—or we learn to resent and be suspicious of differences. We learn to celebrate one another's victories and support one another's efforts—or we learn to compete in ways that undermine rather than dignify those with whom we share time and space.
—Tomlinson and McTighe (2006, p. 45)

Given recent and ongoing demographic shifts, as discussed in Chapter 1, many of our classrooms have become rich tapestries of culture, language, religion, socioeconomic status, and ways of perceiving that are difficult to understand unless we make it a priority to create a climate where being part of a diverse ecology is cause for celebration. According to Charney (2002), being in a community means having "the capacity to care for oneself, for others, and for the world" (p. 15). In creating a community, we educators must hold ourselves accountable for strategically planning ways to bring students together to share their knowledge before, during, and after each lesson. Learners must become aware of the diversity of perspectives, knowledge, and skills that exist within the social and learning classroom space.

Walqui (2000) asserts that in a community of learners, "teachers and students together construct a culture that values the strengths of all participants and respects their interests, abilities, languages, and dialects. Students and teachers shift among the roles of expert, researcher, learner, and teacher, supporting themselves and each other" (Principle #1). If we believe this to be true, how do we set up classrooms that are not solely concerned with the academic dimension of learning? Ask yourself the following questions:

- The last time I taught, what activity did I plan/use that allowed for all students to share a little of themselves—their knowledge or understanding of the new vocabulary words or the concept to be introduced, or their perspective on the issue to be discussed?
- Did I take time to absorb what was shared or reflect on the essence of what the student was trying to share?
- Did I incorporate partner or small team talk that allowed CLD students opportunities throughout the lesson to use their language of choice to share their knowledge, questions, or interpretations with a peer?
- What did I do with the information I gathered? Did I use it to clarify, elaborate, and ask questions as the lesson unfolded?
- How might I use the information and knowledge I gained to guide my thoughts and actions in future lessons?

Answers to these questions help us become more aware that the opportunities we create for using students' language and knowledge to promote learning and the ways we validate and affirm every student can set us on the path to increased student engagement and learning.

In classrooms that constitute a true community of learners, teachers are less likely to have difficulty with classroom management. According to Freeman and Freeman (2002), community-oriented classrooms unify learners through shared experiences. Affirmation and validation of experiences, or academic insights shared before, during, and after the lesson, bring to life the contributions of all learners. By making sure the classroom represents a safe environment and by creating situations that provide opportunities for each student to actively participate during the lesson, educators create the conditions for all members of the learning community to discover the many gifts and assets that each possesses.

Following are a few suggestions for fostering a climate that supports social and academic community in practice:

- Create a climate where every answer can be reevaluated and changed to arrive at the destination.
- Set up conditions and opportunities for members to build both personal and academic relationships.
- Model expectations for participation and turn-taking.
- Remind students that collaboration is key to learning, and no one person (not even the teacher!) has all the answers.
- Use what students produce to advance the learning of the entire class.

Remember that it is relatively unimportant whether answers are right or wrong in the classroom; what matters is that learning is taking place. Keep in mind that we each have different strengths and talents. Not everyone is a great artist; otherwise, we wouldn't have paint by number, clip art, and stencils. Not everyone is great at math, or we wouldn't need accountants, calculators, and computerized spreadsheets. However, together we bring the multitude of talents needed to accomplish our goals—in life and in the classroom.

Classroom Community and the CLD Student

Earlier in this section, I discussed the importance of understanding contextual and situational processes and our power to create a community where the climate of teaching and learning serves to engage the learner. At some point while you were reading, the following thought may have crossed your mind: *If only this author knew my students or taught in my school!* Multiple factors are at play within our classrooms. While some are beyond a teacher's control, there are many others we can try to influence in positive ways. The climate of a classroom community can be affected by factors such as the following.

- Organization of classroom structures
- Social relationships among the students
- Teacher beliefs related to ability grouping
- Social relationships between CLD students and the teacher
- Psychological states of mind of the students and the teacher

The psychological state of mind of the CLD student has a large impact on his or her engagement and motivation in the classroom. The teacher cannot control what happens in a student's life outside the school setting. However, the teacher's understanding of what is happening has profound implications for decisions about contextual and situational processes. These processes include *how* and *when* we differentiate and scaffold for the individual learner. Figure 6.1 builds on what we already know about differentiated instruction (e.g., Tomlinson, 2001) by highlighting aspects of biography-driven instruction that are key to CLD student success.

We educators have the ability to influence the cognitive, behavioral, and affective engagement of our students through the learning contexts and situations that we create (Appleton et al., 2008). Through our words and actions, we communicate our high expectations for each student's learning, and we make clear that we will accompany learners each step of the way. Ultimately, our goal should be to support students to become self-directed learners who have the confidence, knowledge, skills, and learning strategies needed to achieve

FIGURE 6.1
Differentiated Instruction + 1

Differentiating Instruction	Making It Happen	Providing Respectful Work
When planning and implementing instruction, consider:	Differentiate instruction along the lines of:	All student tasks and assessments should be:
• Student readiness • Student interest • Student learning profile	• Content • Process • Product	• Focused on what matters most in the curriculum. • Structured to necessitate high-level thinking. • Equally appealing and engaging to learners.

Traditional Perspective

+1

Biography-Driven Perspective

• Foundations of student biography
  ◦ Sociocultural ◦ Cognitive
  ◦ Linguistic ◦ Academic
• Foundations of language
  ◦ Affective filter ◦ SLA
  ◦ CUP vs. SUP ◦ BICS/CALP
  ◦ L1 and L2
	• Use culturally responsive teaching and learning processes
	• Biography-driven
	• Strategies-rich
	• Promoting positive "states of mind"
		• Designed to promote student gains in language and content
		• Affirming of student knowledge/performance/outcomes
		• Focus of teacher critical reflection (checking our "habits of mind")

their future educational, career, and life aspirations. We can support students to become more autonomous, self-regulated learners as they approach academic tasks "by using relationships, setting up students for success in course tasks (via scaffolding of lessons and attention to developmental level), and orchestrating student opportunities for decision making and other authentically autonomous experiences (Appleton et al., 2008, pp. 378–379).

Common sense suggests, and research clearly shows, that the climate we create greatly influences the cognitive and affective learning outcomes of our CLD students (Appleton et al., 2008; Clandinin & Connelly, 1995; Cummins, 1996; Lackney, 1998; Straits, 2007). As Jensen (2008) notes, "There is no such thing as an unmotivated learner. There are, however, temporary unmotivated states in which learners are either reinforced and supported or neglected and labeled" (p. 119). Educators can consider the questions below, which apply to each of their students, but are particularly important for exploring specific situations and supporting the learning of struggling students and CLD students. A teacher can use the resulting information and ideas to make decisions about pedagogical actions.

• What is happening outside the classroom that is impacting the student during instruction? What can be done to help the student feel more comfortable about the situation?

• What is happening inside the classroom that is impacting the student during instruction? What can be done to alter those conditions?

• If anxiety related to classroom climate is keeping the student from engaging in the lesson, what techniques can be employed to lessen the anxiety the student is feeling?

As Krashen (1982) points out, the student's negative emotions, including anxiety, self-consciousness, boredom, annoyance, alienation, and so forth, constitute an affective filter that can greatly "interfere with the reception and processing of comprehensible input" (p. 468).

We all have had experiences with the reality of the affective filter in our own lives. For example, if you have ever taken a course in which the professor came in and said, "By the end of this semester, only a few of you will be left in the course," you have probably experienced anxiety and fear accompanying the thought that you might fail to achieve your goal, as well as resentment that a teacher would express such indifference to your personal success or failure. As an adult learner, you use the many skills you have gained over the years to lower that anxiety and to turn anger into motivation. You might:

• Use a social strategy, such as self-talk, to calm your nerves.

- Think about the people you know who may have taken the course or find someone in the class with whom you can study throughout the semester.
- Consider taking notes during class and comparing them with your text or someone else's notes.
- Refer to your cognitive belief system, including your positive self-concept as a learner.

These are but a few of the skills you have gained over the years.

As educators addressing the needs of CLD students, we must provide learning conditions that minimize anxiety and maximize learning while at the same time helping students develop the kinds of strategies that support adults in monitoring (and lowering as necessary) their levels of stress and anxiety. Each CLD student in the class will demonstrate his or her reality and needs in different ways at different times. We must be ready to respond and keep students moving forward in their personal development and academic endeavors. By remaining active in our role as a "negotiating agent," we can better respond to students' needs as they transition into the culture, language, and community of our classrooms.

When creating risk-free and low-anxiety learning conditions, educators can do the following:

- Incorporate the language of the student into all aspects of classroom life.
- Value and use the CLD student's culture as a bridge to understanding the curriculum.
- Observe for the CLD student's feelings, attitudes, self-concept, and interaction preferences during all phases of lesson delivery.
- Provide varied opportunities for interaction among *all* students in the classroom, regardless of linguistic or academic ability.
- Use strategies that serve as linguistic and academic supports for the learner.

In addition, lessons that provide *each student* in the classroom with a chance to share from his or her own point of view—and be heard—are more likely to lower the student's affective filter and lead to greater participation. Such opportunities for expression promote students' social adjustment processes, positive attitude toward school, and academic success. Figure 6.2 provides a guide that can be used to support BDI lesson planning.

Biography-Driven Instruction: A Culturally Responsive Method

In the first edition of this text, I referred to biography-driven instruction as an action model. I attempted to provide educators with a description of the key constructs that the research and literature of the field—as well as the research

efforts of our team of researchers in the Center for Intercultural and Multilingual Advocacy—have collectively revealed as fundamental to the academic and linguistic development of CLD students. I strived to provide a roadmap for teachers to follow as they approached instruction in culturally responsive ways. Over the next five years, additional research and additional discussions with public school teachers and administrators across the country informed my decision in the second edition to characterize biography-driven instruction as a *method* for providing culturally responsive pedagogy.

In this third edition, I utilize the biography-driven instructional framework to capture how the four interrelated dimensions of the CLD student biography, situated within the context of the learner's biopsychosocial history, influence and are continually influenced by the teaching and learning dynamics of the classroom. Contextualized within the principles of cultural responsiveness (Gay, 2018) and cultural sustainability (Paris, 2012), the current text more explicitly describes how teachers can use BDI to achieve the goals of liberatory praxis as a result of this humanistic, learner-centered, and adaptable approach to teaching and learning in diverse spaces. The terminology that researchers and educators use to describe perspectives on how to orchestrate teaching and learning in the classroom is anything but uniform. Different individuals define in different ways innumerable terms, such as approach, framework, model, method, strategy, and technique (Herrera & Murry, 2016). In this edition, I clarify how these terms can work together to inform our understanding of instruction.

First, an **approach** is the educator's overarching philosophical orientation to instruction. This orientation reflects at least one research-based or **theoretical framework** for practice, which provides a particular view on human development, learning, or language learning. The theoretical framework(s) likewise inform the key concepts that an educator sees as essential to the teaching–learning process. Together, these concepts represent the **conceptual model of instruction** that the educator brings to his or her teaching. Figure 6.3 summarizes the theoretical and conceptual foundation for BDI.

At this juncture, the educator needs some way of actually implementing in practice what he or she believes to be true about effective teaching. In many typologies, the teacher then selects a method of instruction. Yet, historically, methods have served to constrain what is possible rather than make clear how the beliefs we hold should shape the daily ebb and flow of our instruction (Richards & Rogers, 2014). For this reason, I choose instead to provide the **methodological principles** of activate, connect, and affirm, which teachers use throughout the BDI lesson to continually elicit and build upon students' existing and evolving understandings as they move learning forward.

FIGURE 6.2
BDI Lesson Planning Guide

Facilitating fidelity to our students and the standards

How do the individual biographies of your students impact your approach to this lesson?

Use the guide below to reflect on how the cultural and linguistic biographies of your classroom community intersect with the learning outcomes you plan.

Learning Community (What evidence have I gathered from the Biography Cards?)	Individual Considerations (Elicit from Biography Cards)	"In the Moment" Instructional Decisions (Situational decisions based on how your students respond to the input in the classroom and the instructional outcomes you have planned)

Think about the following questions as you reflect on the learning community in your classroom.
 	
• What considerations for students' socioemotional needs might support them to be engaged learners on this topic?
• What collective experiences do students bring with them that can be an asset to their learning on this topic?
• What are the students' language backgrounds?
• What are some cultural and academic expectations that students might bring to the classroom?
• Have I considered the overall biography of the different parent groups that are represented through my classroom community?
• What information do I have on the ways of thinking and lived experiences of students' families, and how can I utilize it in my lesson planning?
• What academic considerations (scaffolds and extensions) might support students with their learning this week?
• What routines and resources are available (within the classroom and outside) to support students and enhance their learning?
• Is my classroom ecology indicative of the community I wish my classroom to be? Is it set up in such a way that students will be truly willing to learn from one another and unafraid to be risk-takers and productive members of our community?
• Am I ready to use students' cultural and linguistic backgrounds as a sounding board for my classroom community to move forward in academic ways?
	• First week of school—Summer slump is real! (*Consider utilizing students' cultural backgrounds as a way to focus on the activities for Week One.*) Let's move away from questions such as "What did you do over the summer break?" to a more encompassing question such as "What would you like to share with us about your summer break?"
	• Use this week for getting to know the biographies of students. (*Resources: Biography Cards, "I am" poems.*)
	• Create opportunities to teach procedure and routines within the framework of the lesson itself. Remember, too much focus on procedures and routines in isolation can be stressful for some students. (*Consider your seating chart as one option for you to create a community of learners; place students in small groups so they can help each other linguistically and academically.*)
	• Plan specific activities and strategies that can be sent home with students to involve parents in their instructional outcomes.
	• *A word of advice:* Various stories/content might be hard for some students to connect with, considering that students come with varied backgrounds and experiences. You may come across a student who is unable to participate due to the socioemotional effect a given topic might have.
		• Your students' biographies are crucial for you to keep in mind in order to make effective "in the moment" decisions. (*See page 74, Situational Processes: Teaching in the Moment.*)
		• These decisions need to stem from:
		  • Socioemotional frames of mind during the lesson
		  • Student interest level
		  • Opportunities for students to use their native languages to clarify, extend, and/or comprehend the information
		  • Think time vs. wait time
		  • Vocabulary needs of students in the classroom
		  • Overall language needs of students
		• Brain breaks are a great way to provide continued support with comprehension and vocabulary and reroute conversations as needed. Brain breaks are critical for students to re-engage in a task. (*See page 14, Research into How the Brain Learns.*) These brain breaks can take several forms:
		  • Providing students with think time
		  • Asking students to pause and do a quick turn and talk
		  • Integrating activities such as quick writes or quick draws
		Ensure that such decisions are made by focusing on students' individual and collective classroom biography.
		• *A word of advice:* Any instructional decision on your part can become a scaffold for students if you are aware of their socioemotional frames of mind.

(Continued on the next page)

FIGURE 6.2

Continued

Guiding Questions for Planning

Oral Language

- In what ways can I structure opportunities for students to talk, share, provide rationales, engage in discussions, and practice language development outside the time designated by the curriculum? How can I ensure that these opportunities become common academic routines for students to enhance their oral language skills?
- How can I ensure that I am not treating oral language as a separate skill, rather than a skill aligned to and integrated within the other curricular skill sets?
- Oral language is part of comprehension and fluency development. Consider the following:
  - Refer back to the Biography Cards to gauge students' linguistic needs and utilize that information as you group or partner students to practice their oral language skills (*i+Tpsl*). (*See pages 124–125 for discussion of the* i+Tpsl *model.*)

- Have students utilize vocabulary words to practice their oral language.
- As students practice their oral language skills through vocabulary work or questioning, walk around and listen to what students are saying, so you can use utilize what they produce to help them further develop their language.
- As you implement a BDI strategy during the lesson, have students use the ideas they included on the BDI tool to further their oral language skills.
- *A word of advice:* Have students use the BDI tool to enhance their vocabulary development, conceptual development, and overall understanding. By guiding students to utilize the BDI tool comprehensively for their learning, you support them to see how oral language development relates to everything else they are doing in the lesson and realize it is not an isolated skill.

Vocabulary & Comprehension

Questions to consider:
- Do all vocabulary words need as much instructional time? (*See page 99, Not All Words Are Created Equal.*)
- Which vocabulary words should be prioritized? Remember, students may already have some understanding of various words. Use what you know about students' assets as you determine how you will prioritize words within the given list.

- How can I plan instructional conversations around the vocabulary words utilizing *i+Tpsl* structures (*See page 126, Figure 8.6: The Ebb and Flow of* i+Tpsl, *and page 127, Figure 8.7:* i+Tpsl *Grouping Configurations Checklist.*) and Kagan structures so that the vocabulary words do not just stay at the word level, but support students in applying their understanding toward overall comprehension?
- How might I facilitate deeper connections to the vocabulary words using the BDI tool? (*See page 103, Linguistically Speaking: Drawing From Their Words.*)

Foundational Skills

- Remember to refer back to the Biography Cards to make decisions about the foundational skills that students need.
- Instructional processes such as *i+Tpsl* (including pairs, small teams, etc., configured using students' Biography Cards) can be instrumental in supporting foundational skill development.

- Consider the following questions:
  - How can the tool I select be used to bridge and make connections between isolated words and the context of the text?
  - How can I ensure that students are using the BDI tool to document their initial connections to the concept, and then to add and connect more ideas?
  - How can I ensure I am supporting students' development of foundational skills through listening, speaking, reading, and writing?

Grammar & Writing

Questions to consider:
- How can I ensure that grammar skills for students are integrated into their overall language and comprehension development?
- How can I facilitate students' development of grammar skills through listening, speaking, reading, and writing?
- If I do teach a grammar lesson in isolation, how am I utilizing a BDI tool to support the process?
- In what ways am I utilizing processes such as *i+Tpsl*, revoicing, and scaffolding of learning to help my students stay engaged with the grammar lesson? (*See page 130, Revoicing for Clarification and Elaboration.*)

- How can I maximize the BDI tool with students to support their "learning to write" and "writing to learn" processes?
- In what ways am I including point-in-time writing activities to support student processing of information at their own level?
- *A word of advice:* To foster students' comprehension and retention, merge the skills being taught with the main story/content and the BDI tool you choose. As you implement the tool (strategy) in the lesson, utilize it for the development of multiple skills. This supports students' integration of skills, content, background knowledge, and process.

In all areas, consider ways the resources provided in the curriculum can be combined with the BDI tool you select to facilitate collaboration, conversation, and interactions between students, teachers, and text.

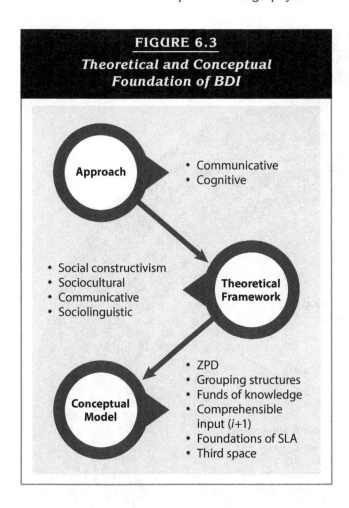

FIGURE 6.3

Theoretical and Conceptual Foundation of BDI

Approach
- Communicative
- Cognitive

- Social constructivism
- Sociocultural
- Communicative
- Sociolinguistic

Theoretical Framework

Conceptual Model
- ZPD
- Grouping structures
- Funds of knowledge
- Comprehensible input (*i*+1)
- Foundations of SLA
- Third space

A **strategy**, *in the traditional sense,* is a collection of related techniques that represents an implementation component of the method. In other words, a strategy reflects a collection of actions that would enable theory-into-practice application of at least one aspect of the method, and one or more concepts of the model. A **technique**, on the other hand, is a specific action or sequence of actions that an educator uses intentionally to achieve a strategic goal.

When implementing biography-driven instruction (BDI), educators intentionally and systematically select a **biography-driven instructional (BDI) strategy** to support students to attain the learning goals of the lesson throughout the three phases of activation, connection, and affirmation. Chapters 7, 8, and 9 highlight the components and processes within these three phases, along with the techniques of *i*+*TpsI*, revoicing, scaffolding, and questioning, among others. BDI strategies are unique combinations of contextual and situational processes and actions for the teacher and student. These strategies provide a through-line for reciprocal teaching and learning *throughout the entire lesson.* BDI strategies incorporate smaller, point-in-time activities, strategies, and techniques along the way. Figure 6.4 illustrates how the biography-driven instructional framework brings culturally responsive and sustaining theory to

life through instruction that embodies the principles of social constructivism.

In previous publications (e.g., MacDonald et al., 2013), BDI strategies have been referred to as Activate, Connect, Affirm (ACA) strategies because of their emphasis on teachers' use of the strategies to guide contextual actions throughout all three phases of teaching and learning:

- Opening (activation)
- Work time (connection)
- Closing (affirmation)

In each phase of teaching and learning, both teachers and students have much to accomplish!

In the **activation phase**, the teacher creates a culturally responsive learning context for the lesson and serves as an active observer. This phase of the lesson cycle is further contextualized as teachers reflect upon the biographies of the learners and the way these biographies become evident in what students produce. Educators begin the lesson by providing open opportunities for students to share what they know about the topic. They offer a "tool in the hand" that provides learners with a "canvas" on which to document their ideas and connections. All students engage to share and record initial insights and connections to the lesson topic, concepts, or vocabulary, based on their background knowledge. Students draw on their previous knowledge and experiences gained in the home, community, and school. The educator observes and documents these links for use throughout the lesson.

In the **connection phase**, the teacher serves as a facilitator and cultural negotiator, supporting students to navigate the curriculum and construct meaning. The teacher confirms/disconfirms students' understandings and revoices connections made so that individual students' words, ideas, and experiences can serve as a springboard for the learning of the classroom community. Throughout this phase, the teacher systematically employs various grouping structures—reflected in the mnemonic *i*+*TpsI*, which is described in Chapter 8—to support students as they work collectively, collaboratively, and individually with the new content and language to develop refined understandings, always relating the known (their existing knowledge, skills, and language) to the unknown (new knowledge, skills, and language). The educator strives to promote both rigor and relevance during lesson activities that integrate listening, speaking, reading, and writing. In addition, he or she monitors students' cognitive processes and affective filters in order to route and reroute each student effectively to ensure that all learners arrive at the target destination and achieve the goals of the lesson.

During the **affirmation phase**, the teacher uses evidence of student understanding and progress to affirm learning. Authentic assessments allow students to build on the successes of the lesson thus far. Students use the hands-on tools

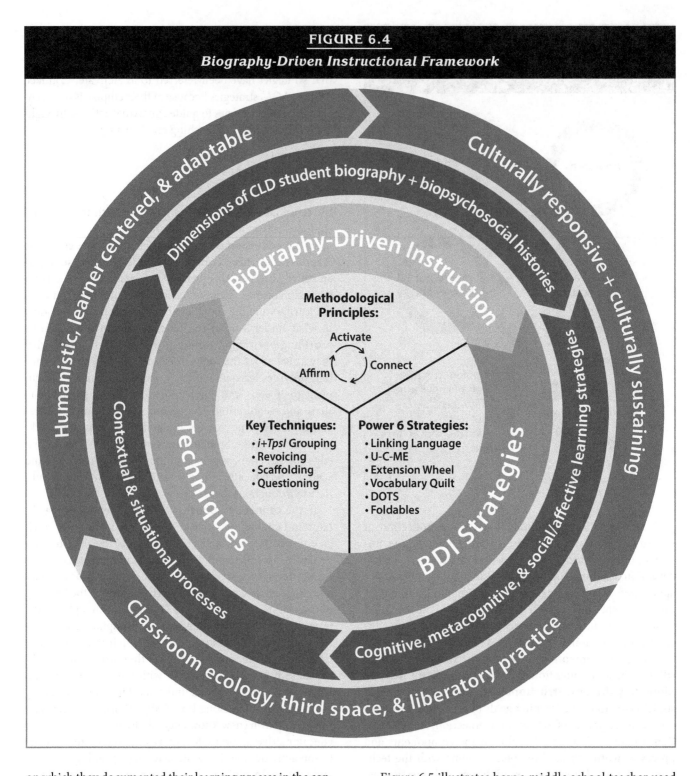

FIGURE 6.4
Biography-Driven Instructional Framework

on which they documented their learning process in the connection phase to scaffold their participation during end-of-lesson assessments. Recognizing the value of both student progress and product, the teacher celebrates growth as well as mastery. He or she also uses evidence of students' individual cognitive processes to address remaining gaps in understanding. As the teacher brings the lesson to a close, he or she guides students to reflect on the effectiveness of their learning processes and strategies for attaining the lesson objectives.

Figure 6.5 illustrates how a middle school teacher used the mind map BDI strategy throughout the activation, connection, and affirmation phases of the lesson. Each of these phases of teaching and learning is further detailed in subsequent chapters. Chapter 7 provides an in-depth look at the activation phase, Chapter 8 explores the connection phase, and Chapter 9 discusses the affirmation phase, highlighting ways to make the learning of all students transparent.

Observe, Facilitate, Affirm

Research has long documented the importance of valuing what every child brings to each act of learning (González et al., 2005; Keefe & Padilla, 1987; Moll & Greenberg, 1990; Vélez-Ibáñez & Greenberg, 1992). As discussed in Chapter 1, many instructional guides exist to support teachers in planning, delivering, and assessing the lesson. However, often lacking is explicit direction on how to take these guides into practice in ways that clarify the multidimensional assets CLD learners bring. Understanding students' existing knowledge and various strengths enables teachers to move away from remediation and toward *acceleration of learning*.

To begin at our CLD students' current levels of competence, we must first assess that level from a perspective that looks for assets rather than deficiencies; that is, we must assume that every student we teach has something to contribute to every lesson. If we use only school-situated data and assessments to inform ourselves about a CLD student's linguistic and academic abilities, we discount the truly dynamic and intricate nature of each individual's second language acquisition and learning process. In Chapters 1 and 3, I discussed the importance of Krashen's (1982) *i*+1 theory of language development and Vygotsky's (1978) construct of learning. Understanding and using these two "ideals" as we plan for teaching requires us to move beyond a superficial, school-situated knowledge of students' assets and into the role of active observer and facilitator of learning. Those who challenge themselves to do so will likely be rewarded by the sight of their CLD students, as well as all their other students, beaming with delight at reaching deeper levels of understanding.

We must become observers and listeners within our own community. Our students have much to share when we provide a risk-free space—a space where CLD students know that if rerouting is necessary, the teacher and his or her peers will provide support to make this happen, without penalty. In such spaces, appropriate strategies and scaffolds help learners connect their background knowledge to the topic of the lesson or the vocabulary being taught. As discussed throughout the remainder of this text, the teacher takes on a responsibility to observe, facilitate, and affirm.

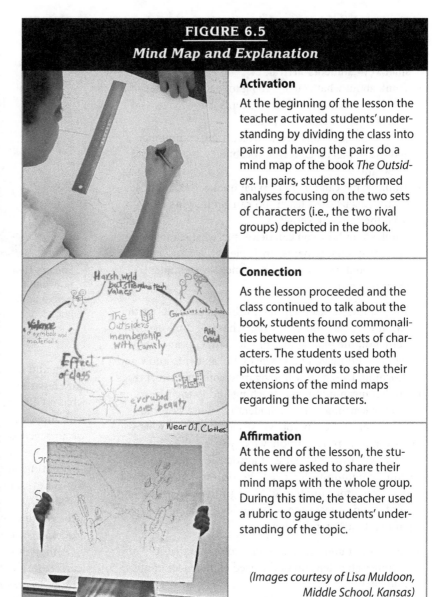

FIGURE 6.5
Mind Map and Explanation

Activation

At the beginning of the lesson the teacher activated students' understanding by dividing the class into pairs and having the pairs do a mind map of the book *The Outsiders*. In pairs, students performed analyses focusing on the two sets of characters (i.e., the two rival groups) depicted in the book.

Connection

As the lesson proceeded and the class continued to talk about the book, students found commonalities between the two sets of characters. The students used both pictures and words to share their extensions of the mind maps regarding the characters.

Affirmation

At the end of the lesson, the students were asked to share their mind maps with the whole group. During this time, the teacher used a rubric to gauge students' understanding of the topic.

(Images courtesy of Lisa Muldoon, Middle School, Kansas)

The Teacher as Participant Observer

In this section, I more specifically discuss how to implement culturally relevant pedagogy within the context of a lesson. You are probably wondering, *How exactly do I plan for instruction that is contextualized and situated with specific considerations for the CLD student biography?* In beginning to answer this question, I ask that you first imagine that you are an ethnographer—a researcher—within your own classroom. Focus your thoughts on what you know about the biographies of your CLD students. What knowledge and understanding does each student bring from his or her previous academic and life experiences (no matter how distant that knowledge may appear from the "standard" you are about to teach)? Now, take a few moments to do the following:

- Think about what you already know from the school-situated biographies you were handed at the beginning of the year, or from what you have collected since your students' arrival.
- Think about what you are going to teach and what you can do to learn more about students' knowledge, as it relates to the topic or vocabulary.
- Pose some questions about the learning community and the new chapter, novel, vocabulary, or concept to be taught.
- Think: What can I gather? What questions can I pose to students before I teach so I can get insights into what they already know?
- Think about how you can delve into what students bring that often remains "invisible."
- Think about ways you will document what students share or learn.

Socorro Herrera engages in a brief, one-on-one conversation with a student. Such informal talks are a great way to gather additional information about the strengths and knowledge that individual students bring to the lesson.

Your aim is to keep an open mind about the "participants" in your classroom—to take what you can learn from reflecting on the biographies of your students and prepare to "ignite" and make public what CLD students know and are learning. Doing so will invigorate your practice, bringing added meaning to your teaching and to their learning, and to the learning of every student in your classroom.

Every step of the way you will strive to consider what you already know, reflect upon what you are hearing, and observe within the social and academic context of your learning community for even the tiniest detail that will inform you about the thoughts, cognitive processes, and state of mind of even the most difficult student. You will begin to ask questions such as:

- How can I build my classroom ecology so that it becomes an extension of the lived experiences of my students?
- How can I best make accommodations throughout this lesson for the levels of language acquisition represented in my classroom?
- Which students have strong academic biographies related to this topic?
- Which students have knowledge of this topic as a result of experiences in their home and/or community?
- What group configurations will be most beneficial given the objectives of this lesson?
- What activity will be most useful for introducing the topic and target vocabulary at the beginning of this lesson?
- Have I made clear my objectives and expectations for this lesson, as well as the directions for specific tasks? (Refer to Chapter 7 for discussion of both content and language objectives.)

According to Massey (1998), this type of reflection forces us to ask ourselves the difficult questions, the questions that

count, and to be open to learning about those who inhabit our classrooms. Rather than jumping to conclusions about what a CLD student is or is not capable of doing alone or with support, we wait until we have collected the data before we proceed on our journey. With the insights we have gained, we are able to route and reroute by clarifying, elaborating, and challenging students as necessary. When we use evidence to inform our instructional actions and decisions, we are better able to ensure that everyone has a chance to achieve the goals of the lesson and arrive at the academic success we want for all our students.

Although we are not technically ethnographers, we can learn from the ideals and methodology of being a *participant observer* and apply these new understandings to our role within the classroom culture we are trying to learn more about. Alexander (2003) describes participant observation as a way of observing the setting, learning about the participants (students), and analyzing documents and artifacts as a means to understanding what is happening at the time. Becoming a participant observer requires the teacher to be totally immersed and involved in the situation. The teacher gathers information about what students know, how they interpret what is to be studied, or gaps that exist in background knowledge, to become better able to truly differentiate the instruction to meet the needs of every student.

The teacher then can use information and knowledge collected and documented to facilitate "instructional bridging and contextualizing," that is, the *scaffolding* of instruction at Krashen's $i+1$ level of language comprehension and production or Vygotsky's zone of proximal development for student learning (see Chapter 1 for discussion of these concepts). Just as a building under construction is less likely to collapse if it is scaffolded by a supporting structure, a student's emergent understanding of a concept is more quickly and effectively built when the teacher takes care to surround it with a supporting framework of existing knowledge. Gay (2018) reaffirms the importance of scaffolding as she draws on the work of others (Davis, 2012; Doyle, 2011; Glasgrow & Hicks, 2009; Howe, 1999; Ormrod, 1995; Rodriguez et al., 2017) to summarize several generally accepted principles of learning.

- Students' existing knowledge is the best starting point for the introduction of new knowledge (principle of similarity).
- Prior success breeds subsequent effort and success (principle of efficacy).
- New knowledge is learned more easily and retained longer when it is connected to prior knowledge, frames of reference, or cognitive schemata (principle of congruity).
- Reducing the "strangeness" of new knowledge and the concomitant "threat of the unfamiliar" increases students' engagement with and mastery of learning tasks (principle of familiarity).
- Organizational and structural factors surrounding how one goes about learning have more powerful effects on the mastery of new knowledge than the amount of prior knowledge one possesses per se (principle of transactionalism).
- Understanding how students' knowledge is organized and interrelated—their cognitive structures—is essential to maximizing their classroom learning (principle of cognitive mapping).
- Expectations and mediations affect performance. If students think they can learn, and receive competent assistance from supporters (e.g., teachers, parents, peers, and other mentors) in the process, they will learn (principle of confidence and efficacy).
- School achievement is always more than academics. Invariably, learning takes place in context, and is influenced by the affective and caring climates of the places or settings where its efforts occur. The social, physical, emotional, psychological, cultural, political, and ethical dispositions, developments, and experiences of the participants in the learning process are significant contributing factors and crucial targets for teaching (principle of holistic education).
- Out-of-school experiences matter, and are resources and filters for in-school learning. These "funds of knowledge, skill, and experience" are assets, building blocks, and leverage for subsequent learning (principle of scaffolding). (p. 204)

These principles highlight the importance of contextualizing our instruction within students' existing knowledge and frames of reference. By using what students know in order to make connections to the new information, teachers support students to see how their existing knowledge, skills, and experiences provide the foundation for new learning. Refer to Chapter 8 for an elaborated discussion of scaffolding in culturally responsive classrooms.

Our observation before beginning a lesson is crucial to our ability to capitalize on not only *what* students know but also *how* they have come to know about the vocabulary, concept, or topic. Gay (2018) states: "It is not enough for teachers to know 'what the learner knows about individual facts and concepts' (Howe, 1999, p. 78). They also need to understand how students come to know or to learn so that they can convey new knowledge through students' own learning systems" (p. 205). Understanding how students derived the information they know gives teachers a link that is stronger than any explanation, visual, or hands-on activity they might have originally planned to use to teach the given concept.

Education has a long history of using terms such as "prior knowledge" and "background knowledge" interchangeably. For many educators, this can be frustrating and confusing, if not misleading. For example, Stevens (1980) defines background knowledge quite simply as "what one already knows about a subject" (p. 151). The definition that Biemans and Simons (1996) provide is slightly more complex: "[prior/background knowledge is] all knowledge learners have when entering a learning environment that is potentially relevant for acquiring new knowledge" (p. 158). Marzano (2004) differentiates between academic background knowledge and all other types of background knowledge. Although he notes that the value of different types of knowledge is dependent on context, he makes clear that the emphasis in schools should be on efforts to build academic background knowledge. The language of these definitions may limit what teachers do in classroom practice, because teachers may assume they already are optimally using students' previously acquired knowledge. Teachers sometimes make comments such as, "This student has very little background knowledge." Yet they may be unable to explain exactly what they mean by such a statement.

Here, I will attempt to respectfully elaborate on the three "roots" of student experience and learning—*funds of knowledge* (home assets), *prior knowledge* (community assets), and *academic knowledge* (school assets)—to clarify the often subtle but important distinctions between the multiple sources of students' previously acquired, or "background," knowledge. These distinctions are drawn to support teachers' observations before, during, and after the lesson. We continuously make connections as we learn new information, linking to what we know on multiple levels in order to assimilate information and modify our understandings. Differentiating between and understanding the types of knowledge students bring to our classrooms supports our efforts to provide students with culturally relevant pedagogy.

Funds of Knowledge

Teachers frequently comment on how little they know about the home lives of their students or how students' home lives do not support what is being taught at school. However, many teachers have discovered the value of home visits and what can be gained from learning about the resources that students acquire from being part of a family, with its unique makeup and dynamics. These assets have been referred to as the **funds of knowledge** that families and students possess, and they have significant implications for classroom practice.

As a theoretical construct, the concept of "funds of knowledge" (Moll, 2019; Moll et al., 1992) has been guiding educators' thought and practice for more than a decade. The term "funds of knowledge" focuses on the wealth of knowledge and assets a student has accumulated from his or her life at home. A student's primary socialization occurs within a group of people who bend, shape, and mold his or her language and ways of thinking and being in the world. The literature defines funds of knowledge as those historically developed and accumulated strategies or bodies of knowledge that are essential to the function and well-being of a household (Moll et al., 1992; Vélez-Ibáñez & Greenberg, 1992). Certain events and experiences occur in the home of any given student that are uniquely tied to his or her understanding of the world, as reflected in native language, primary discourse patterns, traditions, actions, and individual roles. Moll (2019) further characterizes funds of knowledge as a way to challenge the deficit orientation by documenting and re-presenting a family's wealth of knowledge, resources, and strengths.

Discourse, or communicative exchange, is explicitly connected to the "bodies of knowledge" that develop within a student's immediate household and that are unique, and often "secret" or "hidden," from the community or the school. This knowledge is transmitted from generation to generation, understood through a shared lens, and passed on in daily activity. Such knowledge includes, but is not limited to, the cultural features described in Chapter 2. The strategies understood and employed by the student thus represent the historical ways of being and participating within a "cultural unit," that is, the family.

I often say to educators that these ways of being in the world are passed on by osmosis without having to be explicitly explained to the members of the family. We all can think of a family saying, practice, joke, rule, or guiding assumption that makes automatic sense to us in the context of our family but would be difficult to explain to an outsider. These personal examples are microcosms of the larger bodies of

In Hindu households, a brother is supposed to protect his sister and uphold her honor. In this photo, a mother is tying a Rakhi (a thread) around her son's wrist, with his sister looking on. The Rakhi symbolizes the bond of protection that exists between brother and sister. Families also celebrate the bond between siblings by sharing traditional sweets. *(Image courtesy of Pooja Aggarwal, New Delhi, India)*

knowledge that may differ radically among cultural groups. Consider the following scenario:

> I have a very close friend who has a daughter in high school. This young woman is beautiful, intelligent, outgoing, and fully grounded in her cultural identity. As I have watched her grow, I have been fascinated with the ease with which she has learned to live within her cultural reality and the reality of being a teenager in the United States. She fully understands how two worlds may look the same and yet be incredibly different. Her own "culturally prescribed" ways of participating are very different from those of her cheerleading peers. Her parents attend all functions, are very involved in her life, and prohibit dating; she is expected to participate in family life beyond what most teenagers would think is "cool." On a recent 2-hour trip together, we talked about her experiences as a cheerleader and the expectations her mother and father have of her. I asked how she managed to live in both worlds, especially with regard to dating. I found her response something to smile about. She shared that when someone asks about "the ways of doing" within her family unit, she says, "I won't be able to do that." When asked why, she simply responds, "It's very complicated, you see. You'd have to live there to understand."

Funds of knowledge, especially those that relate to culture, are not always capitalized on in the classroom. It is our responsibility, as educators, to set up contextual and situational conditions that provide students with an opportunity to share these often hidden ways of doing that are evident only to those who share a long history with individual students or interact with them on a daily basis. By selecting strategies that make this possible, we integrate information gathering as a natural part of every lesson. Understanding the dynamics that create the richness of what every family—poor or wealthy—possesses sets the stage for moving beyond surface levels of using students' backgrounds and cultures during instruction. As González et al. (2005) note:

> Using the concept of funds of knowledge as a heuristic device provides teachers with a pragmatic avenue to engage with their students' lives. It allows the possibility of seeing beyond the classroom and glimpsing the circulating discourses and shifting fields of power that shape students' lives. (p. 44)

When we create opportunities for families and students to share what is happening in their homes and lives, the resulting insights become resources—*authentic* information we can use to make connections between what the student brings and what is being taught.

The concept of funds of knowledge provides a lens for understanding the primary socialization of students who may come from homes where the culture and the language of their environment are often different from those of the school. When appropriate observations are made in the classroom, educators are provided with a rich tapestry of CLD student assets that are available for knowledge construction processes for the entire learning community. With this in mind, we can begin to look for strategies that will make public what the student knows about vocabulary, topics, and so forth that may support what is going to be taught. Consider the following scenario and reflect on what the teacher learned by using a strategy that provided space for this student's funds of knowledge to be made public in the classroom.

> Mrs. Nowakowski, a 2nd-grade teacher, showed her students the cover of the book she would be reading to them and said, "One of our objectives for today is to use the DOTS strategy to prepare for reading our story of the week, *The Piñata Maker,* by George Ancona." The previous year, Mrs. Nowakowski had learned the DOTS strategy in a graduate level course in ESL methods.
>
> Mrs. Nowakowski then asked the students to reach deep into their memories and "splash" onto their DOTS chart (see photo below) the words or pictures that came to mind. She said they could write in the language(s) of their choice and/or draw pictures. As she walked around the room observing and noting what students were writing, Mrs. Nowakowski noticed that one of the students had written the word "rheumatism," not a typical word for a 2nd-grade student with a limited English vocabulary. She stopped and asked about this "big" word. The student shared that her *abuelita* (grandmother) used to make piñatas in Mexico before coming to live with them. However, she no longer made piñatas because she had rheumatism.

This information was one of those little disclosures that provided Mrs. Nowakowski with a window into her student's immediate connections to the story and the lesson. By providing the students in the class with the opportunity to voice what they were thinking, seeing, or feeling, she was able to listen and observe for student associations that could be used later in the lesson to build trust, community, and academic knowledge.

We must always be aware that long before we come into students' lives, they are living and breathing the history of their innermost circle. The languages they speak, their values, and their beliefs already have been communicated in verbal and nonverbal ways. These have been passed on from one generation to the next through parenting practices that teach social and communicative behaviors. According to Vygotsky (1986), we first understand our identity through the hearts and minds of those who have socialized us to see and feel the world in a certain way.

To understand what our students know and how they communicate that knowledge, we must first understand the cultural constructs that shaped them *before* they arrived in our classrooms. These constructs cannot be understood unless we make a conscious effort to observe our students throughout the lesson as they make sense of what we teach. If we consider what educators and researchers have discussed in relation to a funds-of-knowledge perspective, we then can begin to conceptualize contexts and situations that provide students with opportunities to be contributing members of our classrooms rather than silent observers.

Prior Knowledge

Considering students' **prior knowledge** has long been part of the lesson planning process. Prior knowledge relates to the understandings and knowledge a student has gained as a result of being part of a community. Prior knowledge is anchored in the student's primary socialization in the home and is wedged between what happens at home and what happens in school (Gay, 2018). Current and past economic and social trends (e.g., employment opportunities, political threats) have forced many CLD students to be very mobile, moving from community to community and continually adjusting to new people and new surroundings. Although this does not hold true for all CLD students, for some it redefines our common understanding of the "community" in which a student has been socialized. Therefore, it often holds true that what is learned in the community will be based on where the CLD student and his or her family find themselves at any point in time socially, economically, and linguistically. When the community has resources available to support the family, the student's role(s) often will be different from the role(s) he or she might play in a community where few resources are available to support the family. Students bring the cumulative prior knowledge they have gained from each of the communities in which they have interacted.

In preparing to tap into a student's prior knowledge, the teacher once again takes on the responsibility of becoming a participant observer of the student and family, to understand the literacy and other assets the student has gained from being an active participant in his or her community context(s). A student's prior knowledge is closely tied to the following:

- The social climate of the community
- The role(s) the student has within the family unit
- The status and acceptance of the student's particular group (e.g., ethnic, racial, linguistic, religious, socio-economic)
- The political climate of the community, region, and nation
- Community resources the student and family can access
- The types of experiences and opportunities available in the community

One of the most relevant and yet often overlooked assets that many CLD students bring to the classroom is derived from lived experience of being the only English speaker in their family. Take, for example, the previously discussed scenario in which the teacher's use of the DOTS strategy yielded a student sharing the word "rheumatism" during the activation phase of the lesson. From a funds-of-knowledge perspective, we learned that the student's grandmother had rheumatism. The teacher subsequently asked the student where she had learned how to spell the word, and she shared that she was the only one in the family who spoke English. Therefore, she translated when her grandmother went to the doctor and helped to give her the necessary medicine. The word was written on both her prescription container and the reading materials that were given during doctor visits. **Language brokering**, in which an individual (often a CLD student) serves to "interpret and translate between culturally and linguistically different people and mediate interactions in a variety of situations" (Tse, 1996, p. 226), is just one experience that many students in our classrooms have had in their respective communities.

Experiences in the community enable students to develop prior knowledge that then can be used as a resource when performing different tasks in school. For instance, when students use literacy for purposes related to life circumstances (e.g., filling out job applications, completing lease agreements, applying for services), such experiences contribute to students' literacy development. Though we generally assume that only adults perform such activities, CLD students often undertake them to assist their families. The resulting skills and knowledge can be capitalized on

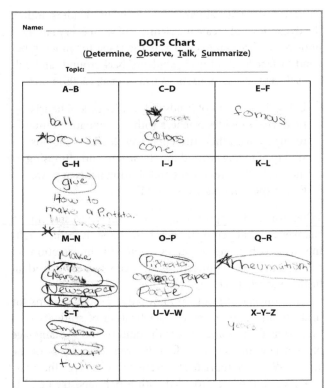

Mrs. Nowakowski's 2nd-grade students created this DOTS chart for the topic "piñata." The chart revealed some unexpected connections and advanced vocabulary, even for students with limited English language knowledge. See Appendix C for a full description of the DOTS strategy. A template for classroom use is available for download from the Teachers College Press website: tcpress.com

during reading and writing lessons. Some students have worked side by side with community members participating in activities that require real-life application of math, science, social studies, and other content areas. Students' prior knowledge about a particular, even unexpected, topic might be quite extensive.

We teachers must consider, however, the effects that the acculturation process can have on students. CLD students often experience the acculturation process in different ways than adults, frequently learning English before their parents. Yet the discrimination they may experience in society can lead to their perception that knowledge and learning can only be gained in school. This perspective, in turn, can lead students to discount their own knowledge. It is up to us first to design opportunities for students to bring their prior knowledge to the surface, and then to validate that knowledge.

Distinguishing between student knowledge acquired inside the home and knowledge gained through participation in the community provides educators with different types of "anchors" for understanding each student. To best accelerate learning, educators need to understand how knowledge gained from the family and community can be used as a bridge to new learning. Connections made to both

A community of learners is solidified through continual opportunities for interaction and sharing. In this photo, Ms. Johnson, a 2nd-grade teacher, is creating conditions in the classroom that can help her learners connect to their prior knowledge. In this lesson, the students were getting ready to focus on the topic *rain forest*. Before the students actually got into the content of the lesson, the teacher activated their prior knowledge by having them first write their individual thoughts about the rain forest on paper and then talk to one another about what they knew. This made the lesson less threatening for the students, gave everyone a chance to share, and provided Ms. Johnson with insights into student knowledge that she could use to make connections to the content. Although this example is from a 2nd-grade class, the process described is effective with learners of all ages, including adults. *(Image courtesy of Denise Johnson, 2nd Grade, Kansas)*

types of lived experiences are much more relevant and can do more to promote students' cognitive connections during the lesson than teacher explanations or descriptions of topics, concepts, or new vocabulary. By selecting and implementing strategies that allow students to share from their funds of knowledge and prior knowledge, actively observing for such insights, and using the information gained during the lesson, we set the stage for students to discover how their knowledge connects to the content. Providing structured, systematic opportunities for students to dialogue with peers regarding these personally relevant connections also promotes cross-cultural communication skills, critical thinking skills, and linguistic and academic development for the entire classroom community.

In teaching, many of us have at least once looked at the curriculum we had to follow and become frustrated with the idea of teaching students whose related knowledge appeared so limited that we had little hope they would be successful in the classroom. We may have moved toward providing impersonal experiences for students by taking them on field trips and bringing in "concrete objects" in an attempt to provide students with experiences we perceived to be relevant to their becoming better prepared to learn

within a prescribed content area. This mode of thinking views learning as the process of accumulating information or experience (Knowles, 1970). To make the best possible use of students' funds of knowledge and prior knowledge, our perspective on learning needs to shift. When we begin to view learning as "conceptual change" (Strike & Posner, 1985; West & Pines, 1985) from the unknown to the known, it becomes more natural to automatically search for existing knowledge to which we can tie new information.

Learning about the knowledge gained by students' socialization in the home and the community, and using it during instruction, helps our teaching to be culturally and linguistically relevant to the student. It demonstrates to students that we care about their lived experiences outside of the school. When we approach instruction with this new perspective, our use of field trips and the virtual reality experiences made possible by technology are more likely to achieve our goals for reaching and teaching CLD students.

Read the following stories, which summarize the experiences of two girls, Thuy and Sonya. Consider the academic value of each student's experiences.

Thuy's Story

Prior to immigrating to the United States from Vietnam, Thuy found herself waiting to hear that her father had earned enough money from working in U.S. beef packing plants to send for the family. During this time, it became the responsibility of the rest of the family to support themselves at home. Thuy's work consisted of selling candy her mother had made the previous evening. During her long hours on the street, she found herself calculating the number of candies she must sell that day to meet the family's needs. At the end of the month, she had to know how much money the family had spent on food in order to determine the amount of candy her mother would still need to make (including considerations for the days/hours of work that were left) in order to pay the rent. When Thuy immigrated to the United States and started school, her teacher never realized that Thuy possessed this kind of experiential mathematical knowledge. Although Thuy excelled in math, she struggled in other areas. Years later, as she sat and recounted her story for a scholarship committee, she expressed her desire to teach math by using student experiences as the basis for what would be taught in school. She clearly had, on her own, realized how pivotal her own prior knowledge was to her academic success.

Sonya's Story

When Sonya was a little girl she was fascinated with numbers. Seeing her learn to count to ten by the time she was one, her parents quickly recognized that she had a gift that needed to be developed. They made sure they bought her toys that supported her love of math, played games with her, and continually pointed out how the world in which she lived was surrounded with mathematical concepts. When she started school, she was immediately tested and provided an opportunity to continue growing. By the time she was a junior in high school, she was taking classes at the local university. She told the scholarship committee that throughout her school years she had been mentored, and that mentoring had helped her to get where she was today. Her goal was to make sure that students who were "gifted" in math would get opportunities to shine in school.

If schools do not consider additional sources of background knowledge, a student's background with formal schooling can create great advantages for some students and great disadvantages for others. As educators, our challenge is to look for ways to create multiple opportunities for CLD students to voice and make public the knowledge they bring from the home and community as well as from previous schooling experiences. Most CLD students do not have problems with processing and storing information; however, if they are not provided with opportunities to be actively part of the learning conversation, we discount the knowledge they bring and leave them at a disadvantage. In such circumstances, in which teachers view CLD students from a deficit perspective (rather than asset perspective), the students are less likely to engage cognitively in the lesson or develop a positive self-concept about their role as learners and contributors to the classroom community.

In Ms. Pate's kindergarten classroom, all the students are exposed to the same content, but the route that each student takes in understanding the content is different. In this photo, students are making connections to vocabulary words from one of their readers. The students were provided with a strategy at the beginning of the lesson in which they were asked to represent their initial understanding of the terms using pictures or words. This necessary step of the lesson is instrumental for activating their knowledge systems and providing the teacher with insights that she can use to increase the comprehensibility of the terms through the remainder of the lesson. After the students had finished the first phase of the strategy, they moved into reading the books. With the help of their teacher, they checked the accuracy of their initial associations, based on the use of the words in context, and then generated additional connections to the words. *(Image courtesy of Katrina Pate, Kindergarten, Kansas)*

Academic Knowledge

In the previous two sections, I attempted to distinguish between what we have come to understand as "funds of knowledge" and "prior knowledge." In this section, I explore "academic knowledge" as part of the conversation on understanding and utilizing CLD student biographies in planning, teaching, and assessing. **Academic knowledge** refers to knowledge that students have acquired in formal educational settings. Academic knowledge reflects the kinds of understandings and skills that traditionally have been highly valued by schools and teachers.

When we make decisions about curriculum and instruction for a given student, we must avoid relying solely on the academic information with which we are provided at the beginning of the year or upon a student's arrival (e.g., enrollment form data, English language proficiency test scores, standardized content-area test scores). Consider the following scenario:

A few years ago, I was asked by an ESL high school teacher to come and model a lesson in her classroom. I accepted the invitation and had a great time interacting with her students. It was evident from the first half of the class that these students had very different biographies and aspirations for the future. Shortly after class, a student came up and asked if I had any connections in the school. I smiled and asked what he meant by "connections." He told me that he recently had moved to the area and wanted to be placed in the AP math courses in the school. He had already taken the highest level of math before moving to the United States from Mexico. He had looked at the books and assignments of the AP courses down the hall and was confident that he could do the work. He said, "They have never asked what I know. What do they have to lose? If I fail because I don't speak English, they can put me back here all day." When I left the classroom, I visited with the counselor, who informed me that until students had reached a certain level of English proficiency, they were not "eligible" for any other class except ESL sheltered instruction.

When we consider a student's academic knowledge, we must remember to take into account not only the experiences the individual has had in the United States but also those in any other country in which he or she was schooled. By reflecting on our current efforts to learn about the academic biographies of our students *beyond traditional assessments,* we become aware of new possibilities for gaining insight into the knowledge our students bring to the classroom.

Knowledge Systems and Background Knowledge

Thinking about *knowledge* from the three perspectives I have discussed in this chapter reframes "what counts" in school and widens our lens to include more in our teaching. Understanding and differentiating among funds of knowledge, prior knowledge, and academic knowledge helps us better understand that *every* student brings something to the lesson that we can connect to as we teach new vocabulary and academic concepts. Knowing what students bring from all three types of knowledge sources informs us as we plan and deliver lessons and assess student learning. It enables us to plot the best path to ensure the academic success of each student.

At the same time, we must remember that funds of knowledge, prior knowledge, and academic knowledge overlap and are intertwined in students' schema. Taken together, these *knowledge systems* represent a student's back-

ground knowledge. According to Lewis (2006), "a system is a collection of parts that interact with each other to function as a whole" (p. 458). Our students begin their life in a family that is full of language, culture, love, and much more, long before they begin to understand and interact with the community. Depending on where their life leads them and the dynamics within their family, they soon begin to interact with a given community in ways that help to mold their understanding of what happens outside the home as well as the implications that the larger society has for their family. This secondary socialization (Cushner et al., 2006) can happen as early as the preschool years and continues into young adulthood. Within these two knowledge systems (funds of knowledge and prior knowledge), educators can find untapped resources to affirm students' language, culture, and life and to promote their linguistic and academic development. Ultimately, these two systems come into contact with formal schooling.

The way we think about these knowledge systems influences our contextual view of teaching and learning, and informs our decisions regarding situational processes during the act of teaching. Figure 6.6 provides a brief review of the defining features of these knowledge systems and illustrates their interrelated nature. To capitalize on these types of background knowledge in the classroom, we must ignite

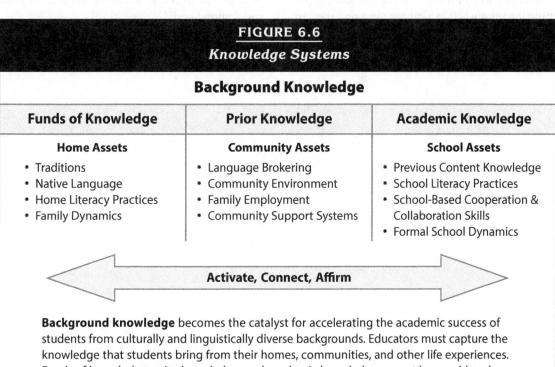

FIGURE 6.6
Knowledge Systems

Background Knowledge

Funds of Knowledge	Prior Knowledge	Academic Knowledge
Home Assets	**Community Assets**	**School Assets**
• Traditions • Native Language • Home Literacy Practices • Family Dynamics	• Language Brokering • Community Environment • Family Employment • Community Support Systems	• Previous Content Knowledge • School Literacy Practices • School-Based Cooperation & Collaboration Skills • Formal School Dynamics

← Activate, Connect, Affirm →

Background knowledge becomes the catalyst for accelerating the academic success of students from culturally and linguistically diverse backgrounds. Educators must capture the knowledge that students bring from their homes, communities, and other life experiences. Funds of knowledge, prior knowledge, and academic knowledge cannot be considered as completely separate sources of knowledge because they are interrelated and each informs the others in multiple ways. Rough boundaries have been drawn to make it easier to ensure that each area is addressed before, during, and after the lesson. Often home and community assets are left on the periphery of teaching, yet when considered and used in practice they become powerful tools for increasing academic achievement.

students' associations with the topic at hand, observe as they share these associations, and validate and elaborate on students' connections to make learning meaningful. As we incorporate these processes into our daily instruction, we begin to think in terms of *biography-driven instruction.*

Reflections on Valuing the Student in Teaching

In some respects, every classroom is a world unto itself— a community that has been created by the teacher in the image of the kind of learning ecology that the teacher believes will best meet his or her goals. In this educational space, conditional and situational processes either enhance or inhibit CLD students' learning. In this chapter, we have learned that teachers who strive to provide biography-driven instruction become participant observers to identify assets that each member of the community possesses. By becoming aware of and using student knowledge as a catalyst for new learning, teachers increase the likelihood of all students achieving academically.

One common myth among educators is related to the presumed lack of knowledge that CLD students have about academic content. The prevalence of this myth calls us to reflect on the value we place on different types of knowledge. If we claim, for example, to value our student's mathematical knowledge gained through the mechanical experience of setting the timing belt in a car, we must find ways to validate and use that knowledge in the learning processes of the classroom. If our thinking is focused exclusively on classroom learning that employs "school valued" knowledge rather than on what we can do with students' existing knowledge, we limit the possibilities for CLD students' success in school.

Teachers often say, "No two days are ever the same, and that's what makes education such a wonderful profession." As we daily provide opportunities for our students to share their thoughts and experiences, we come to a greater understanding of the background knowledge (i.e., funds of knowledge, prior knowledge, and academic knowledge) that each possesses from their life history and from attending school. Yet students will only be willing to make their knowledge public to the degree that we teachers have created spaces where human relationships are valued and learning is built on trust and respect. Motivation, engagement, emotion, and cognition are interrelated, and never exist in isolation when students are learning. Therefore, we must continually navigate our students' states of mind and attend to situational processes throughout the lesson.

Chapter 7 provides additional tools for discovering what each student brings. The strategies that are introduced will solidify what you have learned in this chapter. By listening and observing for glimpses into what students think and know, we allow students to teach us and to provide us with links to their lives that will make our content more relevant and comprehensible.

7 Activation
A Canvas of Opportunity

GUIDING QUESTION

How does the use of strategies focused on helping students disclose what they already know and the ways they are processing language and content support their learning and academic achievement?

See the online Discussion Guide for opportunities to further explore answers to this question and connections to chapter content with a colleague or team. Available for download from the Teachers College Press website: tcpress.com

IN PREVIOUS CHAPTERS, I focused extensively on the importance, even urgency, of understanding CLD learners and the wealth of community knowledge, funds of knowledge, and untapped linguistic and academic knowledge they bring. Each learner arrives at the space with a rich linguistic repertoire and knowledge of the world they live in. This world is full of science, math, literature, and life. What often is absent when we open the lesson is the "activation" of language and knowledge through visual representation, asking questions, and entering into storytelling to gather or "harvest" what is known by the learner. In classrooms, we often view building background as identifying what the learner lacks in order to frontload our teaching through the use of media, visuals, or vocabulary lists. Then we wonder why, even with all the frontloading, the learner doesn't get it. If we think about how it is that a learner enters into cognitive processing, neuroscience quickly points out the need to associate or "velcro" to what is known in order to build to the unknown (Sousa, 2017; Zadina, 2014). It's not about us building for students, it's about the learner activating, making sense and meaning with the words they have available to them and with the knowledge they have gained by breathing language and culture, in and out, every day in their communities and home. Think about the following conversation I had with Ms. Salazar, a 5th-grade teacher:

Teacher: I have tried everything to build background on "government and the Constitution." Videos, pictures, books, you name it, I have used it. They have no background!

My response: Have you asked them who makes the rules, at home, school, community, state, and nation? Given you have students from many countries, ask about the rules in their country. Are they the same or different from those we have in the United States? From their responses, tell a story about how all countries have governments that make up the rules about many things. Pretty simple. From there, use their words to build toward the complexity of government and the academic words we use to talk about the Constitution, branches of government, and what role each plays. Keep building, ebbing and flowing from where they started to where you are taking them, using all the language/words they have available as you together walk the road that is going to take you where you need to go.

Weeks later, I reconnected with Ms. Salazar. She was elated to tell me how her students were performing, engaged, excited, and using both languages seamlessly to get their messages across. She commented, "It's crazy how something that took no time or external resources could get me so far." It's all in the questions we ask and how we open up the pathways to engage our community from where they stand linguistically and academically. It takes *letting go* of so much!

Only by closely attending to and using the assets that the learner brings to our lesson are we able to differentiate instruction for CLD students. Scaffolding of instruction that places the biography of each student at the center of pedagogy has the potential to lead to better classroom management, student engagement, and motivation to learn. The sociocultural and socioemotional spheres that we often talk about wanting to attend to seem to get lost in translation when we plan and deliver instruction. The opening of the lesson is pivotal to what we will attend to during the lesson. We often talk about the unmotivated learner. Yet, we seldom ask what cultural, linguistic, cognitive, and academic assets the individual and community of learners possess that will give us the fertile ground to extend on what is known.

Socioculturally Speaking

According to Palincsar (1998), educators who use a type of **social constructivist approach** create conditions and situational contexts wherein the student drives the discussion and the teacher assumes the role of facilitator, or guide, alongside the learner. Any form of instruction that takes a constructivist approach strives to implement the ideal of "teacher as facilitator" in the classroom. However, what is often missing in constructivist classrooms is facilitation guided by what the learner brings, both culturally and linguistically, to the learning environment. The social constructivist classroom, on the other hand, is one in which the teacher uses what he or she has learned from the student in order to provide more opportunities for all students to fully participate in brainstorming, questioning, and directing student learning in the classroom.

According to O'Dwyer (2006), we must move away from strict adherence to the old pedagogical ideal that placed the teacher in charge of "transmitting knowledge" to students. Although direct instruction on the particulars of a content area is one important aspect of teaching, educators also should become facilitators of student learning. For example, the educator activates what the learner associates with the vocabulary word and considers how that connects with the conceptual knowledge in order to use it as a building block to validate the learner and bridge into new learning. Social constructivist pedagogy involves the facilitation of activities that are communicative, democratic, and student-centered. To become a truly effective facilitator of learning for all students, the teacher must value the CLD learner's experience and knowledge, gained both in and out of the classroom. The teacher's facilitation process begins with learning about and using CLD student knowledge as the "anchor" or "point of departure" for instruction.

In classrooms where the goal is to use the biographies of the students to bridge and connect to new knowledge, the teacher no longer follows the standard pattern, in which the vocabulary is taught using the Frayer model (Frayer et al., 1969) in isolation without using what has been gained from the activation of student knowledge in the opening of the lesson. During the lesson's opening phase, we must be intentional in flipping the script from "Let me teach you the vocabulary words so you will understand," to "Let's build from using these words in context, *yours and mine,* to bridge into the text and the lesson." In the activation phase, the teacher connects student talk in ways that route and reroute learning to arrive at the tar-

Before students entered the formal part of the lesson about leaves, the teacher had the students record and then share in their small groups what they already knew about leaves. The teacher wanted the students to include as much information as they could regarding their ideas about where leaves come from, how they feel, what they look like, how they change, and what they are used for. The teacher then collected the drawings and words to support her explanations of the vocabulary words for the lesson. *(Image courtesy of Kendra Herrera, 3rd Grade, Texas)*

geted destination. Here, the teacher facilitates all levels of academic talk in ways that make public what the learner knows about the topic or vocabulary.

In beginning to address the biographies of the students in our classrooms, we consider instructional factors that:

- Help to ensure that all students have opportunities to share what they know at the opening of the lesson
- Enable teachers to capitalize on student assets and create conditions and situations that scaffold students to become active participants in learning
- Use strategies that naturally scaffold students in reaching their full potential, with the aid of our facilitation

The following tactics are fundamental to the social constructivist teaching strategy:

- Educators make "transparent," or explicit, to students what is going to be taught and how they will be supported in their learning.
- Teachers begin to situationally monitor output and make decisions based on the information about students' needs and assets.
- Teachers provide all students with an opportunity to disclose the knowledge they bring from their home, community, and school using a strategy or tool in the hand.
- Educators make clear to students that there are no right or wrong answers at the beginning of the lesson; there is only activation of each student's existing frame of

reference, or **schema**, so that together the class can begin its journey toward learning.

- Teachers create a low-risk environment in which the learners of the community feel culturally and linguistically validated and respected and trust that their educated contributions, in whatever language(s) they decide to use for disclosure, will be accepted as part of the learning process.

- Educators take part in the "activation" process by observing for insights into students' systems of knowledge (i.e., funds of knowledge, prior knowledge, and academic knowledge) and reflecting on ways such background knowledge can be used as a bridge to vocabulary development, conceptual understanding, comprehension, and validation of self.

These tactics encourage the teacher to go beyond merely setting objectives, telling students what they are to learn, and then proceeding to teach and evaluate student learning. Instead, the teacher facilitates learning through biography-driven instruction guided by BDI strategies, in which he or she brings all the resources of the classroom community to the forefront of the learning process. Accordingly, the teacher strives to publicly acknowledge CLD students' knowledge and supports students in making their thinking processes explicit.

Transparency in Teaching

As discussed in Chapter 6, fostering a supportive classroom ecology means much more than creating an environment that values culture and language in superficial ways, such as posters with inventors from diverse backgrounds or labels for classroom objects in the various languages spoken by students. While these additions are meaningful, ecology involves even greater consideration of the individual students in the class, the curriculum, and the teacher in charge. In our classrooms, we educators set in motion and orchestrate *everything* that happens. We model expectations, respect, and effective communication even as we make decisions about what, why, when, and how the curriculum will be navigated. We are the narrators of the story.

Attention to ecological factors requires that teachers make a concerted effort to make their teaching transparent to students. Consider the following scenario:

After 13 years of teaching, Ms. Sanchez had given up on ordering many books on strategies and getting excited about every make-and-take workshop she attended. She found that once back in the classroom she just didn't have time to figure out where a given strategy fit into her curriculum. She also found that if she used one of the strategies, it took so much energy to explain it, model it, and practice it that it hardly seemed worthwhile. Over time she had begun to see little value in all the strategy "fads" that passed her way.

Yet one day, everything clicked for Ms. Sanchez. After presenting a session at a conference, I was delighted to have Ms. Sanchez come up to me and share, "I never thought about all the things you talked about and how my community of learners is made up of so many dynamic, complex, and interrelated variables. Simply finding an exciting strategy to shove into my existing 'agenda' does little to change much of *what* or *how* I teach. Rather, multiple things have to be considered and changed before I can say that my practice is culturally responsive, sustaining, and relevant. Simply learning a new strategy and using it may or may not lead to learning. Instead, I have to choose my activities based on multiple variables and what is happening in my classroom. The activities I choose to use eventually will become strategies for my students as I make them a part of our classroom routine. Students will need opportunities to practice and apply the strategies multiple times through multiple lessons in order for the strategies to become part of the classroom rhythm. That makes so much sense! If I choose the strategies that work for *my* community, given *my* standards and curriculum and *my* style, and then I collaborate with students to make it work, it just might move my English learners forward to success."

Later I received an e-mail in which Ms. Sanchez told me that she now strategically selects her strategies based on what is going to be taught and how she envisions students will be participating in the learning process. She also takes the time to let the learners in her classroom know the destination!

When planning our instruction for maximum relevance to all students, we first align our standards, curriculum, student biographies, and teaching with a learning strategy. We then explicitly state to students the learning tasks that will be accomplished by using the particular strategy, sharing with them the destination and the stops that will be made along the way. As Kulesz (2007) simply states, "Pedagogy is about making what we teach transparent" (p. 5). Just as knowing our destination and what landmarks to look for helps us feel comfortable as we travel to a new place, by making our instructional intentions transparent, we increase the likelihood that all students will engage in learning (A. D. Anderson et al., 2013). Students will understand the purpose behind the lesson's activities and tasks rather than assuming that some (or all!) are merely included as "busy work." Furthermore, by using students' biographies to connect to the content, it becomes easier to model strategies and discuss how CLD students' background knowledge will contribute to what is to be learned. Making our students aware of what we teachers often keep secret gives them an open invitation to be a full participant in the community and its activities.

FIGURE 7.1
Applying the "D" in DOTS to Our Transparent Teaching

1. Know your standards, content, and curriculum.

- Determine how the curriculum, standards, and materials will impact CLD student learning.
- Set conditions from the onset to harvest students' background knowledge.
- Determine how you will make connections from the known to the unknown.
- Announce to individual students and the community of learners the assets that they already possess that will serve as scaffolds for autonomous learning.

2. Know your community of learners.

- Observe your community of learners and individuals as you enter the lesson.
- Determine the ways they make connections from the known to unknown.
- Call attention to the important information from your lecture, text, and/or visuals.
- Observe for students using their selective attention to "chunk and chew" new vocabulary and concepts.
- Monitor how the lesson changes the students' affective filters.
- Observe for the students' cognitive beliefs regarding their ability to use language and grasp information.
- Recognize how students use language (e.g., spoken, gestures, English, non-English).

3. Understand pedagogy from a biography perspective.

- Set conditions for talk throughout the lesson.
- Make connections that continue to build on students' knowledge.
- Strategically and systematically orchestrate talk throughout the lesson.
- Modify and adapt your curriculum as necessary to provide all students with opportunities to contribute in constructive ways.

4. Announce to your students the destination and what will happen along the way.

- Determine academic routines that enhance student participation.
- Model and acknowledge respectful ways to have students remind one another of the routines that lead to learning.
- Remind students that the overarching mission of the classroom community is to ensure that all members learn and support one another in the learning process.
- Inform students of your learning expectations through the use of language and content objectives.

As discussed in Chapter 6, we can use the DOTS strategy with our students to promote a reciprocal relationship between the learning community and the teacher. This and other BDI power strategies are key to making connections from what the student already knows to new concepts and authentically assessing our students' new learnings. However, the DOTS strategy is not just for students; it also helps us teachers to view our own instruction.

In this chapter, I focus on the "D" in DOTS: *Determine what we and the students know*—at the opening, during the work time, and at the closing of the lesson. Figure 7.1 summarizes key ways we can make the teaching and learning process transparent for the learners in our classroom and outlines how to apply the "D" in DOTS to ensure the clearest communication and expectations between the teacher and the community of learners.

Ideally, transparency in teaching is like retelling an important experience to someone and not wanting to leave out a single detail. You want the other person to feel as though he or she was there with you every step of the way—living the same experience. The same kind of energy, excitement, and attention to detail will help each student to "experience" the content with us. One of the most effective ways to enable transparency in teaching and to ensure that CLD students become active participants in learning is to plan instruction that is guided by an essential question and clear content and language objectives. Although teachers are more familiar with using an essential question to focus student learning, they often have not considered how both types of learning objectives work together to scaffold conceptual understanding, comprehension, and language growth for CLD students.

Content and Language Objectives

Content and language objectives have been discussed in the literature for over two decades as tools for ensuring transparency regarding (a) the concepts to be taught and (b) the ways the content will be practiced and applied during the lesson and then assessed. However, our development of content and language objectives should be guided by both *who* we are teaching and *what* we are teaching.

Content Objectives

According to Mager (1962), clearly identified content objectives serve to empower students by letting them know what is to be learned during the lesson. For the teacher, defining content objectives sets the stage for his or her selection of content, instructional strategies, and materials (Kim, 2007).

Content objectives also provide educators with a basis for assessment at the end of the lesson. As Gronlund (2004) explains, "If the intended learning outcomes are clearly stated, there is no problem in constructing a valid test. Just match the test item to the learning outcome to be measured" (p. 35).

Bear in mind these guidelines when writing content objectives:

- Select the overarching standard to be addressed during the lesson from the national, state, or grade-level standards (Echevarría & Graves, 2015).
- Write your content objectives, aligning them with the national, state, or grade-level standards (Echevarría & Graves, 2015).
- Align content objectives with the key grade-level concepts and vocabulary to be covered in the lesson.
- Scaffold the language used to explicitly share with the class *what* is going to be taught.

Content objectives often come as second nature to educators, given the time they have spent learning about and writing these types of objectives from the beginning of their teacher preparation program and beyond. What often is more difficult and time-consuming is conceptualizing and writing language objectives, that is, letting students know *how* the content is going to be learned.

Language Objectives

I like to think of language objectives as the ways we "bring to life" what we plan to teach our students during the lesson. Language objectives make it necessary for the teacher to take notice of the context and foresee some of the situational processes that may occur during the lesson, given the biographies of the members of the learning community. It takes time to make decisions regarding language objectives that will address the language demands prompted by both the conceptual and academic needs of our CLD students.

According to Numelin (1998) and Snow and colleagues (1989), we can think of language objectives as relating to one of two language categories: **content-obligatory** and **content-compatible**. Content-obligatory language is that which must be understood in order to understand the concept (Kim, 2007); content-compatible language supports the lesson but is not critical to concept learning. For example, in a science lesson on the three fundamental types of rock, *igneous, metamorphic,* and *sedimentary* would be content-obligatory words. Content-compatible words for the same lesson might include *magma, crust,* and *settle.* Content-compatible language can increase CLD students' academic language skills when it is embedded during instruction in community interaction, strategy use, and other classroom activities. With this distinction in mind, suggestions for writing language objectives include:

- Consider the biographies of the students (e.g., stages of SLA) when making decisions about language objectives, that is, decisions about *how* or *by what means* the content objectives will be taught and learned.
- Develop language objectives that reflect the academic language students need to fully participate during the lesson and reach the highest level of learning (Met, 1991).
- Write language objectives that vary between cognitively undemanding and cognitively demanding tasks in order to maximize language development and conceptual understanding during the lesson (Cummins, 2000; Fenner, 2013; Verplaetse, 2002).
- Make decisions about the *language functions* (e.g., compare, summarize), *skills* (e.g., scan text, draft an essay), and *structures* (e.g., questioning patterns, future or past tense verbs) that will be needed to complete the assigned tasks (Echevarría et al., 2016).
- Translate the content objectives into concrete activities that involve listening, speaking, reading, and writing.
- Consider the particular language functions, skills, structures, and grammar that are essential to your content area.
- Write language objectives with teaching activity and student learning strategy in mind that will address both the content and the language needs of your students.
- Think about language objectives as providing students with guidance to achieve the intended outcome of the lesson.

Content and Language Objectives Are for Everyone

A few questions that may be going through your mind at this point are, "Given that language objectives flow from the content objectives, aren't content objectives enough? Will all of this prove to confuse the learner? Will older students think content and language objectives are 'beneath' them?" These are valid questions. The following scenario provides some insight regarding the answers to such questions.

For the courses delivered through our center, at both the undergraduate *and* graduate levels, we write, post, and discuss content objectives as well as language objectives. At the end of one semester, I had a young lady from Korea stop to discuss her experience in the course. She was a doctoral student whose proficiency in English was quite advanced. I was surprised to have her tell me that the most rewarding experience for her throughout the course was our posting of the language and content objectives. She said, "Although I can speak English well, there were times during class that the terms and pace were overwhelming for me. But I always knew that I could pause and wait until we moved on to the next objective! What was important for me, as a student, was always knowing where

FIGURE 7.2
Five Steps for Writing Content and Language Objectives

Step 1

Identify the state **standard**, benchmark, indicator, etc.

Step 2

Identify the **key vocabulary** within the overarching standard.

Step 3

Identify the **content** (or concept within the content) you wish to teach. This is the "**WHAT**" of what you want to teach.

Example: The students will identify the *elements of a short story* within a given text.

Step 4

Once you have identified the "**WHAT**" of the concept, it is time to decide the "**HOW**" of teaching it. This is where you will consider:

- Strategy to be used throughout the lesson
- Language functions to be targeted
- Grouping configurations throughout the lesson
- The four domains of *listening*, *speaking*, *reading*, and *writing*

Step 5

Revisit the content objectives and language objectives as they align with the state standard, and then align the course texts and materials with these objectives.

we were going to end up that day and what was expected of me at the end of the lesson."

In this scenario we see an educated, graduate-level student benefiting from the posting and discussion of content and language objectives. The benefits to CLD students in K–12 classrooms in which I have observed are even more profound. Content and language objectives promote a sense of *hope* and *expectation* for engagement that is of inestimable worth, especially given the sociopolitical climate of schools today. This fact is reflected in academic research: language objectives recently have received a heavier focus, as educators have begun to recognize the need for integrating content and language instruction when meeting the needs of CLD students.

Together, content and language objectives serve as a road map for our instruction. At the beginning of the lesson when they are both posted and orally shared, they let everyone know where the class is going. During the lesson,

they provide us with landmarks along the way as we implement strategies and create opportunities for student interaction throughout the learning process. At the end of the trip, they announce that we have arrived at our destination as we restate the objectives. Figure 7.2 provides a guide that can assist in writing both content and language objectives.

Using Content and Language Objectives to Guide Lesson Preparation

As Echevarría et al. (2008) remind us, "An objective is not a by-product of an activity, but the foundation of one" (p. 27). Strategic and systematic planning is supported by our making decisions about which activity or strategy would best guide students to achieve the content and language objectives of the lesson.

When preparing and conducting a lesson, attention should be given to:

- Selecting a BDI power strategy as a tool for moving CLD students from the known to the unknown. The strategy should provide students with a "through line," connecting the lesson's various activities and tasks, which are employed as a multifaceted effort to promote students' development of conceptual understanding, vocabulary knowledge, and proficiency in all four language domains: listening, speaking, reading, and writing. The power strategy should serve as the building block that naturally scaffolds all learning.
- Focusing on activities that promote engagement and **socio-academic talk** of *all* students throughout the lesson.
- Making preliminary decisions about which *grouping configurations* will meet both the language and the content objectives and in what ways the configurations will be used during strategy implementation.
- Making *all* expectations transparent at the opening, during the work time, and at the closing of the lesson to ensure more students arrive at the destination.
- Planning for both linguistic and academic formative/postinstructional assessment during the lesson.
- Making explicit for students the target language functions and content-specific academic language, as well as ways that listening, speaking, reading, and writing will be part of the lesson.
- Observing, as the lesson unfolds, how the grouping configurations are working to enhance the learning opportunities and engagement of all students. The grouping configurations should be designed—and adjusted mid-course, if necessary—to provide CLD students with multiple opportunities and language models for practicing and applying language (both social and academic vocabulary) and content in varied and meaningful ways.

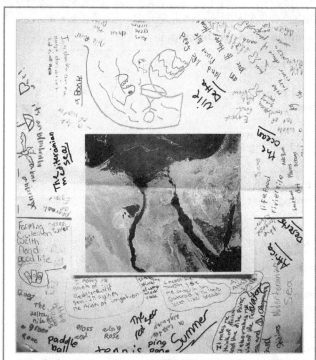

One high school teacher used the Linking Language strategy (see Figure 7.6) to activate students' background knowledge related to a geography lesson. Students were asked to do a "silent quick write" related to each of the visual representations that were placed on four different tables. Upon completing the "silent quick write," students discussed with their small groups what they had written and why. The teacher took this information to support explanation of the topic and vocabulary for the lesson. These conversations became sources of connections throughout the lesson.

The overlay graphic organizer depicted in Figure 7.3 can be used to simplify thinking about biography-driven instruction that uses activities and strategies to attend to the lesson's content and language objectives during the activation, connection, and affirmation phases of instruction. The sample lesson plan included exemplifies how teachers can plan lessons that integrate—in systematic, intentional ways—the biography-driven pillars of promising practices.

Linguistically Speaking: How Vocabulary Fits Into the Picture

Vocabulary is touted as the one essential ingredient for comprehension of text (Gottardo & Mueller, 2009; Tompkins, 2012; Vaughn & Linan-Thompson, 2004). Many frameworks and models exist for selecting and teaching vocabulary to grade-level and CLD students, including those of Marzano (2004), Beck and colleagues (2002), and Calderón (2007). (The work of Beck et al. and Calderón will be discussed in detail in the sections that follow.) Yet in many classrooms that I visit, educators continue to lament

how difficult it is to move students forward when they come to school with such "limited vocabulary." The teachers say there is not enough time in the day to fill in all the gaps necessary to meet the many vocabulary demands of the curriculum. They note that some students seem to lack linguistic ability in their native language as well as in English. "How will I ever meet these students' academic needs?" teachers often ask with distress in their voices.

What frequently prompts some of these concerns is a perspective on vocabulary that views language as a set of words that must be part of the linguistic makeup of each student. This perspective leads teachers to devote the majority of their time and attention to detecting "deficiencies" in students' word knowledge and then scrambling to help them "catch up." A perspective that leads to more productive efforts involves recognizing that *all* students bring large vocabularies. The difference in vocabulary knowledge that exists among our students often lies in the *kinds* of words they know. According to Schifini (1994), we each have words that make us individuals—words that help us express who we are and what we know. These same words can be used to teach academic concepts and corresponding academic words.

Biography-driven instruction provides us with a guide for setting the context and observing situational processes in order to determine CLD students' current linguistic resources. Students have gained their vocabulary knowledge from language use in the home and community, prior schooling, and other linguistic interactions. Once we know the words students *do bring* to our classrooms, we can better create opportunities for introducing new academic words during instruction. Effective vocabulary instruction, delivered in the course of teaching our curriculum's content-area concepts, requires that we educators study and explore words in order to make the best decisions about which words to teach, how to teach them, and ways we can build on what lies within CLD students' schemas to make links to their conceptual knowledge and linguistic repertoire.

Not All Words Are Created Equal

Beck and colleagues (2002), in their work on vocabulary development with native English-speaking students, present vocabulary words by classifying them into three tiers, which are used to explain the varying levels of difficulty among words. According to Beck and colleagues, Tier 1 words (e.g., *sun, rain, clouds*) for native English speakers do not require direct instruction because they are words that such students generally know prior to entering school. Tier 2 words are words with which students are already conceptually familiar (e.g., *temperature, front, moisture*). That is, native English speakers would be able to explain Tier 2 words using words that they already know, but they might not possess the exact academic term necessary to refer specifically to the concept. These Tier 2 words are important

FIGURE 7.3a
Biography-Driven Lesson Planning: Overlay

Three Phases of Teaching and Learning: Student Outcomes

Activation (Opening)	**How do the strategies implemented at the opening of the lesson:** • Activate and document students' background knowledge? • Provide opportunities for students to share, or make public, what they know? • Support students in making meaningful links to new learning? • Enable pre-assessment of the known? • Create conditions for students to connect their life experiences to new learning? • Allow students to use all their communicative resources (L1, L2, nonlinguistic representations) to express what they know?	**Know Your Community**
Connection (Work Time)	**How do the strategies implemented during the work time of the lesson:** • Promote students' use of listening, speaking, reading, and writing skills to ensure equitable access to the content? • Provide scaffolds for student learning? • Create conditions that encourage learners to practice and apply new vocabulary and concepts in meaningful and interactive ways? • Engage students in a variety of grouping configurations to promote dialogue that leads to linguistic and academic development? • Allow students to utilize translanguaging to support communication, comprehension, and expression? • Provide opportunities for formative assessment of cognitive processing and language use as students articulate, clarify, elaborate, and provide rationales? • Create opportunities for students to share and use their culture-bound ways of knowing and learning? • Support students to come to a thorough understanding and take ownership of the new information?	**Work with Your Community**
Affirmation (Closing)	**How do the strategies implemented at the closing of the lesson:** • Showcase the end results of students' effort and learning throughout the lesson? • Allow students to individually demonstrate their new understandings? • Encourage students to reflect on how the strategy supported and advanced their learning? • Provide opportunities for post-instructional assessment of planned outcomes that leads to meaningful application of learned language and concepts? Lift the classroom community by validating and celebrating the learning and language growth of all members?	**Reciprocal Accountability**

ZPD
Capitalizing on Academic Potential

***i*+1**
Utilizing Student Language

Biography-Driven Pillars of Promising Practices

Classroom Ecology	Vocabulary	Strategies	*i+Tpsl*	Checking Habits of Mind
Create a context conducive for orchestration of equitable access to the curriculum in a way that values all students' potential.	Select and use target vocabulary that supports progression from the known to the unknown based on learners' background knowledge and conceptual connections leading to comprehension.	Use strategies as tools to document linguistic and academic progress in order to differentiate instruction and scaffold student learning.	Systematically use ongoing techniques to promote application, rehearsal, and advancement of linguistic and academic development through socio-academic talk throughout the lesson.	• L1/L2 biography • State of mind • Bridge BICS to CALP • Situational accommodations • Revoicing • CLD student biography • Documented evidence of knowledge and learning • Standards-based outcomes

Traditional Lesson Components

• Standards • Objectives • Accommodations	• Materials • Essential Question • Vocabulary	• Learning Activities • HOT Questions (**H**igher **O**rder **T**hinking)	• Guided Practice • Independent Practice	• Assessment • Home Learning

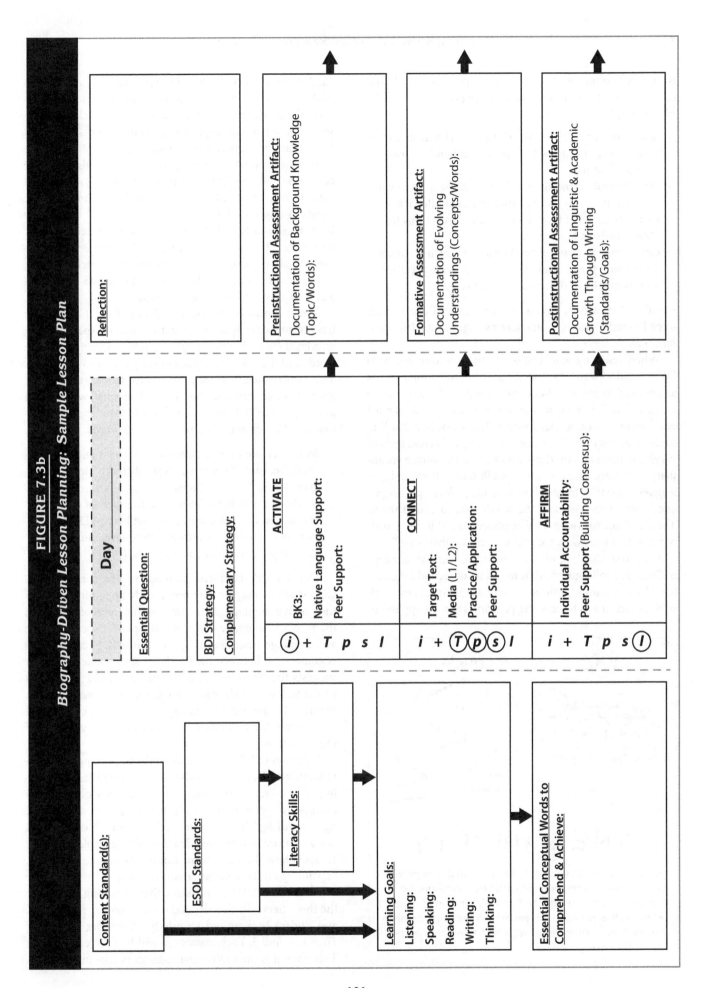

FIGURE 7.3b
Biography-Driven Lesson Planning: Sample Lesson Plan

Reflection:

Preinstructional Assessment Artifact:
Documentation of Background Knowledge (Topic/Words):

Formative Assessment Artifact:
Documentation of Evolving Understandings (Concepts/Words):

Postinstructional Assessment Artifact:
Documentation of Linguistic & Academic Growth Through Writing (Standards/Goals):

Day _____

Essential Question:

BDI Strategy:
Complementary Strategy:

ACTIVATE
BK3:
Native Language Support:
Peer Support:

(i) + T p s l

CONNECT
Target Text:
Media (L1/L2):
Practice/Application:
Peer Support:

i + $(T)(p)(s)$ l

AFFIRM
Individual Accountability:
Peer Support (Building Consensus):

i + T p s (l)

Content Standard(s):

ESOL Standards:

Literacy Skills:

Learning Goals:
Listening:
Speaking:
Reading:
Writing:
Thinking:

Essential Conceptual Words to Comprehend & Achieve:

to the development of mature language users. Beck and colleagues (p. 19) introduce the following considerations for identifying Tier 2 words:

- *Importance and utility:* Words that are characteristic of mature language users and appear frequently across a variety of domains.
- *Instructional potential:* Words that can be worked with in a variety of ways so that students can build rich representations of them and of their connections to other words and concepts.
- *Conceptual understanding:* Words for which students understand the general concept but provide precision and specificity in describing the concept.

Finally, Tier 3 words have a low frequency of use and are often limited to specific content areas (e.g., *barometric, nimbus, meteorology*).

When selecting words to teach, the question becomes "Why would I want my students to understand *these* words as opposed to others?" Beck and colleagues (2002) suggest that Tier 2 and Tier 3 words are the ones that educators must emphasize over basic Tier 1 words. Tier 2 words, according to these authors, are those that can be applied across texts of varying content areas and also are heard in the spoken vocabulary of mature language users. Additionally, Beck and colleagues emphasize the need for students to develop a heightened awareness regarding the words that surround them. These authors further note that students need to use words repeatedly if the words are ever to become "their own."

Calderón (2007) applies the tiered vocabulary concept of Beck and colleagues within the arena of second language learning, providing a three-tiered vocabulary framework with guidelines as to how the principles can be applied to

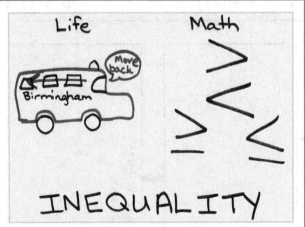

Providing students with an opportunity to define polysemous words using both linguistic and nonlinguistic representations can help scaffold their learning of these words. In this example, the teacher had the students relate the math vocabulary word *inequality* to their own background knowledge.

CLD students who are still in the process of acquiring English. Calderón reminds educators not to make assumptions about which words CLD students might already possess in their new language. Although in most cases it is safe to assume that native English-speaking students will be familiar with most age-appropriate Tier 1 words, the same cannot be said for CLD students. CLD students might need explicit instruction if they are not familiar with these basic words in English. However, CLD students will most likely know these words in their native language. Therefore, Tier 1 words are relatively easy to teach to CLD students. Educators can show pictures of these words to impart meaning, or the words can be translated into the student's native language to make the meaning apparent.

Tier 2 words, according to Calderón (2007), frequently have **cognates** in Spanish. Therefore, Spanish speakers have an advantage in that they might already be familiar with the words and the concepts represented by the word in English. Tier 2 words include content-area words that are used across a variety of academic contexts as well as small words, such as *by, if,* and *so,* that are essential to CLD students' comprehension. Calderón maintains that Tier 2 words

> do not receive as much attention as Tier 1 and Tier 3 words because ESL teachers typically teach Tier 1, and mainstream teachers focus on Tier 3 (content key) words. It's our hypothesis that the lack of explicit instruction of Tier 2 words is what keeps ELLs from moving on to Tier 3 words and thus developing reading comprehension of content texts. (p. 31)

Tier 3 words comprise content-specific concepts that CLD students may or may not already be familiar with in their native language, depending on their level of literacy in the primary language. Once again, Spanish speakers have an advantage when learning Tier 3 words, because many cognates exist between the two languages. Calderón (2007) suggests that these words/concepts be pre-taught to CLD students, using their native language whenever possible. Figure 7.4 elaborates on ways Spanish cognates can be used as resources for students' learning of vocabulary in each of the three tiers.

Calderón (2007) also discusses the importance of **polysemous words**, that is, words that can have different meanings depending on the context in which they occur. Some examples of polysemous words include "*power, cell, radical, right,* [and] *leg*" (p. 32). Tiers 1, 2, and 3 each can contain words that are polysemous. Teachers should explain to CLD students how the same word can have multiple meanings, depending on the context or content area.

Calderón (2007) emphasizes that "selecting words for the three tiers will also depend on the subject, grade level, and student background knowledge. *There are no lists for Tiers 1, 2, and 3. Each classroom will be different*" (p. 33). Therefore, it is imperative that educators take into account

FIGURE 7.4
Spanish Cognates Across Vocabulary Tiers

Tier 1 Cognates

Many words that end with *-ción* in Spanish can have the same meaning in English. Keep in mind, Tier 1 words are usually concepts that CLD students will already possess in their native language, although they may not be familiar with the *word* in English.

> *information* ⇒ *información*
> *preparation* ⇒ *preparación*
> *contribution* ⇒ *contribución*

Tier 2 Cognates

Tier 2 words, according to Calderón, frequently have cognates in Spanish. Therefore, Spanish speakers have an advantage in that they might already be familiar with the words and the concepts represented by the word in English.

> *disaster* ⇒ *desastre*
> *determine* ⇒ *determinar*
> *object* ⇒ *objeto*

Tier 3 Cognates

According to Calderón, "Literate Spanish speakers have a great advantage over monolingual English speakers with Tier 3 words because many cognates are high frequency words in Spanish but low frequency words in English (e.g., *coincidence/coincidencia, absurd/absurdo, concentrate/concéntrate,* and *fortunate/afortunado*" (p. 33).

Source: Adapted from Calderón (2007).

Cognates for Conceptual and Linguistic Understanding

Cognates have long been touted as a port of entry for students' transfer of conceptual and vocabulary knowledge from the native language to English. August and colleagues (2005) call attention to the importance of using students' first language as a resource for their understanding of new vocabulary and academic content during the lesson. Cognates are defined by August and colleagues as words in two languages that are similar "orthographically and semantically" (p. 52). Cognates can be used to support word recognition and entry into academic words within all three levels of tiered vocabulary. When students are taught to be aware

of how their language compares to the English language, they are more likely to view their language as an asset to learning. Students' native language can assist their understanding of many words that initially may appear to teachers to be too difficult for CLD learners.

Yet cognates are only an instructional asset when teachers guide CLD students in comparing and contrasting English with the language(s) they already know. This does not mean that teachers must become experts in every language represented in their classroom. However, teachers should encourage students to become "word detectives," and teachers themselves should be continually on the lookout for any language similarities that could be useful in helping students understand vocabulary and content.

Some educators comment on their hesitancy to use cognates in their practice because, as they do not speak the language of their students, they are unsure whether a word is a true cognate or a "false cognate"—that is, a word that sounds the same in two languages but has very different meanings in each language. Some examples of false cognates between English and Spanish are *embarrass* and *embarazada* (pregnant) and *exit* and *éxito* (success). Although we should be aware that false cognates exist, the use of cognates in teaching has proven to have many more benefits than drawbacks in inching CLD students toward greater comprehension. Figure 7.5 provides a list of English–Spanish cognates tied directly to content that have been collected from practicing teachers.

Linguistically Speaking: Drawing From Their Words

Research by Beck and colleagues (2002) and Calderón (2007) has helped to reinforce the importance of thinking about vocabulary in systematic and strategic ways. If we want students to have access to words that will accelerate their comprehension of academic content, then what we do with vocabulary during instruction matters. For many teachers, this involves a new way of thinking. Consider the insights of Ms. Lopez:

> For all the talk we have in schools on individualized and differentiated instruction, I had never thought that students would have different takes on the vocabulary I was teaching. I always had my list, based on what the book gave me, and that is what I taught. We talked about the words, read them in the book, looked in the dictionary, and finally drew a picture that would help the students remember them. Like robots, my students knew the drill. This year has been one of uncovering, discovering, and getting to know how my students think and what they know about the words. I've been amazed at how much I assumed and how wrong I was about their limited knowledge of English.

not only their CLD students' academic needs, but also the sociocultural, cognitive, and linguistic dimensions of their biographies when deciding which words to teach.

FIGURE 7.5
English–Spanish Cognates

Subject: ENGLISH

Abbreviation / Abreviación
Analogy / Analogía
Anecdote / Anécdota
Audience / Audiencia
Bibliography / Bibliografía
Biography / Biografía
Comprehension / Comprensión
Debate / Debate
Definition / Definición

Dialogue / Diálogo
Edit / Editar
Expression / Expresión
Novel / Novela
Allegory / Alegoría
Alliteration / Aliteración
Characterization / Caracterización
Chronological Order /
    Orden cronológico

Contrast / Contraste
Criticism / Criticismo
Description / Descripción
Descriptive language /
    Lenguaje descriptivo
Purpose / Propósito
Coherence / Coherencia
Cohesion / Cohesión
Exposition / Exposición

Subject: GENERAL HISTORY

Agriculture / Agricultura
Asia / Asia
Chronology / Cronología
Colonial government /
    Gobierno colonial
Colony / Colonia
Constitution / Constitución
Declaration of Independence /
    Declaración de independencia
Expansion / Expansión
Expedition / Expedición

Hemisphere / Hemisferio
History / Historia
Idea / Idea
Independence / Independencia
Justice / Justicia
Liberty / Libertad
Mayan calendar / Calendario maya
Middle class / Clase media
Minority / Minoría
Society / Sociedad
Civil rights / Derechos civiles

Cultural tradition /
    Tradición cultural
Cuneiform / Cuneiforme
Era / Era
Immigration / Inmigración
Pioneer / Pionero
Vote / Voto
Industrial revolution /
    Revolución industrial
Oral tradition / Tradición oral

Subject: MATH

Addition / Adición
Base / Base
Circle / Círculo
Circumference / Circunferencia
Classes of triangles /
    Clases de triángulos
Convert / Convertir
Decimal / Decimal
Diagram / Diagrama
Distance / Distancia
Division / División

Area / Area
Cardinal number / Número cardinal
Constant / Constante
Dispersion / Dispersión
Dividend / Dividendo
Equation / Ecuación
Perimeter / Perímetro
Prism / Prisma
Simplification / Simplificación
Absolute value / Valor absoluto
Equivalent fractions /
    Fracciones equivalentes

Experimental design /
    Diseño experimental
Geometric pattern /
    Patrón geométrico
Linear equation / Ecuación lineal
Logarithm / Logaritmo
Matrix / Matriz
Negative exponent /
    Exponente negativo
Subtraction algorithm /
    Substracción algorítmica

Subject: SCIENCE

Air / Aire
Conductor / Conductor
Ecosystem / Ecosistema
Formula / Fórmula
Gamma ray / Rayos gamma
Gas / Gas
Observation / Observación
Organism / Organismo
Science / Ciencia
Atom / Átomo

Balance / Balance
Cellular response / Respuesta celular
Condensation / Condensación
Digestive system / Sistema digestivo
Gravitational energy /
    Energía gravitacional
Photosynthesis / Fotosíntesis
Precipitation / Precipitación
Semiconductor / Semiconductor
Viscosity / Viscosidad

Asexual reproduction /
    Reproducción asexual
Atomic energy / Energía atómica
Experimental control /
    Control experimental
Hypothesis / Hipótesis
Meiosis / Meiosis
Protein / Proteína
Refraction / Refracción
Solubility / Solubilidad

In differentiated instruction, educators strive to make adaptations to their teaching to meet the needs of the particular individuals in the classroom. What this looks like during vocabulary instruction often tends to be a shade of gray, because teachers frequently continue to use the same worksheet or technique to teach vocabulary to all students, regardless of biography.

When selecting target vocabulary, consideration of the type of vocabulary words being identified directly affects CLD students. Vocabulary words that are merely new labels for concepts that CLD students already understand are approached differently than words that represent new and potentially difficult concepts (Garcia, 2003). Ultimately, the question becomes "When my CLD students finish this lesson, will they be able to tell me the essence of the story or concept I have been teaching, given the words I have selected as the target vocabulary?" Often, teachers will comment that there are too many words to teach. What is important to remember is that some words are taught through "incidental" opportunities, whereas others must be taught "intentionally." Understanding this distinction relieves undue pressure while still ensuring that words needed for content tests and high-stakes tests are made accessible to all students.

Critical to this entire process of selecting and teaching vocabulary words is knowing the biographies of all of our students! More specifically, it is essential that we teachers delve into our CLD students' funds of knowledge, prior knowledge, and academic knowledge. Knowing which concepts the student possesses in his or her native language will help us determine the type of instruction needed to teach key words. For example, if a student has already studied *fotosíntesis* (photosynthesis) in his or her native country, then a simple translation of the English term into Spanish may be all that is necessary to clarify the concept.

When educating CLD students, vocabulary instruction must be approached from the perspective that, although a student may not be proficient in English, he or she is surrounded by English words, words in the native language, and lived experiences that may support the teaching of the academic words. Consider the following scenario:

Saul, a middle school student, had been referred for testing given his slow academic progress. As is customary when I am invited to assess an ELL learner using multiple district assessments in Spanish, I began by getting to know the student prior to formally beginning the testing. That day I asked Saul to share a little about the school and his teachers. I was amazed at how articulate he was regarding his perception about what was right and what was lacking in his education.

First, he told me that not all teachers wanted him to learn. That is, some of his teachers, although they did not speak Spanish, went to great lengths to teach him the academic content so he could be a good student. Some, he said, were not as eager, and he thought they saw him as a slow learner, given his background. Since Saul had not mentioned his ESL teacher, I asked, "What about your ESL teacher?" He responded, "Oh! Her. . . . Well, she must serve lots of students at lots of schools, because she comes in here sweating everyday, pulls out some cards and starts to teach me all these words. We play bingo, memory games, and more games!" he responded. "What would you want to be different?" I asked. He said, "I want her to teach me the words that the mean teachers are not teaching me, the words I need so I can answer the questions. What she is teaching me I learn from my friends, watching TV, and just being here in the United States. I want her to teach me the words I need to be smart, the words to pass the classes so I can be a veterinarian when I grow up!"

Through this conversation, I realized that many of the words that teachers spend significant amounts of time on can be learned incidentally by CLD students—both through out-of-school experiences and through opportunities we provide for students to talk with one another and discuss as a class. Academic vocabulary, on the other hand, must be taught differently. Teachers must be intentional in their planning for explicit vocabulary instruction (Carlo et al., 2004; Fisher & Frey, 2010).

Teachers who set contexts for explicit instruction to teach Tier 1, 2, and 3 vocabulary prior to formally beginning the lesson create ecologies where culture and language help connect vocabulary to the content they teach. Words are selected systematically, taking into account the biographies of the students in the learning community. The number of words selected is limited by the relevance of the words to the most critical information about the concept. To provide students with multiple exposures that are culturally, linguistically, and academically connected to the learners, potential selections of vocabulary words may be further narrowed given the planned contexts. Teachers provide opportunities at the opening, during the work time, and at the closing of the lesson for students to discuss and use new words in multiple settings with a diverse group of their peers.

Students who are provided with opportunities to use words in meaningful ways and in a variety of contexts are much more likely to improve their oral language development, feel safe in voicing their learning, and take ownership of the target vocabulary. Selecting activities and strategies that support students' construction of meaning with the new words, discussing the relationship between the new words and what students already know, and, ultimately, defining these words by making cultural and linguistic links have the potential to improve academic learning for CLD students.

As stated earlier in this chapter, no one single activity or strategy is sufficient for teaching academic vocabulary. As educators, we must be attentive observers of students' culture and language so that we can maximize connections during instruction. In broad and narrow brushstrokes, our teaching can create opportunities for both incidental word learning and intentional word teaching.

Cognitively Speaking: Creating a Canvas of Opportunity for Disclosure

After selecting academic vocabulary words to be taught, educators embark on the path to making decisions about what will happen with these words during the activation, connection, and affirmation phases of the lesson. There are many models for the teaching of vocabulary that include explicit steps for introducing students to the academic content vocabulary. These steps have in common the following characteristics:

- The teacher is in control of the word, as demonstrated by his or her saying it, explaining it, and contextualizing it.
- Students are asked to repeat the word after the teacher to personally experience the word.
- Students work with a partner or team to practice the word.
- Students draw a nonlinguistic representation of the word.
- Students write a definition of the word using their own words.

Models that exhibit these characteristics are more teacher-centered and tend to limit the potential for CLD students to make lasting personal connections to the words as well as fully develop their English language skills.

During observations of lessons, I often see teachers explaining words from their own frame of reference while their students listen as idle participants. Consider the following scenario:

As I sat in the library waiting for the principal to arrive and let me know where to set up for the session on vocabulary development, I was drawn into a 5th-grade language arts class. The topic being addressed was the importance of understanding "sequence" when writing a story. The teacher offered a group of 28 Latino students the following explanation: "I love to cook," she said, "Have you all ever watched a cooking show on television?" The students all nodded in agreement. She continued, "Well, in a recipe, it is very important for you to follow the sequence." All students agreed. "If you don't follow the sequence," she added, "whatever you are cooking will not turn out right." At that time the bell rang, and all the students shuffled out of the classroom.

I was left wondering how many of the students actually had ever watched a cooking show and how many of their mothers used a recipe to cook. For nearly 10 minutes, the teacher had discussed sequence from her own lived experiences and what was important to her. This teacher would have helped her students more if she had asked them to each think to themselves of something they knew how to do or had seen done, like cooking something, or washing, or solving a problem, that had to be done one part or step at a time. Then she could have asked them to write or draw those steps, write numbers to indicate which came first, then second, then third, and explained to students that that was a sequence.

This type of classroom dynamic can be observed across the country in classrooms where students' background knowledge is, though often unintentionally, discounted in the course of instruction. Often we might find ourselves thinking that certain students have not had any contact with the academic words or concepts we are introducing. Yet this question remains: *How will we really know what students know, if we don't give them an opportunity to share their experiences with the new words before we go into our "teacher explanation" of the vocabulary?*

A Canvas of Opportunity: Spaces and Places for the Known

> What students already know about the content is one of the strongest indicators of how well they will learn new information relative to the content.
>
> —*Marzano (2004), p. 1*

Every day teachers begin new lessons based on curriculum guides or prescriptive programs assigned by their school or district. Absent from many of these initial activities are avenues for investigating students' background knowledge and interests. Learning can be thought of as a search for meaning, using formal education and one's own experiences as the foundation for making sense of new information. As the brain interacts with input from the environment, it forms patterns of understanding, or schemas (Caine & Caine, 1991). When the brain encounters new information, it interprets the information using existing schemas. Because these patterns of understanding develop through personal experience, schemas reflect the cultures and experiences of the learner (Quinn & Holland, 1987). More recently, brain research at the Max Planck Institute found that activation of prior knowledge speeds brain recognition of and learning about even the most challenging concepts (Melloni et al., 2011).

What we do during the activation phase of the lesson is important to the engagement and motivation of CLD students throughout the lesson. Many educators, based on their knowledge of or assumptions about students' levels of English proficiency and academic readiness, exclude students from full participation in the learning process by providing limited opportunities for involvement from the beginning of the lesson. According to Rubie-Davies and colleagues (2006), expectations are evident to students in the opportunities that educators provide, "in the affective climate created and in the interactional content and context of the classroom" (p. 430).

When planning a lesson, it is important to consider what will be done to learn about students' background knowledge related to the topic or vocabulary to be introduced. Many current strategies that exist for "activating" student engagement are effective for students who are willing to raise their hand or who are called upon by the teacher to respond to the stimulus. Often absent, however, are opportunities that require *all* students to respond and that hold students accountable—from the beginning of the lesson— for their participation. I refer to teachers' incorporation of such opportunities as creating a "canvas of opportunity" for every student to respond to a teacher prompt through listening, speaking, reading, or writing. Teachers then have a chance to collect from *every* student what he or she might perceive related to what is going to be taught.

For example, once we have selected words for instruction, we must provide students with opportunities to share personal associations and insights related to the vocabulary that might be useful to our instruction of the words throughout the course of the lesson. According to Honig and colleagues (2013), a student's knowledge of a particular word can be described in one of the following ways:

- The student has never seen or heard the word.
- The student has seen or heard the word before but does not know what it means.
- The student vaguely knows the meaning of the word and can associate it with a concept or context.
- The student knows the word well and can explain it and use it.

By allocating a small portion of our time to providing opportunities for students to share their personal connections to the target words, we are more likely to be able to teach/explain vocabulary using CLD students' background knowledge to accelerate learning. This will also support the vocabulary development of native English speakers.

Creating an opportunity for all students to respond before formally getting into the lesson enables teachers to move away from abstract ways of using students' background knowledge and toward specific ways of linking students' culture, language, and experiences to the content and vocabulary. Consider the Linking Language strategy presented in Figure 7.6. This activity provides students with an opportunity to make meaning using their own background knowledge and to make their knowledge public for the

learning community. It is through CLD students' negotiation of what is known and what is being learned that they are able to make sense of new language, vocabulary, and content.

Brain-Compatible Teaching and Learning

According to contextual learning theory, learners are most likely to process what is taught when they can connect it to their own frames of reference and patterns of understanding—their own schemas. The brain naturally attempts to make meaning of what is presented. It will do this by looking for relationships that make sense based on the individual's background.

Current research on how the brain learns has provided a much-needed look at what happens to learners during instruction. These findings may help teachers understand the importance of "igniting" the brain and then using culturally responsive and relevant ways of fueling students' learning. Although the work of many researchers and authors (e.g., Bjork et al., 2013; Bransford et al., 2000; Caine & Caine, 1991; Erlauer, 2003; Hammond, 2015; Jensen, 2006, 2008; Willis, 2006; Zadina, 2014) who focus on brain-compatible learning has informed my efforts, I draw most heavily on the work and writings of David Sousa (2017, for example) in explaining the process by which the brain makes sense of information. Figure 7.7 depicts Sousa's Information Processing Model and provides a simplified look at the overall process the brain goes through when making sense of new information.

According to Sousa (2017), the brain must first notice and perceive something before it can become engaged in

In this classroom, the teacher provided her students with an opportunity to work in small groups to look at pictures related to the topic and make instant connection to the content. These 2nd-grade students were able to record their immediate associations on paper and refer back to them during the learning process. *(Image courtesy of Christine Sloan, Elementary, Kansas)*

FIGURE 7.6
The Linking Language Strategy

Directions

- Select three or four pictures that illustrate key concepts from the lesson (pictures can be taken from the internet, clip art, or magazines, or the actual textbook pictures can be used).
- Tape each picture on the center of a large piece of chart paper (if using the textbook, place the textbook in the center of the chart paper).
- Divide the class into groups of four or five students.
- Instruct the students to write down everything they think of or feel when they look at the picture.
- Allow only 1–2 minutes for students in each group to write.
- Then have the whole group rotate to the next chart/picture.
- Continue until all groups have visited each picture.
- As students are working at each picture, rotate around the room and circle any words that come close to the target vocabulary or actually reflect the academic vocabulary for the day.
- At this time, you can work as a silent observer to reflect upon the knowledge that students bring to the learning community.

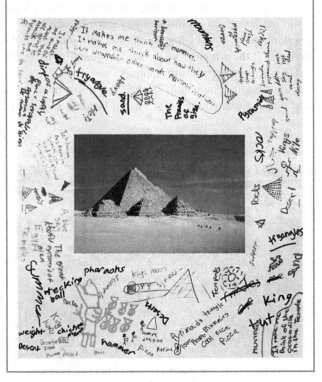

responding to what it is experiencing. If in that split second of stimulation the brain does not connect to the input, the brain's attention will move on to other things. In the classroom context, the stimulus is the introduction of the vocabulary or topic through a strategy that involves active student participation through listening, speaking, reading, or writing. The stimulus is some aspect of the information that the teacher wants students to understand (e.g., visual, written word, spoken word), as perceived through one or more of the learner's five senses. When any aspect of a new concept is introduced, the principles of neuroscience take effect. At this point, one of two things can happen. The new information can be either ignored or perceived by the student. If the new information is ignored or filtered out by the *sensory register,* no information is passed on and it disappears. On the other hand, if the student perceives (notices) this new information, it is passed on to the student's *sensory memory.* If the student perceives the new information through one of his or her five senses, it is stored in sensory memory only for a very short period (only seconds in length).

To increase the likelihood that information from the environment will make it through the filtering process and farther into a student's memory (and eventually, we hope, into the long-term memory), teachers should first activate the student's background knowledge about the topic through the use of multisensory activities and strategies. It is through the activation of the student's long-term memory (the funds of knowledge, prior knowledge, and academic knowledge that he or she already possesses), and through multisensory stimulation, that new information is transferred into the sensory memory and, from there, into the *immediate memory.* At this point, teachers have a window of opportunity in which to help the student make and record as many connections as possible between the new information and the concepts, words, and ideas he or she already knows.

Immediate memory lasts only for approximately 30 seconds. During those 30 seconds we can imagine the brain placing images, emotions, words, sounds, and so forth on a "clipboard" of sorts. The pieces placed on the clipboard come from both the new information that was recently received from sensory memory as well as information related to the learner's past experiences that is stored in his or her permanent memory. Our goal is to have students capture these immediate associations for later discussion and use during the learning process. These sometimes fleeting schematic connections, if documented, can be maintained, built upon, and navigated to help students better remember and understand the new material.

Information that successfully passes from immediate memory to *working memory* is then consciously processed by the learner (processing of information in immediate memory can take place either subconsciously or consciously). According to Sousa (2017), working memory is

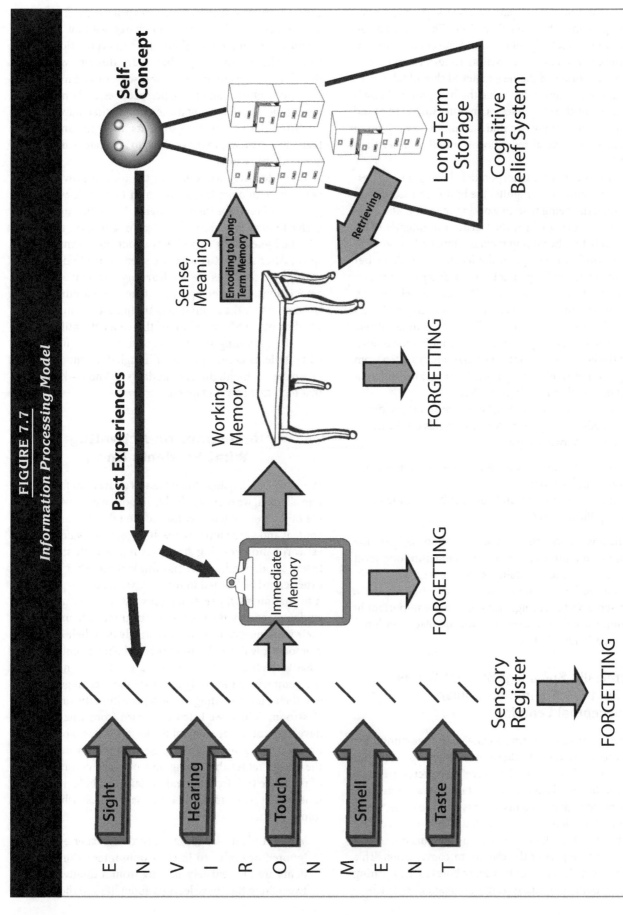

FIGURE 7.7
Information Processing Model

Self-Concept

Long-Term Storage

Cognitive Belief System

Sense, Meaning

Encoding to Long-Term Memory

Retrieving

Past Experiences

Working Memory

Immediate Memory

FORGETTING

FORGETTING

Sensory Register

FORGETTING

Sight

Hearing

Touch

Smell

Taste

E N V I R O N M E N T

Source: Sousa, D. A. *How the Brain Learns*, 5th Ed., p. 45. Copyright © 2017 by Corwin Press. Reprinted by permission of SAGE Publications.

where "we can build, take apart, or rework ideas for eventual storage somewhere else" (p. 51). The information placed on the "work table" of our mind can come from sensory/immediate memory as well as long-term memory. Therefore, repetition of the new material should take place within learning contexts that value the background knowledge the student already possesses. In other words, this kind of repetition does *not* involve students mindlessly repeating isolated facts. Beneficial repetition is *mindful* rather than mindless!

The various activities incorporated throughout the lesson reinforce (and further ignite) the brain's connections to the new material being held in working memory. The average time span during which the learner can intently focus on material before becoming mentally fatigued or bored is dependent on both the age of the learner and his or her motivation. In general, a preadolescent learner can focus on the material for approximately 5–10 minutes, whereas an adolescent or adult learner can focus intently for 10–20 minutes. As Sousa (2017) notes, "For focus to continue, there must be some change in the way the individual is dealing with the item. For example, the person may switch from thinking about it to physically using it, or making different connections to other learnings" (p. 54).

Whether the new material makes it from working memory into a student's long-term storage depends on the learner's assessment of two things:

- Does this make sense? Is it logically coherent in a way that I can understand?
- Does it have meaning? Can I connect it to my life in some significant way?

When the answer to either of these questions is "yes," the likelihood of the information being retained in long-term storage increases. The possibility of storage is greatest, however, when "yes" is the answer to both questions. Finally, between sense and meaning, *meaning* is more important in determining whether information will be placed in long-term storage (Sousa, 2017).

Academically Speaking: Student Words as a Link to Academic Vocabulary and Conceptual Learning

As I have discussed, creating a canvas of opportunity for students to show their background knowledge provides the teacher with insights that have far-reaching effects during the lesson. When teachers take the accumulated word knowledge that students possess and use these words as the point of departure for explanations of academic words, the CLD student's culture and language is much more likely to be part of the classroom conversation. This dynamic, in which every student contributes to the learning of the classroom community, cannot happen if we teachers continue to introduce words and explain them from a limited perspective that puts us in charge without providing avenues for students to share their interpretations of the words. The beauty of opening doors through which students' voices can emerge is in the discoveries we make about students' cultures, languages, perspectives, and understandings of the world. During the lesson, we then have multiple opportunities to return to students' thoughts and reroute them, as necessary, to move them to accurate definitions of the academic words.

Often teachers will question the idea of providing students with an open forum in which they write whatever a given word reminds them of, saying, "Isn't that guessing?" I prefer to liken this part of the learning process to making educated guesses or hypotheses about the meaning of the word. After all, that is what we spend our life doing with words and concepts we are learning. We make tentative associations, test their appropriateness and accuracy given the context, and continue negotiating the meaning of the word or our understanding of the concept until we get it right. By providing these ecological contexts and guiding CLD students as they proceed through different situational processes, we highlight what students *do* know—knowledge that too often goes untapped.

Reflections on Activating What Students Know

When we begin using student assets as avenues for moving into a lesson, we increase the likelihood that we will achieve the objectives we have set for meeting the standards of the content and grade level we teach. By igniting student interest early and choosing strategies that ask all students to listen, speak, read, write, and think about what they have experienced or learned in the past, we set the stage for new information to move from sensory input (stimulus) to students' sensory memory, to their immediate memory, to their working memory, and eventually into their long-term memory. It is through our efforts to help students uncover what they already know that we are able to bring them to the point where they fully negotiate the meanings of words and their understanding of concepts within the safety of the classroom. When we listen and learn from what students have to say at the opening of the lesson, we are able to draw on their background knowledge during the work time of the lesson, rather than using only our own cultural frames of reference to introduce and explain vocabulary and content concepts. Cummins (1996) says it best when he reminds us that

When students' language, culture and experience are ignored or excluded in classroom interactions, students are immediately starting from a disadvantage. Everything they have learned about life and the world up to this point is being dismissed as irrelevant to school learning; there are few points of connection to curriculum materials or instruction and so students are expected to learn in an experiential vacuum. Students' silence and nonparticipation under these conditions have frequently been misinterpreted as lack of academic ability or effort, and teachers' interactions with students have reflected a pattern of low expectations that become self-fulfilling. (pp. 2–3)

In short, the context we create and the opportunities we provide in our classroom must make it clear that we respect and value the experiences and knowledge that each student brings to our learning community. Holding every student accountable for what he or she knows does much to increase student engagement and learning.

Chapter 8 will discuss how to work with target vocabulary during the lesson, using insights gained from observations made in the activation phase. It provides ideas about how we teachers can plan for:

- Using students' native language, experiences, and other assets as points of connection during the lesson
- Orchestrating meaningful student interaction based on student biographies
- Using vocabulary multiple times and in multiple contexts
- Using text to make connections and draw attention to important content-specific vocabulary and concepts

Lessons that are prescriptive in nature and preplanned based solely on the curriculum, without taking into account the learner, begin from a flawed point of departure. Every student in every classroom has something to share. It is up to the teacher to decide whether he or she will give students an opportunity to disclose their knowledge so that those assets can be used in the learning process.

8

Connection

Navigating From the Known to the Unknown

GUIDING QUESTION

What teacher pedagogical actions during the lesson help ensure that student voices are heard and valued as learners make sense of and bring meaning to new information/learning?

See the online Discussion Guide for opportunities to further explore answers to this question and connections to chapter content with a colleague or team. Available for download from the Teachers College Press website: tcpress.com

THE PRECEDING CHAPTER examined core considerations for opening a culturally responsive, sustaining lesson. If we educators want to move beyond a deficit perspective, we must take full advantage of student potential and harvest language and conceptual knowledge based on each student's background knowledge. We can then enter the lesson ready to navigate and negotiate the known. We must align what students bring to the classroom with our standards and objectives so that we are prepared to scaffold and differentiate our lesson, given the observed and documented responses of the learner. Having observed for students' funds of knowledge, prior knowledge, and academic knowledge, we must next make decisions about what to do with the student assets and identified "gaps" in background knowledge. This chapter explores the connection, or "work time" phase (often referred to as the "during" phase) of instruction, when the teacher employs culturally responsive pedagogy during the lesson as he or she uses the information gathered in the opening of the lesson. I discuss why such efforts during instruction are important and describe what this kind of pedagogy looks like in practice.

In hundreds of hours spent collaborating with teachers across the country on preparing and delivering lessons to increase CLD students' motivation, engagement, and academic achievement, I have often observed teachers plan and proceed into the lesson with wonderful strategies for differentiating instruction so that all their students can be successful. Often missing from their preparation, however, is a strategic plan for **contextualization**, or using students' biographies for making decisions about contextual and situa-tional processes and the types of challenging activities that will advance each student's learning (CREDE, 2021). During instruction, teachers may underestimate the importance of their own active listening and documentation as students work to make meaning of the new content. Active listening is essential to our ability to document how students are cognitively processing the information. It is only with these insights that we are able to guide and reroute students as the lesson progresses and respond in ways that lead to a greater level of understanding and student affirmation.

Creating a third space is key to the connection phase of the lesson cycle. In the third space, we as educators stand at the intersection of the curriculum and school, our own positionality and biography, and the biographies, knowledge systems, and biopsychosocial histories of the learners in our community. We support students to navigate the curriculum in ways that highlight the interplay (including tensions) among curricular/dominant ways of viewing, interpreting, and knowing the world and their own ways. How do we do this? The first step is by becoming part of the learning process. This requires our willingness to engage on a personal level with learners, allowing them space to question, connect, and teach us how the content relates to their world. We must be ready to juxtapose our culturally influenced views with theirs, as we work together to come to an understanding of the content that moves us all forward. This is what learning is all about—this is the power of diversity in our classrooms. Diversity of perspective, when combined with opportunities for honest dialogue and collaboration, creates the conditions for liberatory practices. It supports hybridization and co-creation of knowledge, language, and culture by drawing on the collective wealth of assets present in our community (Bhabha, 1994). As teachers navigate student learning, they continually connect what is being taught in school to what is happening in the lives of students, especially as they are making sense of new content and language. It is during this work time phase that educators help students connect the dots between what they already know and what they are intended to learn during the lesson. Teachers employ everything they know about both the science and the art of teaching to support students' development of language and literacy, as well as content knowledge and skills. Teaching that occurs in the third space has a much greater chance of being comprehensible to the learner, because it builds on what he or she already knows.

Transformative Comprehensible Input

According to Krashen (1982, 1984/2005, 1985), providing comprehensible input means giving students language input that is one step beyond their current level of competence and is made understandable through

- Context (e.g., visual aids),
- Extralinguistic information (e.g., nonverbal signals or body language), and/or
- Students' existing knowledge of the world.

Comprehensible input is equally important to both language and content learning (Lucas et al., 2008). Such input ensures that the information being presented by the teacher and negotiated by the learning community is accessible to all students. Providing comprehensible input has long been one of the crucial ways educators have sought to accommodate the linguistic and academic needs of emergent bilinguals. Efforts to provide English learners with comprehensible input have generally focused on four fundamental components: hands-on activities/manipulatives, cooperative learning, guarded vocabulary, and visuals. These components are detailed in Figure 8.1, along with a BDI perspective on each.

Teachers who have emergent bilinguals in their classrooms use these four components to guide their instructional planning and to monitor their delivery of that instruction. For example, teachers may try to control their rate of speech, avoid using idioms, and use supplemental materials to help make the content accessible. Although these are great ways to begin meeting students' needs, traditional ways of providing comprehensible input are not sufficient for sparking engagement and optimal learning. Many other factors (some previously discussed in this text) can inhibit learning. If the contextual and situational processes of the classroom have not been planned with specific consideration for the diverse members of the learning community, anxiety and fear may keep students from fully participating and taking risks in learning. Krashen (1985) finds that language acquisition can occur only when comprehensible input passes through a student's affective filter. In classrooms where teacher lecture is the norm, students may demonstrate low levels of "risk taking" and, at the end of the day, less learning.

More recently, Krashen and Mason (2020) argue that not all comprehensible input is of equal value. Comprehensible input from a biography-driven perspective takes on additional meaning through reciprocal activity in which the teacher draws on knowledge of the student biography as well as observations about how the learner makes sense of and brings meaning to the linguistic and academic input. Transformative comprehensible input requires back-and-forth cycles of listening and responding to students as they process language and content. Learners are supported to comprehend content material through actions that ensure their sociocultural, linguistic, cognitive, and academic needs are met and that connections are made between the new information and what they already know. For instance, merely showing a picture associated with a vocabulary word does not guarantee that the student will make a connection. Rather, the learner must be provided an opportunity to voice, or make public, how he or she is interpreting the visual (Zadina, 2014). Using BDI power strategies that set the conditions or stage for comprehensible input to occur also multiplies opportunities to gain insights into students' background knowledge.

We as teachers then need to make use of the documented evidence of knowledge and learning that we have collected situationally, in the moment. We use these insights to provide each student with $i+1$ linguistic input and to stretch learners to engage academically in their ZPD by employing comprehensible input techniques in purposeful ways during the lesson.

Effective educators focus their efforts, regardless of students' linguistic or academic levels, on the attainment of meaning. They do this by actively engaging students in the learning environment and by implementing strategies that use the words and concepts students *do* know in explaining and elaborating the target vocabulary and content.

Consider the DOTS strategy, which was discussed in Chapters 6 and 7 and is summarized in Figure 8.2 (see also Appendix C). Figure 8.2 illustrates how this strategy requires mutual investment from both the teacher and the student throughout the lesson as they engage in back-and-forth cycles of listening and responding.

In this strategy, students first record their background knowledge connections to the topic in the A–Z boxes of the template. The teacher documents these foundational insights, recognizing them as keys to unlocking greater student understanding throughout the remainder of the lesson. These connections support the teacher to provide comprehensible input in ways that uniquely target individual students' needs, because the connections reflect what was learned about students' funds of knowledge, prior knowledge, and academic knowledge.

The words or illustrations recorded on the DOTS chart provide the teacher with an inside look at how learners made sense of the topic during the activation phase of the lesson. As the lesson progresses into the connection phase, the teacher uses the words, ideas, and concepts shared by the learning community to support comprehensibility of input. Knowledge of students' previous experience with the topic allows us to make informed decisions related to the various components of comprehensible input described in Figure 8.1. Moreover, the structure of the DOTS strategy itself ensures that these components already are built into the lesson.

Specifically, use of the DOTS chart provides each learner with a hands-on tool for:

- Documenting background knowledge in the activation phase
- Making physical connections between words, ideas, and concepts in the connection phase
- Scaffolding talk during classroom discussions
- Supporting self-evaluation and postinstructional assessment of learning in the affirmation phase

Insights gleaned about students' background knowledge in the opening of the lesson also inform our situational decisions about which types of cooperative learning, or which interaction structures (e.g., pair/partner, small team), will best support learning as the lesson moves forward. This documentation also supports our decisions about which

---

FIGURE 8.1
Components of Comprehensible Input

Hands-On Activities/Manipulatives

Definition:	**Benefits:**	**BDI Perspective:**
Cooperstein and Kocevar-Weidinger (2004) explain that through the use of hands-on activities and manipulatives "abstract concepts become meaningful, transferable, and retained because they are attached to performance of an activity" (p. 145)	• Can lead to increased student–student/student–teacher interactions • Create opportunities for students to interact with the subject matter being studied • Activate the sense of touch and thereby increase the likelihood that students will attach meaning to the content they are learning • Provide CLD students at any level of English language proficiency with an outlet for demonstrating their learning (Echevarría et al., 2016)	• Are provided through the context of BDI strategies, which incorporate hands-on tools to support student learning • Afford opportunities for joint productive activity, in which the teacher and students work together to document how the learning community is actively negotiating the curriculum and constructing knowledge, individually and collectively • Provide scaffolds that can be used throughout the lesson cycle to ensure that all learners are supported to attain the lesson objectives

Cooperative Learning

Definition:	**Benefits:**	**BDI Perspective:**
"Cooperative learning is the instructional use of small groups through which students work together to maximize their own and each other's learning" (D. W. Johnson et al., 1994)	• Emphasizes reliance on positive interdependence among learners; the success of each group member is dependent upon that of his or her cooperating peers—one cannot succeed without the others • Encourages students to work together in order to complete specific tasks while simultaneously fostering important social skills • "Cooperative learning is a helpful way to discuss other cultural groups' perspectives, and such groups allow ELLs to feel comfortable speaking while they are developing English fluency" (Lacina et al., 2006, p. 140)	• Is most effective when pairs and small teams are configured to ensure that the assets of each individual member can be used to benefit the learning of other members • Allows students to support one another's learning as they articulate their views, judgments, and processes; ask and answer clarifying questions; and provide rationales • Provides teachers with formative assessment data as students negotiate the *sense* and *meaning* of academic and linguistic input with peers

students should be paired or grouped together to most effectively support each learner's social, linguistic, cognitive, and academic growth.

Teachers implementing the DOTS strategy leave the activation phase with a better understanding of how to guard vocabulary during the work time phase of the lesson. They are able to use students' words as a starting point to scaffold learners toward use of the academic language needed to successfully attain the lesson's objectives. Educators also have an increased awareness of the kinds of visuals that already support CLD student understanding of the topic in personally relevant ways. Incorporating these visuals during instructional conversations illustrates how the experiences of individual students can support comprehension of the lesson for the entire learning community.

The DOTS strategy exemplifies how BDI strategies provide teachers with a supportive frame for ensuring that key components of comprehensible input are provided *naturally* throughout the lesson. We teachers carefully attend to student responses to such scaffolds, increasing or decreasing the level of support or shifting the type of support in order to meet their current learning needs.

Throughout this book, I have provided scenarios, examples, tips, and ideas for educators to consider. It is my hope that you will continue to reflect back on all you have read thus far and utilize those ideas as you think about ways to provide learners with meaningful access through optimal comprehensible input. As students learn from and about the English language through content embedded in a rich context, they develop their English language skills and reach high levels of academic success. In addition, when teachers

---

FIGURE 8.1
Continued

Guarded Vocabulary

Definition:	**Characteristics:**	**BDI Perspective:**
Guarded vocabulary involves efforts to reduce the linguistic load in order to increase comprehensibility of instruction for CLD students (Herrera & Murry, 2016)	• Using speech that is appropriate for CLD students at their specific stage of English language acquisition (Echevarría et al., 2016) • Simplifying sentence structure—using subject, verb, object order versus passive or more complex sentence structures (Echevarría et al., 2016) • Avoiding idioms such as "It's a piece of cake" (Echevarría et al., 2016) • Calling attention to cognates (e.g., information = información) (Echevarría et al., 2016)	• Asking students to record words they associate with the topic provides words that can be used to scaffold academic language development • Providing opportunities for students to document native language connections to the topic supports translanguaging, meaningful use of cognates, and transfer of knowledge from L1 to L2 • Revoicing and elaborating on student connections allow teachers to reduce or increase the linguistic load for members of the learning community

Visuals

Definition:	**Benefits:**	**BDI Perspective:**
"The use of photos, media, computers, drawings, charts, tables, diagrams, and more to illustrate concepts and processes in classroom instruction" (Herrera & Murry, 2016, p. 265)	• Activate CLD students' background knowledge, in their native language or in English, thereby leading to increased reading and listening comprehension (Tang, 1993) • Support comprehension of text; such visuals include graphic organizers, charts, diagrams, and webs that can help CLD students organize their thoughts in a way that is meaningful for them (Echevarría & Graves, 2015) • Supplemental materials, including visuals, can be employed to increase CLD students' comprehension of content-area material (Echevarría et al., 2016)	• Students' illustrations of background knowledge connections to the topic provide insights into visuals that already are personally meaningful for learners • BDI strategy tools often look similar to traditional graphic organizers, but differ in how they are used by the teacher and students throughout all phases of lesson delivery to document visually the step-by-step learning process • Use of visuals throughout the lesson is based on students' responses to instruction, and can include visuals generated or selected by both the teacher and the learners

FIGURE 8.2
DOTS Strategy

I am responsible to . . .

STUDENT (D)

- Determine what I know about the topic/vocabulary before the lesson starts
- Decide what I am learning during the lesson to document what is important as evidence of my learning
- Evaluate what I learned and how I learned it

STUDENT (O)

- Observe for clues the teacher provides on what is important and relevant
- As I read the text, be observant for what the message is and what meaning I bring to the text
- Use selective attention and document my observations, as evidence of what I have learned and where I found the information

STUDENT (T)

Use the tool as a resource to
- Use the vocabulary to discuss my conceptual understanding
- Listen to others and clarify by asking questions
- Consider others' perspectives
- Build consensus.
- Plan, elaborate, clarify, and make connections

STUDENT (S)

Use the tool as a resource to summarize, solve, and/or synthesize the information in writing in order to share what I have learned

DETERMINE **OBSERVE** **TALK** **SUMMARIZE, SOLVE, SYNTHESIZE**

D O T S

When: Before, During, & After

How: Activate, Connect, Affirm

TEACHER (D)

Determine what the student knows—before, during, and after the lesson—by activating, connecting, and affirming knowledge/assets from all knowledge systems. Use the information for *i* +1 (language) and ZPD (academic development) through instructional conversations

TEACHER (O)

- Observe affective filters and information processing by continuously using the DOTS chart to formatively assess
- Use the vocabulary, student talk, and student notes for decision making about scaffolds that would support student learning in the moment

TEACHER (T)

- Set conditions for academic talk to occur (intentional)
- Select structures and grouping configurations that are intentional and based on the needs of each learner
- Provide structured opportunities as springboards for academic talk, and ask higher order questions based on student processing of information
- Use the tool to revoice using the students' words
- Make meaningful links for the classroom community using students' words

TEACHER (S)

Use the tool as a resource to help students summarize, solve, and/or synthesize the information in writing to provide meaningful opportunities to share what has been learned

116

Providing students with a canvas for sharing what they know about a word makes public for the teacher how the student is interpreting what he or she is seeing, hearing, and reading. This then becomes a source of information the teacher can use for bridging the student's knowledge to the content concepts. In this example, one of Mrs. Teran-Pinion's 1st-grade students heard the word "moth" instead of "moss," which was the target vocabulary word. Mrs. Teran-Pinion was then able to work with the student to pronounce and read the word, supporting the student by rerouting her understanding of the word before the lesson. *(Image courtesy of Marisol Teran-Pinion, 1st Grade, Kansas)*

select and implement strategies that position all students as capable contributors to the learning process, students begin to develop a positive cognitive belief system and see the learning activities as true opportunities for engagement.

Activities Versus Strategies

In recent years, there has been a great deal of discussion about the importance of teachers both recognizing the implications of brain research for education and adjusting their instruction to capitalize on the way the brain processes information (e.g., Hammond, 2015; Sousa, 2017; Zadina, 2014). Information that is currently available calls attention to the educational realities of CLD students and the types of experiences and interactions they have in the classroom. At every moment during instruction, students learning a second language experience "input" within two processing spheres, the linguistic and the academic. The more that is done to plan for what I call "broad and narrow brush-strokes of teaching and learning," that is, bold, large-scale actions and fine, detailed words and behaviors that focus on moving students from the known to the unknown, the more we ensure that students have pathways for reaching a thorough understanding of the content by making sense of what is presented and bringing meaning to it.

An **activity** is a teacher-generated opportunity for students to interact with the curriculum. Activities are initiated and facilitated by the teacher to provide students with a hook to connect to the lesson and to move the lesson forward. We teachers use activities to (a) provide a canvas of opportunity for students to share with us what they know from their prior experiences, (b) support students in making connections between what they know and the new material, and (c) provide opportunities for students to demonstrate what they know. Targeted and systematic modeling of activities eventually enables students to use these activities in more independent ways to take responsibility for their own learning.

Strategies should not exist in isolation. A strategy that students have adopted gains effectiveness and becomes a student-owned **learning strategy** through continued, consistent use. In this context, the definition of a strategy according to Afflerbach and colleagues (2008) is "a systematic plan, consciously adapted and monitored, to improve one's performance in learning" (p. 365). As educators, one of our intents is to provide students with skills that support their learning beyond their time in our classrooms. This happens when teachers select activities that have potential beyond scaffolding of lesson content. Eventually, these activities become student-owned strategies that facilitate comprehension and allow students to take responsibility for their own learning.

Figure 8.3 shows how a teacher has used the foldable activity (Herrera, Kavimandan, & Holmes, 2011) as a tool for guided note-taking during a lesson. He moved from teacher-directed, partner, and small-team components to students' individual completion of the task. It was exciting for this teacher when other teachers began to comment about students using the foldable as a study tool in their classrooms. This teacher's CLD students also have commented on how the foldable has helped them earn higher scores in their other classes. Selecting teacher activities and tools that, with practice and application, have the potential to be adopted by the students as their own learning strategies should be one of the central goals of our teaching.

Students can apply a wide range of strategies to comprehend, interpret, and evaluate their learning. They draw on their prior experience, interactions with peers, knowledge of word meaning, and other strategies they have learned to make sense of talk and text. Teachers can move beyond traditional ways of thinking about student learning strategies and use strategies that both support students' content understanding and teach students to utilize their language and cultural experiences. Such practices connect the biography of the learner to cognitive, metacognitive, and social/affective learning strategies that have proven effective in increasing academic achievement for CLD students. Maximizing the benefits of using these types of learning strategies during instruction with students is the focus of discussion in subsequent sections of this chapter.

When I think of learning strategies, I think of the ways many parents coach their children to "work through" difficult times they might have in school. Often I have told my

FIGURE 8.3
From Teacher Activities to Student Learning Strategies

Select teacher activities that have the potential to become cognitive, metacognitive, or social affective strategies for students in the future. In this example, the teacher uses a foldable to guide the students in taking notes in sequence as he presents vocabulary and concepts. *(Image courtesy of James Sparks, High School, Kansas)*

Students are given opportunities to practice using the foldable by comparing what they have written with peers in the classroom. The teacher reminds students to add additional information from the textbook. *(Image courtesy of James Sparks, High School, Kansas)*

After observation, the teacher makes the decision to have students work independently. The students are encouraged to make sense of the information as it relates to their own lives and their own learning needs. *(Image courtesy of James Sparks, High School, Kansas)*

The foldable ultimately becomes a tool to be used to study for a test, to synthesize the information learned, or as a scaffold for responding to questions after the lesson. The tool has become a learning strategy for the student when he or she uses it to support his or her own learning across content areas.

own children to close their eyes and "visualize" what they have been studying in order to remember information when taking a test. These and other little tricks help them to see ways they can recall information, get through giving a speech in front of the class, or call a friend when they do not remember how to solve a difficult equation. Some learning strategies start at home and later are elaborated upon in school. Teachers can explicitly model, practice, and apply the three types of learning strategies detailed in the academic literature: cognitive strategies, metacognitive strategies, and social/affective strategies (see Figure 4.4 for Chamot & O'Malley's [1994] examples of such strategies). When consistently implemented across lessons and content topics, these strategies can lead CLD students to better take responsibility for and control of their own learning.

Cognitive Strategies: Tools in My Hands

Cognitive learning strategies are those tools that students can use to learn through the rehearsal, organization, or elaboration of material. Consider the following scenario and ask yourself: How has this teacher used the mind map as a strategy for guiding student thought from the known to the unknown?

Mr. Hanley was getting ready to start a lesson with his 7th-grade social studies class on what changes a person's character. His objective was to connect students' responses to a novel the class was getting ready to read. He gave each student a piece of blank paper and had them create a basic mind map in which they drew and wrote life events they had experienced that had changed the way they behaved or thought about the world. Examples of such events included becoming the oldest child in the home after an older sibling moved out, moving to a new location, or changing schools and trying to fit into the new school. Students also indicated whether the events and

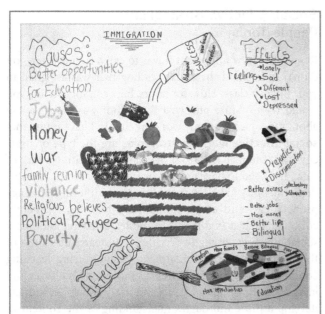

Cognitive strategies support students as they rehearse and retrieve information. In this example, students worked cooperatively to write and draw what they remembered as a group about the concept of "immigration."

circumstances transformed their character in positive or negative ways.

After they had finished this activation phase of the lesson, Mr. Hanley told his class that one of the objectives of the reading for the next week was to add the main characters of the novel to their own mind maps as they read. Using a pen of a different color, the students were to incorporate the individuals in the story and what was happening to them in the novel that was causing them to change the way they behaved and looked at the world (their personal character). Mr. Hanley reminded the students to use both pictures and words to document what was happening in the novel. He also asked them to draw and make notations about any connections between their own lives and the lives or feelings of the characters in the novel.

At the end of their study of the novel, Mr. Hanley's students used yet another color of pen to document whether the changes in the characters in the story had contributed to how things had turned out in the end. Then, using the mind map as a tool, students summarized what had happened in the novel and connected it to their own lives—past, present, and future. In this way, Mr. Hanley demonstrated how a mind map can be used as a tool for keeping notes and making sense of what one is reading. He reminded students that when they are preparing for a test, they can follow five easy steps:

- Jot down everything you can remember about the topic. Write or draw what you remember.

- Look at the study guide you have been provided and determine which questions you would be able to answer, given what you remember.
- Go back to your notes and your text and then add to your mind map what you left out, using pictures and words.
- Use the mind map to study by aligning the questions with the words and pictures you jotted down.
- Create a visual representation of the mind map in your memory.

By using the mind map as an instructional strategy, Mr. Hanley was able to first activate students' permanent memory to gain access to their background knowledge related to the topic. Throughout the remainder of the lesson (and during subsequent lessons), he was then able to facilitate students' learning and explicitly model how the mind map can be a tool for:

- Elaborating on prior knowledge
- Taking notes
- Organizing information
- Summarizing

Metacognitive Strategies: Tools in My Head

Metacognitive learning strategies include those strategies that lead students to monitor their own learning and the success of their in-progress efforts to understand new material. In essence, metacognitive strategies are ways of paying conscious attention to what and how we are thinking. Metacognitive strategies have great potential to enhance CLD students' comprehension during and after the lesson. When teachers ask students to think about the connections they make as they read or as they learn while the teacher or peers talk, they are better able to actively listen and make links to the content and language objectives of the lesson. Metacognitive strategies help to demystify the learning process and to lower CLD students' anxiety, which is often provoked by being in a linguistically demanding learning environment. Consider the following scenario:

Using her story bag strategy, Ms. Kavimandan asked her students to predict which 8 of the 12 words that were listed on the board were going to be in the story. She read the title of the book and showed several of the pictures. She then asked students to write the words they had selected on 3 × 5 cards (one word per card). After writing the words, they were told to write or draw why they thought the selected word was going to be in the story and whether they had heard, seen, or could define the word. Students were encouraged to make an educated guess and write what they thought the word *might* mean.

Ms. Kavimandan then asked the students to place their series of selected words in front of them because they were going to be listening for the words as she read. Their task was to use a strategy that involved applying their selective attention skills to listen for these very important words they had identified. She told them that she would be stopping at different points in the lesson to give them an opportunity to discuss what they had heard about the words and, as a team, they would begin to define the words in context.

Ms. Kavimandan was very explicit about having students understand that when they were learning new vocabulary, the ability to read and know why you are reading is important. She also told them that having questions about what we are reading sometimes helps us not to become overwhelmed with very difficult reading. She proceeded to explain that there are multiple ways to confirm answers to the questions we have. One way is through reading, and another is through listening attentively to what the teacher has to say about a word or topic. Ms. Kavimandan let students know that through the use of metacognitive strategies, they can plan for their learning and continually self-monitor their understanding of what is being read or taught during the lesson.

Explicit instruction on metacognitive strategies supports CLD students in performing metacognitive activities such as the following (N. J. Anderson, 2002; Brown, 1980; Chamot, 2009; Chamot & O'Malley, 1994):

- Clarifying the purposes of reading and the demands inherent to the task
- Identifying significant aspects of a message
- Allocating attention
- Monitoring ongoing activities
- Engaging in review and self-questioning with regard to attainment of goals
- Taking corrective action when necessary
- Recovering from distractions and disruptions

Metacognitive strategies are especially useful for helping all students understand how they can become more efficient learners. Through advance organization, students become *prepared* readers, listeners, and active participants. Through selective attention, students become more *aware* of what they are reading or hearing. By monitoring their comprehension, students become *strategic* in their learning efforts as they read, respond, write, and discuss. Finally, by monitoring their production, students become *reflective* learners and language users throughout the lesson (N. J. Anderson, 2002; Chamot, 2009; Chamot & O'Malley, 1994; Swartz & Perkins, 1987).

Social/Affective Strategies: People Tools

Remember how important it was to call a friend when you didn't understand the dense reading that was assigned in your English class? How, for hours, between socializing, you would try to figure out what the author was really saying about the topic? From my work in schools, I have found that **social/affective learning strategies** are the type of strategy most often absent from the classroom. Citing a lack of time, the need to have control over the classroom, and students' inability to help one another given differing language proficiencies and academic abilities, teachers frequently comment that it is difficult to model, practice, and apply social/affective strategies. Yet these strategies are some of the most effective for creating cohesive, caring learning communities in which differences in students' cultures and languages are valued as assets and used to help all learners develop a more thorough understanding of the content as well as a more global perspective.

A safe, supportive, inquiry-based environment in which students frequently have opportunities to interact with their peers encourages all students to meet our high expectations for learning. What the teacher does to prepare students to work in cooperation with one another, to learn how to ask questions when something is beyond their grasp, and to learn to risk without fear of being ridiculed is of utmost importance. Students should understand that when facing challenging concepts and tasks, they should feel comfort-

Pair work is one way of creating a learning community in a classroom that is low-risk and that emphasizes the importance of teamwork. As students worked in pairs on this strategy, they were encouraged to ask each other questions for clarification and work together to find answers as they moved forward with their learning task. This kind of interaction is important for the creation of a balanced learning community and for the development of social/affective skills.

able with coming together for problem solving. After all, this is how most adults determine how to solve problems when the answer is not evident.

Consider this scenario and reflect on how the teacher is creating opportunities for students to learn social/affective strategies:

> Mr. Rojas always reminds his students that no one in the classroom possesses all the answers, all the time. He continually tells students that one of the greatest gifts that comes from different students using different strategies to arrive at the same answer is that the class always has more than one way of looking at a problem. To prove the point, he selected multiple excerpts from the novel he was introducing, read them to the class, and had the students individually sketch and label each selection he had read. The students then compared their thoughts and ideas, first with a partner and then within small groups. In this way, each student's cultural and linguistic thoughts were made public.
>
> In the groups, the students next worked together to sketch and label what they predicted the novel was going to be about. Mr. Rojas then asked them to discuss within their groups the following questions:

- What were the commonalities in what was heard, sketched, and labeled?
- Were these commonalities derived from personal experiences or school knowledge?
- What were the differences?
- What were the sources of these differences?
- What was the group's prediction, and how were group members able to come to agreement?

This type of activity allows students to value the input of each student as well as clarify and elaborate on concepts. Merely having students turn and talk to a partner at some point in the lesson does not achieve the same results as the planned use of social/affective strategies to promote higher order thinking and relationship-building. Social/affective strategies, when planned with a definite purpose and outcome in mind, can enhance learning and lead to relationships that reach beyond classroom walls.

Social/affective strategies can support CLD students as they generate questions about the content, relate ideas and questions to their own lives, and risk using language (if grouping configurations are strategically planned based on sociocultural, linguistic, academic, and cognitive factors). Students are more likely to engage with the curriculum if they perceive that they have a support system to use during and after the lesson. In short, cognitive, metacognitive, and social/affective strategies enable teachers to gradually release ownership of and responsibility for learning to the learners themselves.

Navigating Socioemotional States of Mind

CLD students, like all students, are eager to become members of the community of learners. However, many CLD students have feelings of failure that stem from perceptions (on their part or on the part of their teachers or peers) of incompetence or inability to fully participate due to language or cultural background. Some students will say, "Why try? I usually fail." In these instances, we can choose either to ignore the student's concern or to think about the context and situational processes we create, making sure that everyone in the classroom experiences success.

For many of our CLD students, the individual's behavior often can be connected to his or her current state of mind. Sometimes we may be seeing the results of fear, anxiety, boredom, apathy, frustration, or confusion. At other times we may sense students' anticipation, excitement, and curiosity. As discussed in Chapter 6, states of mind vary given what is happening in the classroom. Have you ever watched students begin to slump in their chairs after an especially difficult lesson? What do you choose to do when this happens? Tsai and colleagues (2008) write about the importance of the learner's psychological state. A learner's state is affected by both external and situational stimuli. Such stimuli have a stronger impact on creating a positive (or negative) state of mind than do individual learner variables.

The best way to promote positive states of mind for CLD learners throughout a lesson is to do the following:

- Select activities that create situational interest.
- Move into the lesson using strategies that change the general context and situation often enough to support autonomy, facilitate memory processes, and create positive learning interactions.
- Use the native language when needed.
- Provide positive performance feedback.

Figure 8.4 summarizes considerations for the successful navigation of students' states of mind.

From Interest to Practice and Application

Teachers who understand the importance of interest and motivation to the learning process are cognizant of the rhythm and duration of tasks and interactions during a lesson. Given the biographies of our learners, we must plan lessons to ensure that practice and application are chunked into time frames that provide students with time to process what they have been learning. In so doing, we make it possible for students to "work smarter, not harder" and increase the chances that what we have taught will be retained. According to Sousa (2017), if information is going in faster than it can be sorted and placed, it becomes a big pile that may clutter the brain and lead to reduced learning. If the

FIGURE 8.4

Tips for Navigating Students' States of Mind

- Understand that there are thousands of states of mind, both positive and negative.
- Know that states of mind can be changed, because they exist at individual points in time.
- Realize that being aware of what our CLD students are feeling, thinking, and learning helps us tap into their states of mind.
- Remember that when we change negative states of mind to positive ones, we enhance student learning!
- Keep CLD students' affective filters low to promote positive states of mind.
- Provide comprehensible input through varying degrees of linguistically and cognitively demanding tasks.
- Vary group structures (e.g., total group, pairs, small teams, individual) and use purposeful group configurations.
- Incorporate strategic use of the native language.

student cannot make sense of or find personal meaning in what is being taught, little retention will occur. However, by planning lessons that provide students with multiple opportunities for interacting with multiple people along the way as they maximize internal and external resources to grapple with new concepts and vocabulary, we increase the likelihood that students' states of mind will remain positively slanted toward learning (Shein, 2012).

Jensen (2008) advises that if educators want students to learn what they are teaching, they must be aware of their students' states of mind, and navigate them. In addition, we must actively monitor our own state of mind. One of the most easily managed aspects of our situational processes is our ability to configure and reconfigure the context in which we teach, based on our learners' social, emotional, linguistic, and academic needs.

From Individualism, Competition, and Cooperation to Biography-Driven Grouping Configurations

Cooperative learning has been a topic of great interest to educational and sociological researchers for many years. In fact, in 2009 D. W. Johnson and R. T. Johnson noted that more than 1,200 studies had been carried out across 11 decades on the subjects of individualistic, competitive, and cooperative efforts, and this number has continued to grow. Overwhelming evidence clearly illustrates the benefits that cooperative learning has for all group members, when com-

pared with more individualistic or competitive experiences (e.g., Deutsch, 1949; D. W. Johnson & R. T. Johnson, 1989, 2009; D. W. Johnson et al., 1983; Lewin, 1935; Pepitone, 1980; Triplett, 1898). Among these benefits are increases in student productivity, achievement, use of higher order thinking skills, idea generation, long-term retention, transfer of learning from one context to another, as well as higher intrinsic motivation and expectations for success (D. W. Johnson & R. T. Johnson, 2009; R. T. Johnson & D. W. Johnson, 1994).

R. T. Johnson and D. W. Johnson (1994) attest:

Our research and the research of many others dating back to the late 1800s has established that having students work together cooperatively is a powerful way for them to learn and has positive effects on the classroom and school climate. This has been verified by teachers in classrooms from preschool through graduate school. However, the importance of emphasizing cooperative learning in classrooms goes beyond just achievement, positive relationships, and psychological health. (p. 43)

These authors extend their findings to encompass the overall well-being of society, stating that most day-to-day situations require a person to understand and get along with others. Therefore, lessons learned during school-based cooperative learning carry over to situations in the workplace as well as to personal relationships with others. *While competition benefits few, cooperation has the potential to benefit all!*

Biography-Driven Grouping Configurations

It is the office [responsibility] of the school environment to . . . see to it that each individual gets an opportunity to escape from the limitations of the social group in which he was born, and to come into living contact with a broader environment.

—*John Dewey (1916/2007, p. 23)*

Long ago, John Dewey eloquently wrote about the conditional and situational processes that existed for students who came from cultural environments that were different from those of the school setting. He reminded readers that coming into contact with others from diverse backgrounds was essential to the broader development of all students. Today, when we educators are working with learning communities that mirror the diverse society in which we live, we must use a variety of grouping configurations in order to create space for all of our students to come together in learning. By providing students with opportunities to cooperatively learn with and from others whose biographies are different from their own, we provide the learners in our classroom the opportunity to see the world through a different sociocultural, linguistic, cognitive, and academic lens.

In this setting, Mr. Pride separated his class into small teams so that students could discuss the new content with one another. Over the course of the 50-minute science lesson, the students were organized into several different grouping structures and configurations. They began the activation process individually. Next, they moved into pairs, and then transitioned to small teams. During small-team discussion, each team was assigned a topic and team members were asked to become experts on it with help from the other members of their learning community. As the teams worked, Mr. Pride and a paraprofessional rotated around the room to listen to students' conversations. *(Image courtesy of Jeremy Pride, Middle School, Kansas)*

One of the most effective ways to ensure this kind of learning is to design pairs and **small teams** based both on the task and on the biographies of the students. Group configurations that support the teaching of content as well as engage and motivate students require high levels of interaction among all students, regardless of language or academic level. Such interactive student teams do not form without thought and action on the part of the teacher. They must be planned strategically and aligned with the dynamics of human and ecological factors at play during instruction. Configurations that are designed merely for classroom management, or simply to ensure that the class is "doing" cooperative learning, are less likely to promote an ecology where learners' states of mind are anticipated and navigated to create positive cooperative learning results.

Planning for biography-driven grouping configurations involves thinking about the following:

- Insights gained during the first phase of the lesson regarding the assets and needs of the CLD learner and the community. These insights inform decisions about the kinds of grouping structures and configurations that will best meet learners' needs for this lesson.
- Biographies of the individual CLD students
- Skills necessary to complete the task, including academic knowledge and vocabulary
- Time available for employing multiple structures, each with a specific purpose

- Complexity and demands of the curriculum. The more complex and decontextualized the information, the more critical is the students' need for scaffolding and comprehensible input.
- Insights gained during the lesson about students' states of mind

We must always remember to think of engagement and motivation as responses to our willingness to vary instruction, challenge all students, and allow the cultural and linguistic resources of CLD students to be used while they are mastering academic content. In addition, Brock and Raphael (2005) urge educators to recognize the importance of supporting students' learning by using a variety of educational contexts and interaction patterns. These contexts and interaction patterns should be designed to promote both academic and social relationships (Urdan & Schoenfelder, 2006).

Consider the following scenario and ask yourself, "What does this scenario tell us about the power of relationships in academic success?"

After a professional development session involving a group of CLD students and their teachers, a young lady came up to me and shared the following story:

I came to the United States when I was in the 4th grade. I hated going to school every day. I felt so out of place, and everything moved so fast. In Mexico I had been a very smart student; here I felt like a failure. The only thing that saved me was my friend Sophie. I remember my teacher would always move us around a lot to work with different students in the class. My eyes were always full of tears because I thought no one liked me because I was different. I was poor, didn't speak English, and my family was not like everyone else. As we were placed in groups to work, I remember how Sophie always found a way to sit next to me in our groups. She also seemed to want to be my partner. Her smile and voice when she would say, "Don't cry, I'll help you," helped me get through many days. In a few months I will be graduating from high school, and Sophie and I help each other out in lots of ways. I have learned so much from her, and today I can say she is passing her AP Spanish class because she has learned from me. So thank you for telling teachers to use teams/groups in their classes. For people like me, it's a matter of survival!

That day I learned from this young lady that grouping configurations are not only about language and academics. They are about the community and climate that are essential for engagement, motivation, and academic success. At one level they create environments that teach, and at another they develop spaces were students can establish mentoring relationships and friendships, built on trust and respect.

Collaboration with teachers has further solidified my understanding of the power of interaction in the learning environment. When making decisions about which grouping structures and configurations would be best, given the content and language objectives of the lesson as well as the students' biographies, I like to remember the following five steps:

* Start by igniting and documenting what students bring from their background.
* Based on this information, consider the pairs and small teams that likely will move each student forward linguistically and academically during the lesson.
* Consider each student's emotional needs and his or her current state of mind.
* Remember the accountability measures you have selected for the end of the lesson, and consider ways you will want to document the linguistic and academic growth of students during the lesson.
* Remember that you are not grouping solely for student cooperation (i.e., students should not be working only with their self-selected friends). To make the most effective use of your instructional time, you are strategically configuring teams of learners that will support one another in their linguistic, academic, and social development.

Figure 8.5 presents a brief overview of cooperative learning, both from more traditional perspectives and from the perspective of biography-driven instruction.

In culturally responsive pedagogy, the goal is to move from the biography of each student to instruction, and then to have the lesson culminate with the student's awareness of how much he or she has learned linguistically and academically. Meeting this goal requires the use of grouping configurations that keep *all* students engaged and motivated to learn. Our team of researchers refers to this conceptualization of the role of grouping configurations in the teaching/learning process as *i+TpsI*. In the previous edition of this text, *i+TpsI* was introduced as a model for grouping configurations. However, countless classroom visits and multiple discussions with educators have led me in this edition to refer to *i+TpsI* as a technique that supports educators to systematically and situationally plan and implement grouping structures/configurations based on the task, students' biographies and socioemotional states of mind, and the planned learning outcomes for the lesson. What then does *i+TpsI* (pronounced "I plus tipsy") represent?

* **i** (individual student) = The "*i*" refers to the opportunities the teacher provides to students in the opening phase of the lesson to activate their background knowledge (funds of knowledge, prior knowledge, and academic knowledge) and share that knowledge with the

---

FIGURE 8.5
Overview of Cooperative Learning

Cooperative Learning

* Concept of **positive interdependence** predominates, that is, the notion that *without you* and all that *you* have to offer, the task cannot be completed
* Importance of **interdependence** among collaborating students
* **Face-to-face interaction** among participants
* Holding both the **individual and the group accountable** for the outcomes
* Teaching of interpersonal skills and skills needed to work in small groups
* Self-reflection and discussion among group members regarding the effectiveness of group processes

Source: D. W. Johnson et al. (1994).

Kagan Structures

* **Definition:** "A Kagan structure is a **content-free, repeatable sequence of steps** designed to structure the interaction of students with each other and/or the curriculum in ways which align with basic principles and efficiently realize specific learning outcomes" (Kagan, 2000)
* Structures are based on cooperative learning philosophy
* Structures, as discussed by Kagan, are based upon four main principles:
  * Positive interdependence
  * Individual accountability
  * Equal participation
  * Simultaneous interaction

Biography-Driven Cooperative Learning

* **Cognitive:** Fostering cooperative learning opportunities for CLD students that cognitively stretch them to their *i*+1 level. Are students thinking critically about the material or just repeating information?
* **Academic:** Using grouping structures that support CLD students' attainment of the learning objectives. Does the composition of the grouping structures promote CLD students' content understanding and language proficiencies?
* **Sociocultural:** Purposefully arranging conditions that support sharing, cooperation, and collaboration among all students. Are students' funds of knowledge, prior knowledge, and academic knowledge used in the cooperative construction of meaning?
* **Linguistic:** Building upon student knowledge gained through the native language as well as through English. Are students allowed to make contributions to cooperative learning endeavors using both their L1 and L2?

rest of the learning community. These initial schematic connections become students' own unique cognitive scaffolds and serve as building blocks for community knowledge construction as well.

- **T** (teacher-directed, text-driven, total group) = Armed with a new understanding of students' background knowledge that can be used for the explanation of new vocabulary, introduction of new concepts, or adaptation of curriculum or lesson delivery, the teacher enters the work time phase of the lesson. What the teacher has learned from the "*i*" has implications for how he or she will help students move from the known to the unknown. Ultimately, the "*T*" refers to the teacher-directed aspects of the lesson in which the educator teaches the whole, or total, group through activities that are largely text- or standards-driven. During total group instruction, the teacher has the power and responsibility to lead students to a greater depth of content and language understanding as he or she translates curricular standards into practice for learners. Only the teacher brings the content and pedagogical expertise needed to orchestrate instruction in ways that lead to increased student comprehension, given each learner's unique past experiences and knowledge. Fortunately, teachers do not work alone; each student and his or her peers actively contribute throughout the learning process.

- **p** (pairs/partners) = The teacher considers various opportunities for pairs or partners that will accelerate students' learning of language and content concepts. Pair/partner work provides opportunities for students to practice, clarify, use their native language, and elaborate in a context that lowers their affective filters.

- **s** (small teams) = The teacher makes decisions about small teams, in which CLD students will have extended opportunities to build consensus, return to the text to check for understanding, observe and listen to more proficient language models, and rehearse language and content for collective and individual accountability. Small teams are designed to ensure that all students, including CLD learners, have opportunities to teach and to model for peers.

- **I** (individual accountability) = In the closing phase of the lesson (to be discussed in detail in Chapter 9), students should feel more empowered as learners and should possess a greater level of linguistic and academic knowledge. The teacher assesses individual growth, with students being held accountable for what they learned in relation to where they started. Through the validation, encouragement, and affirmation provided by the teacher, students strengthen their cognitive belief system and build more positive perceptions of themselves as capable learners.

This mnemonic reminds teachers that learning is an interactive process that moves from student knowledge, to curriculum learning, and back to the student. This interaction happens through different structures (*i, T, p, s, I*), with pairs and small teams configured in biography-driven ways. Frequent, systematic opportunities for student interaction with the teacher and peers occur through different contexts, conditions, and situations throughout the lesson. Such learning and teaching processes make social and academic talk public for the benefit of the entire learning community. Using strategic grouping configurations increases the chance that each student will share something of significance to the lesson that can then be used as a springboard for meeting the lesson's objectives. Giving students space to move through multiple grouping configurations allows them to engage with individual accountability throughout the lesson. Through intentional, strategic use of grouping structures and configurations, teachers promote student engagement and provide scaffolding and comprehensible input that supports all learners to achieve the learning outcomes of the lesson. Figure 8.6 offers ways to maximize *i+TpsI* grouping configurations to support the ebb and flow of instruction. Figure 8.7 provides a checklist for reflecting on the ways we maximized *i+TpsI* grouping configurations in a given lesson.

"i" *as the Anchor to Learning*

I like to think of every student in every classroom as having something in their background that anchors them to their own learning. Sometimes the link is a stretch, but as breathing and thinking individuals, we are always trying to make sense of the world around us. I spent many years as a second language learner wishing there were just split seconds during instruction when I could say to someone: "I know. . . . I remember when. . . . I know something that looks like that. . . ." Yet most teachers seemed to be in a hurry to teach me something. I often observe the same urgency in the classrooms I visit: "Get your books out. . . . Let's get started. . . . Soon we will be out of time." Sometimes there is a brief "Here it is—make a connection" and then the lesson moves on. When I hear and see this, I wonder how many students in the classroom have something to say, or how many already know something about the vocabulary or topic being explained or introduced.

As discussed in Chapter 7, the activation and documentation of students' background knowledge is an important goal to strive for. As teachers, we first need to become keen observers to record or make a mental note related to what students know from both their experiential and their academic backgrounds. With this information as a resource, we have new tools in the form of pictures, words, or stories from the students that can be used to move the class toward

FIGURE 8.6
The Ebb and Flow of i+TpsI

Helping Students Develop Conceptual Understanding and Boost Language and Academic Development

i+TpsI is a way of maximizing the "ebb and flow" of interaction/academic talk and instructional conversation as it occurs naturally in response to instruction. As you plan, ask yourself if you have been *"Tpsi"* by strategically designing activities, selecting cooperative structures, and "shuffling" grouping structures/configurations based on students' need and potential. The key is to situationally monitor processing, learning, and need (linguistic, academic, cognitive, and sociocultural) to take students to their ZPD. Below is a selection of activities that you might consider utilizing at different points in your lesson as you use *i+TpsI* to maximize your students' potential. Your decisions will be based on:

1. The BDI strategy you choose (outcomes: listening, speaking, reading, writing, thinking)
2. The reciprocal act of entering into social and academic talk—instructional conversation
3. The socioemotional, academic, and linguistic needs of your students

i Activate student background knowledge	T Total class	p Partners	s Small teams	I Individual
What I know about the topic/concept/vocabulary	Teacher-Led, Standards & Text-Driven	Question, Clarify, Elaborate	Perspective Taking, Consensus Building	Written Accountability
Opening	**Work Time**	**Work Time**		**Throughout**
BDI Strategies: • DOTS • Linking Language • U-C-ME • Extension Wheel • IDEA • Mind Maps • Foldables • Pictures and Words • Magic Book	• Whole group discussions • Concept-building • PowerPoints • Socratic seminars • Read alouds • Choral responses	• Listen Right • Think-Pair-Share • Turn and Talk • Shoulder Talk • Read and Review • Stand-Up, Hand-Up, Pair-Up • Partner Skim and Share • Explain to Your Neighbor • Study, Tell, Help, Check • Inside-Outside Circle	• Consensus Builder • Take One, Give One • Take, Compare, Share • Thumb Challenge • Around the World • Team Windows • Jigsaw • All Record Consensus	• Quick Write • Quick Draw • Exit Ticket • 3,2,1 • I Wish, I Question, Next Steps • Cornell Notes • Word Splash • Think and Write • Schema Maps

Postinstructional Task/Assessment

The BDI Strategy/Tool continues to be used to document learning.

Utilize the BDI strategy to set the conditions for this to happen.

Grouping	What did you do to support your CLD students' sociocultural, linguistic, academic, and cognitive dimensions throughout the learning process?
i = Individual student	☐ Student interest in the lesson was sparked through stimulation of one or more of the five senses. ☐ All students were provided with opportunities to document and share their initial connections between the topic and their background knowledge (i.e., funds of knowledge, prior knowledge, and academic knowledge). ☐ Awareness and understanding of learners' biopsychosocial histories informed responses to the ideas and language produced.
T = Teacher-directed, text-driven, total group	☐ Whole-group modeling, discussion, and/or authentic application of learnings in practice occurred. ☐ Whole-group activities were structured to provide explicit opportunities for CLD students to interact with their peers. ☐ Students were provided with opportunities to discuss, synthesize, and infer from their own unique perspectives as they participated in group discussions. ☐ Whole-group activities were strategically designed to provide emergent bilinguals with English language modeling by the teacher and/or more proficient peers as they interacted to enhance their understanding of the text and concepts.
p = Pairs/partners	☐ CLD students worked with partners to support their comprehension of academic tasks through one-on-one discussion and authentic practice and application of content-based learnings. ☐ Emergent bilinguals worked with a more proficient peer who could speak the native language and clarify information in the native language, if needed. ☐ Partners produced a product that demonstrated their understanding of a critical concept or vocabulary term.
s = Small teams	☐ Students worked in small teams so that they could hear multiple perspectives, check their understanding, build consensus, and elaborate on their own schemas. ☐ Teams were purposely configured so that emergent bilinguals were able to see and hear language modeled by more proficient peers. ☐ Small teams were held accountable to demonstrate their learnings informally or formally.
I = Individual accountability	☐ Students independently practiced and applied their learnings. ☐ Individual activities allowed students to demonstrate what they had learned. ☐ Authentic assessments were implemented that enabled emergent bilinguals at multiple language proficiency levels to successfully demonstrate their learnings.

FIGURE 8.7 i+Tpsl Grouping Configurations Checklist

a greater understanding of the vocabulary and content concepts to be taught.

A professor of mine continually reminded us that "from small words come bigger and bigger words." All writing and learning begins with a single picture, word, or story. As future teachers, we had to think about how we would "dig" for the knowledge that students would bring to our lessons. What would we do with student assets we discovered? We had to reflect on how we could use student assets during the lesson to benefit our learners. If we simply left students' background knowledge behind, we limited the potential for academic achievement by our CLD learners. Somehow, we needed not only to uncover experiential and academic knowledge but also to use the information in positive ways. I learned never to discount what my learners brought to the lesson, knowing that if I did, I was discounting their culture, language, and life. This was as true for the students I taught in public schools as it was for the students incarcerated in the youth facilities in which I worked. Becoming familiar with the types of knowledge that our CLD students already have is the first step in being able to address their learning needs. Once familiar with the funds of knowledge, prior knowledge, and academic knowledge they possess, we can use this information to address state standards and the curriculum at hand. In reflecting on ways to encourage students to make connections between what they know and the new information we are teaching, consider the following scenario:

> A few years ago I was co-teaching a lesson in a 5th-grade classroom, where the story was on Thurgood Marshall. The other teacher, Ms. Melton, and I had agreed that we would use the Vocabulary Quilt strategy (see Appendix E) as the activation activity for the lesson. She passed out all the quilts for the students to work in teams of 4. She had strategically placed the students in their teams based on what she knew about their home and school biographies and the objectives of the lesson. We wanted to learn how many of the target vocabulary words, which included terms such as *judge, courthouse, justice,* and *Supreme Court,* the students could relate to past experiences in or out of school.
>
> Ms. Melton asked the students to go to the quilt and then quickly and silently write what was in their brains related to each of the terms. Ms. Melton was visibly excited about what was happening. It seemed that each of the teams had written several words that were directly associated with six of the eight vocabulary words on the quilt. Given what she was hearing and seeing, she asked each of the teams to write a statement related to their life experiences using the target vocabulary words on 3 × 5 cards. That day Ms. Melton not only learned about what this group of students knew about the topic but she also got a glimpse into their daily lives, which included friends, family, or themselves having first-hand immigration and other experiences within the legal system. She learned that there were two terms she would have to focus on during the lesson: *Supreme Court* and *justice.* It also was evident that, together, these students had many life experiences that would be useful for their understanding of the new material.
>
> As the class read the story about Thurgood Marshall during the lesson, Ms. Melton returned several times to the stories students had shared and the words they had written. By the end of the lesson, they knew what *justice* meant in their world. They also understood why the Supreme Court is of such importance to our society.

As teachers, we must remind ourselves that students are not passive recipients but rather active participants in learning. The activation of background knowledge encourages students to be "connection makers" during the lesson,

continually making links between new material and their own background knowledge. These connections are more likely to happen when we intentionally consider the CLD student biography so that the sociocultural, linguistic, cognitive, and academic assets and needs of our CLD students are taken into account throughout the lesson. We make decisions about how to group students and adapt the curriculum at two levels. We make initial decisions going into the first part of the lesson based on what we know about our students' biographies. Later, as we enter the work time phase of the lesson, our decisions are informed by what we have learned as silent observers of our students.

"i" + "TpsI": *Multiple Meaningful Exposures Using the Same Biographical Anchor*

During the lesson, the teacher serves as a facilitator by making connections to the background information he or she gained from students in the activation phase. Connections are made to the objectives of the lesson, the vocabulary, the key concepts, and the overall content. According to Sousa (2017),

> To convince a learner's brain to persist with that [a given] objective, teachers need to be more mindful of helping students establish *meaning*. . . . Past experiences always influence new learning. . . . If we expect students to find meaning, we need to be certain that today's curriculum contains connections to *their* past experiences, not just ours. (p. 57)

Going from the "*i*" into "*TpsI*" requires teachers to consider the kinds of total group, pairing/partnering, and small-team work that will provide the best avenues for students' continued associations, interaction, clarification, and elaboration of the new material. As you read the following scenario, consider how the teacher first encourages every individual in the learning community to share what he or she knows and then uses resulting insights in the construction of knowledge.

> A few years ago I was observing a social studies teacher as he taught a lesson. He very effectively stated his content and language objectives and put out the materials needed for implementing the Vocabulary Quilt strategy (see Appendix E) to activate students' knowledge related to the vocabulary words for the chapter. He proceeded to give students the directions and form student teams, placing students according to where he thought they might be able to learn from one another's culture and language.
>
> Soon after the students had started working on the quilt, he moved over to one of his "intermediate" ELL students and pointed to the word *efficient.* This was one of the eight words that were part of the lesson.

As I, too, moved over, I noticed that the student had drawn a building with many windows. When the teacher smiled and asked about the drawing, the student shared with him that this was where she lived. He asked why she had drawn it for the word *efficient.* The student responded that she lived in an efficiency apartment. The teacher then asked if she knew why it was called an efficiency apartment, and she replied, "No." I wondered what he would do with this exchange as he moved on to other students and noted what they had written. The teacher then returned to the front of the room and jotted on the board some of the words, along with his sketch of the building.

Next, he asked his students to take out their textbooks. This week the focus was on efficient machinery, and he told the students that they were going to further explore the target vocabulary as they read the chapter and as he helped explain the words. The lesson proceeded with some partner reading, with portions of the text being read aloud by the teacher. He stopped at different points and went over to the board to talk about the students' words and their relation to the concepts. I observed that he had yet to point out the building or ask the student to explain her rationale for having drawn a building.

As the lesson began to come to closure, the teacher went over to the student and said, "Today the prize goes to Delia. She drew an efficiency apartment during our Vocabulary Quilt at the beginning of the lesson. Turn and talk to a partner. How is an efficiency apartment like an efficient machine?" After allowing a brief time for partners to share, the teacher then walked over to Delia again and asked her the question. Beaming, she said, "An efficiency apartment uses very little gas and electricity and does not take long to clean, so it's like a machine that does not use too much energy."

"You are a very bright student," he said, "Now, everyone return to your quilt and associate what you wrote at the beginning of the lesson with what you learned. You can use others' ideas since we have been discussing everyone's words during the lesson. Make sure to cross out the words or pictures that do not fit with what we have studied. You have 10 minutes to think and talk in your teams, and then I will ask you to work alone." As the students headed toward their teams, the teacher and I both smiled.

In observations of this teacher and others like him, I have listened to and learned from their use of traditional techniques of scaffolding to support learning in ways that are both culturally relevant *and responsive* to the CLD students in their classrooms.

Scaffolding From Student Words/ Thoughts to New Learning

We never really cognitively understand something until we can create a model or metaphor that is derived from our unique personal world.
—*Eric Jensen (2008, p. 168)*

New ways of orchestrating comprehensible input, as discussed earlier in this chapter, lead to new perspectives on ways teachers can scaffold classroom practice to achieve a higher level of CLD student engagement, motivation, and learning. The biographies of our students affect what they bring to a given lesson, and this background knowledge, in turn, determines how we will use visuals, grouping configurations, meaningful activities, and student language to scaffold our teaching and guard our own language use during instruction. The key is to think of scaffolding as guided by students' biographies. CLD learners will use scaffolds at different times for different purposes. Understanding students' needs and assets informs our decisions about which types of scaffolds will be most effective.

According to Dickson and colleagues (1993), scaffolding of instruction relates to how the teacher provides support for learners through the selection and use of materials, types of tasks, and interactions among students and between students and the teacher. Larkin (2002) notes, "scaffolding is a process in which students are given support until they can apply new skills and strategies independently." Instructional scaffolding has roots in Vygotsky's (1978) notion of the learner initially needing support in the learning process.

After students have been provided with the opportunity to make public the associations they made with the target vocabulary, Mrs. Teran-Pinion begins to have them think about the words in relation to the story that will be read that week. The scaffolding begins as she explains the words in context, begins to define them, and reroutes students' thinking toward the correct meaning of each word. *(Image courtesy of Marisol Teran-Pinion, 1st Grade, Kansas)*

As learning progresses, the support systems that have been employed during the practice and application part of the lesson are gradually removed, allowing the student to take responsibility for independently demonstrating what he or she has learned.

In culturally responsive pedagogy, providing instructional scaffolding goes beyond simply deploying superficial "safety nets" for the learner. Instead, the teacher must be strategic about the types of student support he or she uses during each phase of the lesson. Such supports include the following:

- Language and content objectives
- Activities that activate students' background knowledge about a topic and allow for use of pictorial representations as well as the native language and English
- Associations made throughout the lesson to students' documented background knowledge
- Ongoing opportunities for learners to make full use of their linguistic repertoire through **translanguaging** as they leverage their bilingual/multilingual ways of knowing to engage with complex concepts, build academic language, and express their identities (García & Kleifgen, 2018).
- Grouping configurations that reflect insights gained from both the students' biographies and information shared by students throughout the course of the lesson
- Constructive and positive feedback throughout the lesson designed to increase students' motivation, reduce their anxiety, and route/reroute their thinking

Collective Scaffolding

Difficult and complex tasks are made reachable or attainable through lessons in which students have multiple opportunities to think and rehearse what they are learning in multiple ways. One of the most effective ways to navigate learning for CLD students is to provide them with non-threatening opportunities to voice what they are thinking.

Collective scaffolding involves the teacher's systematic use of Bloom's taxonomy to vary his or her questioning techniques and then allow students to grapple with questions for minutes at a time. At this point, the teacher walks around the classroom actively listening to students negotiate the correct answers to the questions based on the readings, lecture, or other learning (Donato, 1994). By allowing peers to work together in an effort to respond to the questions, the teacher sends the message that there can be more than one correct answer to a question (or at least more than one perspective on how to arrive at the correct answer).

Remember, everyone processes information differently and arrives at the answer at a different time. Releasing questions to students allows more opportunities for students to all get back on the same page before the lesson continues. What an opportunity this provides for us teachers to make an informed assessment of the connections or interpretations all students are making about the content! Ask yourself: "How many questions do I ask? How often during the lesson do I provide risk-free opportunities for students to make public their thought processes?" Figure 8.8 provides some ideas for thinking about the academic talk that is part of the ongoing public conversation of the classroom.

Revoicing for Clarification and Elaboration

Have you ever stopped to listen—*really* listen—to student responses when you ask a question or talk to small teams of students? What are they saying? What cultural and linguistic resources are they using to make sense of the content? Only when we actively listen to the hidden messages of student talk can we guide learners to interact with the content within their zone of proximal development. Great teachers often use the technique of **revoicing** during instructional conversations to reroute, elaborate upon, and validate student responses.

A teacher revoices when he or she listens to what students have to say and re-utters their understanding through repetition, expansion, rephrasing, summarizing, and reporting what was shared (Forman et al., 1998; Krussel et al., 2004; Kwon et al., 2008; Leighton et al., 2021; Suh, 2020). Revoicing is a technique frequently found in the math literature and, as noted by Park et al. (2007), is a "discursive move that teachers use to facilitate students' learning" (p. 4). Other discursive moves used by teachers include telling (e.g., hinting, directing), requesting clarification, and questioning (e.g., challenging, probing) (Krussel et al., 2004). Our revoicing of CLD students' experiential and academic talk can only occur after we have actively observed their language and thought. Therefore, the teacher must be skillful in the orchestration of classroom discussion.

Shein (2012) adds to our understanding of revoicing by highlighting the importance of attending to and including student gestures as well. According to Shein, gestures enable students to ground their "words in the physical world by making references to objects in space and time, and thereby specifying the meaning of the accompanied talk" (pp. 188–189). In addition, gestures can serve a narrative function, supporting language learners and other students to represent ideas that they are not able to adequately express in words. When teachers revoice student gestures along with their verbal language, they validate both ways of expressing meaning.

Teacher revoicing provides CLD students with an opportunity to hear and see the teacher use their words, thoughts, and gestures to clarify or elaborate on what was shared and to make connections with the content. Revoicing therefore allows the teacher to connect student knowledge with content concepts and vocabulary and to model language and reroute student thinking as necessary. O'Connor and

FIGURE 8.8
Capitalizing on Questions to Promote Student Learning

The right kinds of questions can take CLD students beyond factual question/answer responses to $i+1$ responses. By stretching students to $i+1$ responses, the teacher can access the deeper dimensions of the CLD student biography and enable students to elaborate on their learning.

For Questions That . . .	Important Considerations for the Questioner
Build upon CLD Students' Sociocultural Knowledge	• Do questions increase CLD students' connections between prior experiential/academic knowledge and new learning? • Are questions structured in such a way that they enable CLD students to draw upon their own culture/language to make meaningful links to new content? • Do the interactive grouping configurations used within the classroom promote discussion and questioning that encourages CLD students to share sociocultural knowledge?
Scaffold Student Learning	• Are questions posed in a manner that enables the teacher to determine what students are learning? • Can information gained from student responses help guide instruction and inform the educator as to where instruction might need to be revisited? • Do questions inform the teacher about areas in which CLD students might need additional support?
Promote Student Dialogue	• Does questioning engage students in rich dialogue that enhances thinking and learning? • Is questioning structured to promote small team/partner discussions that foster problem solving? • Are students strategically grouped based on their CLD biographies (sociocultural, linguistic, academic, and cognitive) in order to promote rich discussion and extended learning?
Build Critical-Thinking Skills	• Are questions posed that engage students in exploring deeper issues related to the topic? • Do questions push students to think "outside the box" and critically reflect on the implications of their learning? • Are questions posed in such a manner that they promote understanding of the concept rather than regurgitation of facts?
Promote Cognitive Links	• Does questioning promote higher order thinking skills? • Are questions posed in such a way that they take students to $i+1$ by having them *explain the process* they used to solve a problem? • Do questioning processes allow learners to maximize all their communicative resources (e.g., L1, L2, nonlinguistic representations, gestures) to engage in cognitively complex thinking?
Promote Self-Assessment	• Are students encouraged to monitor their own understanding of critical concepts by documenting questions about the content before, during, and after the lesson? • Are students guided to ask questions of themselves so that they can monitor their own learning processes?

Michaels (1996) maintain that revoicing of students' language and thought may lead students to more fully see themselves as part of the learning community and participate in making, analyzing, and evaluating predictions. O'Connor and Michaels (1993) state that revoicing "affords the teacher the tools to coordinate the academic task structure and social participation structure, while simultaneously bringing students into the process of intellectual socialization" (p. 319).

Read the following exchange as the teacher revoices student thinking related to the target vocabulary. Think about how this teacher uses "connected talk" after students have shared their thoughts with peers. Notice the numerous times the teacher revisits the word *justice* and tries to route/reroute students' responses.

> *Teacher:* As the teams talked about "justice," I heard several takes on the word. Let's do a connected talk and see if we can connect our thoughts and come up with how justice fits in with what we have been studying.
>
> *John (with no raising of hands, John starts speaking):* Ahh . . . justice . . . it's umm . . .
>
> *Teacher:* It's hard to explain.
>
> *John:* Yeah.
>
> *Teacher:* You can do it!
>
> *John:* Justice is a part of what you believe and stuff.
>
> *Teacher:* Okay, it is a belief. You're on the right track. Can anybody add to what he said about justice?
>
> *Sophia:* Kinda getting your rights back.
>
> *Teacher:* Okay.
>
> *Sophia:* Being . . . oh, it's hard to explain. When you get free or something, it's like you have your own beliefs. You can be under your own power. You're not under somebody else's . . .
>
> *Teacher (nods head in agreement):* Let's see if somebody else can connect to what you're saying. (points to Natalie)
>
> *Natalie:* Umm . . . sorta like . . . when people get what they deserve. Sorta like if someone died . . . umm . . .
>
> *Teacher:* You can use it . . . Use "justice" with the Holocaust . . . (nods head in encouragement)
>
> *Natalie:* Like the family would want justice from the Nazis. They would want the Nazis to get what they deserved. And the family . . . because, like, relatives died during the Holocaust. They want justice.
>
> *Teacher (points to Sophia):* Does that thinking connect to where your team was going?

According to Forman and colleagues (1998), revoicing makes ideas public for the rest of the classroom. It gives the community an opportunity to hear explanations of words and concepts, negotiate text from multiple perspectives,

reposition their own thoughts, and make changes to their understandings as necessary. Revoicing allows CLD students to hear peers and the teacher discuss and interpret the content multiple times. According to Chapin and colleagues (2003), this gives students "more thinking space and can help all students track what is going on" (p. 2). As teachers navigate what students are thinking and learning, they use curricular and biographical insights to chart the course of their revoicing efforts.

Through revoicing, repetition happens naturally during the lesson. Such repetition provides CLD students with more avenues for participating in the academic conversation. Although revoicing has many potential benefits, especially for students whose first language is not English (Forman et al., 1998), one of the greatest is the opportunity it provides for the teacher to engage with all learners in the classroom.

Confirming and Disconfirming

Often teachers ask me, "Isn't it counterproductive to give voice to what students think a word means?" Some say, "Most ELL students don't have enough English language experience or academic background to know the words I'm going to teach." My reply is, "How can we really know that our students don't know, unless they have been given the chance to fully participate in learning?"

We must continually release learning to the students. Second language learners often hear a word and have a difficult time getting past what they initially thought the word meant. That is why we must provide space for them to talk with one another and come to consensus about the meaning of words in context. As students make sense of the vocabulary and the content, one of the roles of the teacher is to confirm and disconfirm learning. The teacher must confirm or disconfirm students' interpretations of the vocabulary and content during small-team interaction, large-group discussion, and students' completion of tasks individually. Consider the following scenario:

> A CLD student sits in a science class taking notes. While she takes notes, the teacher begins to explain a concept using a "litter box" as an example to bring the vocabulary and concept to life for the students. The CLD student hears "little box" every time the teacher uses the term "litter box." At the end of the lesson she scours the textbook for "little box." She looks at her notes everyplace "little box" appears and still has no clue. She finally works up the courage to go to the teacher and ask where in the book it talks about the "little box" he mentioned in the previous lesson. He looks puzzled and says, "I don't recall. Show me what I was talking about." She shares her notes and the teacher laughs, "I wasn't talking about a 'little box,' I was referring to a 'litter box.' Now, let me explain!"

When we allow students to share their thinking at numerous points throughout the lesson, we increase the likelihood that we will be able to clarify any confusion before it leads students astray and detracts from their learning.

Confirming student learning also legitimizes students' thoughts and understanding. By going back to the text, activity, or tools they have been using since the beginning of the lesson to revisit students' original thoughts, the class is able to see the learning that has taken place and the value that their background knowledge had for the meaning-making process. Consider the following teaching and learning scenario. In what ways is the student's early thinking confirmed and yet disconfirmed, given the new context for the word?

> As Ms. Baker's class talked about the vocabulary words on the quilt, two students in one of the small teams were having quite a discussion about the word *apprentice.* The conversation was between an ELL student and one of the students that had been identified as gifted. The teacher noticed the discussion and walked over. For the word *apprentice,* the ELL student had drawn a television, while the gifted student had written "someone who learns from someone else." They both stated their thoughts on the word while Ms. Baker listened attentively. Then she said, "I think both of you may be right. Let's think about it as we read and discuss the chapter."
>
> During the lesson, Ms. Baker stopped at different points to discuss how words change over time. Very skillfully she revoiced what she had heard from both of the students at the beginning of the lesson. She discussed the television show called "The Apprentice" and how the textbook was defining the word and concept. Toward the end of the lesson, she returned to the two students and had them partner to write about the word *apprentice.* At the end of the lesson, the pair shared that an apprentice was a person who learned a skill from another person. The television show might be called "The Apprentice" because, in a way, the people who are on the show are learning from the lead person. Although the ELL student's original thoughts about the meaning of the word had been disconfirmed, given the context of the lesson, she left the lesson having confirmed two meanings/uses of the word *apprentice* and she now understood their differing contexts.

Using an activation strategy that allows students to make public their word associations before the lesson enables the teacher to revisit and revoice those connections during and after the lesson. When we provide an opportunity for students to share their understanding of a word, distant though that understanding might be from our curricular use of the word, we are better prepared to scaffold the students to a new understanding of the word in the content-area context.

Students Negotiate Meaning

Chapter 1 outlined the relevance and importance of brain research in educating CLD students. Multiple fields, such as sociology, psychology, anthropology, and others, have researched the importance that student biographies play in the academic achievement of students from diverse backgrounds. The current findings from brain research also support this connection. As previously noted, according to Sousa (2017), information is most likely to be stored if it makes sense and has meaning. Students are unlikely to transfer information from their working memory to their long-term memory unless it has meaning to them. Educators need to purposefully select the activities and strategies that they employ to activate students' background knowledge and support meaning-making for each learner.

During the lesson, teachers should provide learners with multiple avenues of exposure to the vocabulary and content, in their efforts to help move the information into students' long-term memory. Willis (2006) states that "the more ways the material to be learned is introduced to the brain and reviewed, the more dendritic pathways of access will be created. There will be more synaptic cell-to-cell bridges, and these pathways will be used more often, become stronger, and remain safe from pruning" (p. 4). Jensen (2006) concurs, saying that "the human brain is designed to interact with the world and make changes, depending on the quality of interaction. If the interactions are positive and sustained, you'll get one set of changes. If the interactions are negative and intense, you get a different set of changes" (p. 12).

Using multisensory strategies with students is essential. "Drill and kill" strategies and the teaching of isolated facts and skills will not lead to student learning. Instead, educators should focus on teaching students how to become thinkers. When students reflect on what they are learning, they delve into their long-term memory to make connections between previously learned information and the new information. These connections are crucial. From a learning perspective, there is no reward in students memorizing material for a test and then forgetting it immediately afterward. Aiding students in the transfer of knowledge from short-term memory (where information can be permanently lost) to long-term memory should be our primary focus. When students demonstrate that they have stored content-area material in their long-term memory, we should continue to refer back to, and make additional connections to, that material to help students keep the information "alive."

Figure 8.9 presents a glimpse of the IDEA strategy (Ignite, Discover, Extend, Affirm) and elaborates on how teachers can use this strategy first to activate students' background knowledge and then to navigate the content-area curriculum, given the insights they have gained into their students' lives (directions for employing the strategy are

IGNITE

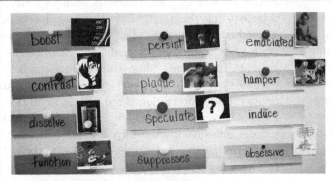

- **Select an activity/strategy that will activate students' funds of knowledge, prior knowledge, and academic knowledge.**

  In this case, IDEA is the selected strategy.

- **Create the space and opportunity for risk-taking—there are no right or wrong answers, only educated guesses taking place.**

  Use visuals to activate students' background knowledge about the academic vocabulary words associated with the topic. Then have students do a "quick and silent write" (or use an alternative method) to document their knowledge of each word. Create the conditions for trust and respect during the activity by reminding the group that there are no right or wrong answers during this phase of the lesson, only "educated guesses" that will be confirmed or disconfirmed during the lesson.

- **Become a participant observer of what students draw, write, or share with peers.**

  Skillfully move around the room "collecting" the thoughts and voices of the classroom learning community to have for future reference. Be perceptive about where to stop and listen, glance, smile, or ask a question. Brainstorm how you will use the information you are seeing and hearing to engage and connect students to the lesson.

DISCOVER

- **Take what you have learned into the lesson to support vocabulary explanation, cultural connections, schematic connections, and validation of individual students.**

  Take every opportunity to go back to the students' words while in the lesson to make sure you validate the knowledge and understandings students brought to the lesson. Support CLD students in connecting their background knowledge with the content. Encourage students to take ownership of the words. Revoice what you hear and interpret to be happening as students respond to the content.

- **Consider the types of grouping structures and configurations that will be possible during the lesson as you teach, address student misconceptions or gaps in understanding, and use formative assessments to reroute your teaching as you navigate students' understanding.**

  Use multiple grouping structures and configurations to promote students' thorough understanding of the topic and to provide opportunities to confirm or disconfirm learning. Structured pairs, for example, often work well during the lesson to contextualize vocabulary in text.

134

FIGURE 8.9
Continued

EXTEND

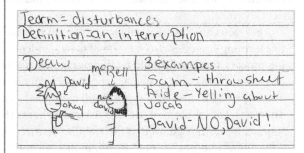

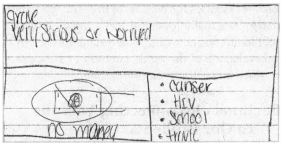

- **Provide multiple exposures to the words and text through listening, speaking, reading, and writing activities designed for students' practice and application of the new words and concepts.**

  Allow students to use both linguistic and nonlinguistic representations as they try to solidify their understanding of the vocabulary and concepts. Multisensory opportunities that emphasize peer discussion and collaboration support CLD students' higher order thinking.

AFFIRM

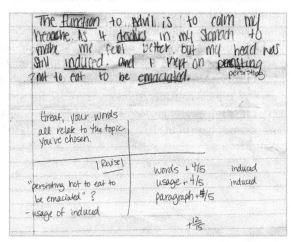

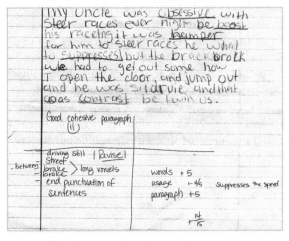

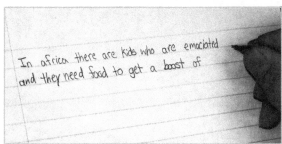

- **Provide opportunities for students to demonstrate individually their understanding of the vocabulary and concepts.**

  Remember to take each student's biography into consideration when designing options for student responses. Try to find a balance between promoting a student's linguistic development and ensuring that his or her response to the task will actually reflect his or her level of content knowledge.

- **Celebrate success!**

  Regardless of the degree to which improvement is still needed, take time to celebrate the progress and accomplishments of the learners in your classroom community. By recognizing the daily successes of your students, you increase their self-confidence as well as their willingness to take risks in making classroom contributions.

(Images courtesy of Joann McRell, Middle School, and Kelly Ledesma, High School, Kansas)

See Appendix F for complete directions for employing the IDEA strategy.

given in Appendix F). This strategy helps to guide students as they negotiate their understanding of the target vocabulary and key content concepts. Joann McRell, a middle school teacher, discusses the benefits of this strategy: "The IDEA strategy is actually [designed for] a higher level of learning of Bloom's taxonomy and requires application, synthesis, and evaluation of the words, contrary to a vocabulary quiz, which is usually rote memorization."

Reflections on Connecting Lessons to Our Students' Lives

This chapter has emphasized the creation of educational opportunities where *one size does not fit all*. Classrooms are much more dynamic when teachers become observers of the assets that each member of the learning community possesses culturally, linguistically, cognitively, and academically. By becoming aware of and using student knowledge as a catalyst for new learning, we increase the likelihood of all students finding both *sense* and *meaning* in the curriculum. In our efforts to help students negotiate meaning, we must find ways to make our instruction comprehensible to each one. To simplify this scaffolding process, we can use the CLD student biography, insights into background knowledge gained in the opening of the lesson, and ongoing student observation as the foundation for our decisions regarding which techniques to use, for which students, and at which points in a given lesson. Moreover, when we intentionally select instructional strategies that guide our implementation of effective grouping configurations and activities, we are better able to orchestrate the conditional and situational processes that are critical to our students' academic success.

Our focus on cognitive, metacognitive, and social/affective learning strategies also is essential to our students' learning process. Our goal should be that our students leave our classrooms better able to manage their own future learning. The information they are learning will continue to change. The facts and skills that we are teaching them, though important, do not guarantee their ability to thrive in the educational and professional world. Rather, we must make the learning *process* more transparent for students, guiding them to see that their own background knowledge is pivotal to their understanding and retention of any new material. As we maximize students' interaction with the vocabulary and concepts we are teaching, we must be cognizant of, and responsive to, our students' (as well as our own) ever-changing states of mind.

Chapter 9 explores the role that review has in providing students with one more chance to make public what they have learned during a lesson. Authentic assessment is critical to our documentation of CLD students' linguistic and academic growth for each lesson, and it ultimately has implications for summative assessments. Throughout that chapter, critical considerations are provided for ways teachers can strategically employ the material used during the work time phase of the lesson to scaffold students to the end of the lesson.

9 Affirmation

Evidence-Based Celebration of Linguistic and Academic Learning

GUIDING QUESTION

What is most important at the end of the lesson: the logistics and end product ensuing from the assessment, or conducting the assessment in a way that its process and progression show the linguistic and academic gains that have occurred for each learner?

See the online Discussion Guide for opportunities to further explore answers to this question and connections to chapter content with a colleague or team. Available for download from the Teachers College Press website: tcpress.com

THE PRECEDING TWO CHAPTERS focused in depth on how to activate students' background knowledge and scaffold instruction to support connections with their new learning before and during the lesson (see Figure 9.1 for a brief overview of critical concepts). In this chapter, I explore how assessment can be woven throughout the lesson, and discuss what final rehearsal and retrieval of vocabulary and conceptual knowledge might look like in the "after" phase of the lesson. Through strategic planning of how to assess students' linguistic and academic growth in all phases of the lesson, we as teachers can affirm student learning or reroute them in a respectful and caring way. Through continual consciousness of CLD students' needs, we can increase the chance that their new academic understandings will be "linked and locked" into their permanent memory. Although there is no magic way of knowing that the information will be there forever, we can do our part to ensure that it is available for future use.

Emotion, Cognition, and Assessment

How often do we see students who seem to understand what we are teaching only to have them fail the final test, leaving us wondering, "What happened?" Often, when we are in the last phase of teaching a lesson, we may neglect to replay in our mind how the student has performed throughout the lesson up to that point. These basic moments of reflection are key; they enable us to determine which activity or strategy will provide the most effective avenue for the learner to "make public" for us the knowledge and understandings he or she has gleaned or constructed from the lesson. Although students must document their learning for our evaluation purposes, assessments should be intentionally designed to lower the anxiety that many students experience when they are asked to recall or produce using traditional assessment tools.

Research has long documented how states of mind impact our ability to retrieve information. Stress, anxiety, and other negative states inhibit learning and have the potential to lock the brain into a decreased production mode (Fredrickson & Branigan, 2005; Sousa, 2017; Zamani & Pouratashi, 2018; Zenasni et al., 2008). Vail (2009) says it best:

> The mere prospect of being asked to read aloud in class is enough to freeze some kids. Having to take a written test or exam, with its combined requirements for memory, reasoning, handwriting, planning and organization, can lock some kids' gears. The sight of a math word problem knocks some kids sideways. Scared kids perform poorly, and don't learn new information well. Anxiety is the enemy of memory. And, sadly, in many of today's classrooms, we see children whose intellectual energies and capacities are drained by negative emotional states. Emotion is the on/off switch for learning.

Given the volume of research on the role that emotions play in our ability to think and perform, I perceive assessment, as it exists today, as a form of pointing out to students all the things they are *not* capable of performing, rather than

FIGURE 9.1
Concepts Critical to Biography-Driven Instruction

Concept	Description
Biopsychosocial history	Refers to the interrelated biological, psychological, and sociological aspects of a learner's background.
Culturally and linguistically diverse (CLD)	The preferred term to describe individuals whose culture or language differ from those of the dominant group.
CLD student biography	Refers to the four interrelated dimensions of a learner—sociocultural, linguistic, cognitive, and academic—that influence his or her academic and linguistic development.
Classroom ecology	Encompasses the interconnected structures, arrangements, events, and processes that influence student and teacher actions and relationships in the classroom.
Contextual processes	How teachers work with the physical setting, curriculum, and community of learners in a classroom to promote trust, respect, engagement, and learning.
Activation phase	Often referred to as the opening of the lesson, the activation phase centers around the opportunities that the teacher provides learners in order to set the stage for the introduction of the lesson. During this phase, the teacher activates students' background knowledge as he or she introduces the lesson vocabulary, topic, or concepts. The teacher creates a risk-free environment for students to share in writing or through non-linguistic representations what they know about the topic or vocabulary/concepts. This activation of background knowledge is critical to setting a context for culturally responsive, sustaining pedagogy that moves teaching away from a deficit perspective and toward an asset perspective.
Background knowledge	Accumulated knowledge related to language and concepts derived from the student's three interrelated knowledge systems: funds of knowledge (home), prior knowledge (community), and academic knowledge (school).
Connection phase	Often referred to as the work time of the lesson, the connection phase is the part of the lesson when the teacher facilitates and navigates conceptual development and language learning by supporting students in constructing knowledge and building the skills necessary to be successful during the lesson. Building on what was learned during the activation phase and documenting the cognitive processes of the learner, the teacher is able to scaffold standards-driven instruction supported by the curriculum. Observation of student learning processes—based on strategic use of strategies that hold the student accountable to write and share about what is being learned—sets the stage for language learning and academic success. In this phase, new knowledge becomes real as students utilize multiple modalities to create joint products.
Transparency in teaching and learning	Teachers explicitly inform students of the learning tasks that will be accomplished by a specific, planned strategy in a lesson, including the destination and the stops along the way. Students respond to the variety of opportunities provided to read, write, listen, and speak by demonstrating their understanding of the concepts and language of the lesson.
Situational processes	How teachers coordinate teaching and learning dynamics in the moment throughout the lesson to increase engagement and guide students to interact and produce in their zone of proximal development.
Socio-academic talk	Speech that results when students interact with peers or the teacher to discuss academic content while simultaneously sharing and capitalizing on their culture-bound ways of knowing, thinking, and applying.
Revoicing	Observing students, listening to what they say, and repeating their understanding (through repetition, expansion, summarizing, or reporting) to validate, encourage elaboration, or reroute student understanding.
Affirmation phase	Often referred to as the closing of the lesson, the affirmation phase reflects the actions of the teacher to use all learning that has been documented throughout the lesson to ask students to authentically share in written form what they have learned. The affirmation phase provides evidence, for both the teacher and the student, that the destination has been reached and the learner has been taken to $i+1$ and into his or her zone of proximal development.

FIGURE 9.2
School-Situated Assessment

Office of Civil Rights (OCR)	Policy-Driven
• Home language survey • English language proficiency tests • Monitoring • Annual testing	• Focus on students' academic achievement • Standardized tests • Reading inventories • Content-based writing samples

Considerations Beyond OCR/Policy	
• Sociocultural • Academic	• Linguistic • Cognitive

celebrating the learning they *have* accomplished during the lesson.

As teachers we are all fully aware of the assessment methods that are imposed upon us, both formal and informal. Figure 9.2 provides a glimpse into the types of assessments that provide point-in-time scores for documenting CLD students' language development and content knowledge. Although such tools provide useful information, learning is much more complex than a paper-and-pencil test can reveal.

Jensen (2008) points out that the prevalent way of thinking about evaluation overlooks some of the most fundamental aspects of what we know about how the brain learns and the way the brain stores information in permanent memory. Relevant to the issue of assessment, Jensen (p. 226) posits the following considerations:

- Learning takes many forms that are not usually assessed (e.g., spatial, temporal, episodic, procedural).
- Memory is highly state- and context-dependent. The location of a test may not be where the information was learned or where the student will need to use the learning.
- Much of our explicit semantic learning requires tremendous repetition and meaning-making to become embedded for long-term retention. On top of that, most explicit learning is at risk for becoming outdated.
- Nutrition and stress make scoring highly variable.
- The brain learns by making mistakes, not by memorizing correct answers.

Jensen (2006) reports that when we are teaching students and having them practice and apply information merely to memorize it and score well on a standardized test, we are limiting the learning that can take place when students learn through trial and error. Involv-ing students in making connections and experimenting with the information being taught increases the likelihood that they will become critical thinkers and use higher-order thinking skills to learn new information.

Connecting the experiential learning process (Kolb, 1984) with neuroscience, Zull (2002) reiterates the importance of allowing learners to maximize the natural learning cycle of the brain. Figure 9.3 illustrates the basic path of a single cycle of learning, including (1) concrete experience (i.e., sensory input), (2) reflective observation (i.e., activation of knowledge systems, in BDI terms), (3) abstract hypotheses (e.g., working with information to assemble language, solve problems, make judgments and evaluations, develop plans), and (4) active testing (e.g., taking action through speaking, writing, interacting). The brain is simultaneously engaged in multiple learning cycles, some that happen in moments and others that might take years to complete. Thus, a teacher's job is to set the stage for assessment that both values the CLD student's efforts thus far to make sense of the new information and provides meaningful feedback to accelerate his or her learning by informing ongoing and subsequent learning cycles.

Throughout this volume you have been guided in pre-assessing what students already know and deciding how to use the resulting insights to foster conceptual and linguistic development. I have discussed the importance of selecting strategies and activities, asking questions that assess student understanding, and reflecting upon new ways to maximize the assets of the learning community to address gaps in student knowledge and understanding. Figure 9.4 sets the

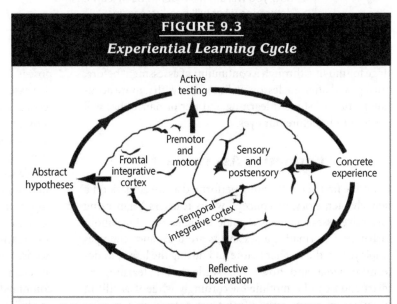

FIGURE 9.3
Experiential Learning Cycle

Source: Zull, J. E. *The Art of Changing the Brain*, p. 18. Copyright 2002 by Stylus Publishing. Reprinted by permission of Copyright Clearance Center.

FIGURE 9.4
Continuum of Assessment

Assessment should be thought of as a process that is ongoing throughout the lesson. Constantly reflect on what was learned at the beginning of the lesson to strengthen new learning during and after the lesson.

Before the Lesson: Formative in Nature

- What does the student bring from prior experiences in and out of school?
- What language is the student using to share what he or she knows?
- What connections to the lesson can be made from what the student has shared?

- Document the student's background knowledge.
- Reflect on ways you can use the information to explain new vocabulary or concepts, transition into the lesson, and reinforce what was learned.
- *This is an opportunity to "get into the student's heart and mind."*

During the Lesson: Formative in Nature

- Take every opportunity to connect the lesson to what you learned during preassessment of the student's knowledge.
- Observe for the student's academic connections and cognitive processing of information as the lesson is taught.
- Document growth in language and academic use of vocabulary as it relates to the lesson objectives and standards.

- Observe for links the student is making with his or her background knowledge. Take every opportunity to strengthen these connections and confirm, disconfirm, or reroute as necessary.
- Provide opportunities for the student to talk, read, and write about the content to give you multiple views of the learning that is taking place.
- *Document, document, document what you are observing!*

After the Lesson: Formative Becomes Summative in Nature

- Take what you have learned and begin to plan for one last review of the vocabulary and concepts to address any remaining gaps in the student's understanding.
- With all observations documented, reflect on how you will affirm what has been learned and determine what will need reteaching.

- Have the student practice with the content by reading, writing, and talking about it before you formally assess.
- Bring together all of the information (preassessment through summative assessment) to make decisions about the final grade.
- *Hold the student individually accountable.*

---

stage for moving through a continuum of assessment before, during, and after the lesson, culminating with a more accurate picture of student learning and performance that will develop right before our eyes.

Formative Assessment

From the first act of teaching performed as we embark on a new chapter, story, or concept, we as teachers begin using formative assessments as a guide to make decisions about instruction. Formative assessments are tools and strategies employed by the teacher before and during the lesson to determine what and how their students are learning so instruction can be modified accordingly while it is still in progress. In many ways, formative assessments can be thought of as a springboard for teaching. Their primary pur-

pose is to increase student learning and engagement. Formative assessments are also pivotal tools for providing student feedback that is meaningful to the individual. The strategies, activities, and questioning techniques used during this time are critical for monitoring the sociocultural, linguistic, cognitive, and academic growth of the CLD student.

We can glean essential information by using preassessment and during-the-lesson strategies that provide natural opportunities for assessing how our students process and store new content. This information becomes the catalyst for creating learning situations that meet students' unique needs. For example, general knowledge of a student's stage of second language acquisition, as described in Figure 9.5, combined with insights about the student's linguistic assets or challenges identified during a specific lesson, provides the teacher with the information he or she needs to make

FIGURE 9.5
Assessment Using P-EP-S-I Ahh!

P-EP-S-I Ahh! is a teacher-friendly mnemonic device to help you recall Krashen's stages of second language acquisition. Knowing which stage your CLD student is in helps you to better plan/implement assessments.

Acronym/Student Behaviors	Teacher Tips
P **Preproduction** • Gain familiarity with sounds, rhythm, and patterns of English. • Rely more heavily on picture clues for understanding. • Respond nonverbally by pointing, gesturing, or drawing.	• **Preassessment:** Use authentic assessments that do not require speech (nonlinguistic), and tap into CLD students' sensory memory by making explicit connections to their previous experiences. • **During instruction:** Pair students with more proficient L1 peers who can translate to support comprehension and assess student understanding informally (e.g., with observation/monitoring of student work) throughout the lesson. • **Postassessment:** Check students' comprehension with performance-based assessments that do not require a lot of speaking or writing in English (e.g., create a visual representation of key vocabulary, act out key points).
E **Early** **P** **Production** • Use one-word type utterances; may verbally identify people, places, and objects. • Manipulate objects and ideas mentally. • Start using knowledge of letter–sound relationships. • Use routine expressions independently.	• **Preassessment:** Use visual cues to preassess CLD students' existing knowledge of key vocabulary terms/concepts. • **During instruction:** Have students work with a partner or small group to label or manipulate visuals and/or real objects that explicitly teach/model key vocabulary and concepts to assess their understanding of these terms in the context of the lesson (e.g., labeling visuals in English using key vocabulary). • **Postassessment:** Have students dictate or write sentences about the key vocabulary/critical concepts to assess their understanding. If the student is proficient in L1, you may have them write in L1 first and then work with someone to translate their sentences into English.
S **Speech Emergence** • Understand grade-level concepts. • Engages in much more independent reading as a result of increased oral language proficiency. • Apply and manipulate writing according to their needs.	• **Preassessment:** Use multiple strategies to assess CLD students' knowledge of key vocabulary/content before the lesson (e.g., visuals, graphic organizers, other hands-on activities). • **During instruction:** Monitor students' comprehension by having them explain, describe, compare, and retell information orally or in writing with a peer or small group (allow for grammatical errors or sporadic L1 usage to express meaning). • **Postassessment:** Provide assessments that focus on communication in meaningful contexts and expression in speech and short writing passages.
I **Intermediate Fluency** • Explore and utilize extensive vocabulary and concepts in content area. • Write and read a wider range of narrative genres and content texts with increased comprehension.	• **Preassessment:** Continue to preassess vocabulary knowledge with contextual/visual support. Students at this stage should also be able to write more about the key vocabulary terms in English. • **During instruction:** Use structured group discussions with concrete/documented outcomes to facilitate more advanced literature studies. • **Postassessment:** Incorporate more writing assessments with an emphasis on linking new learnings to past learnings/experiences.
Ahh! **Advanced Fluency** • Produce language with varied grammatical structures and vocabulary. • Construct multiple hypotheses and viewpoints.	• **Preassessment:** Continue to develop CLD students' academic knowledge by preassessing existing knowledge and building new academic vocabulary. • **During instruction:** Use interactive grouping configurations and multiple authentic assessments of students' work as they practice and apply new learnings. • **Postassessment:** Have students work in pairs/groups/independently to authentically demonstrate learnings via written or hands-on techniques.

> ## FIGURE 9.6
> ### Formative Assessments: Linking to the CLD Student Biography
>
> **Sociocultural Dimension**
>
> - Formative assessments affirm students' learning and give them hope that they can learn academic content with the proper support.
> - Formative assessments can help make explicit links to the CLD students' families by involving them in the assessment process (e.g., a student might interview a family member about his or her immigration experience as part of a social studies unit on immigration).
> - When multiple grouping configurations are used within formative assessment, all students have the opportunity to interact with peers from diverse cultural backgrounds and build links to new content.
>
> **Linguistic Dimension**
>
> - Formative assessments help emergent bilinguals and other CLD students see their growth in acquiring academic language.
> - Formative assessments encourage CLD students to use English vocabulary in meaningful ways.
>
> **Cognitive Dimension**
>
> - Formative assessments allow CLD students to demonstrate learning in multiple authentic and contextually bound ways.
> - Formative assessments enable CLD students to monitor their own learning and see what it is they "got right."
>
> **Academic Dimension**
>
> - Formative assessments allow for ongoing monitoring of CLD students' learning throughout the lesson.
> - Formative assessments help teachers see where there might be gaps in student learning/knowledge that need to be addressed.
> - Formative assessments help students reach end goals.

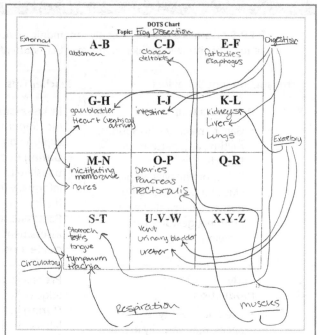

A DOTS chart (shown in Chapter 6 and explained in Appendix C) has been used as a preassessment tool for students and will be carried throughout the lesson as a strategy for learning about frog dissection. The teacher asked students first to come up with all the words they knew about the topic. As the students recorded words on their charts, they were also given an opportunity to discuss their known words with a peer. After this quick preassessment to see where students were in their understanding, the teacher proceeded with the strategy as a during-the-lesson tool with which students made connections to additional words they were learning. Finally, the teacher used the same tool for students' postassessment by asking them to write a summary of the topic using the words from their individual DOTS charts. (*Image courtesy of Brad Fabrizius, High School, Kansas*)

individual accommodations. Accommodations in types of activities used and questions posed are thus guided by what the student knows and is able to produce with scaffolding by the teacher and support from peers. Figure 9.6 elaborates on ways formative assessments enable us to link to students' biographies.

Using Preinstructional Assessment to Inform Our Teaching

In Chapter 7, I discussed how to provide a "canvas of opportunity" for CLD students to make public the knowledge they bring from their experiences in and out of school. In my work with teachers across the country, I have noticed

that this seems to be the most difficult skill to develop. Much of the challenge lies with the perception that there is not enough time to "waste" on learning about the knowledge students already have on a topic or its associated vocabulary. After all, many teachers explain, most of their CLD students come from homes of low socioeconomic status and have limited sources of knowledge that would relate to the curriculum of the school. This way of thinking falls short in understanding just what a wealth of knowledge learners bring to our classrooms—knowledge that can be used to teach the content and accelerate student learning. When we show students that we care about and will utilize what they know, they are more likely to invest in what we are teaching and to perform at a higher level.

Preassessment informs the teacher about what the student brings from each dimension of his or her biography, as related to the vocabulary and topic of the lesson. This, in

Comprehension of grade-level text can be often difficult for second language learners. Having students work together as well as independently to make decisions about what is important in a text passage or chapter supports their understanding of the content. In this Relevance Scale strategy, students first collaborate to identify and record the most important details from the passage. They then rank the details by number to indicate how relevant each is to understanding the passage or retelling the story/concept. *(Image courtesy of Melissa Lunney, 8th Grade, Kansas)*

turn, provides the road map for making connections and decisions about where to stop during the lesson to address gaps that CLD students may have. Preassessment of knowledge makes it possible for us to truly work from the known to the unknown. Insights from preassessment guide our ongoing assessment throughout the lesson and frame the final assessment for determining what each student has learned. Knowing where you are starting will increase the chances that you will be able to successfully navigate the curriculum and actually arrive at your final destination *with your students*! Preassessment before every lesson thus becomes the catalyst for CLD student motivation, engagement, and learning.

Using Formative Assessment During the Lesson

We teachers often become comfortable with our own rhythms of teaching and assessing as we go through a lesson. Bear in mind this word of caution, however: when we become comfortable, we easily can slip into using our comfortable "expectation" lens to assess learning without regard to what we learned during the preassessment phase. We often hear that no assessment is bias-free, and we tend to think about this in terms of the tests that have been developed by companies. However, bias can also exist based on the lens we wear while observing student learning.

Students' willingness and socioemotional state of mind (as discussed in Chapters 6 and 8) and their biopsycho-

social histories (e.g., level of acculturation) have implications for the way they respond to assessment. At times, for example, CLD students may have feelings of anxiety, fear, or frustration resulting from one or more of the following:

- Amount of time the student has been in the country
- Type of ESL/bilingual programming the student is receiving
- Incongruity between U.S. assessment tasks and those used in the country of origin
- Level of linguistic ability in English
- Prior experiences with assessment in school settings
- History of success or failure in the academic subject
- Classroom climate

A CLD student's state of mind has implications for what he or she produces during the lesson. Therefore, we must assess students' motivation and engagement with an eye on their socioemotional state.

By creating a classroom climate that fosters positive thinking, acceptance, and respect, we better ensure that students feel valued as members of the learning community. When we incorporate students' funds of knowledge, prior knowledge, and academic knowledge into the learning process, we build students' self-confidence and encourage them to see themselves as knowledgeable contributors to their own learning as well as that of their peers. And when we challenge students to think complexly in low-risk situations, we help develop learners who understand that wrong answers are part of the learning process and, therefore, are willing to take risks and share how they make sense of new material.

Interaction and Accommodation

The strategies we select to use throughout each phase of the lesson should set the stage for the progression of students' thinking, interaction, and learning. Effective strategies scaffold student learning and provide contexts that make students' cognitive processes more transparent for the teacher. According to Jensen (2008), some aspects of student processes are open for assessment whereas others are more difficult to access. At the end of the day, he states, "it is the cognitive skills—not the content—that will be the primary measure of a student's long-term success" (p. 233). Rather than viewing the final assessment as the only measure that "counts," we can maximize our strategies and time during the lesson to assess those aspects of student progress that often are overlooked.

The use of systematic and structured interaction to help students make public how they are processing and applying the information being taught is crucial for assessment during the lesson. Students should have multiple opportunities to interact with peers through *i+TpsI* grouping configurations as they build on existing cultural, linguistic, cognitive, and academic knowledge and skills. This can be

FIGURE 9.7
Student Interaction Throughout the Lesson

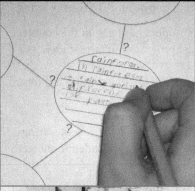

Students begin to engage with the lesson by activating their background knowledge and recording their ideas to be used during the lesson.

The teacher uses the information gained to inform her practice and make explanations and examples more connected to what the students brought from their own backgrounds.

Students are then given an opportunity to practice and apply the new information, providing the teacher with one more glimpse into how they are understanding and processing the new content and language.

Students continue learning and practicing both language and content in small groups. At this point, students are placed with peers that will challenge and support their academic learning and language use.

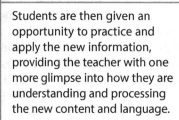

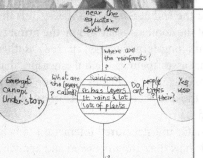

At the end of the lesson, the teacher is able to assess what students have learned and determine which accommodations and groupings were most beneficial for students, given their individual needs.

(Images courtesy of Denise Johnson, 2nd Grade, Kansas)

accomplished when the teacher is aware of and creates opportunities for student talk, as discussed in Chapter 8, where the teacher shares information and then releases it to the class for discussion, clarification, or elaboration. These opportunities can take the form of partner talk that allows students to discuss for a short period what was read or said by the teacher, small-group talk that is structured around solving a problem or coming to consensus on some aspect of the topic, or individual responses to a question that will demonstrate what each student is thinking with regard to the concepts and vocabulary of the lesson.

Such opportunities for students to convey their thoughts and ideas provide us with numerous chances to informally assess and document their application of learning. Furthermore, they provide us with the information we need to actively accommodate our students' assets and needs in our instruction. For example, we often make accommodations for learners based on their demonstrated level of language proficiency during a lesson. We use the information we have gathered to strategically plan for partners and group configurations that will provide scaffolds that ensure the best situational context for our assessment of a student's oral language development and content learning. We also consider other dimensions of the student's biography. For instance, we determine which social contexts will allow optimal levels of social and academic interaction to occur. Figure 9.7 provides a glimpse of ways student interaction can be used throughout the lesson to promote CLD students' learning.

Posing Questions That Count

> Most teachers waste their time by asking questions that are intended to discover what a pupil does not know, whereas the true art of questioning has for its purpose to discover what the pupil knows or is capable of knowing.
>
> —*Albert Einstein*

Questioning is an underutilized tool for assessment in today's classrooms. Observe a master teacher and you will quickly see a facilitator who has perfected questioning techniques that get students where they need to be by challenging them to link to the past, think beyond, and use questions to discover and uncover new learning. Kinsella and Feldman (2005) describe the kinds of questioning that facilitate academic talk for different purposes. Questioning has the potential to engage students in talk that allows for

- Clarification and elaboration of learning
- Review of information as it is taught
- Rehearsal of responses before they are shared with the learning community
- Multiple opportunities for retrieval of information

Structured with a specific purpose in mind, academic questions become useful for revoicing what the students are learning in their own words, as described in Chapter 8, and thus become a tool for providing respectful feedback to CLD students. Structured academic questions promote academic dialogue between partners and within small groups; they nudge students to reach new limits with the questions they themselves pose. Releasing a question to a small group

of students increases the chances that an $i+1$ response will become part of the group answer. As students negotiate answers to difficult questions, they consider others' perspectives, pose questions of the teacher that will guide them in coming to consensus, and evaluate their own lines of thought—skills that are precursors for effective self-questioning as learning occurs.

As students work together to develop responses to questions, the teacher takes on the task of reflectively observing student talk. The teacher gathers insights that will help him or her orchestrate subsequent dialogue to promote student thinking and learning. During this time, the teacher considers what he or she hears in light of what students shared in the preassessment phase and during earlier parts of the lesson. In these moments, the teacher reflects on ways he or she can scaffold to get students back on track, as necessary, by making new connections or revisiting previous links to students' background knowledge and content understanding.

In this image-based text, the student was provided the opportunity to make connections first to her own background knowledge and then to the story the class was reading, *Charlie and the Chocolate Factory*. The student's mind map of this information was then used to write a summary of the story. The teacher encourages students to use the mind map as a cognitive strategy to prompt their thinking when summarizing information. *(Image courtesy of Kendra Herrera, 3rd Grade, Texas)*

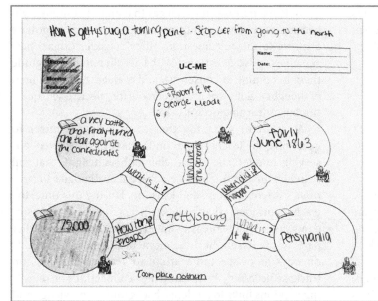

This photo illustrates how the U-C-ME strategy can be used to uncover student understandings and then connect those understandings with the new learning. Students' known knowledge was placed in the middle circle. Next, students were asked to frame questions regarding the topic and place those questions on the spokes. Students continually monitored their learning throughout the lesson, using the questions to guide their thinking. Finally, students placed their learnings in the circles at the ends of the spokes. In this way, the U-C-ME strategy was used at the end of the lesson as a way to assess student learning. (See Appendix H for a full description of the U-C-ME strategy. A template and student academic behavior rubric for classroom use are available for free download and printing from the Teachers College Press website: tcpress.com) *(Image courtesy of Kelly Ledesma, Middle School, Kansas)*

Learning Strategies as a Bridge to Summative Assessment

Student learning strategies have long been overlooked as a tool that teachers can use during formative assessment and as a bridge to summative/postinstructional assessment. Learning strategies can be a great resource for observation and documentation of thinking and learning throughout the lesson. In addition, learning strategies have the potential to promote simultaneous development of both academic knowledge and language skills. As we support CLD students in taking ownership of and monitoring their own learning, we increase the chance that what we teach will become knowledge that students can retrieve in the future.

Application of learning strategies enhances students' comprehension, motivation, and self-esteem and makes transparent for us teachers what has been learned and what needs additional rehearsal. Students who are taught to use learning strategies strategically, systematically, and consistently are empowered to utilize these tools for articulating their learning in multiple ways. The discussion that follows provides a brief introduction to the use of student learning strategies as a source of authentic, informal assessment.

Cognitive Strategies: Aiding the Brain

When teachers model and gradually release cognitive learning strategies for students to use as part of their daily routine, they create ideal conditions for students to share background knowledge and use it to accelerate learning. A natural progression follows: students use what they know, or what they surmise, to make inferences and predictions about the content or text during the lesson. Students can then use the activated schematic associations they have

related to the overall topic to classify and group ideas from the new information. Mind maps, when used as a student learning strategy, provide students with a scaffold for performing all of these learning tasks as well as for summarizing what was learned at the end of the lesson.

Image-based texts support CLD students in their efforts to conceptualize ideas, understand relationships among terms, make sense of their thinking, and better understand what they know (and don't know) about the content. This strategy allows each learner to represent ideas first in pictures and words. Then, with appropriate support and guidance, all students share their thinking and learning through more complex spoken and written forms of communication.

Metacognitive Strategies: Thinking It Through

"There's just not enough time!" How many of us say this to ourselves (or to others) in the context of planning a lesson? It seems as though we always are in such a hurry during every phase of the lesson that we forget to talk about and model how to "think through our learning" as we read and write. By habitually incorporating metacognitive strategies, we can support our students as they plan how they will learn new information. For example, we might teach students how to use their selective attention to focus on what is important or to define vocabulary and content concepts of a lesson. When students are guided to monitor their listening, reading, and writing, they are more likely to be academically successful at the end of the lesson. They can use the same metacognitive skills and strategies during assessment to think about what they know in relation to a prompt and to organize and express this knowledge. CLD students need to be able to evaluate their own learning, and to understand processes that can help them enhance their learning throughout the lesson and reveal it after the lesson. The U-C-ME strategy (see Appendix H) is a straightforward way to embed the skills of planning, focusing, monitoring, and evaluating learning as students proceed through the lesson.

Social/Affective Strategies: Finding Support

The use of social/affective strategies throughout the lesson creates situations in which learners become less dependent on the teacher as they make and elaborate on connections to the critical concepts. Opportunities to work with one or more peers allow students to ask questions for clarification. When teachers configure groups based on students' biographies, they ensure student pairings and groupings that will result in challenging, yet low-risk and supportive environments. The Thumb Challenge (see Appendix G) is a great strategy for having students work together to rehearse vocabulary definitions as well as assess their understanding of how the vocabulary connects to the content. During strategy implementation, the teacher informally assesses learning while moving from group to group to observe. Ultimately, what we see during the lesson is the best predictor of the results we will see after the lesson. The activities and strategies we choose to use during the lesson as tools for formative assessment can become the scaffold for subsequent postinstructional assessments. Figure 9.8 discusses how selected learning strategies can be taken into the final stage of assessment.

Teaching and modeling for students how to use positive self-talk (e.g., *I can do it*; *just breathe*; *relax*) to manage their own emotional responses and states of mind can also increase the likelihood that CLD students will achieve their learning goals throughout the lesson and be able to demonstrate learning during assessment. Figure 9.9 offers a few suggestions for providing students with ideas for self-talk.

Review, Rehearsal, and Retrieval

When the teacher holds every student accountable, learning is enhanced for all students.

The "after" phase of the lesson brings everything together—what has been shared, what has been taught, and what has been learned. Because all students do not start at the same place, it is common sense that they will not all end at the same place. However, every student will have gained valuable knowledge that will keep him or her moving forward.

Confirmation of Learning

Take a moment to think about one of your recent lessons. How much time did you allow at the end of the lesson to provide students with a "dress rehearsal," or final review, before their culminating performance? Did you provide students with an opportunity to voice what they had learned by talking to someone, writing about how they understood the words and concepts, or participating in an interactive activity? Did you give yourself one more chance to listen, observe, and reflect on students' learning?

Reviewing is often left to chance in many classrooms, yet it is the place in the lesson where students can have one last opportunity to confirm their understanding of the vocabulary and concepts and self-assess their overall comprehension of the lesson. It is the teacher's "window peek" into whether the class has met the content and language objectives. According to Sousa (2017), this last rehearsal is the final step for taking information from working memory (practice and application) to permanent memory, where it will be available to students for future use. The Thumb Challenge discussed earlier (and in Appendix G) also can serve as tool for reviewing content before moving into the last phase of assessment.

Remember that "anxiety is the enemy of memory" (Vail, 2009). We help to relieve students' anxiety before the final assessment by providing them with an opportunity to review and rehearse what they have learned. In this way, we better ensure that the assessment will measure what it is intended to assess. Without time for review, our assessments are more likely to reflect the negative effects that students' socioemotional states can have on their performance. Review at the end of the lesson also gives us teachers one more opportunity to address any gaps that may still exist in student learning.

Summative Assessment: A Celebration and Elaboration of Learning

Having made expectations for learning transparent from the beginning of the lesson, the teacher's next task is to plan a gallery of opportunities for the students to exhibit what they have accomplished. The products that students are asked to develop might vary, based on the data gathered from formative assessments. The teacher's goal is to create opportunities to celebrate what students know and to encourage them to elaborate on their academic and linguistic learning.

Consider the following insights from the biographies of three emergent bilinguals and ask yourself how their end-of-lesson assignments might differ.

- *Alberto* is fluent in the English language for social purposes. He still has difficulty with new academic words. He enjoys reading to the class and is eager to translate when others need help. He processes information best when he is allowed to retell using his own words, rather than completing worksheets or answering end-of-chapter questions in the text.
- *Iram* can return to materials used during the lesson and produce definitions of vocabulary words and content

FIGURE 9.8
Taking Strategies to the Final Stage of Assessment

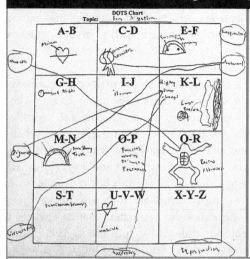

DOTS Strategy

- **Preassessment:** Have students individually record their ideas and document connections between their background knowledge and the topic.
- **During the lesson:** Have students connect their known words to the target vocabulary words.
- **Summative assessment:** Have students write a summary of the topic using the words from their DOTS chart along with the target words for the topic.

See Appendix C for complete directions for employing the DOTS strategy.

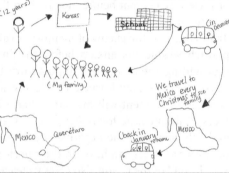

Mind Map

- **Preassessment:** Activate students' background knowledge by asking them to write/draw their schematic for the topic.
- **During the lesson:** As students use information from the text/lesson to elaborate on and add new ideas to their mind map, informally assess students' expansion of ideas.
- **Summative assessment:** Have students create a written summary of their learning, including new concepts, vocabulary, and skills.

See Appendix D for complete directions for employing the Mind Map.

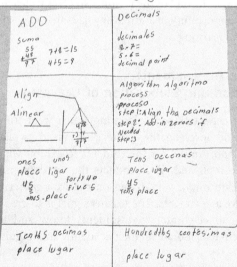

Vocabulary Quilt

- **Preassessment:** Activate what the student associates with the words.
- **During the lesson:** Observe to assess student learning related to academic concepts and linguistic skills.
- **Summative assessment:** Have students use their understanding of the words on the quilt to create individual summaries, which are scored as part of final assessment.

See Appendix E for complete directions for employing the Vocabulary Quilt.

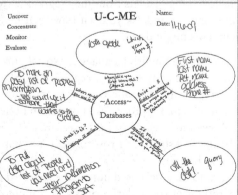

U-C-ME

- **Preassessment:** <u>Uncover</u> students' schematic connections to the topic.
- **During the lesson:** Have students create questions to better <u>**concentrate**</u> their learning.
- **Summative assessment:** Have students <u>**monitor**</u> their comprehension by answering the questions they created. <u>**Evaluate**</u> students by having students use their responses to the questions to summarize their learning in sequence.

See Appendix H for complete directions for employing U-C-ME.

concepts in context. He still is very much in need of a scaffold during the assessment phase. A tangible aid provides him with a sense of security as he uses his third language (English) to put his thoughts on paper.

- *Fatima* prefers to work alone and can easily generate definitions or sentences as they relate to concepts learned. She does well taking the sentences and elaborating on what was learned orally with a partner. She

still has difficulty with grammar. The sentences she creates provide a tool that can be used to practice grammatical structures.

In the context of a lesson in which the teacher is using the Vocabulary Quilt strategy (described in Chapter 8; see Appendix E for a complete strategy description) to assess students' ability to use the target vocabulary to retell about the key concepts of the lesson, the three students might be asked to demonstrate their learning by completing the following tasks:

- *Alberto* is asked to write a detailed outline of what he learned about the topic, incorporating the target vocabulary, and then orally share his report with the class.
- *Iram* is asked to write what each vocabulary word means in the context of the lesson. He is allowed to use his completed vocabulary quilt as a resource, which includes his original thoughts about the words along with his new understandings.
- *Fatima* is asked to incorporate the vocabulary words as she writes a summary of what she learned about the topic. As part of the process, she will have a peer read her summary and underline in pencil any parts that are especially confusing. Fatima will then make minor revisions to enhance the clarity of her summary.

This kind of summative assessment moves beyond traditional conceptualizations of what postinstructional assessment looks like in practice. Figure 9.10 presents ideas for summative assessment tasks that can be used to help CLD students' progress toward their linguistic and academic goals.

FIGURE 9.9
Student Self-Talk

The frequent testing and assessment of CLD students often serve to raise their affective filter. As a result, some students experience mental blocks or acute anxiety, resulting in teachers misunderstanding or underestimating what they really know or are able to do. Moreover, when taking a test or talking to a teacher, emergent bilinguals tend to overtly monitor their speech in English and become exceedingly self-conscious about their accent or routine grammatical errors. For these reasons, it is critical for the professional to teach CLD learners how to use the self-talk strategy.

The following are examples of self-talk:

- **You can do it!**

  When taking a test or working in a group, emergent bilinguals may feel too intimidated and embarrassed to participate, because they think their English proficiency is not compatible or comprehensible to other students. Often they give up and opt to stay silent. Teachers should consistently encourage students to believe in themselves. By telling students, "You can do it!" you can prompt them to think, "I can do it!"

- **Making a mistake is better than not talking at all!**

  CLD students may be hesitant to share their ideas. Emergent bilinguals often are intimidated when speaking with a teacher or in front of the class. Teachers should let CLD students know that it is okay to make mistakes. You can help them feel safe in making mistakes by complimenting them when they have the courage to speak and share their ideas. Make it clear that what matters is hearing their ideas and opinions, which support the learning of the entire community.

- **So what?**

  A great way to boost confidence in CLD students is to have them repeat the words, "So what?" Yes, your answer was wrong, so what? Now you know the right answer. That's how you learn. Nobody knows everything! Yes, your opinion was challenged by others, so what? That's the fun part of the lesson. Let others know what you know.

Ms. Mayerske, the learning coach, works with 6th-grade students after a lesson on Roman history. She is reviewing the vocabulary words with students and using this time to confirm/disconfirm students' understanding of the words. This opportunity for student review also allows her to see which words need to be re-taught. *(Image courtesy of Jackie Mayerske, Elementary Resource Room, Kansas)*

FIGURE 9.10
Summative Assessment Tasks

Informal Summative Assessments
- Portfolios/E-portfolios
- Writing summary of concepts/topics
- Group project
- Unit grade
- Teacher-created tests

Formal Summative Assessments
- End of chapter tests
- Mid-term and final exams
- Policy-driven tests

Feedback based on postinstructional assessments should be provided to students in ways that both acknowledge moments of excellence and recognize errors made—appreciating them as markers that indicate the route along which re-teaching can occur. In this way, thinking and learning do not end with assessment. Rather, assessment provides the redirection needed for the learning process to continue as a shared responsibility between the teacher and the student. We teachers continually strive to move students one step beyond their current knowledge, skills, and understandings by situating their learning within the context of past performance and helping them envision possibilities for their future endeavors.

Rethinking Our Aim: Testing and Grades Versus Teaching Through Assessment

Teachers always comment about my idealistic view as a researcher, educator, and author, given the demands and agenda of those who "control" what happens in schools and classrooms. My response is that in order to be ethical and caring educators, we must approach teaching, learning, and assessment by valuing what students know and are capable of accomplishing. When educators only care about standardized tests and grades, we fail to value what students really know.

Merely testing provides teachers with a one-moment-in-time view of CLD students' knowledge. Most testing does not take into account the learner's biography or the ways testing outcomes are affected by each student's starting point. Not taking into consideration the student's biography makes end-of-lesson assessments inherently biased. Although there is much talk about differentiation of instruction, pressure exists in most classrooms to teach and test grade-level curriculum through a fast-paced, drill-and-practice approach that leaves behind the learners most in need of differentiated instruction and assessment. Those practices stand in stark contrast to what research tells us about the need for pedagogy that validates and builds on CLD students' background knowledge and experiences.

Think about the sequence of learning and assessment employed in the Pic-Tac-Tell strategy (Herrera, Kavimandan, & Holmes, 2011; Herrera et al., 2017) illustrated in Figure 9.11. Reflect on what can be gained from using authentic assessment throughout all three phases of instruction. Ask yourself, How might what I learn about my students *throughout* the lesson lead to a more accurate assessment of what they have learned *as a result* of my lesson?

Grades often have a negative impact on both learning and community. They frequently result in an environment that is individualistic, competitive, and detrimental to students' creativity and critical thinking. A grade does not increase learning. It merely lifts some students, diminishes others, and encourages all students to view learning as a process of identifying what the teacher deems most important and then efficiently reproducing those facts and perspectives on assessment tasks. Much more can be accomplished when we strive for the development of a cohesive community of learners working together with a common mission.

CLD students experience true access to education when instruction and assessment are biography-driven and holistic in nature, rather than focused on mastery of isolated or decontextualized pieces of information. As Jensen (2008) notes, "The brain is not very good at learning isolated information, especially when it is devoid of any joy or meaning" (p. 178). By providing students with the kinds of learning contexts and situations described in this text, we foster their intrinsic motivation and hope of success. This confidence in learning will translate into measurable academic achievement and better performance in the classroom as measured

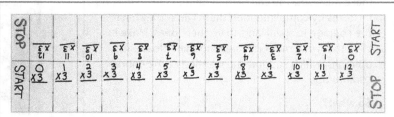

Depicted here is an example of a math concept strip Ms. Barton used with her class when implementing the Thumb Challenge strategy (see Appendix G). The students worked in pairs to review and assess the multiplication facts they had learned. Students moved their thumbs from one multiplication fact to the next taking turns. As students did this, Ms. Barton went around the room listening to her students practice and discuss their learning.

—*Cheryl Barton, Special Education Resource, Kansas*

FIGURE 9.11
Pic-Tac-Tell

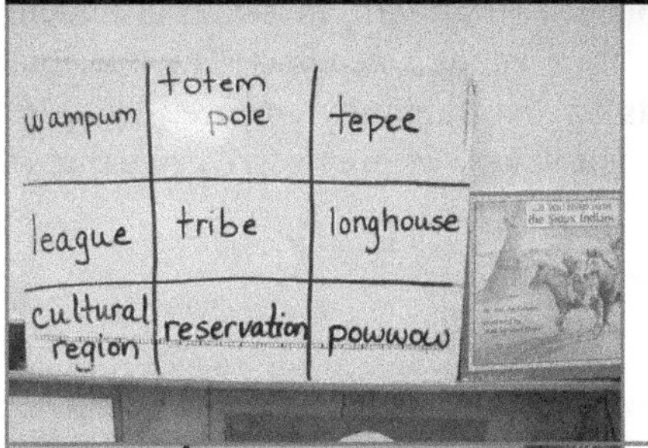

	Taking the words from the vocabulary quilt, the teacher has created a grid using the words to move from the "before" and "during" phases of the lesson to one last review and then individual accountability. Using the quilt, the teacher and the students review the words together.
	The teacher then moves to having the students work in groups to discuss the words in relations to the concepts that were covered during the lesson. She observes for the ways students use the words with one another, keeping in mind what she has learned about each student throughout the lesson.
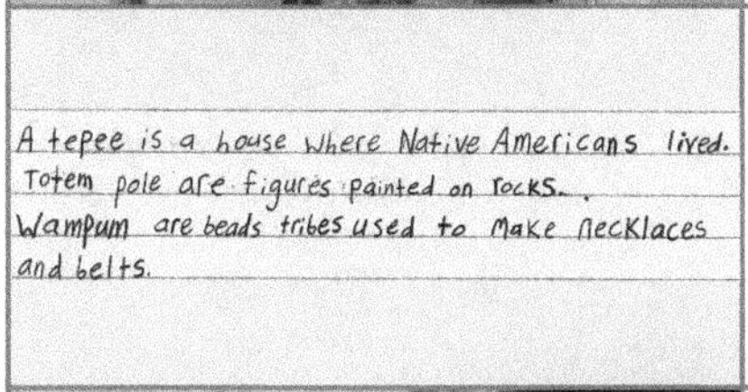	Next, the teacher has students practice writing short paragraphs using their words and the target vocabulary. The words must be used correctly in the context in which they were learned.
	At the end of the lesson, after multiple opportunities for practice and application, the student is ready to be held accountable for his or her learning. In Pic-Tac-Tell, students are asked to write their own paragraph related to the content. The teacher, having observed students along the way, provides a more accurate final assessment.

(Images courtesy of Leah Wisdom, 6th Grade, Kansas)

- Develop assessments that are focused on producing thinking and learning
- Use assessment results to provide feedback that supports students' future learning

One of our greatest challenges today is convincing students that assessment does not have to be, and indeed *should not be*, dehumanizing. We must redefine assessment as an indicator of progress that values each learner's point of departure. Assessments should inform our instruction and guide us to make sound decisions regarding ways we can continue to build on CLD students' assets to increase their achievement and support their development as lifelong learners.

Reflections on Affirming Student Learning Through Assessment

Great teachers empathize with kids, respect them, and believe that each one has something special that can be built upon.

—Ann Lieberman

Transparency in teaching and end-of-lesson celebration and elaboration increase student engagement and create a community in which learners know they can succeed. This perception alone can have a tremendous influence on the socioemotional state of mind and motivation of the CLD student. It is much easier to encourage and support students who know they have been provided with all the conditions, situations, and tools to be successful. When we implement strategies throughout the lesson that provide optimal $i+1$ conditions for learning, students come to the end of the lesson ready to demonstrate their new understandings and skills on postinstructional assessments. Such assessments take on a new look when the CLD student biography is the guiding force behind individual accountability. Postinstructional assessments culminate the lesson and allow us to provide feedback beyond a grade.

A move toward biography-driven assessment will require us to revisit our own patterns and habits of teaching and assessment. By focusing more on students' thinking and learning and less on meeting externally imposed agendas (which frequently are the agendas of individuals

by grading systems. It is our responsibility as educators to think about what we want for our classrooms and to begin balancing school politics with what we know is right for the learners. This will require us to:

- Create a classroom ecology that provides CLD students with a safe place for making public their thoughts and ideas
- Configure groups that teach
- Orchestrate student dialogue through questions that challenge
- Move students beyond the mentality that only "correct" answers count

who lack the preparation to understand culturally responsive, sustaining pedagogy), we transform our classrooms into true communities of care and learning. While the long-term goals remain the same, the path I am asking you to take looks *and feels* very different. As a result, students are more likely to develop positive beliefs about themselves as learners, experience greater academic success in the classroom, and increase their achievement on standardized tests as well! As CLD students reap the benefits of internalized learning strategies, more in-depth comprehension of content, and lowered affective filters, enhanced performance outcomes on "standard" measures of student achievement often are a happy side effect. The more we maintain our focus on the humanity and well-being of CLD students, the more likely we are to arrive together at our destination.

10 Biography-Driven Pedagogical Action

Voices of Care, Hope, and Academic Achievement

GUIDING QUESTION

How does an emphasis on reflective practice and standards for effective pedagogy provide us with a blueprint for creating meaningful teaching and learning experiences?

See the online Discussion Guide for opportunities to further explore answers to this question and connections to chapter content with a colleague or team. Available for download from the Teachers College Press website: tcpress.com

Cultural pedagogy therefore creates the possibility of education being personal, and thus collective or social change, as well as intellectual challenge and the pursuit of knowledge, is possible. Recognizing and developing education as a cultural practice creates an opportunity for students to engage actively in a change process that aims to influence positively the way that they understand and relate to one another.

—*Debra Manning (2006, p. 54)*

AT THE END of this book and the end of your school day, it will be important to ask: What have I accomplished today to make the world a better place for all students? This is the question that really matters in teaching. Not long ago, before I had any thoughts of writing about my work in schools, I was being interviewed by a person who wanted to know what it would take to decrease the dropout rate, engage and motivate students, and give CLD students the "push" they needed to achieve academic success. My response was not what the interviewer expected to hear.

I explained that during my years in collaborating with both pre-service and in-service teachers, my only goal was to move them beyond the I-don't-see-color, or colorblind, perspective toward seeing the *cargas* and *regalos* (gifts and challenges) that CLD students bring to the classroom. Rather than seeing students from a deficit perspective, we should begin the journey toward educating them as if they were the next president of the United States. I told the interviewer that this was more important than any theory or

strategy teachers would learn from participating in a course or professional development. I said that assumptions about what is possible need to be examined for their validity. What really matters is the biography of the teacher and how that influences their teaching and CLD students' learning.

The interview continued, with my responses always coming back to knowing students' biographies, meeting students where they are academically, captivating students' hearts and minds, and knowing who they really are, including their dreams and aspirations. It was evident after 10 minutes that not only was the interviewer frustrated with my answers but also that he wanted me to provide him with some magic answer that was not so touchy feely. Finally, the frustration with my responses got to him and he asked, "Aren't you a little too idealistic about what is possible with these students? They have so many problems in their home, they are so behind, and their parents don't really care about education."

I smiled and reminded him that it is in the idealistic world that teaching happens, because there are no limitations placed on what can happen. When you believe it is possible, you approach curriculum and the learner from a different perspective. As a teacher, you keep looking at what research has to say and setting up the learning environment to ensure no student is left behind. This, I have observed, happens most often in rural and urban, rich and poor schools with teachers who are idealistic, who are passionate, and who care about their students. Through their teaching, such educators provide opportunities for everyone to have access, hold high expectations, and create low-risk environments where everyone is held accountable for learning. Then it becomes less about the curriculum and more about the student, hope, and academic achievement.

As a teacher educator, I have to ask myself if this is, indeed, too idealistic to make it part of the plan for teaching and learning. Yet, many who have committed a lifetime to writing about culturally relevant pedagogy in schools have documented through their work *how* and *when* it happens. Sonia Nieto, Guadalupe Valdés, Luis Moll, Geneva Gay, and many others continue to encourage teachers to realize that *all* students can and will learn if provided the conditions to do so.

What then is it that keeps us educators trapped in a box? Could years of research be so wrong that many in political circles discount what they have to say? I believe the alternative to be true. Politics and politicians often are driven by agendas that are economic rather than humanistic in nature. So much time is spent focusing on what does not work that CLD students are lost in the debate. Culturally relevant pedagogy begins with understanding CLD students and their families. It ends with teachers' ability to think outside the box, to think beyond limitations, to make no more excuses, and to provide equitable opportunities for CLD students to be successful in school. Teachers who are committed to proving the status quo wrong—and who have the necessary passion and commitment—have the potential to shift current political agendas and provide those all-important opportunities in today's schools.

A Different Type of Agenda

The complex and dynamic nature of our schools today requires a capacity to move beyond prescriptive programs and laundry lists of characteristics and behaviors that are to be expected from different cultural groups. Rather, educators must be prepared to understand the biographies of their students and the implications those biographies have on practice. Becoming informed is the first and most important step toward becoming a culturally responsive teacher. This means finding the time and doing what it takes to make the biography of the CLD student a priority within our classrooms and schools. As educators, we must understand the contexts in which we teach, and we must use the assets that students bring from home and community to create conditions and situations in our classrooms that value *all* knowledge.

One of the most significant goals of this book is to move teachers beyond the myth that what is presented in high-quality courses or professional development training for CLD students is *just good teaching* for all students. If this were true, more of our schools across the country would be performing significantly better than they currently are. Gay (2018) reminds us:

Many educators still believe that good teaching transcends place, people, time, and context. They contend it has nothing to do with the class, race, gender, ethnicity, or culture of students and teachers. This attitude is manifested in the expression "Good teachers anywhere are good teachers everywhere." Individuals who subscribe to this belief fail to realize that their standards of "goodness" in teaching and learning are culturally determined and are not the same for all ethnic groups. (p. 29)

If we continue to think, "Oh, it's just good teaching," we discount the rich diversity that students bring to our classrooms and buy into the one-size-fits-all mentality. A movement away from this, as discussed and described in this book, is about getting to know the student and his or her family beyond superficial interest surveys, questionnaires, home language surveys, or other point-in-time snapshots of what students know, like, and can do. Our decisions and actions in our professional practice must create opportunities for us and our students to learn not only about the content, but also about each other as unique individuals.

BDI and Research-Based Standards

Since our research and implementation work began, BDI has continued to be a theory-into-practice framework for culturally responsive and sustaining pedagogy that is situated at the intersection of care, hope, and achievement. In the real world of increasingly diverse and complex schools and communities, it is difficult for teachers to effectively deliver on the goals of the framework/model without progressively developing their own dispositions and agency. To genuinely understand the CLD student's multidimensional biography is to *care* about her or him as an individual, to actively learn relevant aspects of the child's background knowledge anchored in his or her home cultural socialization, community membership (in the U.S. or abroad), and experiences as a learner (and often an emergent bilingual) in educational settings.

Caring is not a *"pobrecito"* mindset, where the learner is viewed through a deficit lens and the teacher can see only the limiting aspects of the student's circumstances. Caring also is not about the teacher being the "savior," coming to *give* students what they need to succeed. Instead, caring is about us as teachers seeing the potential in learners and recognizing that the knowledge and experiences they already have are the catalysts for their learning. Students need us to believe in them and to help them to see what is possible. Biography-driven instruction is a pedagogy of hope driven by the strengths and assets the family and learner bring.

For CLD students, BDI strategies are a powerful way to make hope tangible—hope that their prior experiences and schooling will not be overlooked in redundant instruction; hope that they can use their home language to learn another, as a part of classroom interactions and dialogue; hope that their funds of frequently untapped knowledge will allow them to participate at grade level; hope that the sacrifices of their family to provide their children a better education will not be in vain. Hope fuels CLD engagement with learning, language acquisition, and ultimately, academic achievement.

Yet, K–12 teachers in the United States are often under intense technocratic and time-intensive pressure to cover all of the curricula, irrespective of the population being served; to prepare learners for complicated formal and summative assessments; and to ensure that all students (including those whose primary language is not English) perform well on these complex and decontextualized assessments. As a result, teachers sometimes put aside what they know is effective pedagogy for CLD learners in order to meet the deficit-driven mandates required to "fix" the perceived problems that families and learners bring, by applying programs, models, curricula, and interventions. What to do in this educational context in which we find ourselves today becomes the question. It has become increasingly important to ask ourselves why we entered this service profession. In our rush to check off a laundry list of agendas, how often do we let go of the knowledge we have that can move students toward meaningful academic achievement? Among those who validate this concern are members of the National Board for Professional Teaching Standards (NBPTS), Teachers of English to Speakers of Other Languages (TESOL), and other professional organizations that prioritize defensible goals for preservice and in-service teachers.

In the past 20 years, our research has documented the impact that biography-driven, culturally responsive and sustaining instruction has on the socioemotional and academic achievement of the learner. Building on the *Standards for Effective Pedagogy and Learning* developed by the Center for Research on Education Diversity (e.g., CREDE, 2021; Tharp & Dalton, 2007; Tharp et al., 2000), we have guided teacher development and practice, supporting teachers to differentiate their practices for CLD learners to promote consistent, sustainable literacy development, language growth, and academic gains.

The CREDE standards are the product of more than a decade of research and analyses that have yielded five *transnationally effective* touchstones for differentiated teaching practices (Tharp & Dalton, 2007). These standards emphasize persistent, systematic classroom observation as a means to enhancing the responsiveness of teachers' facilitation of learning. They have served as a theoretical framework for research on teachers' efficacy with CLD and other underserved learners (e.g., Murry et al., 2015; Yamauchi et al., 2013). Each of the CREDE standards is evidence-based, defensible, and briefly discussed in the narratives that follow.

Contextualization
Making Meaning Through Relevance

In a BDI sense, contextualization is foundational to conceptual learning as well as literacy and language development. Teachers who maximize it begin to learn about the background of their students, focusing on their sociocultural, linguistic, cognitive, and academic biographies. What a teacher knows and learns about the student provides multiple entry points for learning. From creating a Biography Card to setting conditions during the lesson that provide all community members with opportunities to engage using what they know, teachers who maximize contextualization during instruction use student assets as points of departure for accessing academic content.

Critical for teachers of CLD students is an understanding of the learner's background knowledge systems. Three knowledge systems are especially relevant to contextualization: the student's funds of knowledge (rooted in the family), prior/experiential knowledge (grounded in the community), and academic knowledge (developed in the school). When the teacher believes that all students possess background knowledge and is intentional in finding ways to bring it to light, then the result is a wealth of assets available for learning.

Teachers also provide contextualization by using the identified assets of learners to locate commonalities across students that might foster or be used to maximize a caring community of learners. Each student enters the learning experience with both assets and challenges. For example, one student might be strong linguistically because she is an emergent bilingual but prove challenged by learning mathematics. Because students who are challenged in a particular subject may learn as much, or more, from a more capable/experienced peer as they do from their teacher (Walqui & van Lier, 2010), they should be regularly encouraged and facilitated to share and exchange ideas, perspectives, and questions. Use of a BDI strategy throughout the lesson provides a scaffold for learners' sharing of language, skills, and knowledge with the teacher and their peers.

By activating students' background knowledge, making connections between the known and the unknown, and affirming student/family assets as the foundation for what is learned, educators contextualize the new academic concepts and language. Applications to the real world also are more likely to be made when classroom learning experiences *begin* with what students know, which is already situated in the real world. In this kind of classroom ecology, students develop a cognitive belief system in which they see themselves as valuable, capable learners.

Instructional Conversation
Teaching Through Dialogue

Through instructional conversations, teachers and their students engage in dialogue that initiates and sustains the sharing of ideas and knowledge. The teacher elicits student talk by questioning, listening, rephrasing, and providing opportunities for student-led discussion to emerge from the natural rhythm and progression of BDI classroom learning. During dialogic sharing, the teacher listens and observes for insights into students' background knowledge, their meaning-making processes, and the intended message of the language produced. She or he monitors for opportunities to support the learner in drawing and elaborating upon connections between what is already known and the academic content. These connections, once made public for the classroom community, can be revoiced by the teacher to affirm learning, support content comprehension, scaffold language use, and crystallize connections that serve to advance attainment of the learning outcomes.

When students are encouraged to become active participants and teachers are willing to release the tight hold they oftentimes have over the flow of the conversation, learners and teachers together have opportunities in the third space to co-construct shared understandings of the content. In this type of instructional conversation, everyone's social and academic stories matter. The educator's caring is made evident through interactions and communicative interchanges that demonstrate interest in the students' language, literacy, and cultural ways of being and knowing. Paris and Alim (2014) have argued that such validation operates to help sustain the culture of the student's family and community.

Collaborative, small-group conversations among peers provide students with extended opportunities for academic talk. As they use the conceptual vocabulary to discuss the topic at hand, they serve as language models for one another. These discussions also provide the teacher with the social language (BICS) used by students that can then be used to scaffold toward increasingly complex and decontextualized academic language (CALP) (Cummins, 1981). Pivotal to this process is allowing students to articulate their views, judgments, and processes and to provide rationales. It is through the articulation of their rationales that students are continually stretched toward higher-order thinking and more elaborate use of language. When thinking is made public, the entire learning community can benefit.

Language and Literacy Development
Prioritizing Cross-Cultural Communication

Situating language and literacy development within CLD students' ways of knowing and "reading the world" (Freire & Macedo, 1987) allows learners to build from the foundation of oracy and literacy in their homes and communities.

The language that students bring to the classroom reflects the history of their lives. It is the medium through which they make sense of their individual experiences and social interactions with others. The literacy practices of the family support the functioning of the household and are often embedded in community interactions that bring joy and a shared sense of belonging. In stark contrast are the conditions in U.S. schools, which historically have asked CLD students to leave their cultures and languages at the door and instead learn through the lenses of other people and communicate using other people's words. Learning environments of this sort serve to silence and marginalize students, along with their experiences, languages, and literacies. They are expected to be autonomous learners, after having been deprived of the ability to use their conceptual frames of reference and their full linguistic repertoire.

From a BDI perspective, this standard encourages multilingualism and biliteracy, especially through translanguaging. Students are encouraged and provided purposeful opportunities to use their L1 as a scaffold for English learning, all the while valuing the role of the native language as a learning and life resource in its own right (L1). Theory and research in the field have repeatedly stressed the value of approaching students as *emergent bilinguals* by enabling them to simultaneously develop both their L1 and L2 language proficiencies (e.g., Byers-Heinlein & Lew-Williams, 2013; Collier & Thomas, 2009; Genesee, n.d.; Howard et al., 2018). CLD learners benefit from reading and writing tasks that allow them to use their culture-bound ways of comprehending, communicating, and expressing themselves as a springboard for language and literacy development. Language and literacy processes and products, such as those that result from use of BDI strategies, validate learners and their cultures and languages (Murry et al., 2021). In short, they engage the *whole learner* in the meaning-making process.

BDI provides opportunities for integrated development of listening, speaking, reading, and writing skills, especially through collaborative partner and small-team interaction. Key to language and literacy is creating contexts in which members of our community of learners are able to learn from one other. Literacy and language development are intertwined with our identity as learners, and by engaging in conversation with others, students are able to share about themselves and gain alternative perspectives on language and text. When we create a classroom ecology that sets conditions for students to raise questions, express opinions, take risks, explore ideas, and examine their own thinking, we expand their opportunities for *i*+1 input, multiple exposures to conceptual vocabulary, and opportunities for authentic language use. This type of active engagement provides the context for our own use of questioning, rephrasing, and modeling to assist language and literacy development.

Joint Productive Activity
Teacher and Students Producing Together

Joint productive activity prioritizes production focused on a common goal among all participants of the learning community. Through collaborative problem-solving with the teacher and peers, the learner is engaged in the development of a joint product. The teacher is present to the learning and facilitates by engaging, monitoring, and providing feedback. Creating contexts that nurture common experiences, where outcomes/products are socially co-constructed, has the potential to lead to improved CLD student academic achievement, hope for academic success, and confidence to engage with someone who is not culturally and linguistically like themselves.

Joint productive activity is scaffolded through BDI strategies and contributes to content learning, literacy development, and second language acquisition in contexts and situations where:

- Multifaceted student collaborations target a particular problem, a common goal, or a collectively created product.
- Grouping configurations and structures are the result of the teacher's awareness and consideration of students' biographies, encompassing, for example, their shared interests, diversity of cultures, range of language proficiencies, and familiarity with the academic content.
- Facilitation by the teacher is responsive to students' assets or needs, made possible by actively listening to and observing for ways students are comprehending the language and making sense of the content throughout the lesson.

Pivotal to joint productivity is creating a classroom ecology in which the learning of CLD students is fostered through the structures, arrangements, events, and processes of the classroom. Two types of processes influence an ecology. *Contextual processes* set the conditions for content learning and language acquisition/development through joint productivity as the teacher maximizes the physical setting, the curriculum to be taught, and the community of learners. *Situational processes* are the means through which the teacher orchestrates teaching and learning dynamics "in the moment." These two processes work interdependently to either cultivate or inhibit liberatory learning and development necessary to student success.

Joint productive activity that contributes to culturally responsive and sustaining teaching ensures that students engage as equal members through grouping arrangements according to *i+TpsI* throughout the lesson cycle. For the teacher, consideration of the intended outcomes of the lesson, the content, the complexity and language demands of the task, student readiness, and other factors serves to guide how instruction will unfold and what classroom conditions/situations are needed to optimize learning. Moving from "*i*" (what is known) to total group—and then releasing partners and small teams who jointly and productively question, clarify, and connect what they know to the vocabulary and conceptual knowledge—allows learners to advance toward greater understanding. Throughout the lesson, teachers use insights from what students produce in order to scaffold connections, affirm learning, and modify instruction as needed.

Challenging Activities
Teaching Higher-Order and Critical Thinking Skills

The Common Core State Standards, among others, suggest that it is increasingly vital to teach academic skills and cognitive processing, including higher-order thinking skills and evidence-based argumentation, along with content. These activities are designed by the educator to stretch all students toward their zones of proximal development in cognition (Herrera & Murry, 2016; Tharp & Dalton, 2007; Vygotsky, 1978). In structuring and implementing challenging activities for emergent bilinguals and other CLD students, it is necessary to maintain low affective filters and nurture a sense of hope among students as they progressively build and exercise their prowess for cognitive complexity. Teachers facilitate student understanding of rigorous academic content by planning appropriate accommodations (e.g., providing a tool in the hand, incorporating partner work) and informally assessing their responses in order to use that information during the lesson (Herrera, Kavimandan, & Holmes, 2011; Herrera et al., 2017).

Explicit content and language objectives provide learners with transparency with regard to where the lesson is heading. When challenging activities are aligned with standards for content and language development, learners know they being asked to engage in respectful work rather than "busy work." BDI strategies incorporate and scaffold challenging activities and promote higher-order thinking. As they implement BDI to support learning, teachers:

- Provide opportunities for students to brainstorm, document, and build upon their connections to background knowledge
- Ask thought-provoking *who, what, when, where, why, and how* questions
- Incorporate multiple perspectives on a topic or focus
- Encourage peer collaboration (e.g., through pairs or small groups)
- Prompt students to connect different ideas and engage in thoughtful decision-making
- Reward creativity
- Facilitate difficult conversations

Depending on the activity and context, teachers incorporate opportunities for student choice, integrate technology, and utilize assignments that require imaginative thinking.

Throughout the lesson, teachers refer to posted learning objectives, using them as checkpoints for learning of the classroom community. Highly effective teachers observe, facilitate, and affirm even incremental gains in students' conceptual understanding, skill development, and language acquisition. Students are scaffolded in their learning, and in their ability to recognize their own growth, through the use cognitive, metacognitive, and social/affective learning strategies. When such strategy use is combined with consistent feedback to confirm/disconfirm learning and prompt higher-order thinking, students develop increased agency as learners.

IT IS THROUGH the consistent use of the CREDE-aligned, biography-driven strategies described in this book, utilizing the processes summarized in the indicators of Figure 10.1 (pages 169–174), that teachers will be able to effectively impact all of their learners, especially CLD students. Teachers who receive professional development that focuses on these strategies tend to outperform their counterparts on the Inventory of Situationally and Culturally Responsive Teaching (ISCRT) (Herrera, Perez, et al., 2011; MacDonald et al., 2013; Murry et al., 2015), a tool that is meant to reflect BDI practices. High performance by teachers in use of these strategies increases the likelihood that students will advance both linguistically and academically (MacDonald et al., 2013; Perez et al., 2012). Figure 10.2 (page 175) shows how all of these concepts—along with others from previous chapters—work together. This diagram provides a visual representation of BDI concepts as *one cohesive unit* that should be employed throughout the entire lesson, rather than as a series of fragmented pieces to be merely considered or implemented only occasionally at convenient times. Ultimately, biography-driven instruction should be seen as a way to engage students from the moment they enter our classrooms until long after they have left. Teachers can use Figure 10.3 (page 176) both to self-assess how they relate to critical aspects of effective pedagogy and to plan for implementation. The following stories highlight the experiences of educators in the field who have changed their practices to reflect the ideals of biography-driven instruction. They describe the positive impact of their change in mindset and use of BDI principles and strategies on their teaching and their students' learning.

Action and Transformation: The Schoolwide Impact of BDI

To convey the magnitude of transformation potential that biography-driven instruction holds for learners, teachers, and entire systems, I share this account of Samuel E. Spaght Science and Communications Magnet, an elementary school in Wichita, Kansas. This story is not mine. Rather, it is told by Dr. Robin Cabral, who has long facilitated BDI professional development with teachers at this school, in collaboration with the principal, Kristina Bowyer. Together, these individuals have joined forces to share the school's journey toward enhanced educational practices, contextualized within the sociopolitical dynamics that over time have both challenged and embraced what it means to foster student success.

Knowing a bit of the school's history is important to understanding the depth of change in mindset that was required to alter the trajectory of the learning taking place within. This school, referred to by the community simply as "Spaght," reflects a history similar to that of many schools affected by pervasive structural and educational inequities over time. Established in the early 1900s, Spaght (then Ingalls) quickly expanded to accommodate a growing and increasingly diverse town. Social and economic forces (i.e., redlining) heavily influenced where families chose and/or were allowed to settle. In 1957, Ingalls's population was more than 50% Black. By 1969, only one White child attended school from this attendance area.

In 1971, Wichita entered into a busing agreement with the U.S. Department of Education's Office for Civil Rights. Ingalls became one of several schools in predominantly Black areas to be closed entirely or have most students reassigned outside of the community to achieve racial integration. White students were encouraged to volunteer for busing, with a much smaller percentage chosen by lottery for reassignment to schools such as Ingalls. Inside the walls, Ingalls became majority White. It was no longer a neighborhood school, and no longer as accessible to, or representative of, the geographical community.

During the 1990s, Ingalls was designated a World Knowledge Magnet, then contracted as charter school before reestablishment as Spaght Accelerated Magnet. In 2008, the Wichita school board voted unanimously to end 37 years of mandatory busing. While busing had sought a positive goal, Black students had always comprised the majority of those bused across town to achieve integration. Most applauded the change away from busing but some worried that schools would resegregate and, in doing so, would no longer be able to provide a high-quality education for all. Inherent to these concerns were both the realities of past inequities but also an implication that predominantly Black schools would fail without a balance of White representation. It was within this context that Spaght Multimedia Magnet became the recipient of grants designed to provide access to top technologies and, in doing so, became a greater attraction for students from outside the neighborhood. Racial integration was an ongoing ideal.

Deemed a Science and Communications Magnet in 2014, Spaght experienced more change in demographics. Culturally and linguistically diverse families moved into the area. As a result, Spaght became designated as an ESOL instructional site. Additional CLD students are now bused into Spaght for participation in this ESOL program.

These years of increased cultural and linguistic diversity coincided with the adoption of MTSS (multi-tiered system of supports), whereby universal screenings and protocols guide student placements in structured academic programs within the school. MTSS (and RTI [response to intervention]) systems are designed to provide "spot treatment" of academic needs through tiered interventions *in addition to* core instruction in which 80%–85% of students experience success. Spaght staff were, however, among early adopters misinterpreting that the school's entire population required intensive support. It was not unusual to hear comments such as "This whole school is tier 2/3" or "Our students aren't yet ready for core." Core instruction is where *all* students learn together about content, despite differences in skills. Core is akin to home, where the entire family watches, enjoys, and learns from a movie, even if not everyone reads subtitles at the same speed. In this case, a focus on discrete skills was reducing learners' opportunities for core instruction.

Despite added funds and layers of curricula intended to bolster outcomes, achievement at Spaght floundered. By 2018, it ranked last, 55th of 55 district elementary schools. Teachers were frustrated, feeling that everything was being done to "fill gaps" but nothing worked. Some expressed that maybe nothing could.

Introduction of BDI

Across town, a few teachers at schools in historically ESOL neighborhoods began using BDI. Improvements in achievement, parent participation, and climate stood out from schools in similar areas that were using the same "universal" curriculum. Could BDI move the needle at the district's lowest-performing school? District administrators thought it might.

Contextually, it was difficult for Spaght staff to hear about "one more thing" to do while juggling new programs, protocols, technology, and accountability expectations. The climate had already deteriorated to the point that it was not uncommon to hear insults hurled between students and staff. Staff comments revealed low expectations (academic/behavioral) and preconceived notions that students were bound for failure in the form of early parenthood, unemployment, or crime. Attitudes were reinforced within a climate of mutual disrespect. A proactive behavioral program was in place but poorly implemented. Many expressed beliefs that Spaght challenges resulted from Spaght stu-

dents. Behaviors were countable infractions rather than opportunities for reflection.

In the 2018–2019 school year, Spaght reported 3,017 occurrences of disruptive behavior, fighting, insubordination, and battery on pupil or battery on staff. Many resulted in office time as well as in/out-of-school suspension. Students were missing out on a significant amount of instruction. That same year, only 6.93% of Spaght students met levels of proficiency associated with college and career readiness on Kansas state assessments.

Perceiving the reinforcing nature of low expectations, the district committed more deeply to BDI for the following year. The administration conveyed the message, "We believe in families, students, and teachers. BDI will foster creation of positive learning spaces. It's not going away."

An additional challenge posed that year was the adoption of a new reading curriculum. Teachers who had begun to implement BDI strategies the year before struggled to translate use of those tools within the prescribed tasks, pace, and scripts of the new material. District and publisher trainings emphasized fidelity through delivery of the curriculum in set ways, right down to the minutes dedicated for each component skill. Through this lens of instruction, BDI did not seem to fit. Frustrated teachers pushed back against BDI, but district leaders held on to their support, determined to do so at least until sufficient data could be gathered.

Observations in classes and during professional development were encouraging, but mixed. Several teachers reported increased engagement and student conversation. Others struggled with long-held beliefs that the ideal classroom is silent, that only the teacher may speak, and that "good listening" is passive. While some teachers found excitement in trying the BDI strategies, others resisted anything that felt like a loss of control. It was easier to adopt use of strategy templates than the processes they were designed support.

Noticing this trend, Spaght's new administrator requested a reset on BDI. Many staff were new, so it proved an authentic opportunity to revisit the *why*. Implementation would need to be deepened across grade levels to leverage instruction schoolwide.

Teachers continued meeting for professional development (PD) in grade-level teams for the rest of the year. These teams always included the ESOL and special education teachers supporting those classes. PD discussions around student work artifacts and video clips of BDI instructional practices allowed teachers to experience the learning power of *i+TpsI* firsthand. Among the most common takeaways was, "I need to let my students talk." Coaches also benefitted from reframing PD as opportunities for teachers to activate, connect, and affirm new learning via this process. How might discussions around a "tool in their hands" lead to more durable understandings and creative applications of the *why*?

(upper left) Grade 1 learners in Ms. Condray's class share their connections with the four seasons. Having opportunities to collaborate with peers and articulate their thinking supports students' comprehension, critical thinking, and language development.

(lower left) Families of students in Ms. Perdue's 1st-grade class document their connections and experiences related to the topic. They engage with the student at home to activate background knowing using the BDI Linking Language strategy. Each family member involved writes their name on the shared poster.

(lower right) Family members added to the self-portraits that students created in order to share assets and characteristics of the learners or comments about what the students love.

Affirmation

Throughout this school year, teachers engaged in more deliberate discussions of academic and behavioral data. What changes were noted? How did these data jibe with student work and participation in class? For teachers discouraged by Spaght's perennial last place among district schools, it was exciting to see evidence of BDI gaining traction and growth in achievement. Teachers were being *successful* at teaching. Students were *learning*. Fewer students were being sent from, or leaving, class. These were initially small celebrations, but each was an affirmation of practice—*an affirmation of Spaght.*

As more teachers sought the power derived from student connections, families were increasingly embraced as partners. Students' lives outside of school were affirmed as sources of knowledge and as assets for learning in school. Home projects completed with adult collaboration were no longer viewed as "cheating" or "dependence" but as indices of family involvement and potent conversations around academic content. The momentum continued.

Midway through spring break 2020, students and teachers received word that schools would not reopen. COVID-19 outbreaks had grown to pandemic proportions and communities were required to shelter at home. Societal inequities that had never really gone away impeded access again for students at schools like Spaght. Working parents in the service sector still went to work; others lost jobs. Students stayed home, many without supervision, technology, utilities, food, and sometimes the safety needed to participate educationally with peers. Digital dependence and its structural divides deepened disparities, but Spaght teachers *leaned into* this new space. In doing so, they discovered firsthand the day-to-day challenges some students face that dwarf homework completion or even the ability to simply stay awake. They also learned that if we educators pay attention, students' lives are anything but barren. What is going on in their worlds does relate to learning at school. Teachers who are aware of and prepared to respond to students' background knowledge find that it can be maximized to enhance the learning of all students. The challenges and richness experienced during this atypical year made use of BDI even more relevant. School did not resume fully for another year, and even then, with barriers to communication unknown before the pandemic (e.g., masks, partitions, restricted interaction structures).

In 2021, Spaght chose to continue its efforts to double down on BDI. Comfortable implementers took on the role of nurturing new staff. As with students, the entry point for teachers is simply *wherever one happens to be.* And the school trajectory? The arrow points up, and the numbers speak for themselves.

District ranking:
- In 2018, Spaght ranked 55th of Wichita's 55 elementary schools.
- By 2021, it ranked 33rd.

Student achievement:
- In 2018, 6.93% of students achieved state assessment levels on track for college and career readiness.
- By 2021, that percentage rose to 35.16%.

Learner behavior:
- In the 2018–2019 academic year, 3,017 behavior incidents classified as disruptive, fighting, insubordination, and battery were reported to have occurred at Spaght.
- During the 2020–2021 year, the number of incidents decreased to 187.

The story of Spaght is exciting. Spaght families matter to the school community, and their engagement supports this shared perception. Spaght teachers continue to use BDI, leveraging it to unleash the potential the students possess and continually reflecting on their instructional practices. Most importantly, Spaght students are on their way—writing a future of *hope.*

Voices From the Field

The accounts that follow reflect the voices of administrators and teachers who have chosen to step outside the box and create ecologies that are grounded in the lives of the students they teach. Gay (2018) defines culturally responsive teaching as "using the cultural knowledge, prior experiences, frames of reference, and performance styles of ethnically diverse students to make learning encounters more relevant to and effective for them" (p. 36). I have chosen to include in this final chapter the voices of individuals who have inspired me to continue my work in schools. Through their vision, commitment, and passion, I have been affirmed

in my efforts to pursue the "idealistic" world in which CLD students are supported in achieving academic success.

These reports are taken from the districts with which I have worked the longest and where I have had time to see systemic transformative results. Other districts around the country, from Oregon to Pennsylvania, Texas to South Carolina, are adopting BDI principles and tools as an overlay to the ESL programs they are using, and they, too, are beginning to feel the excitement that you will hear in reflections that follow. Readers who start incorporating biography-driven instruction and assessment are also invited to share their experiences with me.

The administrators and teachers represented here have taken their knowledge and acted to do what is right for students, regardless of the consequences. For example, by going from a pull-out program to a more inclusive learning community that considered the biographies of students who represented 49 different languages, Hillcrest Elementary created an ecology of respect for their students and families. The road was not easy. Yet, through ongoing conversation and dedication to an "idealistic" goal, a new type of instructional conversation resulted for teachers and students in all classrooms.

Although we often hear that change cannot happen at the high school level, two administrators from Salina South High School share their journey of change. With high expectations for all, Salina South is rethinking the education of their CLD students. Without excuses, they have moved forward in building communities of learners, where more opportunities are provided for students to learn from one another. Evident in this ecology is the value placed on all students' biographies.

The next two voices are those of educators who have lived and experienced what it means to be biography-driven. They speak with openness and honesty about the joys and struggles of finding ways to make their classrooms and schools places where every student of every background can be at home. By collaborating with students, families, and colleagues, these educators have found ways to make their professional practice relevant and responsive to the assets and needs of their CLD students.

The final voice is that of a Kansas Teacher of the Year. Caring begins with making connections with kids, and this educator recognizes that you cannot care for all children in the same way. Each learner needs a particular kind of care, based on his or her experiences, strengths, and challenges. This is especially true in classrooms such as hers, in which the learning community reflects significant diversity with regard to cultures, languages, recency of arrival, home lives, ability, trauma, and previous access to formal schooling. Despite institutional and sociopolitical influences that create decreased autonomy for teachers (e.g., to make decisions about how to use the curriculum, to select resources for supporting learners), her desire to humanize instruction propels her to continually respond to and leverage students' biographies.

Tammy Becker, Principal
Hillcrest Elementary, Lawrence, Kansas

Learning for All, Whatever It Takes

Transforming the curriculum for our culturally and linguistically diverse students and, as educators, rethinking our perspectives on these students was no easy task. But when we discovered we were doing an inappropriate job of instructing nearly half of our student population, we knew something had to change. Some of our teachers started thinking of how we could make our school community inclusive of all our students. As we started working with the needs of students, we found that the students do not see differences. They see each other as individuals all coming together. At our school and in the classroom we recognize our differences, but it doesn't set us apart.

The initial idea of working toward a classroom community came in 2003, when a group of our staff began taking professional development that eventually led to professional dialogue within our building about the way we handled the instruction of our students. At that time, we were pulling CLD students out of the classroom to work on materials different from what was happening in their grade-level classroom. That meant removing, at times, 300 CLD students from their 200 English-speaking peers—likely leading to stigmatization of the CLD students.

The more we worked with students, the more we realized that the Celias, Mohammeds, and Joses of the world need more than just being pulled out of the classroom and seeing a new face every 30 minutes. Not only was this a costly practice, but it also didn't recognize any of the CLD students' academic knowledge in their native language. We saw students from many Arabic countries sit in the library during the lunch hour and refuse to go to the cafeteria. We also saw that some of our students would refuse to participate in any Halloween-related activities. As we started asking "why" about many of these unfamiliar practices, we found ourselves with no answers.

The more we reflected on these challenges, the more we started thinking that since our students were being divided among so many teachers, none of our teachers really were aware of the biographies of our students. All we knew was that we had this student whose parents had filled out a home language survey and the district had done a LAS (language assessment) on them. We placed the students based on the numbers they received for their LAS scores. And when the students were pulled from their grade-level classrooms, they missed out on the content being taught, and we only continued to hinder their progress. That was a turning point in making learning a true reality for a lot of our students. We knew we needed to bring the students back into the general classroom; we needed to help them acquire academic language skills, while also exposing them to the content-area curriculum.

In 2004 we began using sheltered instruction, and within 2 years all students were included in the general classroom. This truly was the beginning of making students feel like they were a part of our community. From that time onward, we decided as a school that we can no longer make assumptions, and it is now our moral responsibility to support our students when they sit out at lunch hour during the month of Ramadan or don't participate in Halloween activities due to their cultural backgrounds.

During the process of implementing this program, I experienced resistance from both teachers and parents who thought that having ESL students in the classroom would take away from other students' learning. But by inviting parents to be a part of the school and being open about the changes and the research supporting our decisions, many parents began to see that when CLD students are in the classroom, not only do they benefit, but so does the rest of the school population. Now students work more collaboratively—across language and culture barriers—and share what they know, because now *we* know that when students work cooperatively, they enhance their ability to learn and retain what they have learned.

Every day I walk down the hallway of the school and know this is my vision, and each day I learn something new from our students. We are honored to have students in our school and classrooms who truly make our school a community of learners. Culture and language have become integral parts of our curriculum. Just the other day, our 6th-grade students together voted not to have any snacks in the classroom during Ramadan so our Muslim students don't feel excluded when the others are eating. This would not have happened in the classroom if the teachers did not share the vision of "Learning for all, whatever it takes."

Even now, years after we completely implemented the program, I know that we must make a continual effort to provide culturally responsive teaching. That means supporting our teachers and providing more than a one-time professional development session. It takes time and commitment to make sure all our teachers are able to meet the needs of every single student. All our teachers receive intensive training, including observation and feedback and ongoing professional development to learn new instructional strategies. We encourage collaboration between grade-level teachers and hold student-progress reviews, which provide a time for educators to work as a team to identify ways to help their CLD students achieve academic success.

I know that facing a classroom in which half the students are English learners can be daunting. But I know it can be done, when we all work together to help *all* our students succeed.

Dr. George Troutfetter and Gary White, Assistant Principals

Salina South High School, Salina, Kansas

Valuing the Student Begins With Valuing the Native Language

Oliver Wendell Holmes wrote, "Every language is a temple, in which the soul of those who speak it is enshrined." As assistant principals at a school where English is a second (or third) language for a quarter of the student population, this statement highlights how important it is that educators respect students' language. When you respect language, you respect the person. From our experiences of shifting our own perspectives and redesigning programming for culturally and linguistically diverse students, we've learned the importance of respecting each student's first language.

We're almost ashamed to admit that for years we neglected the ESL population at our school. The first-year ESL students attended half days of ESL instruction and then were sent home, because we didn't know what to do with them. Students who spoke a language other than English in the general classroom were often referred for disciplinary action, because we assumed that if they weren't speaking English, they were off task. Now, after much professional development and training, we know just how wrong and culturally ignorant we were.

By understanding the difference between BICS and CALP, we came to realize that students acquire social language skills before academic language skills. Just because we might hear CLD students speaking English in the hallway to a friend doesn't mean that they will excel in the classroom. In fact, they might still struggle in an academic setting. But when we support students' L1, their second language acquisition comes faster.

Now we've created a more culturally friendly environment—one that values CLD students' first language and celebrates our diversity. For instance, we have bilingual teacher assistants to provide staff support. These assistants are often upper-level CLD students who help teachers translate and modify materials, bridge the language gap for students, and also earn credit for their work. Not only do these students gain valuable experience, but we also validate their L1 and show them the value of their language skills.

Perhaps most importantly, we've given these students a sense of hope. To be included now is to be equal; we are not going to lower the bar or let our CLD students slip through the cracks. We provide support with translation software and classroom materials in various languages. CLD students are also intentionally placed in certain classrooms. ESL instructors and counselors meet to discuss students' schedules, ensuring that CLD students are in a classroom with an ESL-certified instructor or, at the very least, that they are placed in classrooms with two or three students who speak the same language and can act as a support system. Even by utilizing content and language objectives, we move beyond thinking "I taught it and they just didn't get it." Now we reexamine *why*. And most of our teachers also realize that it is good teaching for *all* our students.

Our preliminary assumptions that students can't learn math or science until they learn English have been completely disproved. We've moved far beyond thinking we couldn't serve our CLD students in the general classroom because they'd be a detriment to the rest of the school. Having CLD students in the classroom has enriched our environment and broken down barriers between all the cultures in our community.

Scott Calder, English Teacher

Olathe North High School, Olathe, Kansas

From Self-Congratulation to Critical Self-Reflection

Every teacher believes that his or her skill level falls somewhere between good and great on the self-evaluation continuum. It is easy to understand that teachers find a comfort in the axiom that "good teaching is good teaching." Teachers honestly, but naively, insert themselves into the equation and feel a sense of satisfaction that they can meet the needs of all students in their classroom under the generic umbrella of "best practices."

I had been teaching high school English for 25 years. During all this time, I had numerous hours of self-reflection and self-congratulation, and I knew that I was a good teacher. As I did this, I never really thought about the many variables that should be considered regarding the academic and linguistic needs of CLD students. As I started working more with the needs of students, I reflected upon their linguistic and academic biographies. One of the first aspects that I reflected upon was the difference between conversational and educational English language. When I had a student in class who did not speak English at home, but did use conversational English in the classroom, I assumed that the student would understand the nuances of the educational language within the context of assignments, discussions, and written responses about the current topic. My thought was that if the student was not doing well on the task, he was just not trying hard enough. This led to several assumptions on my part as I continued with the learning process of my students.

Through coursework, however, I was guided to *critically reflect* on my professional practice. I was forced out of my "good teacher" comfort zone and started challenging myself to be empathetic with my CLD students who needed support to meet the challenges of learning content material with their age-level peers. In an effort to learn more about the academic and linguistic needs of my students, I continuously reflected upon the many issues surrounding them.

The more I started working with the students, the more I started implementing scaffolding techniques for teaching my CLD students. I learned how to structure collaborative learning groups to accommodate my second language learners based on their biographies.

During all this time, I had to rethink my philosophy of working with students many times. As I implemented various methods to front-load vocabulary words when introducing difficult literature, I had to reflect upon the students and what they were bringing with themselves. During my numerous discussions with colleagues and reflections upon students' needs, I came up with the most valuable teaching device: a personal biography questionnaire. Students' responses to the questionnaire provided me with the insights I needed to support CLD students who had conversational English skills but lacked knowledge of educational terms or had not learned how to analyze content literature. An understanding of students' biographies truly led me to focus on my students and helped me think of ways to bring student voices into the classroom.

The more I thought about my students, the more my teacher's world opened up. One of the first revelations came up during my English class. Our class was reading Edgar Allen Poe's "The Black Cat," and my native English-speaking students were creating higher level and insightful literary collaborative learning group assessments about how the narrator had alcohol, domestic, and animal abuse issues. But I noticed that the CLD students were not strong contributors to the group work. After the lesson, when I reflected upon the students and the lesson itself, I realized that the book was full of specifics that related to an American context of various issues.

In my efforts to balance this situation in my room, I spoke with two of my CLD students and asked them to recommend a scary story they knew that also had a moral message. They immediately thought of "La Llorona." I found an English translation of the tale, and when we had class discussions and group work, my Mexican students became the leaders of class. The climate of the classroom changed immediately. The CLD students' self-confidence soared, and the native English-speaking students were empathetic to the plight of analyzing the literature of a different culture.

The Mexican students taught the class that "La Llorona" is more than a scary story; it is a preventive tale that teaches children to stay away from fast-flowing waters, to not talk with strangers, and to come into the house before nightfall. None of these nuances of the story were picked up on by the native English-speaking students. We had great discussions following the story. Some of my American-born learners were able to share out their own experiences of scary stories with their parents. The discussion that followed in my classroom was truly reflective of a community of learners.

I now incorporate many accommodations to aid my CLD students, but the most valuable is when I speak with the students about their native literature and infuse it into the curriculum to support my standard pieces of literature. The CLD students are gaining confidence in analyzing the standard pieces, and the native English speakers are enjoying expanding their view of literature through a whole new world of heroes and villains. This is truly what creating a sense of global community is all about.

I am glad that my CLD students are learning from the strategies I incorporate to help with academic and linguistic needs. After having implemented various techniques for a long time, I now am continually reflecting upon the many needs of my students and looking for various ways to incorporate the biographies of my students in the content. I try to make this a year-round focus for my students rather than a one-time affair, where we only talk about cultural celebrations once a year. This is something that needs to be embedded into the curriculum every single moment of the day so that the students can truly work as a community. It is this that gives me the vision to be always moving forward with the students in their academic and linguistic development. I have had several students talk to me about the connections they now are able to make with the content.

Every day our students remind us of the need for us to make instruction a reality for them. As I walk the hallways of my school and listen to the students talk in multiple languages and represent different cultures, it makes me proud to be a teacher and a member of our school community that welcomes and accepts students from every part of the world. I know that this will not be possible if we don't keep an open mind and an open heart regarding the students and their biographies.

Denise Johnson, 2nd Grade
Hillcrest Elementary, Lawrence, Kansas

Connecting With Parents—
Connecting to Biographies

At Hillcrest we have gone through various cycles of transformation in understanding our students and what they bring. Going through this transformation, we have all come together now, as a school, in trying to do what's right for our students and do the best we can to educate them and make them the students of our global community. There were times when the path to reaching this goal was very challenging. At least that was my experience here at Hillcrest, when we were transitioning from a pull-out program to a push-in program. After facing and overcoming multiple challenges, we now realize what a benefit this new model has been to our CLD students.

I still remember the days when half my class would be gone for most of the day. As my students left, the rest of the class—including myself—would find it so hard to really consider the CLD students a part of our classroom community. When the students came back to the room, they felt distant and lost in the class. Now, when they're no longer being pulled out of the classroom and pulled to different places, I've seen my CLD students excel socially and academically. Keeping them in the classroom for the full day has helped their language acquisition immensely. And perhaps just as importantly, these students now feel like they are part of the classroom and part of a family. They have a home and this is something we really need to focus on.

As a result of having CLD students in the classroom, more and more teachers in our school are having dialogues regarding students and their biographies. A connection with the student's family and culture is a critical component in teaching the whole child. I think a little fear of the unknown can be an obstacle for both parents and the teacher. The parent often feels uncomfortable because of the language barrier and because they have to come into an unfamiliar environment. So, that means the teacher needs to go to the home. Home visits are important to make the connection work and ease the nervousness.

I now understand the importance of connecting with CLD students' parents. For example, we've had a student from Vietnam in our school since kindergarten. Year after year, we discussed how we could make Judy more a part of the classroom community. When Judy got to 2nd grade, we knew we had to do something different. We had to come together as a school community to find out more about Judy. At one meeting we decided to conduct a home visit. We knew it was not going to be an easy task, especially since the parents don't speak the English language, but it had to be done to help them see that we truly cared.

At the home visit, we instantly found the connection with Judy and her parents. She is now a part of the classroom the way we want her to be. From this, we learned that it's still possible to make a connection. If you can get Mom and Dad to see that you care about their child, you're already helping your students immensely. I might not be able to communicate extremely effectively in person, but by trying various methods of communication, such as e-mail, newsletters, and phone calls, I have more opportunities to show the parents how much I care.

Throughout my time at Hillcrest, I have found many other ways, in addition to home visits, to get to know my CLD students. For example, during my first year at Hillcrest, I had three students from Saudi Arabia. The three boys and their parents taught me about Islam and the traditions of their culture. I am a practicing Catholic, but understanding other religions has always intrigued me. I knew that gaining an understanding of their religion was something that I had to do in order to truly connect with their biographies. So, when I was invited to their parties, of course I said yes.

These parties were for women and children only. We talked and ate. The food was unbelievable, and I was privy to many of the ways of the Islam culture. This was truly an experience that helped me better understand one aspect of my classroom community. My students enjoyed introducing me, their teacher, to their family and friends. We had made a connection. The parents trusted me. The boys knew I cared, and I learned so much. This experience definitely paved the way for me to create a relationship and an understanding in my classroom that was appreciated by my students and their parents.

The more I have reflected on the biographies of my students, the more I have been able to get their biographies to become a part of the everyday academic experience in my classroom. One interesting experience that I recently had was when my student from Pakistan brought her father in to teach with me. He was a master teacher/principal in his country. He took notes and pictures of my lesson and activity and I took pictures and notes about his lesson. He even put together a PowerPoint presentation explaining Ramadan. The presentation fit perfectly with our cultural awareness objective. The family is now back in Pakistan and we still e-mail.

Last year, I had two American Indian children in my room. They were quiet, did not participate much, and their assessments were low. These children could have been overlooked because they are so quiet and well behaved. Yet, these students were examples of children who were not connected to school. I found out to which tribe the two children belonged, and I called the parents. Even though they had been reluctant to share in previous phone calls, this time I asked about them and their culture. I encouraged them to come into the classroom. One parent did. That particular parent became my connection to literature that day. She spoke about the Navajo Indian tribe, and I then read a story called "Annie and the Old One." We talked about the connections and that allowed my two quiet students to be spotlighted. We discussed the vocabulary from the story, and the mom helped me to illustrate to the students what many of the words meant. That afternoon we all learned about the Navajo people, made real connections to literature, and gained a greater understanding of the importance of everyone being a part of the class.

As we have transitioned at our building and reflected upon the needs of students, we also have experienced many challenges. For example, last summer I was given the opportunity to teach summer school to five ESL students. The money to teach was there, but transportation was not. This was becoming a true challenge for some of the families, as they wanted the students to come, but transportation was causing issues and making their participation difficult. I started talking to the moms about how to get their children to school. Only two of the parents were able to transport due to work schedules and lack of transportation. After several phone calls and introductions, we were able to work out a car pool. The connections I made with the parents were a critical component in the success of the program. At the end of the summer, I had our business partners donate massages to the two parents that drove for the car pool. It was a treat for all, knowing that we had found a way to overcome this obstacle. We had shared a vision of providing for the needs of these students and, by working together, we accomplished our goal.

Susanne Stevenson, 4th Grade
Kansas Teacher of the Year
Beeson Elementary, Dodge City, Kansas

I wonder if you've ever taken a close look at a coconut. Having lived in Kansas all my life, this fruit is very foreign to me. The outer shell feels rough, it has nicks and bruises from its journey to get to me, and it's challenging to crack open, but if you listen carefully, you know there's something incredibly special on the inside.

An encounter with a student, whom for today's purposes we'll call David, changed my perception of coconuts. David entered my 4th-grade classroom with no formal education, a language barrier, and an unknowable amount of trauma. We started learning letter names as a foundation for his journey of learning to read, using one of my favorite children's books, *Chicka-Chicka-Boom-Boom,* as our anchor text. We read the book, chanted the words, and found the letters around our classroom and school. At the end of the week, I decided to bring in a real coconut for us to explore as an extension activity. I had to find a YouTube video that explained how to open a coconut with a hammer and a screwdriver because, again, I had no background knowledge of a real coconut. I came to school fully prepared to give David an experience that I hoped would stick with him for many years, but what I found is that this experience would be one that changed *my* life forever.

As I proceeded to use the hammer and screwdriver to crack open the coconut, David was incredibly invested in helping me. Suddenly he exploded with all this language, as if he had been itching to get it out all along. He had never been so confident in his English language abilities before this moment. For the first time in my classroom, I saw David come alive. He *knew* what he was talking about and was determined to share it with me.

After we got the coconut open, we shared the water inside and I could see in his eyes the comfort and joy of being with family back home that this water reminded him of. David began to tell me about his life in Guatemala, about the ranch that he worked on with his grandfather, and about the many memories he had of cracking open coconuts on his own. It was amazing to me how something as simple as a coconut could transport David back to a place full of so much comfort, love, and joy. He was able to become

Susanne Stevenson provides learners with individualized support and scaffolding.

immersed back in those emotions, bring them into our classroom, and use them to connect to his new learning. It took the simple act of bringing a coconut into the classroom to bridge my world and David's. His funds of knowledge allowed him to share, teach, and inspire not only himself, but me as well.

This moment is one that will stick with me forever. It made me wonder, How often do our culturally and linguistically diverse students feel a bit like that coconut? They may feel they are in a foreign place, they may have nicks and bruises from their journey, and they are likely tough to crack open. But each and every one has something valuable, worthy, and important to share. It is our jobs as educators to crack open that coconut and allow our students' voices to be heard. Once we've done so, there's no telling what the next chapter will be, for ourselves or for our students. Each moment like this reveals the power of progress.

Too often, the way in which we analyze schools and students does not account for progress. Our most vulnerable students and many of our schools are seen as "low achieving," even when their progress and growth are incredible. When we neglect the celebration of progress, we are failing to recognize our students and ourselves as whole people, with multiple stories to tell.

As an educator, I am a harvester of knowledge, always looking for ways to reveal the knowledge that students hold within themselves. I am tasked daily with showing the student, and the world, that the knowledge we have inside of us is valuable and worthy. For students and teachers, it is easy to get stuck in the mindset of "I'm not as good as ____." Looking to our left or right to see how we compare to others around us should not be our concern. Our circumstances and stories are not the same. As long as we are moving forward, what we are *doing* is enough. We are all working together in the pursuit of progress. Community will always be greater than competition, and together, *we* are enough.

Through the Eyes of a Student

In the following narrative, an educator who has used BDI strategies for 15 years captures the voice of a CLD student who feels stuck in a system where no one cares. Drawn from actual events, this is an imagined view of a CLD student's perspective on her time in our educational system. As you read this scenario, consider how you would respond to this student. Would you act in the same way? Would you get frustrated and walk away? Would you continue to show love, compassion, and hope?

Because No One Ever Cared

I'm stuck in an Alt Placement school because no one ever cared. None of my teachers ever gave me a chance or helped me. And I'm not talking about here at the "School for Bad Kids." I'm talking about elementary school, middle school, and even high school. I'm 16 and don't know what my future holds. I don't really care what happens. I'm just trying to survive. No one has ever cared. Why should I?

Today, a white teacher came to see me. She told me I had to take an English test. I immediately told her I wasn't taking the @#$%$ test. And I meant it. I wanted no part of it. Every year, it's the same thing and nothing changes. I have to take this stupid English Proficiency Test every year. Every year, I purposely do bad on it. I don't care. They don't care. Why should I?

I'm gonna give this teacher a hard time. She'll run outta here just like all the others. I give her 15 minutes max before she runs outta here frustrated and crying like a little baby. I make them run. It always works this way for me. Don't let anyone see me, know me. No one's gonna hurt me. Because no one has ever cared. So, why should I?

She talks to me about my abilities. She thinks I can do well on this exam. How would she know? She doesn't know me. Who does she think she is? No one has ever believed in me. They just tell me to do my work. No excuses. No one ever believed in me. Why should I?

So, the first thing this lady tells me to do is write. Really? I hate writing. I ain't doing this. No WAY! I'm gonna tell her that, too.

"I ain't doing this," I tell her gruffly and angrily. She's patient with me. She doesn't tell me to just do it.

"Why not?" she asks.

The first prompt asks me to write a letter to my principal to explain why my teacher should get the "Teacher of the Year" award. Really? Are they kidding me? Teacher of the Year? Yeah, not so much.

"I've never had a good teacher," I gruffly respond.

She looks shocked when I tell her this.

"Really?" she questions. "Maybe not here in the Alternate School, but what about at the high school?"

"Nope."

"OK, then," she says confidently, "What about middle school?"

"NOPE!"

"Surely there was a teacher in elementary school that cared about you. That took an interest in you? That helped you?" she asks, hoping for a positive answer, which I can't give her.

"What part of NO don't you understand? No one ever cared about me."

She seems shocked at my response. Perplexed. I think I'm off the hook and won't have to complete this stupid test.

"OK, then," she says. "I want you to write a letter to the principal telling him what an injustice has been done to you that you've never had a good teacher in all your years of schooling and that NO ONE deserves the award and WHY."

"I'm not doing that!" I tell her, hoping she'll let me off the hook and back off.

"Yes, you have to. Someone needs to read your story," she exclaims.

I cross my arms and refuse to do it. She walks behind me and puts both hands on my shoulders and whispers, "I can't wait to read what you write."

Why should she care? Should I?

I sit, arms crossed, for 5 minutes, and then I decide to tell her what I really think. I pick up my pencil and start composing a letter to the principal, citing all the bad teachers I've had and why they were bad. I'm writing. The words are flowing out of me. It isn't even hard to express what I'm feeling. Before I know it, I have a full page of words, feelings, and expressions. I have told my story. How no one ever took the time to take an interest in me, and that I thought I was worth it. I felt that teachers should care about me and what I had learned. Someone should have paid attention to me. Someone should have cared. I did!

The white teacher walks around the room while I write. As she makes her rounds, she walks in front of my desk. She stops in front of me and begins reading my work, upside-down. I watch her as she reads. I can't believe what I see. She has tears in her eyes. Tears! Why does she care? Do I care?

I watch her wipe her eyes and exit the room. Through the glass pane in the door, I see her crying. CRYING! Whatever I wrote, it brought her to tears. Does she understand me? I think she cares about how I feel. Is that possible? She doesn't even know me.

I see her wipe the tears and re-enter the room. I brought her to tears but she's not running away. She's coming back. Here she comes.

She places her arms on my shoulders, gives a firm squeeze and quietly says, "That's an amazing story. You should write more often. Thank you for your effort."

She walks away, paying attention to the other students in the class. She looks back at me and winks. She does care! I care!

Final Reflections

Every day, educators across the country enter their classrooms ready to achieve what they have spent a lifetime preparing to do—educate *all* students regardless of the challenges they may face. As discussed earlier, too often political agendas and school dynamics complicate our efforts to move forward and do the best work we can with students and families. Still, we must continue to forge new paths that will lead to the classrooms, schools, districts, and world we envision for our children.

Knowing a good story when they see one, in recent decades those in Hollywood have dramatized the lives of educators who have succeeded in spite of overwhelming odds. Some of these stories are based on real teachers who saw their students not as empty vessels waiting to be filled with academic content mandated by benchmarks or standardized tests, but as individuals who need meaningful educational experiences to succeed. By taking the responsibility to learn about their students, the learners' families, and the community in which they taught, these teachers were able to look at their students as individuals and recognize that each has unique academic potential. Armed with this background information, the teachers were able to passionately advocate for the right to approach instruction in a way that would not punish the student but instead would awaken, challenge, and motivate the learner.

Not surprisingly, this same thread runs through the academic literature, as well as our own lives as students. The teachers who knew us first as individuals changed our lives. Decades of study, working in classrooms, and my own life experiences have shown me that the only effective approach to meeting the needs of all learners—especially those who are culturally and linguistically diverse—is to accept responsibility for learning about the individuality of each one. In this book, I have addressed several key considerations that successful teachers can intentionally act upon to enhance student motivation, engagement, and learning. These considerations include (a) critically reflecting on our own socialization to identify assumptions, (b) understanding how these assumptions affect how we teach, (c) translating theoretical fundamentals into our own practice, (d) planning effective strategies that link students' background knowledge to new learning, and finally (e) using appropriate assessments to determine academic progress. Such considerations effectively enable teachers to integrate their differentiated practices with programs, models, and curricula currently in use within the school.

The consequential impact of such actions cannot always be operationalized or measured in numbers. We must embark on a journey *with* our students. The first step is to check for roadblocks—attitudes and assumptions that might impede our own motivation, engagement, and learning. Such roadblocks may result from our own socialization or may be the natural result of working under the harsh and confining conditions prevalent in many of our schools. Too often we are led to believe that certain students can only be motivated if we threaten their existence, remind them daily of their failure to learn, and ultimately push them out of school. We can help clear these roadblocks for ourselves and for others by continuing to build our own knowledge and skills, creating networks with other teachers and community members, and then advocating for the rights of our students.

Defensibility of practice takes place at two levels, head (research) and heart (passion). The head takes theory into practice, using strategies, techniques, and tools such as those described in this book, and devising creative new approaches as unique as the classroom ecology and as individual as each teacher. The heart is touched by the eagerness and potential each student brings to the classroom. We develop a connection and affection for our students as we work toward a common goal. Care and concern guide us in employing the strategies and processes we have learned to ensure that *all* students have access to academically challenging and individually meaningful educational experiences. In challenging the status quo and becoming advocates, we can make a difference in the way our schools and classrooms accommodate the different learning needs of all of our students. The heart takes care never to forget the calling to become a teacher—and the strength of love in that call.

FIGURE 10.1

Inventory of Situationally and Culturally Responsive Teaching (ISCRT)

State	Teacher Name	Date
District	Grade Level(s)	Observer
School	Content Area(s)	Start: ___
	No. of ELL Students	Total Students	End: ___

Lesson Overview

Lesson Topic:

Lesson Summary:

Classroom Environment / Setup

- ☐ Rows w/ individual desks
- ☐ Groups w/ 3 to 5 desks
- ☐ Pairs w/ 2 desks
- ☐ Other

ELL Language Proficiency   *No. of Students*

- ☐ Beginning ___
- ☐ Intermediate ___
- ☐ Advanced ___
- ☐ Fluent

Strategy Implemented

- ☐ Active Bookmarks
- ☐ All in the Box
- ☐ All on My Clipboard
- ☐ Consequence Wheel
- ☐ DOTS Chart
- ☐ Extension Wheel
- ☐ Foldables
- ☐ Hearts Activity
- ☐ IDEA
- ☐ Linking Language
- ☐ Listen Sketch Label
- ☐ Magic Book
- ☐ Mind Maps
- ☐ Mini Novela
- ☐ Pic-Tac-Tell
- ☐ Picture This
- ☐ Pictures and Words
- ☐ Relevance Scale
- ☐ Story Bag
- ☐ Three Facts and an Opinion
- ☐ Thumb Challenge
- ☐ Tri-Fold
- ☐ U-C-ME
- ☐ Vocabulary Quilt
- ☐ Word Drop
- ☐ Other: ___

Opening / Work Time / Closing

(Continued on the next 5 pages)

Figure 10.1 (pages 169–174) copyright © 2010 Socorro G. Herrera, Kevin G. Murry, Shabina K. Kavimandan, Melissa A. Holmes, and Della R. Perez

FIGURE 10.1
Continued

I. Joint Productive Activity

	Not Observed 0	Emerging 1	Developing 2	Enacting 3	Integrating 4
		The teacher:	The teacher:	The teacher:	The teacher:
LE	A. No evidence of a respectful learning environment	A. Creates an environment that **respects students as individual learners**	A. Creates a **culturally and linguistically** respectful learning environment	A. Creates a **low-risk** learning environment that **values diverse perspectives**	A. Orchestrates **conditions and situations** to ensure that students collaborate as **equal members** in a low-risk **learning community**
TC	B. No collaboration between teacher and students	B. **Collaborates with students,** but no evidence of a joint product	B. Collaborates with **whole class** to create a **joint product,** or students collaborate on a joint product in **pairs or small groups**	B. **Collaboratively guides small groups** of students, especially those who need **higher levels of support,** to create joint products	B. Collaborates with students to create joint products that **integrate language and content standards**
TPSI	C. Students work independently of one another	C. Provides **minimal** opportunities for **student interaction**	C. Provides **occasional structured opportunities** for student interaction	C. Provides **frequent** structured opportunities for **purposeful** student interaction	C. Provides **consistent** structured opportunities for purposeful student interaction that **promotes development of the CLD student biography**
PGD	D. Pairs or groups students based on random grouping or student self-selection	D. Pairs or groups students based on **one dimension of the CLD student biography**	D. Pairs or groups students based on **two or three dimensions** of the CLD student biography	D. Pairs or groups students based on two or three dimensions of the CLD student biography **as appropriate for the task/activity**	D. Pairs or groups students based on **all four dimensions** of the CLD student biography as appropriate for the task/activity
AC	E. No connections between the activity and the lesson	E. Makes **minimal connections** between the strategy/activity and the lesson	E. Makes **occasional relevant** connections between the strategy/activity and the lesson	E. **Frequently uses insights** from the strategy/activity to make connections, **affirm learning, or modify instruction as needed**	E. **Consistently** uses insights from the strategy/activity to make connections, affirm learning, **and** modify instruction as needed

Notes:

LE = Learning Environment   TC = Teacher Collaboration   TPSI = Total Group, Partner, Small Group, Individual   PGD = Partner/Grouping Determination   AC = Activity Connections

Adapted from Doherty et al. (2002).

FIGURE 10.1
Continued

II. Language & Literacy Development

	Not Observed 0	Emerging 1	Developing 2	Enacting 3	Integrating 4
		The teacher provides:	*The teacher provides:*	*The teacher provides:*	*The teacher provides:*
LSRW	A. Instruction is dominated by teacher talk and students are passive listeners	A. Listening (L), speaking (S), reading (R), & writing (W) activities with **minimal opportunities for students' academic language development**	A. L, S, R, & W activities with **occasional** opportunities for students' academic language development	A. **Frequent** opportunities for **student expression** and academic language development in activities that **integrate** L, S, R, & W	A. **Consistent** opportunities for student expression and academic language development in **higher-order thinking** activities that integrate L, S, R, & W
QRM	B. No use of questioning (Q), rephrasing (R), or modeling (M) to assist language and literacy development	B. **Minimal** use of Q, R, or M to assist language and literacy development	B. **Occasional** use of Q, R, or M to assist language and literacy development	B. **Frequent** use of **purposeful** Q, R, **and** M to assist language and literacy development	B. **Consistent** use of purposeful Q, R, and M to assist academic language and literacy development and to build students' capacities to **pose questions about their own thinking**
L1	C. No evidence of native language in environment or instruction	C. **Minimal** evidence of native language **in environment and/or instruction**	C. **Occasional** opportunities for **students to use their native language** during the lesson	C. **Frequent, explicit, purposeful** opportunities for students to use their native language during the lesson **in ways that support academic learning**	C. **Consistent, systematic** opportunities for students to use their native language during the lesson in ways that support **academic language and literacy development**
LBK	D. No references to students' prior knowledge and background experiences related to language and literacy development*	D. **Minimal** references to prior knowledge and background experiences related to language and literacy development*	D. **Occasional** references to prior knowledge and background experiences related to language and literacy development*	D. **Frequent** references to prior knowledge and background experiences related to **academic language** and literacy development*	D. **Consistent use of students' culture-bound ways of comprehending, communicating, and expressing themselves as a springboard** for academic language and literacy development*

Notes:

*PA = Phonemic Awareness; P = Phonics; V = Vocabulary; F = Fluency; C = Comprehension.

LSRW = Listening, Speaking, Reading, Writing   **QRM** = Questioning, Rephrasing, Modeling   **L1** = Native Language   **LBK** = Background Knowledge of Language/Literacy

Adapted from Doherty et al. (2002).

171

FIGURE 10.1
Continued

III. Contextualization

	Not Observed	0	Emerging	1	Developing	2	Enacting	3	Integrating	4
			The teacher:		The teacher:		The teacher:		The teacher:	
BK3	A. No preassessment of students' academic knowledge about the topic		A. Conducts **preassessment of only students' academic knowledge** about the topic		A. Conducts preassessment of students' **funds of knowledge, prior knowledge, and academic knowledge** about the topic **or key content vocabulary**		A. Conducts preassessment that provides **all students** the opportunity to **share/document** their funds of knowledge, prior knowledge, and academic knowledge about the topic or key content vocabulary		A. Conducts preassessment that provides all students the opportunity to share/document their funds of knowledge, prior knowledge, and academic knowledge about the topic **and key content vocabulary; documents students' background knowledge for use throughout the lesson**	
A/CL	B. Focus is solely on content delivery		B. Provides **minimal** opportunities for students to share with peers content-related connections to their background knowledge		B. Provides **occasional** opportunities for students to share with peers content-related connections to their background knowledge		B. Provides **frequent** opportunities for students to **share/document** their content-related connections to their background knowledge **and purposefully listens/observes as students share/document**		B. Provides **consistent** opportunities for students to share/document their content-related connections to their background knowledge and **uses insights gleaned to highlight student assets, support academic learning, and maximize the community of learners**	
BIO	C. New information is presented in an abstract, disconnected manner		C. Makes **minimal** connections between students' **sociocultural, linguistic, cognitive, and academic dimensions and the new academic concepts**		C. Makes **occasional** connections between students' sociocultural, linguistic, cognitive, and academic dimensions and the new academic concepts		C. Makes **frequent and purposeful** connections between students' **individual biographies,** including what was learned about their knowledge and experiences from home, community, and school, and the new academic concepts		C. **Systematically** makes **consistent** and purposeful connections between students' individual biographies, including what was learned about their knowledge and experiences from home, community, and school, and the new academic concepts, **with applications to the real world**	

Notes:

BK3 = Funds of Knowledge (family), Prior Knowledge (community), Academic Knowledge (school)   **A/CL** = Assets/Community of Learners   **BIO** = CLD Biography Connections

Adapted from Doherty et al. (2002).

FIGURE 10.1
Continued

IV. Challenging Activities

	0 Not Observed	1 Emerging	2 Developing	3 Enacting	4 Integrating
		Teacher instruction and strategy use:	*Teacher instruction and strategy use:*	*Teacher instruction and strategy use:*	*Teacher instruction and strategy use:*
ACOM	A. No accommodations for linguistic or academic levels	A. Provides **minimal** accommodations based on students' linguistic and academic levels	A. Provides **occasional structured** accommodations based on students' linguistic and academic levels	A. Provides **frequent** structured accommodations based on students' linguistic and academic levels that build upon **culture-bound patterns of knowing, learning, and applying**	A. Provides **consistent, systematic** structured accommodations based on students' linguistic and academic levels that build upon culture-bound patterns of knowing, learning, and applying
CO/LO	B. Makes no reference to lesson objectives	B. Includes **verbally stated or posted lesson objectives that reflect content standards**	B. Includes verbally stated **and** posted **content and language objectives that** reflect content standards	B. Includes content and language objectives that (1) are verbally stated and posted, **(2) reflect content and language standards, and (3) are revisited during the lesson**	B. Includes content and language objectives that (1) are verbally stated and posted, (2) reflect content and language standards, and **(3) are interwoven throughout the lesson**
S/E	C. Strategies/activities are not aligned to standards and do not reflect expectations	C. Includes strategies/activities **that are aligned to standards and that reflect vague expectations**	C. Includes strategies/ activities that are aligned to standards and that reflect **clear expectations**	C. Includes **challenging** strategies/ activities that are aligned to standards and that reflect clear expectations	C. Includes challenging strategies/ activities that reflect **skillful integration of multiple standards, clear expectations, and higher-order thinking skills**
AF	D. Does not consider students' states of mind/affective filter	D. **Minimally** attends to students' states of mind/affective filter	D. **Occasionally** monitors students' states of mind/ affective filter and **adjusts instruction accordingly**	D. **Frequently** monitors students' states of mind/affective filter and adjusts **instructional conditions** accordingly	D. **Consistently** monitors the states of mind/affective filter **of individual students and of the whole group** and adjusts instructional conditions **and situations** accordingly
FB	E. Provides no feedback on student performance	E. Provides **minimal** feedback on student performance	E. Provides **occasional** feedback on student performance **to confirm/ disconfirm learning**	E. Provides **frequent** feedback on student performance to confirm/ disconfirm learning and **to advance student learning**	E. Uses **systematic formative assessment** to provide **consistent** feedback on student performance to confirm/disconfirm learning and to advance student learning

Notes:

ACOM = Accommodations **CO/LO** = Content Objectives & Language Objectives **S/E** = Standards/Expectations **AF** = Affective Filter **FB** = Feedback (formative assessment)

Adapted from Doherty et al. (2002).

FIGURE 10.1
Continued

V. Instructional Conversation

	0 Not Observed	**1** Emerging	**2** Developing	**3** Enacting	**4** Integrating
		With individuals and small groups of students, the teacher:	*With individuals and small groups of students, the teacher:*	*With individuals and small groups of students, the teacher:*	*With individuals and small groups of students, the teacher:*
ESTK	A. Lecture predominates	A. Uses **questioning to elicit student talk**	A. Elicits student talk with questioning, **listening, and rephrasing**	A. Elicits student talk with questioning, listening, rephrasing, and **explicit modeling of turn-taking and questioning structures**	A. Elicits student talk about the content through **student-led discussion and questioning**
KTU	B. Teacher responds in ways that validate students	B. Responds in ways that **minimally promote higher-order thinking and individual connections from the known to the unknown**	B. Responds in ways that **occasionally** promote higher-order thinking and individual connections from the known to the unknown	B. Responds in ways that **frequently** promote higher-order thinking and individual connections from the known to the unknown	B. Responds in ways that **consistently** promote higher-order thinking, **elaboration of connections** from the known to the unknown, **and application beyond the classroom**
BICS/ CALP	C. Teacher conversation is not on topic	C. **Uses BICS and/or CALP to discuss the content/topic;** provides **minimal opportunities for academic talk among students**	C. **Uses CALP** to discuss the content/topic and provides **occasional** opportunities for academic talk, **including use of key content vocabulary,** among students	C. Provides **frequent** opportunities for academic talk, including use of key content vocabulary, in which the **teacher bridges between student talk and academic language**	C. **Facilitates consistent** opportunities for **student-led academic conversations using key content vocabulary**
REV	D. Incorporates no revoicing of students' learning	D. Includes **minimal** revoicing of learning, limited to **repeating students' words**	D. Includes **occasional** revoicing of learning, limited to repeating **and/or rephrasing** students' words	D. Includes **frequent** revoicing of learning that **challenges students to solidify or expand upon connections to the academic content and vocabulary**	D. Includes **consistent** revoicing of learning that challenges students to solidify, expand upon, **and make deeper connections** to the academic content and vocabulary
SAV	E. Does not invite students to articulate their views/judgments/processes	E. Provides **minimal** opportunities for students to articulate their views/judgments/processes	E. Provides **occasional** opportunities for students to articulate their views/judgments/processes **and provide rationales**	E. Provides **frequent, purposeful** opportunities for students to articulate their views/judgments/processes and provide rationales	E. Provides **consistent, structured** opportunities for students to articulate their views/judgments/processes and provide rationales

Notes:

ESTK = Eliciting Student Talk KTU = Known to Unknown BICS/CALP = Basic Interpersonal Communication Skills/Cognitive Academic Language Proficiency
REV = Revoicing SAV = Students Articulate Views

Adapted from Doherty et al. (2002).

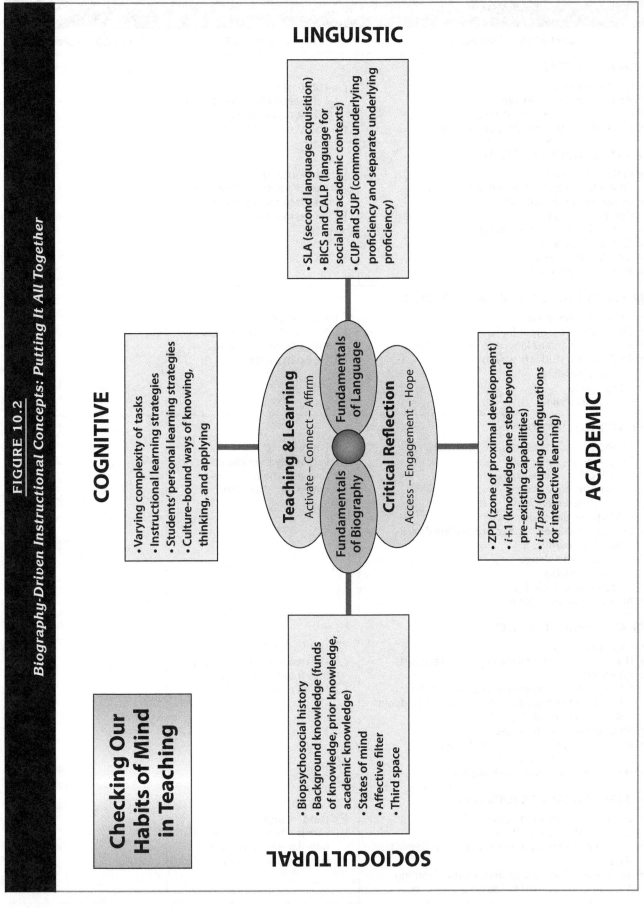

FIGURE 10.2

Biography-Driven Instructional Concepts: Putting It All Together

LINGUISTIC

- SLA (second language acquisition)
- BICS and CALP (language for social and academic contexts)
- CUP and SUP (common underlying proficiency and separate underlying proficiency)

COGNITIVE

- Varying complexity of tasks
- Instructional learning strategies
- Students' personal learning strategies
- Culture-bound ways of knowing, thinking, and applying

Teaching & Learning
Activate – Connect – Affirm

Fundamentals of Language

Fundamentals of Biography

Critical Reflection
Access – Engagement – Hope

ACADEMIC

- ZPD (zone of proximal development)
- *i*+1 (knowledge one step beyond pre-existing capabilities)
- *i*+*TpsI* (grouping configurations for interactive learning)

Checking Our Habits of Mind in Teaching

SOCIOCULTURAL

- Biopsychosocial history
- Background knowledge (funds of knowledge, prior knowledge, academic knowledge)
- States of mind
- Affective filter
- Third space

For a version of this diagram listing page numbers for primary discussions of these concepts in the text, see Appendix I.

FIGURE 10.3
Critical Aspects of Effective Pedagogy

Aspect of Effective Pedagogy	How I Relate to This	How I Will Implement
REFLECTIVE PRACTICE • Critical reflection • Asset/potential perspective • Culturally responsive teaching • Biography-driven teaching and learning	☐ I understand it. ☐ I am ready to implement and take it to the next level. ☐ I need more support.	
JOINT PRODUCTIVE ACTIVITY • Classroom ecology • Contextual and situational processes • *i+Tpsl* grouping configurations • Conditions for ZPD • Scaffolding (teacher and peer) • Teacher strategies • Learning strategies • Academic dimension	☐ I understand it. ☐ I am ready to implement and take it to the next level. ☐ I need more support.	

LANGUAGE AND LITERACY DEVELOPMENT
• Linguistic dimension
• Comprehensible input ($i+1$)
• Maximize L1 and L2 language proficiencies
• Capitalize on students' ways of
  ◆ Communicating
  ◆ Expressing
  ◆ Comprehending
	☐ I understand it.
	☐ I am ready to implement and take it to the next level.
	☐ I need more support.	

CONTEXTUALIZATION
• Make connections to students' individual biographies:
  ◆ Sociocultural dimension
  ◆ Linguistic dimension
  ◆ Cognitive dimension
  ◆ Academic dimension
• Uncover, document, and utilize students' background knowledge:
  ◆ Funds of knowledge
  ◆ Prior knowledge
  ◆ Academic knowledge
• Activate, connect, affirm
	☐ I understand it.
	☐ I am ready to implement and take it to the next level.
	☐ I need more support.	

CHALLENGING ACTIVITIES
• Cognitive dimension
• Use content and language objectives/essential question to
  ◆ Share target outcomes at beginning of lesson
  ◆ Highlight the essentials of the lesson at midpoint
  ◆ Revisit learning at the end
• Student learning strategies
• Vary complexity and difficulty of tasks
• Monitor students' states of mind
• Formative and summative feedback
	☐ I understand it.
	☐ I am ready to implement and take it to the next level.
	☐ I need more support.	

INSTRUCTIONAL CONVERSATION • Build on the known to guide students to the unknown throughout the lesson • Structured opportunities for student academic talk ($i+Tpsl$) • Revoice to value, extend, and advance learning • Ask questions beyond hands-up questioning	☐ I understand it. ☐ I am ready to implement and take it to the next level. ☐ I need more support.	

Glossary

academic dimension One of the four dimensions of the CLD student biography. Includes facets of the student's received curriculum and instruction from prekindergarten to high school classrooms and throughout higher education pursuits. Essential to this dimension are factors related to the individual's opportunities for access, engagement, and hope; these can be more difficult to uncover, but they often hold the key to understanding student reactions, given current curriculum, instruction, and academic policy.

academic knowledge One of the three background knowledge systems. Includes knowledge acquired in formal educational settings.

activation phase Taking place during the opening of a lesson, this phase of teaching and learning provides the culturally responsive teacher with opportunities to actively engage students in the new lesson. Teachers observe and document students' connections between the lesson concepts and vocabulary and their background knowledge, which might be drawn from home, community, and/or previous schooling experiences.

activity A teacher-generated opportunity for students to interact with the curriculum. Activities are initiated and facilitated by the teacher to provide students with a hook to connect to the lesson and to move the lesson forward.

additive programs Bilingual educational programs that focus on the positive cognitive effects of CLD students' learning of both the native language and the new language. With this approach to language learning, students continue to become proficient in the first language as well as the new language.

affective filter A theoretical construct that can be thought of as an imaginary wall positioned between the student and language input. This wall rises—blocking input—when the student experiences negative feelings such as stress, anxiety, or frustration. Conversely, the student's wall lowers and language input is best perceived (and ideally comprehended) when he or she has positive classroom experiences and feels safe, confident, motivated, and affirmed.

affirmation phase Taking place during the closing of the lesson, this phase of teaching and learning provides the teacher with opportunities to use evidence of student understanding and progress to acknowledge learning. Recognizing the value of both student progress and product, the teacher celebrates growth as well as mastery. He or she also uses evidence of students' individual cognitive processes to address remaining gaps in understanding.

approach The educator's overarching philosophical orientation toward instruction that reflects at least one research-based or theoretical framework for practice and that allows the teacher to then select an instructional method consistent with his or her philosophy.

asset perspective A mindset that consistently identifies and actively affirms the cultural identities of CLD students and their families (including cultural beliefs, values, and experiences), use of multiple languages, and diverse ways of knowing and interacting in the world.

background knowledge A student's accumulated knowledge and skills that can be used to accelerate learning and that have been acquired through three distinct but related knowledge systems: funds of knowledge (home), prior knowledge (community), and academic knowledge (school).

basic interpersonal communication skills (BICS) Language needed to interact in social contexts, which incorporate nonverbal cues that support spoken language comprehension and production.

behaviorist theories Learning theories that focus solely on observed student behaviors and which reflect the belief that learning is merely the acquisition of new behaviors in response to environmental stimuli and rewards.

biography-driven instruction (BDI) framework A research-based instructional framework that captures how the four interrelated dimensions of the CLD student biography, situated within the context of the learner's biopsychosocial history, influence and are continually influenced by the teaching and learning dynamics of the classroom. BDI applies the principles of cultural responsiveness (Gay, 2018) and cultural sustainability (Paris, 2012) to achieve the goals of liberatory praxis as a result of this humanistic, learner-centered, and adaptable approach to teaching and learning in diverse spaces.

biography-driven instructional (BDI) strategy A unique combination of processes (contextual and situational) and actions (teacher and student) that guides reciprocal teaching and learning throughout the entire lesson. BDI strategies incorporate smaller, point-in-time activities, strategies, and techniques along the way.

biopsychosocial history A term used to refer to the biological, psychological, and sociological aspects of an individual's background.

classroom ecology The structures, arrangements, events, and processes that influence student and teacher action (and reaction) in the classroom. In contrast to the more limited concept of classroom environment, classroom ecology moves beyond the physical aspects of the classroom to emphasize the human element, highlighting the interconnectedness of the multiple agents and aspects at play.

classroom environment The physical aspects of the classroom, including elements such as the arrangement of chairs and desks, bulletin boards, wall decorations, and so forth. Contrasts with the concept of classroom ecology, which emphasizes the human element.

CLD student biography Evolved from the prism model, this concept accounts for the challenges and processes associated with each of the four dimensions of the culturally and linguistically diverse student: the sociocultural, linguistic, cognitive, and academic dimensions. Educators who implement biography-driven instruction attend to the traditional, school-initiated responses to each dimension, as well as the culturally responsive ways each dimension can be leveraged to accelerate the student's linguistic and academic development.

CLD Student Biography Card A tool on which teachers document crucial aspects of a student's school-situated and home/community-bound biography. This information can be later used to support informed instructional decisions regarding grouping configurations, curricular connections to student interests, content and language scaffolds, and so forth.

cognates Words with a common language ancestor that have similar form and meaning (e.g., insects [English] and insectos [Spanish]).

cognitive academic language proficiency (CALP) Language needed to succeed in academic contexts that provide minimal contextual clues and to perform tasks, such as summarizing and synthesizing, that require use of abstract language.

cognitive belief system An individual's comprehensive view of the world and how it works that is influenced by the total of all that is in long-term memory (e.g., socialization, lived experiences, individual thought processes).

cognitive dimension One of the four dimensions of the CLD student biography. Includes what the students know, how they make sense of new information, and how they apply learning in personally meaningful ways. This dimension also highlights the student's background knowledge (including assets and understandings acquired in the home, community, and school). Related to the sociocultural dimension.

cognitive learning strategies Processes and tools that support physical or mental manipulation of material (e.g., through rehearsal, organization, or elaboration). A student uses these strategies to increase comprehension and retention of new content and language.

collective scaffolding The scaffolding that students provide one another through collaborative negotiation of language and meaning as they work together in pairs or small teams to answer a question posed or jointly produce toward a common goal.

common underlying proficiency (CUP) A theoretical construct that suggests that a student's background knowledge and skills acquired through his or her native language will inform and be transferred to the individual's development of knowledge and skills and performance in another language.

comprehensible input New language information that CLD students receive and are able to understand that is one level above their current level of proficiency. If the learner is at level i, then input at $i+1$ is the best for language learning. The new language material is understandable to students because the teacher has taken measures to ensure that connections are made between the new information and what the learners already know.

conceptual model of instruction The accumulated concepts central to the research-based theoretical frameworks that comprise the foundation for an educator's approach to instruction.

connection phase Taking place during the work time of the lesson, this phase of teaching and learning allows teachers to support students in navigating the curriculum in order to construct meaning. The educator confirms/disconfirms students' understandings and revoices connections made so that individual students' words, ideas, and experiences serve as a gateway to new learning by the entire classroom community. Throughout this phase, the teacher systematically uses intentional grouping structures and configurations to support students as they work collectively, collaboratively, and individually with the new content and language to develop refined understandings.

content-compatible The type of language that reflects vocabulary that can be taught within a lesson but is not essential to content proficiency.

content-obligatory The type of language that reflects vocabulary that is absolutely necessary for a student to comprehend and discuss the content of a lesson.

contextual processes   The means through which educators interact with the physical setting in which they teach, the curriculum, and the classroom community of learners to set the stage for teaching and learning.

contextualization   The teacher's use of student biographies both to support learners' meaningful connections to new language and content and to make decisions about contextual and situational processes, including the implementation of challenging activities that will advance each student's learning.

critical reflection   The act of identifying and examining one's assumptions in order to determine the validity of the assumptions in the current context as well as the influence of one's socialization (and resulting beliefs and values) on those assumptions. As a result of this process, individuals have the opportunity to modify reactions to others or situations as needed.

culturally and linguistically diverse (CLD)   The favored term to refer to individuals whose culture and language are different from those of the dominant group.

deficit perspective   A mindset that focuses on students' needs and limitations rather than on their sociocultural, linguistic, cognitive, and academic strengths and assets. This mindset perpetuates an attitude of hopelessness in regard to both the teacher's ability to provide effective accommodations and the student's ability to reach his or her academic potential.

Discourse   Although *discourse* commonly refers to written or spoken communicative exchange, *Discourse* (with a capital D) refers to the shared ways of thinking, believing, communicating, knowing, interacting, and so forth to which a student has been apprenticed through his or her home culture and community experiences.

emergentist theories   Learning theories that emphasize a student's cognitive efforts to make sense of the linguistic environment in which he or she interacts, and the intertwined nature of language knowledge development and language use.

funds of identity   The historically accumulated, socially distributed, and culturally developed resources that are key to a person's self-understanding, self-definition, and self-expression. The individuality of the learner, as well as their socially situated relationships and activities, are among influences that determine which resources are most relevant and useful.

funds of knowledge   One of the three background knowledge systems. Includes the wealth of knowledge and resources accumulated from one's life in the home with family.

***i+Tpsl* model**   A conceptualization of the role of grouping configurations in the teaching/learning process. The lesson progresses from an opening phase promoting activation of knowledge for the individual student ("*i*") through a connection phase involving teacher-directed, text-driven, total group ("*T*") work, pairs/partners ("*p*") work, and small teams ("*s*") work. The lesson culminates in a closing phase focused on individual accountability ("*I*") through validation, encouragement, and affirmation by the teacher.

information processing theories   Learning theories that emphasize both the automatic and the controlled cognitive operations that students use as they process knowledge during learning.

input hypothesis   According to Stephen Krashen (1984/2005), CLD students' best progress in second language acquisition occurs when the information to which they are exposed is one level higher than their current level of proficiency.

language brokering   The efforts of an individual to serve as an interpreter, translator, and cultural mediator in interactions between two parties who do not share a common language or culture.

learning strategy   A thought process, behavior, or procedure a student uses to help comprehend new concepts and language.

linguistic dimension   One of the four dimensions of the CLD student biography. Includes the learner's proficiency in the first and second languages (and any additional languages) and highlights his or her capacity to comprehend, communicate, and express in each language.

meaning perspectives   A teacher's belief system, which has developed over the course of a lifetime and has been influenced by his or her socialization and ongoing experiences in a particular family, community, and larger world context (biography). An important influence on a teacher's decisions related to classroom environment and ecology.

metacognitive learning strategies   Processes and tools that prompt one to intentionally plan, undertake, and evaluate learning. Used by a student to increase comprehension and retention of new content and language.

methodological principles   Instructional delivery processes (i.e., activate, connect, affirm) that lie at the core of biography-driven instruction. These principles allow for teacher responsiveness to situational contexts. By comparison, a "method" typically is a more rigid set of procedures used to operationalize a conceptual framework or model for classroom practice. Methodological principles and methods reflect the guiding theoretical framework(s) and align with the educator's philosophical orientation to instruction. Strategies and techniques are systematically chosen to accomplish desired outcomes/tasks while aligning with the educator's approach to instruction.

polysemous words   Words or phrases that are capable of having multiple meanings, depending on the context in which they are used.

positionality   One's relative location in society reflective of the multiple identities that the person has chosen, or those that have been imposed on the individual by societal/external forces, which has implications for power and access.

prior knowledge   One of the three background knowledge systems. Includes knowledge acquired as a result of being part of a community.

prism model   Four interdependent and complex dimensions of the student—the sociocultural, linguistic, cognitive, and academic dimensions—that serve as the foundation for understanding his or her linguistic and academic growth. Developed by Thomas and Collier (1995, 1997).

responsive assistance   An in-the-moment response/scaffold individualized to assist the learner in achieving academic success.

revoicing   The teacher's act of rerouting, expanding upon, or validating students' responses in order to advance the learning of individual students as well as the learning of the larger community of learners.

scaffolding   A variety of tools, strategies, and techniques used by the teacher to support the student's progression to a deeper understanding of concepts while simultaneously building his or her capabilities to become a more independent learner.

schema   (schemas or schemata, pl.) The ways in which one stores, processes, and understands units of knowledge, including the organization of and relationships between categories of information.

separate underlying proficiency (SUP)   The theoretical construct that assumes that languages operate independently; thus, no knowledge or skills are transferred between the L1 (first, or native, language) and L2 (second language).

situational processes   The means through which teachers orchestrate teaching and learning dynamics in the moment. These processes apply to every student and teacher action and reaction within the classroom, including those that are not anticipated. The teacher mediates these actions and reactions by continuously navigating and negotiating students' biographies as well as the lesson objectives.

small teams   Strategically configured groups of three to five students who work collectively and collaboratively on a purposeful activity during a lesson to achieve a common goal.

social/affective learning strategies   Processes that support positive emotions and often leverage the benefits of peer collaboration. Used by a student to increase comprehension and retention of new content and language.

social constructivist approach   An approach to instruction that reflects the perspective that learning is promoted best when students drive the discussion and the teacher assumes the role of a facilitator who maximizes the bio-graphical assets of the learners to provide opportunities for all students to engage fully in the lesson.

socio-academic talk   Speech that results when students interact with peers or the teacher to discuss academic content while simultaneously sharing and capitalizing on their culture-bound ways of knowing, thinking, and applying.

sociocultural dimension   One of the four dimensions of the CLD student biography. Includes the student's social and cultural variables, which influence how he or she navigates academic successes. This dimension is critical to understanding the whole student and how the other three dimensions work. Considered the "heart" of the student biography.

state of mind   The psychological mood, disposition, or perspective that one inhabits. Generally a temporary, conscious or unconscious mindset.

strategy   Traditionally defined as a collection of related techniques that represents an implementation component of a method. More specifically, a strategy is a collection of actions that would enable theory-into-practice application of at least one aspect of the method (and one or more concepts of the overarching conceptual model).

subtractive programs   Academic programs for English learners with a primary focus on CLD students learning the second language. When so much emphasis and value are placed on the second language, CLD students tend to lose proficiency in the native, home language.

technique   A specific action or sequence of actions that an educator uses intentionally to achieve a strategic goal.

theoretical framework   Provides a particular view on human development, learning, or language learning. Informs the key concepts that an educator sees as essential to the teaching–learning process.

third space   Classroom conditions that reflect responsiveness to the contributions of individual learners and the voice of the collective learning community. The teacher engages in the sense-making process with students. Together, they jointly negotiate discourse and knowledge, utilizing all linguistic and cultural repertoires of practice. Third space is an indicator of culturally relevant, responsive, and sustaining classrooms.

translanguaging   The dynamic and creative use of one's entire linguistic repertoire to make meaning and engage with others.

zone of proximal development (ZPD)   Vygotsky's (1978) theoretical construct that depicts the space between what a student is independently capable of achieving and the level of achievement possible with the help of peers. When concepts fall within this space, or zone, new learning is most likely to occur. The zone continually shifts as the student grasps new concepts and works with them independently, rather than needing support from the teacher or peers.

Appendices

Templates, rubrics, and a checklist for Appendices B through H, as well as a template for
the Hearts Activity (described in Figure 2.5, page 27), are available for free download and printing
from the Teachers College Press website: tcpress.com

Critical Reflection Using the Reflection Wheel Journal

	A.1. Guide

Heading	Directions
Event(s)/Behavior(s)	**One or two paragraphs** that briefly describe an article, a critical event, a response, a reaction, or a question about course content. The event description should be purely descriptive; it should not include assumptions, judgments, or rationalizations about the event.
Feelings	**Bulleted list** of the feelings (*minimum of three*) that were elicited by/during the journal event. Feelings should be single words (e.g., happy, sad, confused, upset). No explanation is required.
Thoughts	**One or two paragraphs** of narrative that *describe your thoughts* in relation to the description provided in the event(s)/behavior(s) section. Thoughts should convey your thinking at the time you experienced the event/behavior.
Learnings	*Step One:* **Identify at least two or three assumptions**. Assumptions should start with the following lead-in statements: • I assumed . . . • A potential bias I had . . . *Step Two:* **One paragraph** (*minimum*) that checks the validity of assumptions identified in Step One. To do this: • Refer back to course readings, session presentations, and/or discussions with informed colleagues. • Consider the context in which you practice, and/or the context/point of view of the author(s) of what you read (or in the case of a critical incident, the actor(s) who took part in the event). • Elaborate on your assumption checking; do not simply state whether assumptions were invalid or valid. *Step Three:* **One paragraph** (*minimum*) that describes the influence of your prior socialization on actions, feelings, and thoughts. You are looking for links back to your background.
Application	*Step One:* **One paragraph** (*minimum*) that describes the way you have grown personally/professionally. You can elaborate by discussing personal perspectives and learnings, or you can discuss how you apply learnings professionally (e.g., continued research, collaboration with colleagues). *Step Two:* **One paragraph** (*minimum*) that describes your applications to professional practice. Include specific examples of strategies you can implement in your professional practice/classroom that will have a direct impact on students.

Remember: Reflection Wheel Journals are meant to help educators check their own habits of mind by engaging in a specific series of reflective steps.
Therefore, *individual growth is the goal—never judgment!*

Ms. Keith, *Elementary, Kansas*

Event(s)/Behavior(s)

Why do CLD students get additional attention and accommodations for learning relative to those for non-CLD students who struggle with the same academic skills? At the elementary school where I teach, there is an extremely high population of CLD students. These students are given extra help with work during reading intervention times and pulled out during the reading block for small group instruction. Non-CLD students are not receiving the same attention or small group instruction. Both the CLD and non-CLD students are struggling with the same academic skills.

Feelings

- Upset
- Irritated
- Disappointed

Thoughts

I think CLD students do get additional resources that non-CLD students do not receive. It is upsetting to know I have to go through more red tape to get non-CLD students the academic help they also need. These students struggle with academics but do not qualify for Special Education classes because they are not low enough. I know there are monetary resources to provide these extra provisions for CLD students; however, it is irritating to know not everyone can benefit from it. I wonder if more funds could be found to benefit all students, not just those with a label, such as CLD students. It is disappointing to know a teacher has to put forth even more effort to see all students succeed without the additional resources for everyone to use.

Learnings

Step One: I assumed the teaching of CLD students would be harder from an academic aspect (not understanding the concept) and not due to a lack of understanding of the language (vocabulary and meanings).

I assumed that students who spoke and read English well didn't need the extra help with academic skills or understanding of various materials.

Step Two: Based on my assumptions about the language barrier and academic understanding, I have a different perspective with this class. If students do not have a true grasp of the English language, teaching CLD students various materials and skills would just be surface understanding and not go any deeper. According to Herrera and Murry's [2005] book, *Mastering ESL and Bilingual Methods,* CLD students face many sociocultural challenges. "The CLD student must adjust to a new country, city, or neighborhood . . . must adapt to a new education system . . . must cope with nuances of the school's culture . . . which can inhibit the performance of a CLD student in the classroom" (p. 13). Without taking into account these factors, how can I teach students academic skills for reading, math, science, and social studies, as well as social skills? Connections need to be made between the students' first language and their second language for deeper understanding. Language acquisition is the key to CLD students' success in the classroom, and using the Prism Model helps me take the whole student into account.

In assuming CLD students who speak and read English don't need additional help, another perspective has been shown. I have noticed from professional experience that those students who speak and read English well do not always understand what they have read. They are not able to make a connection with their background knowledge of the material for full understanding. Slang words used in various reading materials are difficult for many CLD students to understand because they cannot make a mental picture or find the words in their native language. CLD students need to be given more strategies to understand the concepts; by using techniques like picture clues, vocabulary will benefit CLD students and still benefit those who have a better grasp of the English language.

Step Three: Based on my own background, I grew up in the era of CLD students being given additional help that would benefit everyone. I remember feeling slighted because these students were excelling in the classroom and I was struggling, yet they got the extra time. At that time, I felt angry because I wanted the extra help. As an adult teaching in a predominantly culturally and linguistically diverse school, I have a different perspective from my adolescence. My background experiences colored my viewpoint of CLD students. I believe it is important for CLD students to get the additional resources to be productive members of society; understanding the culture and academics of the school is the first step.

Application

Step One: I have grown in a professional aspect. My eyes have opened to new ideas and viewpoints to benefit my students. The new perspectives I have been exposed to will benefit all my students. My school provides CLD students with additional resources to make them successful in the classroom and in society. What I need to do is take what the ESOL teachers in my building are doing and incorporate their strategies into my classroom lessons. Personally, I believe I have done a disservice to my first group of CLD students last year by not taking into account the diversity of my students. Last year, I used a few strategies in daily activities, however not to the extent my students truly needed. I hope I will be given many different strategies to engage my CLD and non-CLD students for academic success.

Step Two: I will make use of many of the strategies I have been taught so far in this class. The strategies are easy to adapt to the demanding curriculum already in place for my school district. My personal favorite strategy, the vocabulary foldable, is easy to use in many areas of academics, like reading, math, and science. Another strategy I have already used in my classroom is my life in pictures and words. I learned a lot about all my students with this. I need to take into account the grade level I am working with to change some strategies to accommodate my students' abilities. For example, the vocabulary quilt can be challenging due to the fact that many of my students do not have the academic and linguistic background to draw a picture of the vocabulary words. Many of the students are being exposed to these words for the first time in their reading books. But I can see how revisiting these words later in the week or later on would be a wonderful way to pull those vocabulary words out of working memory into permanent memory. I look forward to learning many more strategies for my students to use.

For detailed instructions for filling out the Biography Card, see pages 68 and 69.

Name:

Age:

Grade:

Country of Origin:

Time in USA:

L1: _____
R: _____
W: _____

**L2 Proficiency
(LAS/IPT/Other):**
O: _____
R: _____
W: _____
SLA: _____

Student Processing:

Learning Preferences:

Prior Academic Experiences:

Preferred Grouping:

School-Situated

**Sociocultural Dimension
Home + Community + School =
♡   Background
Knowledge**

**Linguistic Dimension
Valuing L1 & L2**

**Cognitive Dimension
Implications for Practice**

**Academic Dimension
+   State of Mind   –**

Biography-Situated

DOTS Strategy (Determine, Observe, Talk, Summarize)

Overview

The DOTS strategy provides a window that allows students, through pictures and words, to make public their immediate connections with a topic. Used throughout the lesson, DOTS helps students link new learning to build on existing knowledge. For additional details on how to implement the DOTS strategy, please refer to Chapter 8.

Phase	Directions	Benefits to CLD Students
Activation (Opening) **D** **Determine** what I know	• Give students a blank DOTS Chart at the beginning of the lesson. • Have students place the name of the topic/concept that will be taught at the top of the chart. • Start by asking students to write things they know about the topic/story, putting each word, term, or phrase in the box of the letter with which it starts. • Students can be encouraged to write in their native languages or to draw to show their understanding. • Allow only 3–5 minutes for students to write/draw. • Students should be able to explain why they added individual words to the chart.	• Empowers students to tap into their background knowledge and bring information they can share. • Can be applied to any content area. • Creates a context for students to publicly share connections they make to the lesson topic.

Connection (Work Time)
 	
O **Observe** and make connections to what I am learning from teacher/text
 	
T **Talk** to peers
	• Have students write the target vocabulary around the outside of the chart as the words are introduced during the lesson or before getting into the text, lecture, or PowerPoint.
	• Have students make associations with the words inside their charts with those outside the chart to demonstrate connections to the vocabulary words and extend learning.
	  ◆ Students can demonstrate associations physically by drawing lines between the words that they connect.
	  ◆ Have students share their associations with a partner or small group, because such discussion helps to solidify connections.
	• Students can add words that come up during the lesson, as well as words from text used for a reading.
		• Scaffolds students' learning to support their making sense and bringing meaning to text, teacher talk, and peer conversation.
		• Gives students a personal scaffold to use throughout the lesson.
		• Supports the learner in building both social language and academic language.

Affirmation (Closing)
 	
S **Summarize** what I have learned
	• Ask students to use their chart to do the following types of tasks depending on their language proficiency:
	  ◆ Use the chart as a tool to write definitions.
	  ◆ Use the vocabulary to complete a fill-in-the-blank/cloze exercise.
	  ◆ Use the vocabulary to write a paragraph.
	• The teacher can create a checklist or a rubric to assess students' understanding of the vocabulary words or the paragraphs they created.
		• Provides students with a tool in their hands for writing, problem solving, creating, clarifying, or elaborating on what has been learned.

A template for classroom use is available for free download and printing from the Teachers College Press website: tcpress.com

Mind Map

Overview

The Mind Map is an instructional strategy that can be used as a tool for documenting students' linguistic and academic growth throughout the lesson. Mind maps can be extremely helpful in providing students with a way to express their understanding through linguistic and nonlinguistic representations.

Phase	Directions	Benefits to CLD Students
Activation (Opening)	• At the beginning of the lesson, ask students to create a mind map where they can put everything they know about the concept through linguistic and nonlinguistic representation (i.e., words and pictures). • Once the students have created their mind maps, encourage them to share with each other what they have drawn or written. • Observe as students share, to gain insights about their background knowledge about key concepts.	• Provides students with a means to focus on their prior knowledge in a meaningful way. • Allows students to make linguistic and nonlinguistic connections to new information.
Connection (Work Time)	• Have students add new information and make connections between the things already on their mind maps and the new material they are learning. • Monitor students' understanding by closely observing the new connections they are making during the lesson.	• Helps students learn how to discover meaning on their own and how to make meaning out of new concepts.
Affirmation (Closing)	• At the end of the lesson, have students once more add to their mind maps by summarizing key points of their new learning—through pictures as well as words. • As a way of extending students' learnings, have them share their mind map with a peer, a small group, or even the whole class. • As a further extension, after the students have completed their mind maps, ask them to use that information to create persuasive or expository paragraphs that summarize what was learned during the lesson. • The teacher can create a rubric to assess students' understanding as demonstrated in their work with their mind maps.	• Provides students with a scaffold with which they can document and summarize key learning and concepts.

A student academic behavior rubric for classroom use is available for free download and printing from the Teachers College Press website: tcpress.com

APPENDIX E

Vocabulary Quilt

Overview

The Vocabulary Quilt lets students activate background knowledge about vocabulary they will need for new learning. By updating their quilts throughout the lesson, students will strengthen connections with newly acquired information.

Phase	Directions	Benefits to CLD Students
Activation (Opening)	• Choose eight vocabulary words based on their relevance to the lesson. • Create blank vocabulary quilts by folding a large sheet of paper horizontally and vertically to produce eight boxes. • Divide students into groups of four or five and give each group a vocabulary quilt. • Have students write each vocabulary word in a separate box on the quilt. • Explain to students that each individual should quick-write (in English or their native language) and/or draw in the box for each vocabulary word whatever comes to mind when he or she reads the word. • Give students 3–5 minutes to write something for each word. It may be helpful to have each student use a marker or pen of a different color. • Provide students with the opportunity to discuss in their groups the rationales for the associations they made.	• Provides students with the opportunity to share based on their background knowledge. • Incorporates both linguistic and nonlinguistic representations. • Allows for use of the native language. • Talk with peers allows for associations to be made.
Connection (Work Time)	• Post the vocabulary quilts to make "interactive word walls" that students can continually revisit during the lesson. • Give students sticky notes they can use to write down additional information about the key vocabulary words as they encounter them in class readings or in the text. • Have students add to their quilts new information gleaned from class or small-group discussion. • Working as a facilitator, refer to students' vocabulary quilts and revoice the connections between students' initial associations and added text-related knowledge. • Confirm/disconfirm associations from preassessment.	• The focus on key vocabulary allows learners to selectively attend to the targeted words in relation to the content/standard. • Revisiting the students' words/images written during the opening of the lesson reminds students that what they know can often be associated with what they are learning.
Affirmation (Closing)	• Have students work together in small groups to define an assigned subset or all of the vocabulary words one last time. • Have groups share with the class the definitions they generated. • Have students individually or in pairs write a paragraph summarizing what was learned. • For limited English speakers, the following adaptations can be made to the writing activity: • Have students dictate the sentences to a teacher, paraprofessional, or peer who can write them. • Allow students to write in their native language. • Pair the students with more proficient peers who can help them write the paragraph in English. • The teacher can create a checklist or a rubric to assess students' understanding of the definitions or the paragraphs they created.	• Allows students to demonstrate their integrated knowledge of the vocabulary and content. • Allows accommodation for students who have limited ability to write English.

A student academic behavior checklist for classroom use is available for free download and printing from the Teachers College Press website: tcpress.com

Ignite, Discover, Extend, Affirm (IDEA)

Overview

The IDEA strategy enables the teacher to activate students' background knowledge and then guide them in navigating the content-area curriculum. The strategy promotes synthesis and application of vocabulary, rather than rote memorization.

Phase	Directions	Benefits to CLD Students
Activation (Opening) **I** **Ignite**	• Select five to seven key vocabulary words that are related to the same concept. • To **ignite** students' understandings of these words, have them think about what they already know about the words. ◆ Showing students visuals of the words will help to activate their understandings of the words. • Have students discuss what they already know with a partner or in a small group.	• Uses students' prior knowledge as the basis for "igniting" understanding of new vocabulary.

Connection (Work Time)
 	
D   **Discover**
	• Students **discover** the meaning of the words as they are taught in context by:
	  ◆ Talking about the words within the context of the lesson.
	  ◆ Reading a text/story in which the words appear.
	  ◆ Generating and writing definitions of the words within the context of the lesson.
	• Be sure to have students make connections back to their initial ideas discussed during the "Ignite" phase.
		• Helps students learn how to discover meaning on their own and make meaning out of the new concepts.

Affirmation (Closing) **E** **Extend** **A** **Affirm**	• As a way to **extend** students' learning, have them create links between individual words by creating a vocabulary chain, where they organize vocabulary word cards (one vocabulary word per card) to show a connection/link between the vocabulary words/concepts. ◆ Students can first do this orally, by sharing the links with peers and then with the teacher to **affirm** their understanding. • Have students independently use all of the vocabulary words to write a paragraph that shows their understandings. Allow students to draw their connections if they are in the preproduction or early production phase of second language acquisition. • The teacher can create a rubric to assess students' understandings of the words, as demonstrated in the paragraphs students wrote.	• Helps students extend on their learnings through listening, speaking, reading, and writing.

A student academic behavior rubric for classroom use is available for free download and printing from the Teachers College Press website: tcpress.com

Thumb Challenge

Overview

The Thumb Challenge allows learners to practice language through interaction and to support each other in extending understanding of the target vocabulary or concepts. During strategy implementation, the teacher has the opportunity to informally assess learning by observing student interactions.

	Directions	Benefits to CLD Students
Onomatopoeia **Metaphor** **Simile** **Alliteration**	• Take two sentence strips or a piece of paper and write the key vocabulary words or critical concepts on both sentence strips or sides of the paper. If sentence strips are used, tape them together after the vocabulary words have been written on them. • Make sure to write the same words/key concepts on both sides so the students are practicing the same words. • Have students sit facing each other, with the sentence strips/paper between them. • Ask both students to hold the sentence strips/paper together with a thumb and index finger with a thumb on the first word on each side. (Note: The words should be the same and in the same order for both students. For example, Alliteration would be the first word on the strips shown at the left.) • Have one student start by reading the first word/concept and then stating the definition/meaning of the word/concept. • If the student who began first struggles or does not know a word/concept, the other student starts sharing from the very first word. As the second student shares his or her definition/meaning, the first student's comprehension is stretched to the next level. • If the second student cannot complete the words/concepts, the first student begins again with the first word. • The student who finishes first is the winner. • Be sure to tell students that if at any point they are both unable to figure out a word, they can raise their sentence strip in the air as a signal that they need help from the teacher. • As the students are sharing, the teacher can go around and listen to students' comments and check for understanding. • If many students struggle with a certain word, bring the whole group back and review that particular word again with the entire class. • **Teacher Tip:** Laminate sentence strips with key vocabulary so they can be used repeatedly.	• Provides a great review/ assessment activity for students across content areas. • Students do not have to rely on their ability to write their responses. Instead, they can state them orally. • The fact that students can challenge each other at any point stretches them to a higher cognitive level as they must justify their responses. • The focus is on engaging students and moving beyond factual knowledge to demonstrate learning in a participatory manner. Such participation makes thinking public and extends student learning and use of content-based English vocabulary.

A student academic behavior rubric for classroom use is available for free download and printing from the Teachers College Press website: tcpress.com

Uncover, Concentrate, Monitor, Evaluate (U-C-ME)

Overview

U-C-ME is a tool that allows students to demonstrate their prior knowledge and connections to the particular topic or concept by writing down everything they know or have experienced that is related to the topic or concept at the opening of the lesson. During the work time of the lesson, students' attention is focused on specific information, and growth is monitored during the closing of the lesson.

Phase	Directions	Benefits to CLD Students
Activation (Opening) **U Uncover**	• Give students a blank U-C-ME template at the beginning of the lesson. • Have students write the name of the topic/concept that is the focus of the lesson around the outside of the center oval. • Ask students to write down everything they "bring to the table" or know about the topic/concept inside the center oval. ◦ Encourage students to write down information in their native language if they prefer. • Allow only 2–3 minutes for students to write.	• Uncovers what students already know, enabling them to build from the *known* to the *unknown*.
Connection (Work Time) **C Concentrate**	• Once students have finished with the uncovering phase, have them think of specific questions they may have about the topic. Model this first by posing sample questions for two or three of the spokes. ◦ Generate questions that require students' higher order thinking skills. • Have students pose their own questions on the remaining spokes. These questions will become the guide for student learning. • During instruction, make sure to concentrate on information that can be used to answer students' questions. • To guide students, it may be helpful to create a whole-class U-C-ME template on which key learning can be documented.	• Helps students learn how to focus on critical concepts during the lesson.

Affirmation (Closing)
 	
M   Monitor
 	
E   Evaluate
	• Have students monitor their learning by placing responses to each of the questions posed in the corresponding ovals.
	• Final evaluation of student understanding can be done by having students use what was in the ovals to summarize what they learned about the topic or concept:
	  ◦ In written form (persuasive or narrative paragraph).
	  ◦ In oral conversations with a peer (discussing what was learned and where or how it was learned).
		• Provides students with a scaffold they can use to document and summarize key learning.

A template and a student academic behavior rubric for classroom use are available for free download and printing from the Teachers College Press website: tcpress.com

Quick Guide to Biography-Driven Instructional Concepts

LINGUISTIC

- SLA (second language acquisition) (pp. 35–40, 42–43, 48–49, 141)
- BICS and CALP (language for social and academic contexts) (pp. 36–37, 177, 178)
- CUP and SUP (common underlying proficiency and separate underlying proficiency) (pp. 39–40, 178, 180)

COGNITIVE

- Varying complexity of tasks (pp. 50–52)
- Instructional learning strategies (pp. 78–79, 178, 180)
- Students' personal learning strategies (pp. 54–56, 117–121, 146–147, 179)
- Culture-bound ways of knowing, thinking, and applying (pp. 57–59, 143–144)

Teaching & Learning
Activate – Connect – Affirm

Fundamentals of Language

Fundamentals of Biography

Critical Reflection
Access – Engagement – Hope

ACADEMIC

- ZPD (zone of proximal development) (pp. 12–13, 180)
- *i*+1 (knowledge one step beyond preexisting capabilities) (pp. 12–13, 37–38, 113–117, 178–179)
- *i*+*Tpsi* (grouping configurations for interactive learning) (pp. 124–129, 179)

Checking Our Habits of Mind in Teaching

SOCIOCULTURAL

- Biopsychosocial history (pp. 19–25, 178)
- Background knowledge (funds of knowledge, prior knowledge, academic knowledge) (pp. 86–92, 106–111, 177, 179, 180)
- States of mind (pp. 65, 76–78, 121–122, 137–139, 143, 180)
- Affective filter (pp. 38–39, 77–78, 177)
- Third space (pp. 14, 112–113, 180)

List of Instructional Aids Available Online

Discussion Guide, Templates, Rubrics, and Checklist

For classroom use, the items listed below are available for free download and printing from the Teachers College Press website: tcpress.com

Chapter-by-Chapter Discussion Guide for *Biography-Driven Culturally Responsive Teaching*

Hearts Activity: Template
(For instructions for implementing this strategy, see Figure 2.5, page 27)

CLD Student Biography Card: Template
(For instructions for implementing this strategy, see Figures 5.2 and 5.3, pages 68 and 69)

DOTS Strategy (Determine, Observe, Talk, Summarize): Template
(For instructions for implementing this strategy, see Appendix C, page 185)

Mind Map: Student Academic Behavior Rubric
(For instructions for implementing this strategy, see Appendix D, page 186)

Vocabulary Quilt: Student Academic Behavior Checklist
(For instructions for implementing this strategy, see Appendix E, page 187)

Ignite, Discover, Extend, Affirm (IDEA): Student Academic Behavior Rubric
(For instructions for implementing this strategy, see Appendix F, page 188)

Thumb Challenge: Student Academic Behavior Rubric
(For instructions for implementing this strategy, see Appendix G, page 189)

Uncover, Concentrate, Monitor, Evaluate (U-C-ME): Template *and* Student Academic Behavior Rubric
(For instructions for implementing this strategy, see Appendix H, page 190)

References

Afflerbach, P., Pearson, P., & Paris, S. G. (2008). Clarifying differences between reading skills and reading strategies. *The Reading Teacher, 61*(5), 364–373.

Ainley, M., & Ainley, J. (2011). Student engagement with science in early adolescence: The contribution of enjoyment to students' continuing interest in learning about science. *Contemporary Educational Psychology, 36*(1), 4–12.

Akmajian, A., Farmer, A. K., Bickmore, L., Demers, R. A., & Harnish, R. M. (2017). *Linguistics: An introduction to language and communication* (7th ed.). MIT Press.

Alcoff, L. M. (2006). *Visible identities: Race, gender, and the self.* Oxford University Press.

Alexander, B. (2003). (Re)visioning the ethnographic site: Interpretive ethnography as a method of pedagogical reflexivity and scholarly production. *Qualitative Inquiry, 9*(3), 416–441.

Alim, H. S., & Paris, D. (2017). What is culturally sustaining pedagogy and why does it matter? In D. Paris & H. S. Alim (Eds.), *Culturally sustaining pedagogies: Teaching and learning for justice in a changing world* (pp. 1–21). Teachers College Press.

Aljaafreh, A., & Lantolf, J. P. (1994). Negative feedback as regulation and second language learning in the zone of proximal development. *The Modern Language Journal, 78*(4), 465–483.

Anderson, A. D., Hunt, A. N., Powell, R. E., & Dollar, C. B. (2013). Student perceptions of teaching transparency. *Journal of Effective Teaching, 13*(2), 38–47.

Anderson, L. W. (Ed.), Krathwohl, D. R. (Ed.), Airasian, P. W., Cruikshank, K. A., Mayer, R. E., Pintrich, P. R., et al. (2001). *A taxonomy for learning, teaching, and assessing: A revision of Bloom's Taxonomy of Educational Objectives* (Complete ed.). Longman.

Anderson, N. J. (2002). *The role of metacognition in second language teaching and learning.* Washington, DC: ERIC Clearinghouse on Languages and Linguistics. (ERIC Digest No. EDO-FL-01-10)

Appleton, J. J., Christenson, S. L., & Furlong, M. J. (2008). Student engagement with school: Critical conceptual and methodological issues of the construct. *Psychology in the Schools, 45*(5), 369–386. doi.org/10.1002/pits.20303

August, D., Carlo, M., Dressler, C., & Snow, C. (2005). The critical role of vocabulary development for English language learners. *Learning Disabilities Research & Practice, 20*(1), 50–57.

Babad, E. (1993). Teachers' differential behavior. *Educational Psychology Review, 5,* 347–376.

Ballard & Tighe. (2004). *IDEA Proficiency Test (IPT).* Author.

Beck, I. L., McKeown, M. G., & Kucan, L. (2002). *Bringing words to life: Robust vocabulary instruction.* Guilford.

Benson, S. (2010). I don't know if that'd be English or not: Third space theory and literacy instruction. *Journal of Adolescent and Adult Literacy, 53*(7), 555–563. doi.org/10.1598/JAAL.53.7.3

Berlak, H. (2003). *The "No Child Left Behind Act" and teaching reading* [Policy brief]. EPSL-0304-107-EPRU. Education Policy Research Unit, Education Policy Studies Laboratory, College of Education, Arizona State University. nepc.colorado.edu/sites/default/files/publications/EPRU-0304-20-RW.pdf

Berman, P., Chambers, J., Gandara, P., McLaughlin, B., Minicucci, C., Nelson, B., et al. (1992). *Meeting the challenge of language diversity: An evaluation of programs for pupils with limited English proficiency* (Executive summary, Vol. I). BW Associates.

Bhabha, H. K. (1994). *The location of culture.* Routledge.

Biemans, H. J. A., & Simons, P. R. (1996). Contact-2: A computer-assisted instructional strategy for promoting conceptual change. *Instructional Science, 24*(2), 157–176.

Bjork, R. A., Dunlosky, J., & Kornell, N. (2013). Self-regulated learning: Beliefs, techniques, and illusions. *Annual Review of Psychology, 64,* 417–444.

Bloom, B. S. (Ed.), Engelhart, M. D., Furst, E. J., Hill, W. H., & Krathwohl, D. R. (1956). *Taxonomy of educational objectives: The classification of educational goals. Handbook I: Cognitive domain.* David McKay.

Boggs, S. T. (1985). The meaning of questions and narratives to Hawaiian children. In C. B. Cazden, V. H. John, & D. Hymes (Eds.), *Functions of language in the classroom* (pp. 299–327). Waveland.

Bondebjerg, I. (2017). The creative mind: Cognition, society and culture. *Palgrave Communications, 3*(1), article 19. doi.org/10.1057/s41599-017-0024-1

Borrell-Carrió, F., Suchman, A. L., & Epstein, R. M. (2004). The biopsychosocial model 25 years later: Principles, practice, and scientific inquiry. *Annals of Family Medicine, 2*(6), 576–582.

Bowers, C. A., & Flinders, D. (1990). *An ecological approach to classroom patterns of language, thought, and culture.* Teachers College Press.

Bransford, J. D., Brown, A. L., & Cocking, R. R. (2000). *How people learn: Brain, mind, experience, and school.* National Academy Press.

Brock, C. H., & Raphael, T. E. (2005). *Windows into language, literacy, and culture: Insights from an English language learner.* International Reading Association.

Brophy, J. E. (1982). How teachers influence what is taught and learned in classrooms. *Elementary School Journal, 83*(1), 1–13.

Brown, A. L. (1980). Metacognitive development and reading. In R. J. Spiro, B. C. Bruce, & W. F. Brewer (Eds.), *Theoretical issues in reading comprehension* (pp. 453–481). Lawrence Erlbaum.

Brownell, R. (Ed.). (2000a). *Expressive One-Word Picture Vocabulary Test.* Academic Therapy Publications.

Brownell, R. (Ed.). (2000b). *Receptive One-Word Picture Vocabulary Test.* Academic Therapy Publications.

Bruner, J. (1996). *The culture of education.* Harvard University Press.

Buzan, T. (1983). *Use both sides of your brain: New techniques to help you read efficiently, study effectively, solve problems, remember more, think clearly.* E. P. Dutton.

Byers, P., & Byers, H. (1985). Nonverbal communication and the education of children. In C. B. Cazden, V. P. John, & D. Hymes (Eds.), *Functions of language in the classroom* (pp. 3–31). Waveland.

Byers-Heinlein, K., & Lew-Williams, C. (2013). Bilingualism in the early years: What the science says. *Learning Landscapes, 7*(1), 95–112.

Caine, R. N., & Caine, G. (1991). *Making connections: Teaching and the human brain.* Association for Supervision and Curriculum Development.

Calderón, M. (2007). *Teaching reading to English language learners, Grades 6–12: A framework for improving achievement in the content areas.* Corwin Press.

Carlo, M. S., August, D., McLaughlin, B., Snow, C. E., Dressler, C., Lippman, D., et al. (2004). Closing the gap: Addressing the vocabulary needs of English-language learners in bilingual and mainstream classrooms. *Reading Research Quarterly, 39*(2), 188–215.

Center for Research on Education, Diversity & Excellence (CREDE). (2021). *The CREDE five standards for effective pedagogy and learning.* manoa.hawaii.edu/coe/credenational/the-crede-five-standards-for-effective-pedagogy-and-learning/

Chamberlain, S. P. (2005). Recognizing and responding to cultural differences in the education of culturally and linguistically diverse learners. *Intervention in School and Clinic, 40*(4), 195–211.

Chamot, A. (2009). *The CALLA handbook: Implementing the cognitive academic language learning approach* (2nd ed.). Addison-Wesley.

Chamot, A., & O'Malley, J. M. (1994). *The CALLA handbook: Implementing the cognitive academic language learning approach.* Addison-Wesley.

Chapin, S. H., O'Connor, C., & Anderson, N. C. (2003, Fall). Classroom discussions using math talk in elementary classrooms. *Math Solutions Online Newsletter, 11.* mathsolutions.com/documents/0-941355-53-5_L.pdf

Charney, R. S. (2002). *Teaching children to care: Classroom management for ethical and academic growth, K–8* (Rev. ed.). Northeast Foundation for Children.

Chater, N., & Manning, C. D. (2006). Probabilistic models of language processing and acquisition. *Trends in Cognitive Sciences, 10*(7), 335–344.

Cholewa, B., Goodman, R. D., West-Olatunji, C., & Amatea, E. (2014). A qualitative examination of the impact of culturally responsive educational practices on the psychological well-being of students of color. *The Urban Review, 46*(4), 574–596. doi.org/10.1007/s11256-014-0272-y

Christensen, L. (2000). *Reading, writing, and rising up: Teaching about social justice and the power of the written word.* Rethinking Schools.

Clandinin, D. J., & Connelly, F. M. (1995). *Teachers' professional knowledge landscapes.* Teachers College Press.

Coffield, F., Moseley, D., Hall, E., & Ecclestone, K. (2004). Learning styles and pedagogy in post-16 learning: A systematic and critical review. *Learning and Skills Research Centre.* hdl.voced.edu.au/10707/69027

Collier, V. P., & Thomas, W. P. (2009). *Educating English learners for a transformed world.* Fuente Press.

Cooper, H., & Good, T. (1983). *Pygmalion grows up: Studies in the expectation communication process.* Longman.

Cooperstein, S. E., & Kocevar-Weidinger, E. (2004). Beyond active learning: A constructivist approach to learning. *Reference Services Review, 32*(2), 141–148.

Critchlow, D. E. (1996). *Dos Amigos verbal language scales.* Academic Therapy Publications.

Cummins, J. (1981). The role of primary language development in promoting educational success for language minority students. In C. F. Leyba (Ed.), *Schooling and language minority students: A theoretical framework* (pp. 3–49). Evaluation, Dissemination and Assessment Center, CSULA.

Cummins, J. (1996). *Negotiating identities: Education for empowerment in a diverse society.* California Association for Bilingual Education.

Cummins, J. (1998). Language issues and educational change. In A. Hargreaves, A. Lieberman, M. Fullan, & D. Hopkins (Eds.), *International handbook of educational change* (pp. 440–459). Kluwer Academic.

Cummins, J. (2000). *Language, power, and pedagogy: Bilingual children in the crossfire.* Multilingual Matters.

Cummins, J. (2008). BICS and CALP: Empirical and theoretical status of the distinction. In B. Street & N. H. Hornberger (Eds.), *Encyclopedia of language and education* (2nd ed., Vol. 2: Literacy, pp. 71–83). Springer Science + Business Media LLC.

Cushner, K., McClelland, A., & Safford, P. (2006). *Human diversity in education: An integrative approach* (5th ed.). McGraw-Hill.

Darling-Hammond, L., Flook, L., Cook-Harvey, C., Barron, B., & Osher, D. (2020). Implications for educational practice of the science of learning and development. *Applied Developmental Science, 24*(2), 97–140. doi.org/10.1080/10888691.2018.1537791

Davis, B. M. (Ed.). (2012). *How to teach students who don't look like you: Culturally relevant teaching strategies* (2nd ed.). Corwin Press.

Delpit, L. D. (1988). The silenced dialogue: Power and pedagogy in educating other people's children. *Harvard Educational Review, 58*(3), 280–298.

Delpit, L. (2006). *Other people's children: Cultural conflict in the classroom.* The New Press.

Demanet, J., & Van Houtte, M. (2012). Teachers' attitudes and students' opposition: School misconduct as a reaction to teachers' diminished effort and affect. *Teaching and Teacher Education, 28*(6), 860–869.

Deutsch, M. (1949). A theory of cooperation and competition. *Human Relations, 2,* 129–152.

Dewey, J. (2007). *Democracy and education: An introduction to the philosophy of education.* NuVision. (Original work published 1916)

Díaz-Rico, L. T. (2008). *Strategies for teaching English learners* (2nd ed.). Allyn & Bacon.

Dickson, S. V., Chard, D. J., & Simmons, D. C. (1993). An integrated reading/writing curriculum: A focus on scaffolding. *LD Forum, 18*(4), 12–16.

DiGiacomo, D. K., & Gutiérrez, K. D. (2017). Seven chilis: Making visible the complexities in leveraging cultural repertoires of practice in a designed teaching and learning environment. *Pedagogies: An International Journal, 12*(1), 41–57. doi.org/10.1080/1554480X.2017.1283992

Dinsmore, D. L., Alexander, P. A., & Loughlin, S. M. (2008). Focusing the conceptual lens on metacognition, self-regulation, and self-regulated learning. *Educational Psychology Review, 20*(4), 391–409. doi.org/10.1007/s10648-008-9083-6

Doherty, R. W., Hilberg, R. S., Epaloose, G., & Tharp, R. G. (2002). Standards performance continuum: Development and validation of a measure of effective pedagogy. *Journal of Educational Research, 96*(2), 78–89. doi.org/10.1080/00220670209598795

Donato, R. (1994). Collective scaffolding in second language learning. In J. P. Lantolf & G. Appel (Eds.), *Vygotskian approaches to second language research* (pp. 33–56). Ablex.

Doyle, T. (2011). *Learner-centered teaching: Putting the research on learning into practice.* Stylus Publishing.

Duncan, S. E., & DeAvila, E. A. (1990). *Language Assessment Scales.* CTB/McGraw-Hill.

Duncan, S. E., & DeAvila, E. A. (1998). *Pre-Language Assessment Scale 2000.* CTB/McGraw-Hill.

Dunn, R. (1990). Understanding the Dunn and Dunn learning styles model and the need for individual diagnosis and prescription. *Reading, Writing, and Learning Disabilities, 6*(3), 223–247. doi.org/10.1080/0748763900060303

Dunn, R., & Dunn, K. (1993). *Teaching secondary students through their individual learning styles: Practical approaches for Grades 7–12.* Allyn & Bacon.

Echevarría, J., & Graves, A. (2015). *Sheltered content instruction: Teaching English learners with diverse abilities* (5th ed.). Pearson Education.

Echevarría, J., Vogt, M., & Short, D. J. (2008). *Making content comprehensible for English learners: The SIOP® model* (3rd ed.). Allyn & Bacon.

Echevarría, J., Vogt, M., & Short, D. J. (2016). *Making content comprehensible for English learners: The SIOP® model* (5th ed.). Allyn & Bacon.

Eisner, E. W. (1998). *The kind of schools we need: Personal essays.* Heinemann.

Ellis, N. C. (2002). Frequency effects in language processing. *Studies in Second Language Acquisition, 24,* 143–188.

Ellis, N. C. (2006a). Language acquisition as rational contingency learning. *Applied Linguistics, 27,* 1–24.

Ellis, N. C. (2006b). Selective attention and transfer phenomena in L2 acquisition: Contingency, cue competition, salience, interference, overshadowing, blocking, and perceptual learning. *Applied Linguistics, 27,* 164–194.

Ellis, N. C. (2007). The associative–cognitive CREED. In B. VanPatten & J. Williams (Eds.), *Theories in second language acquisition: An introduction* (pp. 77–95). Lawrence Erlbaum.

Ellis, R. (1997). *SLA research and language teaching.* Oxford University Press.

Engel, G. (1961). To the editor. *Psychosomatic Medicine, 23,* 426–429.

Engel, G. (1977). The need for a new medical model: A challenge to biomedicine. *Science, 196*(4286), 129–136.

Engel, G. (1980). The clinical application of the biopsychosocial model. *American Journal of Psychiatry, 137,* 535–544.

Erlauer, L. (2003). Emotional wellness and a safe environment. In *The brain-compatible classroom: Using what we know about learning to improve teaching.* Association for Supervision and Curriculum Development.

Esteban-Guitart, M., & Moll, L. C. (2014). Funds of identity: A new concept based on the funds of knowledge approach. *Culture & Psychology, 20*(1), 31–48. doi.org/10.1177/1354067X13515934

Faltis, C. J., & Hudelson, S. J. (1998). *Bilingual education in elementary and secondary school communities: Toward understanding and caring.* Allyn & Bacon.

Fenner, D. S. (2013). *Implementing the Common Core State Standards for English learners: The changing role of the ESL teacher. A summary of the TESOL International Association convening April 2013.* tesol.org/docs/default-source/advocacy/ccss_convening_final-8-15-13.pdf?sfvrsn=8

Fisher, D., & Frey, N. (2010). *The value of intentional vocabulary instruction in the middle grades* [White paper]. f.hubspotusercontent40.net/hub/95641/file-16105551.pdf/douglas_fisher_whitepaper_download.pdf

Forman, E. A., Larreamendy-Joerns, J., Stein, M. K., & Brown, C. A. (1998). "You're going to want to find out which and prove it": Collective argumentation in a mathematics classroom. *Learning and Instruction, 8*(6), 527–548.

Frayer, D., Frederick, W. C., & Klausmeier, H. J. (1969). *A schema for testing the level of cognitive mastery.* Wisconsin Center for Education Research.

Fredrickson, B. L., & Branigan, C. (2005). Positive emotions broaden the scope of attention and thought–action repertoires. *Cognition and Emotion, 19*(3), 313–332. doi.org/10.1080/02699930441000238

Freeman, Y. S., & Freeman, D. E. (2002). *Closing the achievement gap: How to reach limited-formal-schooling and long-term English learners.* Heinemann.

Freire, P. (1970). *Pedagogy of the oppressed.* Continuum International Publishing Group.

Freire, P., & Macedo, D. (1987). *Literacy: Reading the word and the world.* Bergin & Garvey.

Frey, W. H. (2021, August 13). *New 2020 census results show increased diversity countering decade-long declines in America's white and youth populations.* Brookings Institution. brookings.edu/research/new-2020-census-results-show-increased-diversity-countering-decade-long-declines-in-americas-white-and-youth-populations/

Gaddy, B. (Ed.). (1999). *Including culturally and linguistically diverse students in standards-based reform: A report on McREL's Diversity Roundtable 1.* Mid-Continent Research for Education and Learning. (ERIC Document Reproduction Service No. ED455335)

Garcia, E. E. (2003). *Student cultural diversity: Understanding and meeting the challenge.* Houghton Mifflin.

García, O. (2017). Translanguaging in schools: Subiendo y bajando, bajando y subiendo as afterword. *Journal of Language, Identity & Education, 16*(4), 256–263. doi.org/10.1080/15348458.2017.1329657

García, O., Johnson, S. I., & Seltzer, K. (2017). *The translanguaging classroom: Leveraging student bilingualism for learning.* Caslon.

García, O., & Kleifgen, J. A. (2018). *Educating emergent bilinguals: Policies, programs, and practices for English learners* (2nd ed.). Teachers College Press.

García, O., & Wei, L. (2014). *Translanguaging: Language, bilingualism and education.* Palgrave Pivot.

Gardner, H. (1992). *Multiple intelligences.* Volume 5, 56. Minnesota Center for Arts Education.

Gardner, H. (1993). *Multiple intelligences: The theory in practice.* Basic Books.

Gates, M. L., & Hutchinson, K. (2005). *Cultural competence education and the need to reject cultural neutrality: The importance of what we teach and do not teach about culture.* Paper presented at the College of Education, Criminal Justice, and Human Services (CECH) Spring Research Conference, University of Cincinnati, OH.

Gay, G. (2000). *Culturally responsive teaching: Theory, research, & practice.* Teachers College Press.

Gay, G. (2002). Preparing for culturally responsive teaching. *Journal of Teacher Education, 53*(2), 106–116.

Gay, G. (2010). *Culturally responsive teaching: Theory, research, & practice* (2nd ed.). Teachers College Press.

Gay, G. (2018). *Culturally responsive teaching: Theory, research, and practice* (3rd ed.). Teachers College Press.

Gee, J. P. (1990). *Social linguistics and literacies: Ideology in discourses.* Falmer Press.

Gee, J. P. (2001). A sociocultural perspective on early literacy development. In S. Neuman & D. Dickinson (Eds.), *Handbook of early literacy research* (pp. 30–42). Guilford.

Genesee, F. (n.d.). *The home language: An English language learner's most valuable resource.* colorincolorado.org/article/home-language-english-language-learners-most-valuable-resource

Glasgrow, N. A., & Hicks, C. D. (2009). *What successful teachers do: 101 Research-based classroom strategies for new and veteran teachers.* Corwin Press.

Goldenberg, C. (2008, Summer). Teaching English language learners: What the research does—and does not—say. *American Educator, 32*(2), 8–44. aft.org/sites/default/files/periodicals/goldenberg.pdf

González, N., Moll, L., & Amanti, C. (2005). *Funds of knowledge: Theorizing practices in households, communities, and classrooms.* Lawrence Erlbaum.

Good, T. L. (1987). Teacher expectations. In D. C. Berliner & B. V. Rosenshine (Eds.), *Talks to teachers* (pp. 159–200). Random House.

Gorski, P. C. (2010). Unlearning deficit ideology and the scornful gaze: Thoughts on authenticating the class discourse in education. *EdChange.* edchange.org/publications/deficit-ideology-scornful-gaze.pdf

Gottardo, A., & Mueller, J. (2009). Are first- and second-language factors related in predicting second-language reading comprehension? A study of Spanish-speaking children acquiring English as a second language from first to second grade. *Journal of Educational Psychology, 101*(2), 330–344. doi.org/10.1037/a0014320

Gronlund, N. E. (2004). *Writing instructional objectives for teaching and assessment* (7th ed.). Pearson.

Guerra, C. (1996). Krashen's *i+1* issue revisited from a Vygotskian perspective. *TESOL-GRAM (The Official Newsletter of Puerto Rico TESOL), 23*, 7–8.

Gutiérrez, K. D. (2008, April/May/June). Developing a sociocritical literacy in the third space. *Reading Research Quarterly, 43*(2), 148–164.

Gutiérrez, K. D., Baquedano-López, P., & Tejeda, C. (2003). Rethinking diversity: Hybridity and hybrid language practices in the third space. In S. Goodman, T. Lillis, J. Maybin, & N. Mercer (Eds.), *Language, literacy, and education: A reader* (pp. 171–187). The Open University.

Gutiérrez, K. D., & Johnson, P. (2017). Understanding identity sampling and cultural repertoires: Advancing a historicizing and syncretic system of teaching and learning in justice pedagogies. In D. Paris & H. S. Alim (Eds.), *Culturally sustaining pedagogies: Teaching and learning for justice in a changing world* (pp. 247–260). Teachers College Press.

Gutiérrez, K. D., & Rogoff, B. (2003). Cultural ways of learning: Individual traits or repertoires of practice. *Educational Researcher, 32*(5), 19–25. doi.org/10.3102/0013189X032005019

Gutiérrez, K., Rymes, B., & Larson, J. (1995). Script, counterscript, and underlife in the classroom: James Brown versus Brown v. Board of Education. *Harvard Educational Review, 65*(3), 445–471.

Hagevik, R., Aydeniz, M., & Rowell, C. G. (2012). Using action research in middle level teacher education to evaluate and deepen reflective practice. *Teaching and Teacher Education, 28*(5), 675–684.

Hammond, Z. (2015). *Culturally responsive teaching and the brain: Promoting authentic engagement and rigor among culturally and linguistically diverse students.* Corwin.

Harcourt Assessment. (2003). *Stanford English Language Proficiency (SELP) Test.* Author.

Hayes, J., & Allinson, C. W. (1993). Matching learning style and instructional strategy: An application of the person–environment interaction paradigm. *Perceptual and Motor Skills, 76*(1), 63–79. doi.org/10.2466/pms.1993.76.1.63

Heath, S. B. (2000). Linguistics in the study of language in education. *Harvard Educational Review, 70*, 49–59.

Henriques, G. (2015, October 30). The biopsychosocial model and its limitations. *Psychology Today.* psychologytoday.com/us/blog/theory-knowledge/201510/the-biopsychosocial-model-and-its-limitations

Herrera, S. (1996). The meaning perspectives teachers hold regarding their Mexican American students: An ethnographic case study. *Dissertation Abstracts International, 56*(12), 4643. (CD-ROM) Abstract from ProQuest File: Dissertation Abstracts Item AAC 9610795.

Herrera, S. G., Cabral, R. M., & Murry, K. G. (2013). *Assessment accommodations for classroom teachers of culturally and linguistically diverse students* (2nd ed.). Allyn & Bacon.

Herrera, S. G., Cabral, R. M., & Murry, K. G. (2020). *Assessment of culturally and linguistically diverse students* (3rd ed.). Pearson.

Herrera, S. G., Kavimandan, S. K., & Holmes, M. A. (2011). *Crossing the vocabulary bridge: Differentiated strategies for diverse secondary classrooms.* Teachers College Press.

Herrera, S. G., Kavimandan, S. K., Perez, D. R., & Wessels, S. (2017). *Accelerating literacy for diverse learners: Classroom strategies that integrate social/emotional engagement and academic achievement, K–8* (2nd ed.). Teachers College Press.

Herrera, S. G., & Murry, K. G. (2005). *Mastering ESL and bilingual methods: Differentiated instruction for culturally and linguistically diverse (CLD) students.* Allyn & Bacon.

Herrera, S. G., & Murry, K. G. (2016). *Mastering ESL/EFL methods: Differentiated instruction for culturally and linguistically (CLD) students* (3rd ed.). Pearson Education.

Herrera, S., Perez, D., Kavimandan, S., Holmes, M., & Miller, S. S. (2011, April 8–12). *Beyond reductionism and quick fixes: Quanti-* tatively measuring effective pedagogy in the instruction of CLD students [Paper presentation]. American Educational Research Association Annual Meeting, New Orleans, LA, United States. aera.net/Events-Meetings/Annual-Meeting/Previous-Annual-Meetings/2011-Annual-Meeting

Herrera Terry, D. (with BESITOS students). (2004). *Student voices: Two short plays on the Latin@ educational experience* [DVD]. Kansas State University.

Hiebert, E. H. (1991). Introduction. In E. H. Hiebert (Ed.), *Literacy for a diverse society: Perspectives, practices, and policies* (pp. 1–6). Teachers College Press.

Honig, B., Diamond, L., & Gutlohn, L. (2013). *Teaching reading sourcebook* (Updated 2nd ed.). Consortium on Reading Excellence.

Hood, B., Howard-Jones, P., Laurillard, D., Bishop, D., Coffield, F., Frith, D. U., et al. (2017, March 12). No evidence to back idea of learning styles. *The Guardian.* theguardian.com/education/2017/mar/12/noevidence-to-back-idea-of-learning-styles

Howard, E. R., & Christian, D. (2002). *Two-way immersion 101: Designing and implementing a two-way immersion education program at the elementary level.* Center for Research on Education, Diversity & Excellence (CREDE). University of California.

Howard, E. R., Lindholm-Leary, K. J., Rogers, D., Olague, N., Medina, J., Kennedy, B., Sugarman, J., & Christian, D. (2018). *Guiding principles for dual language education* (3rd ed.). Center for Applied Linguistics. cal.org/resource-center/publications-products/guiding-principles-3

Howe, M. J. A. (1999). *A teacher's guide to the psychology of learning* (2nd ed.). Blackwell.

Hughes, M. T., & Talbott, E. (Eds.). (2017). *The Wiley handbook of diversity in special education.* Wiley-Blackwell.

Hymes, D. H. (1972). On communicative competence. In J. B. Pride & J. Holmes (Eds.), *Sociolinguistics: Selected readings* (pp. 269–293). Penguin.

International Literacy Association. (2017). *Second-language learners' vocabulary and oral language development* [Literacy leadership brief]. Author. literacyworldwide.org/docs/default-source/where-we-stand/ila-second-language-learners-vocabulary-oral-language.pdf?sfvrsn=67f9a58e_6

Jensen, E. (2006). *Enriching the brain: How to maximize every learner's potential.* John Wiley & Sons.

Jensen, E. (2008). *Brain-based learning: The new paradigm of teaching* (2nd ed.). Corwin Press.

Ji, L., Zhang, Z., & Nisbett, R. E. (2004). Is it culture or is it language? Examination of language effects in cross-cultural research on categorization. *Journal of Personality and Social Psychology, 87*(1), 57–65.

Johnson, D. W., & Johnson, R. T. (1989). *Cooperation and competition: Theory and research.* Interaction Book.

Johnson, D. W., & Johnson, R. T. (2009). An educational psychology success story: Social interdependence theory and cooperative learning. *Educational Researcher, 38*(5), 365–379.

Johnson, D. W., Johnson, R. T., & Holubec, E. (1994). *Cooperative learning in the classroom.* Association for Supervision and Curriculum Development.

Johnson, D. W., Johnson, R. T., & Maruyama, G. (1983). Interdependence and interpersonal attraction among heterogeneous and homogeneous individuals: A theoretical formulation and a meta-analysis of the research. *Review of Educational Research, 53*(1), 5–54.

Johnson, R. T., & Johnson, D. W. (1994). An overview of cooperative learning. In J. S. Thousand, R. A. Villa, & A. I. Nevin (Eds.), *Creativity and collaborative learning: A practical guide to empowering students and teachers* (pp. 31–44). Paul H. Brookes Publishing.

Joy, S., & Kolb, D. A. (2009). Are there cultural differences in learning style? *International Journal of Intercultural Relations, 33*(1), 69–85. doi.org/10.1016/j.ijintrel.2008.11.002

Jussim, L., Smith, A., Madon, S., & Palumbo, P. (1998). Teacher expectations. In J. E. Brophy (Ed.), *Advances in research on teaching: Expectations in the classroom* (Vol. 7, pp. 1–48). JAI Press.

Kagan, S. (2000, Fall). Kagan structures—Not one more program: A better way to teach any program. *Kagan Online Magazine.* kaganonline.com/free_articles/research_and_rationale/274/Kagan-Structures-Not-One-More-Program-a-Better-Way-to-Teach-Any-Program

Kavanagh, K. M., & Fisher-Ari, T. R. (2020). Curricular and pedagogical oppression: Contradictions within the juggernaut accountability trap. *Educational Policy, 34*(2), 283–311. doi.org/10.1177/0895904818755471

Keefe, S., & Padilla, A. M. (1987). *Chicano ethnicity.* University of New Mexico Press.

Khong, T. D. H., & Saito, E. (2014). Challenges confronting teachers of English language learners. *Educational Review, 66*(2), 210–225. doi.org/10.1080/00131911.2013.769425

Kieran, L., & Anderson, C. (2019). Connecting universal design for learning with culturally responsive teaching. *Education and Urban Society, 51*(9), 1202–1216. doi.org/10.1177/0013124518785012

Kim, S. (2007). *Exploring the self-reported knowledge and value of implementation of content and language objectives of high school content-area teachers.* Unpublished doctoral dissertation, Kansas State University, Manhattan. hdl.handle.net/2097/357

Kinsella, K., & Feldman, K. (2005). *Narrowing the language gap: Strategies for vocabulary development.* teacher.scholastic.com/products/authors/pdfs/Narrowing_the_Gap.pdf

Knowles, M. S. (1970). *The modern practice of adult education: Andragogy versus pedagogy.* Association Press.

Kolb, D. (1984). *Experiential learning: Experience as the source of learning and development.* Prentice Hall.

Krashen, S. D. (1981). *Second language acquisition and second language learning.* Pergamon Press.

Krashen, S. D. (1982). *Principles and practice in second language acquisition.* Pergamon Press.

Krashen, S. D. (1985). *The input hypothesis: Issues and implications.* Longman.

Krashen, S. D. (2005). Bilingual education and second language acquisition theory. In C. F. Leyba, *Schooling and language minority students: A theoretico-practical framework* (3rd ed., pp. 47–75). Legal Books. (Original work published 1984)

Krashen, S. D. (2009). *Principles and practice in second language acquisition* (Internet ed.). (Original work published 1982) sdkrashen.com/content/books/principles_and_practice.pdf

Krashen, S., & Mason, B. (2020, May). The optimal input hypothesis: Not all comprehensible input is of equal value. *CATESOL Newsletter, 53*(5). catesol.org/v_newsletters/newsletter_7745937.htm

Krashen, S. D., & Terrell, T. (1983). *The natural approach: Language acquisition in the classroom.* Pergamon Press.

Krätzig, G. P., & Arbuthnott, K. D. (2006). Perceptual learning style and learning proficiency: A test of the hypothesis. *Journal of Educational Psychology, 98*(1), 238–246. doi.org/10.1037/0022-0663.98.1.238

Kressler, B., & Cavendish, W. (2020). High school teachers' sense-making of response to intervention: A critical practice analysis. *Education and Urban Society, 52*(3), 433–458. doi.org/10.1177/0013124519848032

Krogstad, J. M. (2019, July 31). *A view of the nation's future through kindergarten demographics.* Pew Research Center. pewresearch.org/fact-tank/2019/07/31/kindergarten-demographics-in-us/

Krussel, L., Springer, G. T., & Edwards, B. (2004). The teacher's discourse moves: A framework for analyzing discourse in mathematics classrooms. *School Science and Mathematics, 104*(7), 307–312.

Kuhrt, L. (2007, Fall). The forgotten half: Those who do not succeed in American schools. In D. Allen, P. O'Shea, J. Kaufman, & P. Baker (and the students of Old Dominion University's ECI 301), *Social and cultural foundations of American education* (3rd ed., Chapter 7). en.wikibooks.org/wiki/Social_and_Cultural_Foundations_of_American_Education

Kulesz, P. P. (2007). Transparent teaching: A pedagogy for success. *Scholarship and Creativity Online: A Publication of the Texas College English Association.*

Kwon, O. N., Ju, M. K., Rasmussen, C., Park, J. H., & Cho, K. H. (2008, July). *Roles of teacher's revoicing in an inquiry-oriented mathematics class: The case of undergraduate differential equations.* Paper prepared for a Topic Study Group of the 11th International Conference on Mathematical Education, Monterrey, Mexico.

Lacina, J., New Levine, L., & Sowa, P. (Eds.). (2006). *Helping English language learners succeed in pre-K–elementary schools.* Alexandria, VA: TESOL.

Lackney, J. A. (1998, June). *12 Design principles based on brain-based learning research.* Paper presented at the CEFPI Midwest Regional Conference.

Ladson-Billings, G. (1994). *The dreamkeepers: Successful teachers of African American children.* Jossey Bass.

Ladson-Billings, G. (1995a). But that's just good teaching! The case for culturally relevant pedagogy. *Theory into Practice, 34*(3), 159–165.

Ladson-Billings, G. (1995b). Toward a theory of culturally relevant pedagogy. *American Educational Research Journal, 32*(3), 465–491. doi.org/10.3102/00028312032003465

Ladson-Billings, G. (2009). *The dreamkeepers: Successful teachers of African American children* (2nd ed.). San Jossey-Bass.

Ladson-Billings, G. (2017). The (r)evolution will not be standardized: Teacher education, hip hop pedagogy, and culturally relevant pedagogy 2.0. In D. Paris & H. S. Alim (Eds.), *Culturally sustaining pedagogies: Teaching and learning for justice in a changing world* (pp. 141–156). Teachers College Press.

Langer, J. A. (1991). Literacy and schooling: A sociocognitive perspective. In E. H. Hiebert (Ed.), *Literacy for a diverse society: Perspectives, practices, and policies* (pp. 9–27). New York: Teachers College Press.

Larkin, M. (2002). *Using scaffolded instruction to optimize learning.* eric.ed.gov/?id=ED474301

Larsen-Freeman, D. (2018). Looking ahead: Future directions in, and future research into, second language acquisition. *Foreign Language Annals, 51*(1), 55–72. doi.org/10.1111/flan.12314

Lau v. Nichols, 414 U.S. 563 (1974).

Leighton, C. M., Ford-Connors, E., Proctor, C. P., & Wyatt, J. (2021). Teacher talk that supports young multilingual students' participation in exploratory discourse. *Reading Psychology,* 1–20.

Lewin, K. (1935). *A dynamic theory of personality.* McGraw-Hill.

Lewis, J. P. (2006). *The project manager's desk reference* (3rd ed.). McGraw-Hill.

Lightbown, P. M., & Spada, N. (2013). *How languages are learned* (4th ed.). Oxford University Press.

Lindholm-Leary, K. (2014). Bilingual and biliteracy skills in young Spanish-speaking low-SES children: Impact of instructional language and primary language proficiency. *International Journal of Bilingual Education and Bilingualism, 17*(2), 144–159. doi.org/10.1080/13670050.2013.866625

Linnenbrink-Garcia, L., & Pekrun, R. (2011). Students' emotions and academic engagement: Introduction to the special issue. *Contemporary Educational Psychology, 36*(1), 1–3.

Linquanti, R. (1999). *Fostering academic success for English language learners: What do we know?* San Francisco: WestEd. Available at wested.org/online_pubs/Foster_Academic_Success_092309.pdf

Lucas, T., Villegas, A. M., & Freedson-Gonzalez, M. (2008). Linguistically responsive teacher education: Preparing classroom teachers to teach English language learners. *Journal of Teacher Education, 59*(4), 361–373.

MacDonald, G. L., Miller, S. S., Murry, K., Herrera, S., & Spears, J. D. (2013). Efficacy of ACA strategies in biography-driven science teaching: An investigation. *Cultural Studies in Science Education, 3*(8), 889–903. doi.org/10.1007/s11422-013-9517-4

Mager, R. F. (1962). *Preparing instructional objectives.* Fearon Press.

Manning, D. (2006). Constructing meaning and metaphor for cultural pedagogy. *International Journal of Pedagogies and Learning, 2*(1), 48–62.

Marcus, L. (1977). How teachers view student learning styles. *NASSP Bulletin, 61*(408), 112–114.

Marzano, R. J. (2004). *Building background knowledge for academic achievement: Research on what works in schools.* Association for Supervision and Curriculum Development.

Massey, A. (1998, September). *The way we do things around here: The culture of ethnography.* Paper presented at the Ethnography and Education Conference, Oxford University Department of Educational Studies (OUDES).

Mays, L. (2008). The cultural divide of discourse: Understanding how English-language learners' primary discourse influences acquisition of literacy. *The Reading Teacher, 61*(5), 415–418.

McCarthey, S. J. (2000). Home–school connections: A review of the literature. *Journal of Educational Research, 93,* 145–152.

McDaniel, E. R., Samovar, L. A., & Porter, R. E. (2012). Using intercultural communication: The building blocks. In L. A. Samovar, R. E. Porter, & E. R. McDaniel (Eds.), *Intercultural communication: A reader* (13th ed., pp. 4–19). Wadsworth Cengage Learning.

McLaughlin, B. (2012). *Second-language acquisition in childhood: Vol. 2. School-age children* (2nd ed.). Psychology Press.

Mehta J. (2013). The penetration of technocratic logic into the educational field: Rationalizing schooling from the progressives to the present. *Teachers College Record, 115*(5), 1–36. nrs.harvard.edu/urn-3:HUL.InstRepos:33063309

Melchert, T. (2013). Beyond theoretical orientations: The emergence of a unified scientific framework in professional psychology. *Professional Psychology: Research and Practice, 44*(1), 11–19.

Melloni, L., Schwiedrzik, C. M., Müller, N., Rodriguez, E., & Singer, W. (2011). Expectations change the signatures and timing of electrophysiological correlates of perceptual awareness. *The Journal of Neuroscience, 31*(4), 1386–1396.

Memari, M., & Gholamshahi, A. (2020). Attitudinal and affective classroom ecology and atmosphere. *Applied Linguistics Research Journal, 4*(2): 1–14.

Met, M. (1991). Learning language through content; learning content through language. *Foreign Language Annals, 24*(4), 281–295.

Mezirow, J. (1991). *Transformative dimensions of adult learning.* Jossey-Bass.

Mezirow, J. (2018). Transformative learning theory. In K. Illeris (Ed.), *Contemporary theories of learning: Learning theorists . . . in their own words* (2nd ed., pp. 114–128). Routledge.

Mohr, K. A. J., & Mohr, E. S. (2007). Extending English-language learners' classroom interactions using the response protocol. *The Reading Teacher, 60*(5), 440–450.

Moje, E. B., Ciechanowsku, K. M., Kramer, K., Ellis, L., Carillo, R., & Collazo, T. (2004). Working toward third space in content area literacy: An examination of everyday funds of knowledge and Discourse. *Reading Research Quarterly, 39*(1), 38–70.

Moll, L. C. (2019). Elaborating funds of knowledge: Community-oriented practices in international contexts. *Literacy Research: Theory, Method, and Practice, 68*(1), 130–138. doi.org/10.1177%2F2381336919870805

Moll, L. C., Amanti, C., Neff, D., & González, N. (1992). Funds of knowledge for teaching: Using a qualitative approach to connect homes and classrooms. *Theory into Practice, 31*(2), 132–141.

Moll, L. C., & Greenberg, J. (1990). Creating zones of possibilities: Combining social contexts for instruction. In L. C. Moll (Ed.), *Vygotsky and education* (pp. 319–348). Cambridge University Press.

Muñoz-Sandoval, A. F., Cummins, J., Alvarado, C. G., Ruef, M., & Schrank, F. A. (2005). *Bilingual Verbal Ability Tests Normative Update (BVAT-NU).* Riverside.

Murry, K. G., Herrera, S. G., Miller, S. S., Fanning, C. A., Kavimandan, S. K., & Holmes, M. A. (2015). Effect of transnational standards on U.S. teacher education. *FIRE: Forum for International Research in Education, 1*(3), 41–63. eric.ed.gov/?id=EJ1133939

Murry, K. G., Holmes, M., & Kavimandan, S. (2020). Approximating cultural responsiveness: teacher readiness for accommodative, biography-driven instruction. *Forum for International Research in Education, 6*(2), 103–124. eric.ed.gov/?id=EJ1248095

Murry, K., Kavimandan, S., Herrera, S., & Holmes, M. (2021). Phenomenological research on BDI use in highly diverse classrooms. *Teacher Education Quarterly, 48*(2), 7–35.

National Research Council & Institute of Medicine. (2004). *Engaging schools: Fostering high school students' motivation to learn.* Committee on Increasing High School Students' Engagement and Motivation to Learn. Board on Children, Youth, and Families, Division of Behavioral and Social Sciences and Education. The National Academies Press. nap.edu/catalog/10421/engaging-schools-fostering-high-school-students-motivation-to-learn

Newmann, F. M., Wehlage, G. G., & Lamborn, S. D. (1992). The significance and sources of student engagement. In F. M. Newmann (Ed.), *Student engagement and achievement in American secondary schools* (pp. 11–39). Teachers College Press.

Nieto, S. (1992). *Affirming diversity: The sociopolitical context of multicultural education.* Longman.

Nieto, S. (2000). *Affirming diversity: The sociopolitical context of multicultural education* (3rd ed.). Addison Wesley Longman.

Nieto, S. (Ed.). (2005). *Why we teach.* Teachers College Press.

Nieto, S. (2011). *Affirming diversity: The sociopolitical context of multicultural education* (6th ed.). Addison Wesley Longman.

Nieto, S., & Bode, P. (2018). *Affirming diversity: The sociopolitical context of multicultural education* (7th ed.). Pearson Education.

Numelin, K. (1998). The importance of sequencing and planning when integrating language and content. *ACIE Newsletter, 2.* carla.umn.edu/immersion/acie/vol2/Bridge2.1.pdf

Nyikos, M., & Hashimoto, R. (1997). Constructivist theory applied to collaborative learning in teacher education: In search of ZPD. *Modern Language Journal, 81,* 506–517.

O'Connor, M. C., & Michaels, S. (1993). Aligning academic task and participation status through revoicing: Analysis of a classroom discourse strategy. *Anthropology and Education Quarterly, 24*(4), 318–335.

O'Connor, M. C., & Michaels, S. (1996). Shifting participant frameworks: Orchestrating thinking practices in group discussion. In D. Hicks (Ed.), *Discourse, learning, and schooling* (pp. 63–103). New York: Cambridge University Press.

O'Dwyer, S. (2006). The English teacher as facilitator and authority. *TESL-EJ, 9*(4). tesl-ej.org/ej36/a2.pdf

Ogbu, J., & Simons, H. D. (1998). Voluntary and involuntary minorities: A cultural–ecological theory of school performance with some implications for education. *Anthropology and Education Quarterly, 29*(2), 155–188.

O'Malley, J. M., & Chamot, A. U. (1990). *Learning strategies in second language acquisition.* Cambridge University Press.

Ormrod, J. E. (1995). *Human learning* (2nd ed.). Prentice Hall.

Ortega, L. (2009). *Understanding second language acquisition.* Hodder Education.

Ortega, L. (2011). SLA after the social turn: Where cognitivism and its alternatives stand. In D. Atkinson (Ed.), *Alternative approaches in second language acquisition* (pp. 167–180). Routledge.

Ovando, C. J., Combs, M. C., & Collier, V. (2011). *Bilingual and ESL classrooms: Teaching in multicultural contexts* (5th ed.). McGraw Hill.

Oxford, R. L. (1990). *Language learning strategies: What every teacher should know.* Newbury House/Harper Collins.

Palincsar, A. S. (1998). Social constructivist perspectives on teaching and learning. *Annual Review of Psychology, 49,* 345–375.

Papadatou-Pastou, M., Gritzali, M., & Barrable, A. (2018). The learning styles educational neuromyth: Lack of agreement between teachers' judgments, self-assessment, and students' intelligence. *Frontiers in Education, 3,* 105. doi.org/10.3389/feduc.2018.00105

Papadatou-Pastou, M., Touloumakos, A. K., Koutouveli, C., & Barrable, A. (2021). The learning styles neuromyth: When the same term means different things to different teachers. *European Journal of Psychology of Education, 36*(2), 511–531. doi.org/10.1007/s10212-020-00485-2

Paris, D. (2012). Culturally sustaining pedagogy: A needed change in stance, terminology, and practice. *Educational Researcher, 41*(3), 93–97. doi.org/10.3102/0013189X12441244

Paris, D., & Alim, H. S. (2014). What are we seeking to sustain through culturally sustaining pedagogy? A loving critique forward. *Harvard Educational Review, 84*(1), 85–100. doi.org/10.17763/haer.84.1.982l873k2ht16m77

Paris, D., & Alim, H. S. (Eds.). (2017). *Culturally sustaining pedagogies: Teaching and learning for justice in a changing world.* Teachers College Press.

Park, J. H., Park, J. H., Kwon, O. N., Ju, M. K., Rasmussen, C., & Marrongelle, K. (2007, February). *Roles of revoicing in an inquiry-oriented mathematics class: The case of undergraduate differential equations.* Paper presented at the Conference on Research in Undergraduate Mathematics Education, Mission Valley, CA. sigmaa.maa.org/rume/crume2007/papers/park-park-kwon-rasmussen-ju-marongelle.pdf

Pashler, H., McDaniel, M., Rohrer, D., & Bjork, R. (2008). Learning styles: Concepts and evidence. *Psychological Science in the Public Interest, 9*(3), 105–119. doi.org/10.1111/j.1539-6053.2009.01038.x

Pepitone, E. (1980). *Children in cooperation and competition.* Lexington Books.

Perez, D., Holmes, M., Miller, S., & Fanning, C. (2012). Biography-driven strategies as the great equalizer: Universal conditions that promote K–12 culturally responsive teaching. *Journal of Curriculum and Instruction, 6*(1), 25–42.

Plyler v. Doe, 457 U.S. 202 (1982).

Porter, R. E., & Samovar, L. A. (1991). Basic principles of intercultural communication. In L. A. Samovar & R. E. Porter (Eds.), *Intercultural communication: A reader* (6th ed., pp. 5–22). Wadsworth.

Quinn, N., & Holland, D. (1987). *Cultural models of language and thought.* Cambridge University Press.

Ramirez, J. (1992). Executive summary. *Bilingual Research Journal, 16*(1–2), 1–62.

Ramírez, M., III, & Castañeda, A. (1974). *Cultural democracy, bicognitive development and education.* Academic Press.

Reid, D. K. (1996, Summer). 1995 CLD Distinguished Lecture: Narrative knowing: Basis for a partnership on language diversity. *Learning Disability Quarterly, 19*(3), 138–152.

Richards, J. C., & Rogers, T. S. (2014). *Approaches and methods in language teaching.* Cambridge University Press.

Rodriguez, E. R., Bellanca, J. A., & Esparza, D. R. (2017). *What is it about me you can't teach: Culturally responsive instruction in deeper learning classrooms.* Corwin Press.

Rogowsky, B. A., Calhoun, B. M., & Tallal, P. (2015). Matching learning style to instructional method: Effects on comprehension. *Journal of Educational Psychology, 107*(1), 64–78. doi.org/10.1037/a0037478

Rohrer, D., & Pashler, H. (2012). Learning styles: Where's the evidence? *Medical Education, 46*(7), 634–635. doi.org/10.1111/j.1365-2923.2012.04273.x

Romero, S. (2021, May 20). Texas pushes to obscure the state's history of slavery and racism. *The New York Times.* nytimes.com/2021/05/20/us/texas-history-1836-project.html

Rotatori, A. F., Bakken, J. P., Burkhardt, S., Obiakor, F. E., & Sharma, U. (Eds.). (2014). *Special education international perspectives: Biopsychosocial, cultural, and disability aspects* (Advances in Special Education, Vol. 27). Emerald Group.

Rubie-Davies, C., Hattie, J., & Hamilton, R. (2006). Expecting the best for students: Teacher expectations and academic outcomes. *British Journal of Educational Psychology, 76*(3), 429–444.

Saleebey, D. (2001). *Human behavior and social environments: A biopsychosocial approach.* Columbia University Press.

Säljö, R. (1996). Mental and physical artifacts in cognitive practices. In P. Reiman & H. Spada (Eds.), *Learning in humans and machines: Towards an interdisciplinary learning science* (pp. 83–96). Pergamon/Elsevier.

Sapir, E. (1968). The status of linguistics as a science. In D. G. Mandelbaum (Ed.), *Selected writings of Edward Sapir in language, culture, and personality* (pp. 160–166). University of California Press.

Schifini, A. (1994). Language, literacy, and content instruction: Strategies for teachers. In K. Sprangfenberg-Urbschat & R. Pritchard (Eds.), *Kids come in all languages: Reading instruction for ESL students.* International Reading Association.

Segalowitz, N. (2003). Automaticity and second languages. In C. J. Doughty & M. H. Long (Eds.), *Handbook of second language acquisition* (pp. 382–408). Blackwell.

Semrud-Clikeman, M. (2015). *Research in brain function and learning: The importance of matching instruction to a child's maturity level.* apa.org/education/k12/brain-function.aspx

Shein, P. P. (2012). Seeing with two eyes: A teacher's use of gestures in questioning and revoicing to engage English language learners in the repair of mathematical errors. *Journal for Research in Mathematics Education, 43*(2), 182–222.

Smith, R. C. (2002). The biopsychosocial revolution: Interviewing and provider–patient relationships becoming key issues for primary care. *Journal of General Internal Medicine, 17*(4), 309–310. doi.org/10.1046/j.1525-1497.2002.20210.x

Snow, M., Met, M., & Genesee, F. (1989). A conceptual framework for the integration of language and content in second/foreign language instruction. *TESOL Quarterly, 23*(2), 201–217.

Snyder, C. R. (2002). Hope theory: Rainbows in the mind. *Psychological Inquiry, 13*(4), 249–275.

Snyder, C. R., Harris, C., Anderson, J. R., Holleran, S. A., Irving, L. M., Sigmon, S. T., et al. (1991). The will and the ways: Development and validation of an individual-differences measure of hope. *Journal of Personality and Social Psychology, 60*(4), 570–585.

Sousa, D. A. (1995). *How the brain learns: A classroom teacher's guide.* National Association of Secondary School Principals.

Sousa, D. A. (2011). *How the brain learns* (4th ed.). Corwin Press.

Sousa, D. A. (2017). *How the brain learns* (5th ed.). Corwin Press.

Souto-Manning, M. (2012). Teacher as researcher: Teacher action research in teacher education. *Childhood Education, 88*(1), 54–56. doi.org/10.1080/00094056.2012.643726

Stahl, S. A. (2002). Different strokes for different folks? In L. Abbeduto (Ed.), *Taking sides: Clashing on controversial issues in educational psychology.* McGraw-Hill.

Stevens, K. C. (1980). The effect of background knowledge on the reading comprehension of ninth graders. *Journal of Reading Behavior, 12*(2), 151–154.

Straits, W. (2007). "She's teaching me": Teaching with care in a large lecture course. *College Teaching, 55*(4), 170–175.

Strike, K. A., & Posner, G. J. (1985). A conceptual change view of learning and understanding. In L. H. T. West & A. L. Pines (Eds.), *Cognitive structure and conceptual change.* Academic Press.

Suh, H. (2020, July). Preparing mathematics teachers to teach English language learners: What we know and what we can do. *The Educational Forum, 84*(3), 200–209.

Swartz, R., & Perkins, D. (1987). *Teaching thinking skills: Theory & practice.* Freeman.

Tang, G. M. (1993). Teaching content knowledge and ESOL in multicultural classrooms. *TESOL Journal, 2*(2), 8–12.

Tharp, R. G., & Dalton, S. S. (2007). Orthodoxy, cultural compatibility, and universals in education. *Comparative Education, 43*(1), 53–70.

Tharp, R. G., Estrada, P., Dalton, S. S., & Yamauchi, L. (2000). *Teaching transformed: Achieving excellence, fairness, inclusion, and harmony.* Westview Press.

Thomas, W. P., & Collier, V. P. (1995). Language-minority student achievement and program effectiveness studies support native language development. *NABE News, 18*(8), 5, 12.

Thomas, W. P., & Collier, V. P. (1997). *School effectiveness for language minority students* (NCBE Resource Collection Series No. 9). National Clearinghouse for Bilingual Education. files.eric.ed.gov/fulltext/ED436087.pdf

Thomas, W. P., & Collier, V. P. (1999). Accelerated schooling for English language learners. *Educational Leadership, 56*(7), 46–49.

Thomas, W. P., & Collier, V. P. (2002). *A national study of school effectiveness for language minority students' long-term academic achievement.* Center for Research on Education, Diversity & Excellence (CREDE). eric.ed.gov/?id=ED475048

Thomas, W. P., & Collier, V. P. (2012). *Dual language education for a transformed world.* Fuente Press.

Tomlinson, C. A. (2001). *How to differentiate instruction in mixed-ability classrooms* (2nd ed.). Association for Supervision and Curriculum Development.

Tomlinson, C. A., & McTighe, J. (2006). *Integrating differentiated instruction and understanding by design.* Association for Supervision and Curriculum Development.

Tompkins, G. E. (2012). *Fifty literacy strategies: Step by step* (4th ed.). Pearson.

Triplett, N. (1898). The dynamogenic factors in pacemaking and competition. *American Journal of Psychology, 9,* 507–533.

Tsai, Y., Kunter, M., Lüdtke, O., Trautwein, U., & Ryan, R. M. (2008). What makes lessons interesting? The role of situational and individual factors in three school subjects. *Journal of Educational Psychology, 100*(2), 460–472.

Tse, L. (1996). The effect of language brokering on home–school communication. *Journal of Educational Issues of Language Minority Students, 16,* 225–233.

Urdan, T., & Schoenfelder, E. (2006). Classroom effects on student motivation: Goal structures, social relationships, and competence beliefs. *Journal of School Psychology, 44*(5), 331–349.

Vail, P. L. (2009). *The role of emotions in learning.* greatschools.org/gk/articles/the-role-of-emotions-in-learning/

Vaughn, S., & Linan-Thompson, S. (2004). *Reading: Effective instructional activities for elementary students.* Association for Supervision and Curriculum Development.

Vaughn, S., Martinez, L. R., Wanzek, J., Roberts, G., Swanson, E., & Fall, A.-M. (2017). Improving content knowledge and comprehension for English language learners: Findings from a randomized control trial. *Journal of Educational Psychology, 109*(1), 22–34. doi.org/10.1037/edu0000069

Veissière, S. P., Constant, A., Ramstead, M. J., Friston, K. J., & Kirmayer, L. J. (2019). Thinking through other minds: A variational approach to cognition and culture. *Behavioral and Brain Sciences, 43.* doi.org/10.1017/S0140525X19001213

Vélez-Ibáñez, C. G., & Greenberg, J. B. (1992). Formation and transformation of funds of knowledge among U.S. Mexican households. *Anthropology and Education Quarterly, 23*(4), 313–335.

Verplaetse, L. S. (2002). How content teachers interact with English language learners. *TESOL Journal, 7*(5), 24–28.

Vygotsky, L. S. (1956). *Selected psychological investigations.* Izdatel'stvo Akademii Pedagogicheskikh Nauk SSSR.

Vygotsky, L. S. (1962). *Thought and language.* MIT Press. (Original work published 1934)

Vygotsky, L. S. (1978). *Mind in society: The development of higher psychological processes* (M. Cole, V. John-Steiner, S. Scribner, & E. Souberman, Eds.). Harvard University Press.

Vygotsky, L. S. (1986). The genetic roots of thought and speech. In A. Kozulin (Trans. & Ed.), *Thought and language* (pp. 68–95). MIT Press.

Walqui, A. (2000). *Strategies for success: Engaging immigrant students in secondary schools.* (EDO-FL-00-03) eric.ed.gov/?id=ED442300

Walqui, A., & van Lier, L. (2010). *Scaffolding the academic success of adolescent English language learners: A pedagogy of promise.* WestEd.

Waxman, H. C., & Tellez, K. (2002). *Research synthesis on effective teaching practices for English language learners.* Mid-Atlantic Laboratory for Student Success. (ERIC Document Reproduction Service No. ED474821)

Weinstein, R. S. (2002). *Reaching higher: The power of expectations in schooling.* Harvard University Press.

Wertsch, J. V. (1998). *Mind as action.* Oxford University Press.

Wessels, S., Holmes, M., & Herrera, S. (2011). The role of preservice teachers' meaning perspectives and schemes in a study abroad experience. *Multicultural Learning and Teaching, 6*(2). doi.org/10.2202/2161-2412.1089

West, L. H. T., & Pines, A. L. (Eds.). (1985). *Cognitive structure and conceptual change.* Academic Press.

Will, M. (2019, September 5). Teachers still believe in 'learning styles' and other myths about cognition. *Education Week.* edweek.org/teaching-learning/teachers-still-believe-in-learning-styles-and-other-myths-about-cognition/2019/09

Willingham, D. T., Hughes, E. M., & Dobolyi, D. G. (2015). The scientific status of learning styles theories. *Teaching of Psychology, 42*(3), 266–271. doi.org/10.1177/0098628315589505

Willis, J. (2006). *Research-based strategies to ignite student learning.* Association for Supervision and Curriculum Development.

Willis, J. (2010). The current impact of neuroscience on teaching and learning. In D. A. Sousa (Ed.), *Mind, brain, and education: Neuroscience implications for the classroom* (pp. 45–68). Solution Tree Press.

Willis, J., & Willis, M. (2020). *Research-based strategies to ignite student learning* (Rev. ed.). Association for Supervision and Curriculum Development.

Wlodkowski, R. J., & Ginsberg, M. B. (1995). A framework for culturally responsive teaching. *Educational Leadership, 53*(1), 17–21.

Woodcock, R. W., McGrew, K. S., & Mather, N. (2001). *Woodcock-Johnson III Tests of Achievement.* Riverside.

Woodcock, R., Muñoz-Sandoval, A. F., Ruef, M., & Alvarado, C. G. (2005). *Woodcock-Muñoz Language Survey Revised (WMLS-R).* Riverside.

Yamauchi, L. A., Im, S., & Mark, L. (2013). The influence of professional development on educators' instructional conversations in preschool classrooms. *Journal of Early Childhood Teacher Education, 34*(2), 140–153.

Young, T. A., & Hadaway, N. L. (Eds.). (2006). *Supporting the literacy development of English learners: Increasing success in all classrooms.* International Reading Association.

Zadina, J. N. (2014). *Multiple pathways to the student brain: Energizing and enhancing instruction.* Jossey-Bass.

Zamani, A., & Pouratashi, M. (2018). The relationship between academic performance and working memory, self-efficacy belief, and test anxiety. *Journal of School Psychology, 6*(4), 25–44.

Zenasni, F., Besançon, M., & Lubart, T. (2008). Creativity and tolerance of ambiguity: An empirical study. *The Journal of Creative Behavior, 42*(1), 61–73. doi.org/10.1002/j.2162-6057.2008.tb01080.x

Zull, J. E. (2002). *The art of changing the brain: Enriching the practice of teaching by exploring the biology of learning.* Stylus Publishing.

Index

Subjects

Cited Authors

About the Author

DR. SOCORRO HERRERA is a professor in the Department of Curriculum and Instruction, College of Education at Kansas State University and serves as the Executive Director of the Center for Intercultural and Multilingual Advocacy (CIMA). She is certified in elementary education, bilingual education, and school counseling. As an international keynote speaker, district consultant, and trainer of trainers, she has collaborated with teachers across the country and the world to chart new paths to academic success for culturally and linguistically diverse (CLD) learners. Her research focuses the role that personal histories of the learner, family, and teacher play in literacy development and culturally responsive, sustaining pedagogy; reading strategies; and teacher preparation for diverse classrooms. Dr. Herrera has authored seven textbooks and numerous articles for publication in journals such as *Bilingual Research Journal, Journal of Hispanic Higher Education, Journal of Research in Education, Journal of Latinos and Education, Journal of Curriculum and Instruction, International Journal of Multicultural Education, Teacher Education Quarterly,* and *Urban Education.*